D1274587

Childcraft

The How and Why Library

Volume 15

Guide for Parents

World Book–Childcraft International, Inc.

A subsidiary of The Scott & Fetzer Company

Chicago London Paris Sydney Tokyo Toronto

Childcraft—The How and Why Library
(Reg. U.S. Pat. Off.)

Merchandise Mart Plaza, Chicago, Illinois 60654

Printed in the United States of America
ISBN 0-7166-0180-X
Library of Congress Catalog Card No. 79-88042

Acknowledgments

The publishers of *Childcraft* gratefully acknowledge the following artists, photographers, publishers, agencies, and corporations for illustrations in this volume. Page numbers refer to two-page spreads. The words *"(left)," "(center)," "(top)," "(bottom),"* and *"(right),"* indicate position on the spread. All illustrations are the exclusive property of the publishers of *Childcraft* unless names are marked with an asterisk (*).

1: Robert Keys
12-13: Phoebe Dunn
14-15: Inger McAbe, Rapho Guillumette *
16-17: *(left)* Susan Perl; *(right)* diagram, Product Illustration; *Childcraft* photos
18-19: Phoebe Dunn
20-21: Susan Perl
22-27: Phoebe Dunn *
28-29: *Childcraft* photo
30-43: Phoebe Dunn *
44-45: Susan Perl
46-49: Phoebe Dunn
50-51: *(left)* Phoebe Dunn; *(right)* Susan Perl
52-57: Phoebe Dunn
58-59: *(left)* Susan Perl; *(right)* Phoebe Dunn *
60-69: Phoebe Dunn
70-71: Susan Perl
72-73: *(left)* Phoebe Dunn; *(right)* Susan Perl
74-85: Phoebe Dunn
86-87: *(left)* Susan Perl; *(right)* Phoebe Dunn *
88-97: Phoebe Dunn *
98-99: *(left)* Susan Perl; *(right)* Phoebe Dunn
101-109: Phoebe Dunn *
110-128: Charles Moser
130-133: Adapted through courtesy of Nancy Bayley
145-147: Charles Moser
162-163: Julius E. Ginsberg, M.D. *
168-169: *Childcraft* photo; diagram, Mary Ann Olson
172-173: *(left)* Lewis Shapiro, M.D. *; *(right) Childcraft* photo
174-175: Photo, Rick White; diagram, Mary Ann Olson
176-177: Kinuko Craft
178-179: *(left) Childcraft* photo; *(right)* Children's Memorial Hospital, Chicago *
180-181: *(top, left to right)* Division of Dermatology, University of Arkansas Medical School *, John H. Gerard, NAS *; *(center, left to right)* William B. Allen, Jr., NAS *, Woodrow Goodpaster, NAS *; *(bottom, left to right)* Charles Mohr, NAS *, John E. Stonitch, NAS *
182-183: Anthony Ravielli
184-185: Eric V. Gravé *
186-187: *(left)* Shriners Hospital for Crippled Children *; *(bottom right) Childcraft* photo; *(right) Childcraft* photo courtesy Bailey N. Jacobson, D.D.S., M.S., and Sheldon W. Rosenstein, D.D.S., M.S.D.
188-191: Anthony Ravielli
192-193: Charles Kallick, M.D. *
194-195: *(left)* Charles Kallick, M.D. *; *(right)* Anthony Ravielli
196-197: *(left)* John Curtin, M.D. *; *(right)* Richard L. Jacobs, M.D. *
198-199: James Smestad
204-205: *(left)* Charles Kallick, M.D. *; *(right) Childcraft* photo
208-209: *(top)* Anthony Ravielli; *(bottom) Childcraft* photos
210-211: Lowell Stumpf
212-213: Carol Ann Bales
214-215: *(left) Childcraft* photo courtesy of Beltone Electronics; *(right)* Carol Ann Bales
218-219: *Childcraft* photo; diagram, Mary Ann Olson
220-221: *(left)* Lewis Shapiro, M.D. *; *(right)* Anthony Ravielli
222-223: *(left) Childcraft* photos; *(right) Childcraft* photo; diagram, Mary Ann Olson
226-227: *Childcraft* photo
228-229: Anthony Ravielli
230-231: *(left)* Charles Kallick, M.D. *; *(right) Childcraft* photos; diagrams, Mary Ann Olson
232-233: *Childcraft* photo
234-235: *(left)* Private medical collection *; *(right)* Lester V. Bergman & Assoc. *
236-237: *(left)* Anthony Ravielli; *(right)* John Curtin, M.D. *
238-239: Eric V. Gravé *
240-241: *Childcraft* photo; Anthony Ravielli
242-243: *Childcraft* photo
244-245: *(left)* photo, Rick White; diagram, Mary Ann Olson; *(right)* Private medical collection *
246-247: Anthony Ravielli
250-251: *(left)* Charles Kallick, M.D. *; *(right)* Kenrad Nelson, M.D. *
252-253: Lewis Shapiro, M.D. *
254-255: Charles Kallick, M.D. *
256-257: Mary Ann Olson
258-259: *(left)* Lewis Shapiro, M.D. *; *(right)* Stuart Markson
260-261: *(left)* Anthony Ravielli; *(right) Childcraft* photos
262-263: *Childcraft* photos
266-267: Hugh Spencer, NAS *
270-271: *(top, left to right)* Nick Drahos *, Nick Drahos *; *(center)* John H. Gerard *; *(bottom, left to right)* John H. Gerard *, Walter Chandoha *
272-273: *Childcraft* photos
274-275: Charles Kallick, M.D. *
276-277: Lewis Shapiro, M.D. *
278-279: *(left)* Private medical collection *; *(right)* photo, Shriners Hospital for Crippled Children *; diagram, Mary Ann Olson
280-281: *(bottom left)* Kinuko Craft; *(top left) Childcraft* photo; *(right) Childcraft* photo; diagram, Mary Ann Olson
282-287: *Childcraft* photos
288-289: Anthony Ravielli
290-291: Private medical collection *
292-293: *(left)* Presbyterian–St. Luke's Hospital *; *(right) Childcraft* photos; diagrams, Mary Ann Olson
294-295: *(left) Childcraft* photos; diagrams, Mary Ann Olson; *(right)* Anthony Ravielli
296-297: Lewis Shapiro, M.D. *
298-299: *(left) Childcraft* photo; diagram, Mary Ann Olson; *(right)* Charles Kallick, M.D. *
302-303: Lewis Shapiro, M.D.*
All illustrations on pages 306-319 are reproduced from Volumes 1 through 14. Full illustration acknowledgments appear in each of those volumes. The illustration on page 310 *(bottom)* is from the book, *Winnie-the-Pooh* by A. A. Milne, illustrated by E. H. Shepard, copyright 1926 by E. P. Dutton & Co., Inc., renewal 1954 by A. A. Milne, reprinted by permission of the publishers and Methuen & Co. Ltd.

Heritage binding cover—all *Childcraft* photos by Phoebe Dunn

Preface

This volume of *Childcraft* is designed to help you meet the challenge of parenthood. It is divided into four sections: (1) Growth and Development; (2) For Special Consideration; (3) a Medical Guide; and (4) a Guide and Index to Childcraft.

Growth and Development describes how children develop from birth to the early teen-age years. This description helps you understand your child and provides guidelines for solving some of the problems that arise at each stage of development.

For Special Consideration deals with subjects that may affect you or your child at any stage in the child's life—choosing a baby sitter, moving, growth, the working mother. It deals with problems of a special nature that, fortunately, touch the lives of only some parents—such as mental retardation, physical handicaps, and drug addiction. Also included are two helpful lists. The first catalogs agencies and organizations that you may want to contact for additional or special help. The other is a collection of books for further reading.

The Medical Guide contains more than 200 articles dealing with a child's health, safety, and well-being. The articles are alphabetically arranged for quick and efficient use. Cross references are included to help you locate information you may have difficulty finding. *See also* entries appear at the end of many articles to lead you to related topics for additional information.

The last section is a Guide and Index to *Childcraft*.

Obviously, no one person is qualified to give expert advice on all the subjects presented in this volume. For this reason, the editors sought the assistance of more than 25 physicians, psychiatrists, educators, and dentists. The result of their work is a body of information that we feel will give you a good understanding of your child's behavior, and confidence in your abilities to guide him through the crucial years leading to adulthood.

Volume 15

Guide for Parents

Contents

Contributors

A person whose name appears in front of an article either wrote it originally or became responsible for its accuracy by critically reviewing the work of another. In the Medical Guide, articles are followed by the initials of the responsible contributor. This list also includes doctors who contributed photographs to the Medical Guide.

Section One: Growth and Development

Berson, Minnie P., B.A., M.A., Ed.D.
Professor of Elementary Education and Director, Early Childhood Programs,
Illinois State University
Author, *Opening, Mixing, Matching*

Blaine, Graham B., Jr., A.B., M.D.
Assistant in Psychiatry, Adolescent Unit,
The Children's Hospital Medical Center (Boston)
Author, *Are Parents Bad for Children?*

Diamond, Eugene F., M.D.
Clinical Professor of Pediatrics,
Loyola University (Chicago)

Hymes, James L., Jr., A.B., M.A., Ed.D.
Specialist in Early Childhood Education
Author, *The Child Under Six; Teaching The Child Under Six*

Redl, Fritz, Ph.D.
Professor Emeritus, Wayne State University
Author, *When We Deal with Children*

Smith, Lendon H., B.A., M.D.
Author, *The Encyclopedia of Baby & Child Care*

Weinberger, Howard L., M.D.
Associate Professor,
Department of Pediatrics,
State University of New York (Syracuse)

Section Two: For Special Consideration

Bayley, Nancy, B.S., M.S., Ph.D.
Consulting Psychologist,
University of California (Berkeley)
Author, *Development of Motor Abilities During the First Three Years*

Chess, Stella, M.D.
Professor of Child Psychiatry,
New York University School of Medicine
Author, *Introduction to Child Psychiatry*

Cone, Thomas E., Jr., B.A., M.D.
Senior Associate of Clinical Genetics,
The Children's Hospital Medical Center (Boston);
Clinical Professor of Pediatrics,
Harvard Medical School

Dittmann, Laura L., B.S., M.A., Ph.D.
Professor, Institute for Child Study,
University of Maryland

Jenkins, Gladys Gardner, B.A., M.A.
Lecturer Emeritus, Department of Home Economics, University of Iowa

LeShan, Eda, B.S., M.A.
Contributing Editor, *Woman's Day*
Author, *The Conspiracy Against Childhood; Sex and Your Teenager*

Lis, Edward F., B.S., M.D.
Professor, Department of Pediatrics,
University of Illinois College of Medicine; Director, Center for Handicapped Children,
University of Illinois Hospital

Myklebust, Helmer R., B.A., M.A., Ed.D.
Adjunct Professor of Education,
University of Illinois (Chicago Circle)
Author, *Progress in Learning Disabilities*

Schulman, Jerome L., B.A., M.D.
Head, Division of Child Psychiatry,
Children's Memorial Hospital (Chicago)

Torrance, E. Paul, A.B., M.A., Ph.D.
Head, Department of Educational Psychology and Alumni Foundation Distinguished Professor, University of Georgia
Author, *Education and the Creative Potential; Gifted Children in the Classroom*

Walters, James, B.A., M.A., Ph.D.
Professor, Child and Family Development,
University of Georgia

Walters, Lynda, B.C.E., M.S., Ph.D.
Assistant to the Editor,
The Family Coordinator

Section Three: Medical Guide

The planning and editing of all articles in the Medical Guide was supervised by Dr. Don M. Hoffman, Chief Pediatric Resident, Rush-Presbyterian-St. Luke's Medical Center, 1969-1970; presently Practicing Pediatrician, Elmhurst Clinic, Elmhurst, Illinois.

(**C.F.F.**) Ferguson, Charles F., A.B., M.D., FACS
Senior Otolaryngologist (retired),
The Children's Hospital Medical Center (Boston)

(**J.J.G.**) Gartland, John J., A.B., M.D.
James Edwards Professor of Orthopaedic Surgery and Chairman of the Department,
Jefferson Medical College of Thomas Jefferson University

(**M.G.**) Green, Morris, A.B., M.D.
Lesh Professor and Chairman,
Department of Pediatrics,
Indiana University School of Medicine;
Physician-in-Chief, James Whitcomb Riley Memorial Hospital for Children

(**T.M.H.**) Holder, Thomas M., M.D.
Chief, Section of Cardiothoracic Surgery, Department of Surgery,
The Children's Mercy Hospital (Kansas City)

(**J.S.H.**) Hyde, John S., M.D.
Clinical Associate Professor of Pediatrics,
Rush-Presbyterian-St. Luke's Medical Center

(**S.L.K.**) Katz, Samuel L., M.D.
Professor and Chairman,
Department of Pediatrics,
Duke University Medical Center

(**A.M.M.**) Margileth, Andrew M., B.S., B.A., M.D.
Professor of Pediatrics,
George Washington University

(**F.O.**) Oski, Frank, B.A., M.D.
Professor and Chairman of the Department of Pediatrics,
State University of New York (Syracuse)

(**H.D.R., Jr.**) Riley, Harris D., Jr., B.A., M.D.
Professor of Pediatrics, Department Head
University of Oklahoma Health Sciences Center;
Medical Director of Children's Memorial Hospital (Oklahoma City)

(**R.O.S.**) Scholz, Roy O., B.S., M.D.
Assistant Professor of Ophthalmology,
Johns Hopkins University

(**A.G.S.**) Swanson, August G., B.A., M.D.
Director of Academic Affairs,
Association of American Medical Colleges,
Washington, D.C.

Photo Contributors to the Medical Guide

Curtin, John W., M.D.
Professor of Surgery and Chief of the Departments of Plastic Surgery,
University of Illinois College of Medicine and Rush-Presbyterian-St. Luke's Medical Center

Ginsberg, Julius E., S.B., M.D.
Professor Emeritus,
Northwestern University Medical School

Jacobs, Richard L., B.A., M.S., M.D.
Associate Professor of Orthopedic Surgery,
University of Illinois College of Medicine

Jacobson, Bailey N., D.D.S., M.S.
Assistant Professor of Orthodontics,
Northwestern University Dental School

Kallick, Charles A., M.D., FAAP
Chief, Section of Infectious Diseases,
Cook County Hospital (Chicago)

Nelson, Kenrad E., A.B., M.D.
Associate Professor,
Department of Preventive Medicine and Community Health,
University of Illinois College of Medicine

Rosenstein, Sheldon W., D.D.S., M.S.D.
Associate Professor of Orthodontics,
Northwestern University Dental School

Shapiro, Lewis, M.D.
Clinical Professor of Dermatology,
College of Physicians and Surgeons,
Columbia University

Spaeth, Ralph, M.D.
Clinical Professor of Pediatrics
University of Illinois College of Medicine

Section One

Growth and Development

The New Baby: Birth to 18 months

A baby is such a small thing to make such a big difference in your life. Soft and cuddly, the new baby is something to be proud of. But the little one also means 2 A.M. feedings, rashes and drooling, and diapers that always are wet. First tooth, first fever, first step, first fall—they are all part of your new baby. But they are also part of a very special challenge that you as a parent accept—the challenge of caring for a helpless but loving lightweight, of guiding and helping the child become a strong and independent human being who will someday also want to accept a real challenge.

By Dr. Howard L. Weinberger, M.D.

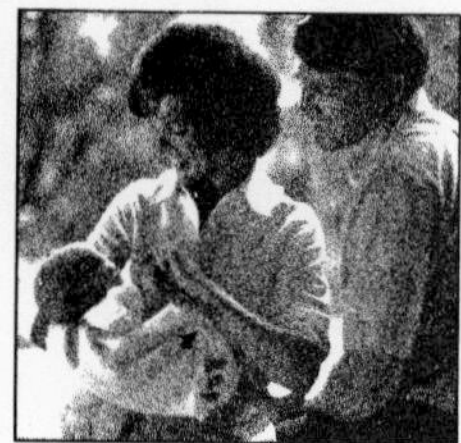

Portrait of the baby

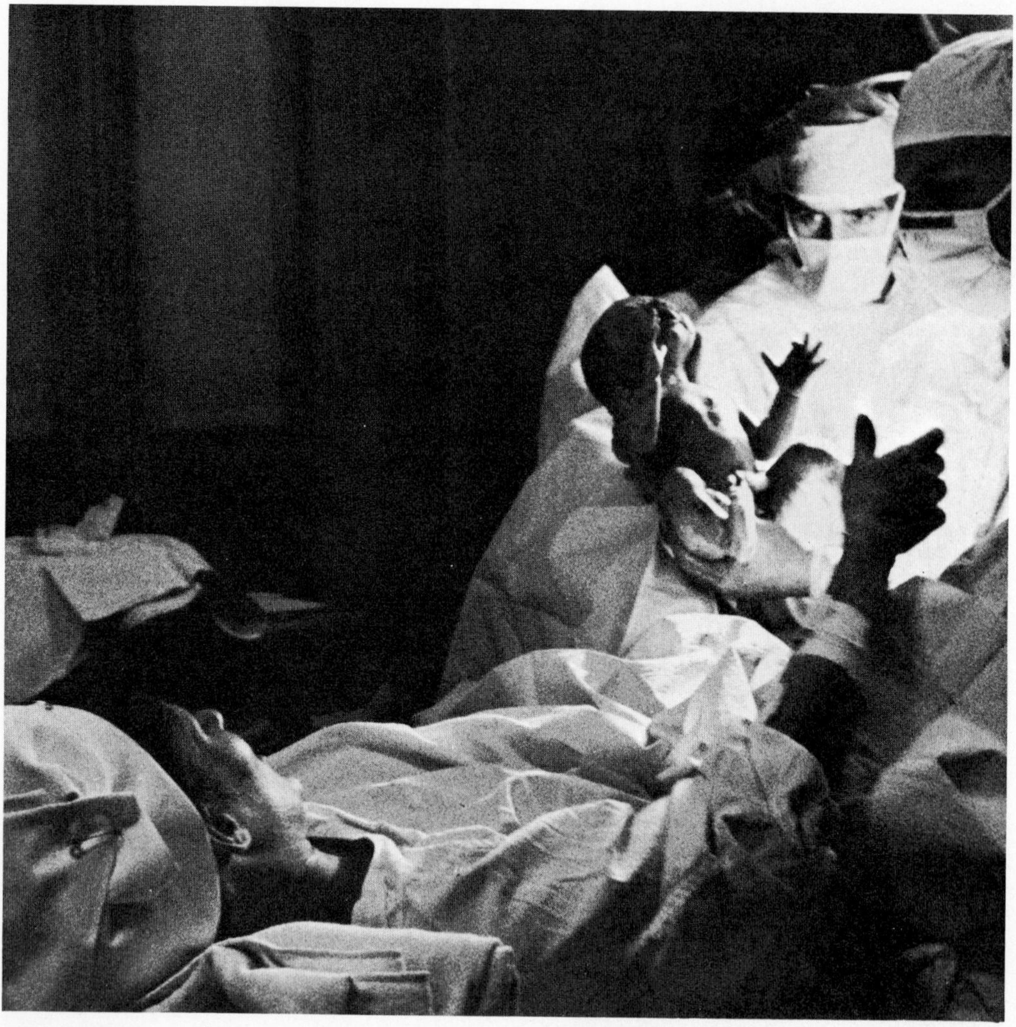

The long months of waiting and wondering are over—the baby is born. The infant looks so weak, so helpless, so dependent.

Suggestions for layette and baby equipment

For baby's wardrobe

Booties or socks, 2 or 3 pairs
Bunting, or coat and hood
Diapers, 3 to 4 dozen cloth diapers or weekly supply of disposable diapers
Sacks and kimonos, 4 to 6 each
Safety pins
Shirts and nightgowns, 4 to 6 each
Sleeping bag, 1 or 2
Sweater, 1 or 2
Waterproof pants, 4

For baby's bed

Basket, bassinet, or crib
Crib blankets, 2 lightweight and 1 winter-weight
Crib bumpers, 1 set
Crib pads, 4 to 6
Crib sheets, 3 or 4 (or pillow slips if you use a basket or bassinet)
Mattress, firm
Mattress cover of heavy plastic, or waterproof sheeting

For baby's room

Baby scale
Chest of drawers
Diaper pail
Night light
Playpen and pad
Rectal thermometer
Rocking chair for parent

For baby's bath

Bath towels and washcloths, 3 or 4 each
Brush and comb
Receiving blankets, 3 or 4
Tray with sterile cotton swabs and cotton balls, mild soap, baby oil, lotion, and baby powder
Tub, plastic or inflatable, and small table

For baby's formula

Bottles, plastic with liner inserts, or: 8 to 10 eight-ounce (240 milliliter) for bottle-fed baby; 2 or 3 if a breast-fed baby has extra feedings
2 or 3 four-ounce (120 milliliter) bottles for orange juice or water
Bottle warmer
Brushes, bottle and nipple
Funnel
Measuring and mixing spoons
Measuring cup
Nipples and caps for all bottles, with a few extra for emergencies
Sterilizer
Tongs

When baby goes out

Baby carriage or stroller
Car bed or car seat
Carriage robe or blanket
Diaper bag

The first time you see your baby will be shortly after he or she is born. He may be quiet and sleepy, or he may be crying lustily. His head may appear pushed out of shape because the skull bones are soft and pliable. His skin may be beet-red and coated with a cheesy substance that will wash off.

Some newborns have almost no hair. Others are born with long, soft hair that rubs off during the first few weeks of life and is replaced by their normal hair. Your baby's eyes may be puffy, especially after the eye drops that doctors use to prevent infection. His hands and feet are probably wrinkled and may be blue or mottled.

All in all, he hardly looks like the bundle of joy you have been picturing for the last several months. Were the magazines wrong? Where are the healthy skin, the bright blue eyes, the ribbons in the hair? And where was the smile of recognition when the nurse put him in his mother's arms?

Be patient. This is the baby's first day in the world, and he is not quite groomed for an official reception. Give him time. And give yourself time. The joys, and hard work, of parenthood are just beginning.

Caring for the baby

Almost all new parents handle their babies as though they are water-filled balloons —ready to burst. These parents are usually overconcerned about care of the baby's navel, his nails, the soft spots in the baby's skull, and (if the child is a boy) the circumcised penis.

The navel seldom calls for more than ordinary care. Immediately after birth, the doctor ties the umbilical cord, then carefully cuts it off close to the baby's body. The small piece of cord still attached to the baby is called the umbilical stump. It dries up and falls off in about a week, leaving the navel to heal. In rare cases, a drop of blood will appear on the stump or around the navel. Dab this away with sterile cotton and report it to your doctor. Keep the area around the stump dry and clean. Until the stump falls off, and until the navel is healed, your doctor may recommend sponge baths for the baby. Occasionally, the stump may become irritated and cause redness around the navel. If this happens, an infection may be present. Call your doctor.

Your baby will scratch himself frequently unless you keep his nails clipped short. If you cannot keep him still enough to cut them while he is awake, cut them when he is least active—while he is asleep.

The soft spots are areas in the baby's skull where the bones have not yet come together. A very tough membrane covers and protects these areas. Ordinary handling and washing of the baby's head and scalp will do no harm.

A few drops of blood may appear on the penis for a day or so after circumcision. For the first few days, apply Vaseline, petrolatum, or some other soothing ointment, and cover loosely with a small, sterile piece of gauze. After a few days you can wash the penis with sterile cotton and a mild soap. Do not apply alcohol because it may sting. Talcum powder may also be irritating. Report any signs of blood to your doctor.

Sleeping

During the first few weeks, your baby will probably sleep from feeding to feeding. But as he gets older, his sleep time diminishes. At first he is awake more in the afternoon. Then he sleeps less during other times of the day. By the time he is a year old, he will probably take only two naps a day—one in the morning and one in the afternoon.

Most newborns are not disturbed by lights or by some noise and activity around them, but the baby should, if possible, have a room by himself. When space is limited, he can still be somewhat separated from the rest of the room by a room divider or a screen. The new baby is most comfortable in a small, close place—a bassinet, a small crib, or even a dresser drawer lined with a pad. When he is older, he needs a high-sided crib.

Bathing

You do not have to bathe your baby every day (three times a week is fine), and bath time does not have to come at the same

Neither phone nor doorbell nor barking dog should distract you when bathing your baby.

time every day. But, whenever you do bathe your baby, remember his safety. Never leave him on a high place from which he could tumble. And never leave him alone when he is in a tub of water. Place everything you need for the baby's bath and dressing within easy reach ahead of time so that you will not have to turn your back to find a towel or a pin or an undershirt.

Either an ordinary, small plastic tub or an inflatable plastic tub placed on the kitchen table lets you bathe the baby while you are standing. This position is more comfortable and safer than bending over a full-sized tub.

Line the tub with a diaper or towel to keep the baby from sliding around. Use only a small amount of water until you get used to handling the baby. The water should be about body temperature, or 98° F. (37° C), which will seem neither hot nor cold when you test it on your wrist or inner elbow. With one hand under the baby's head, and the other under his buttocks or grasping his legs, lower him into the tub. Let him sit in the tub, leaning back a little. Support his head by holding your arm behind his neck and gripping his arm under his armpit. Wash his face first, without soap. Then, with soap, wash his scalp and the rest of his body. When you are done, lay him on a towel and dry him by patting rather than by rubbing.

At each bath, wash the scalp with a mild soap, then comb the scalp with a fine-tooth comb. This helps prevent cradle cap (a crust that forms on the baby's scalp).

Whenever you bathe a baby girl, clean between the folds of the labia where a cheesy substance accumulates. With boys who are not circumcised, your doctor may suggest that you gently push back the foreskin at each bathing to clean the head of the penis, and to ensure that the foreskin does not stick to the head.

Diapers

You may need more than 3 to 4 dozen diapers a week for the first several weeks, particularly if you use the diapers for extra purposes such as burping. Disposable diapers and diaper liners are becoming more popular, and are especially handy when traveling. A diaper service for the first

Fold the diaper as shown above. Boy babies wet the front of their diapers. Girl babies wet the back of their diapers. Place the thickest fold where it is needed.

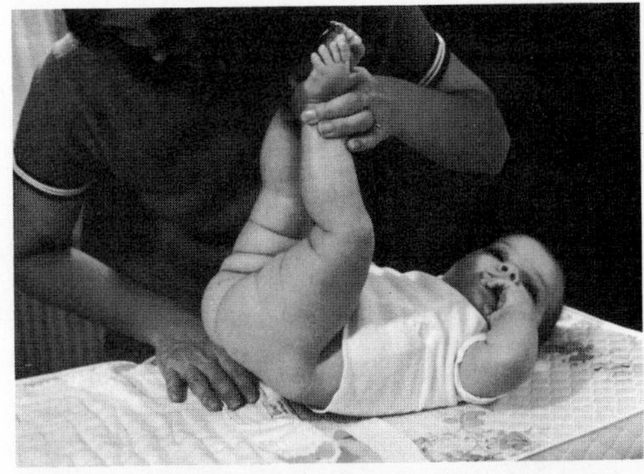

Take hold of the baby's ankles and lift the legs. Then slip the folded diaper under the baby's hips. You may want to work one side of the diaper under and then the other.

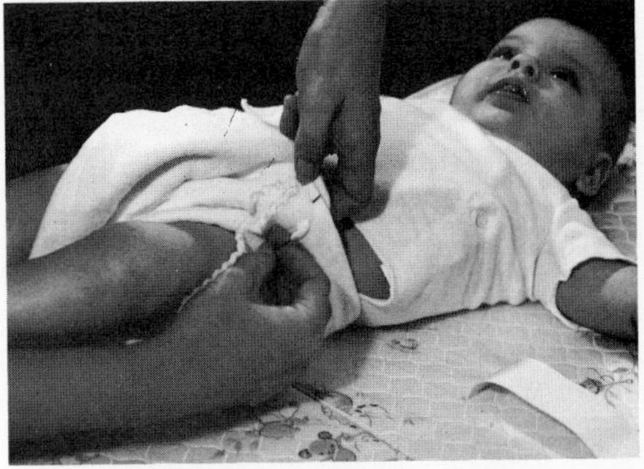

Lap the back fold of the diaper over the front fold. Hold two fingers under the folds next to the baby's skin to prevent sticking the baby with the diaper pin. Then do the same on the other side.

few months, is a great help. The service not only assures you that the diapers are thoroughly clean, but saves you the daily washing and drying.

When changing the baby, never lay down an open safety pin. Always close the pin immediately after you remove it from the baby's diaper. The baby may pick up the safety pin, put it in his mouth, and swallow it. Closed safety pins may pass easily through the baby's bowels and out of his body. An open safety pin is more likely to get stuck.

Each time you change your baby's diaper, wash the diaper area, using cotton balls dipped in lukewarm water. (Do not use alcohol unless your doctor advises it. Alcohol may irritate the skin.) This cleansing of the diaper area is particularly important after each bowel movement. Generally, do not use rubber or plastic pants until the baby is a few weeks old. The pants retain moisture and heat, which may cause diaper rash. If your baby seems to wet a great deal, use two diapers, especially at night.

One way of burping is to hold the baby against your shoulder and pat the child on the back.

Feeding the baby

Whether you breast-feed or bottle-feed, doctors usually recommend following a modified demand feeding schedule during the baby's first few weeks. The baby usually takes two to three ounces (60 to 90 milliliters) of milk at each feeding. Then he sleeps and awakens in about three hours for the next feeding. As the baby grows, his stomach capacity increases. At 8 to 12 weeks, he will take five or six ounces (150 to 180 milliliters) at a feeding, and require only five or six feedings every 24 hours.

Babies sometimes spit up their feeding, usually just a few minutes after they have finished. This may be just a dribble of several drops of milk. If spitting up happens more than one-half hour after the feeding, it will probably be a cheesy material that smells sour because the stomach juices have already started to curdle the milk for digestion. Do not be alarmed. These babies usually weigh enough for their age. The spitting-up probably is caused by an overflow from a full stomach.

In some cases, the baby spits up early during the feeding. His stomach may be filled with air from crying or from improper feeding techniques. If this seems to be the case, burp the baby before and several times during feeding. Once the baby is fed, hold him upright on your lap or over your shoulder (with a diaper or cloth to protect your clothing) and pat or rub his back until he has burped well. Or prop him up against a cushion for 15 to 20 minutes after the feeding. Never feed a baby by propping a bottle in his crib. Not only do you and he miss the mutual pleasure of feeding, but you run the risk of his choking on the milk.

Weaning

Wean your baby gradually from the breast or the bottle, allowing him plenty of time to get used to his new way of eating.

He will decide for himself when he is ready. All you have to do is follow his lead. When he is around 5 or 6 months old, give him a cup to play with. Then, one day, offer him a few sips of milk from it. Gradually, over the next several weeks, he may learn to enjoy drinking from a cup. At each feeding, offer him as much milk from the cup as he will take. Then, allow him to nurse, or offer him a bottle. After a while omit the daily breast- or bottle-feeding that he is least interested in. This is usually the breakfast or lunch feeding. Offer him only the cup at this time. After a week, omit another breast- or bottle-feeding, if the baby is willing. Then, in another week, omit the last of the feedings by breast or bottle.

The baby's willingness to be weaned may not be constant. When he is teething or has some illness, he may revert to the bottle. He may be entirely weaned when he is a year old, or he may cling to his evening bottle for a longer time. It may be comforting to note that it is rare to see a child entering school with a bottle in his lunch box.

Solid foods

Many mothers regard the introduction of solid foods as the surest sign that their babies are growing up. Some feel that solid foods make babies sleep better and longer at night. But feeding of solids may be started too early. In some cases, when a spoon touches the front part of the baby's tongue, the tongue rapidly attempts to push the spoon out. Too early attempts are also generally frustrating and messy, since most of what does get into the child dribbles right back out again. The frustration involved in overcoming the baby's efforts to fend off food can set up a poor eating pattern. Mealtimes should be pleasant experiences, not battles between opposing forces.

When your baby is about 2 or 3 months old, he should accept a spoon in his mouth. At this time, start strained foods in small amounts, increasing the amounts as the baby's capacity and interest increase. Since milk has very little iron in it, the first foods introduced should be cooked, strained cereals with iron added to them. A teaspoon of rice cereal mixed with enough of the baby's formula to give it a smooth consistency is an excellent first food. Although the rice may be relatively tasteless to you, it offers a new and important experience for your baby. He feels a new consistency on his tongue. Some mothers add the cereal to the milk in the baby's bottle, but this deprives the baby of a pleasurable learning experience. Rice cereal is good to start with since it is unlikely to cause allergic or other reactions (such as diarrhea). After a few days, oatmeal, barley, wheat, and, last of all, mixed cereals can be introduced one at a time.

After cereals, introduce other strained foods, one food at a time. Then, if any reaction occurs—such as a rash or diarrhea—you can easily identify the offending food.

This table can be used as a guideline for introducing your baby to solid foods.

Age	Food
2-3 months	Cereals: Rice, oatmeal, barley, wheat, mixed cereals
	Fruits: Applesauce, pears, bananas
3-4 months	Vegetables: Carrots, squash, peas, sweet potatoes, spinach, beans
5-6 months	Meats and eggs: Lamb, chicken, beef, liver, veal; egg yolk

Introduce junior foods (still mostly strained, but with some chunks of food) when the child has one or two primary teeth (6 months old or later). Some babies prefer to skip junior foods and go directly to mashed potatoes, cottage cheese, eggs, hamburger, and other table foods. Most babies at this age also enjoy hard cookies and toast. By the time they are a year old, most children enjoy sucking and gnawing at a chicken bone or lamb chop.

Mealtimes

After he is a year old, your child may appear to eat less, even though he is becoming increasingly more active. A mother who complains that her child is not eating may be surprised to discover that he is gaining weight. At this age, the tremendous growth rate which has taken place during the baby's first year tapers off. And since he can move

"They're off and running!" is the starting cry of many a meal when baby learns to walk.

around more, the child has relatively less time for eating. Often a considerable amount of ingenuity is required to prevent mealtimes from deteriorating into a chase or a battleground.

The 1-year-old should be eating about three times a day and learning the meaning of mealtime. Feed him at the table at about the same time as the rest of the family. To avoid too much disruption, you can feed him most of his meal first, then let him have dessert with the family. Give him small portions that he can finish. If he is still hungry, give him second helpings. This technique avoids the situation where the 1-year-old is faced by a seemingly overwhelming amount and choice of foods, a situation that forces him either to surrender and be stuffed full, or to rebel and not eat at all.

Encourage your child to feed himself. Give him bite-sized portions that are easy to handle. Do not expect him to be adept with a spoon and fork. Expect a fairly messy high chair, clothing, and baby after each meal. However, some limits must be set. Do not let him throw food around. And if he does not finish enough of his meal at mealtimes, do not leave food around for him in case he gets hungry. This only encourages between-meal snacking and leads to more difficulty at the next meal.

Sometimes a 1-year-old begins to drink more and more milk at the expense of meats, vegetables, and other foods. This may follow an illness during which he drinks only milk, or because he is teething. But most often it occurs as a result of mealtime conflicts. The mother finds the bottle a simple solution to getting what she feels are adequate calories into the child. But, milk lacks iron. If this "simple solution" continues beyond a few weeks, the child may suffer serious iron deficiency leading to anemia.

Growth and development

Every child is an individual. He grows and develops at his own rate. Two children in the same family are no exception. One may walk when he is only 9 months old, but the other may save his first step for his first birthday. Generally, however, the growth and development of a child can be fairly well predicted. For more information, see GROWTH on page 133.

The first month

The average newborn weighs from 6½ to 8 pounds (3 to 3.5 kilograms) and is anywhere from 18 to 22 inches (45 to 55 centimeters) long. The baby's first move toward growth usually begins with a weight loss. In the first three to five days, he may lose up to 10 per cent of his weight. This occurs because he is losing more fluids than he is getting at his feedings. There is no need to worry. The baby usually regains his birth weight by the end of his second week.

The first few weeks of your baby's life are taken up almost completely by eating and sleeping, and crying when hungry, wet, or otherwise uncomfortable. His breathing while he is asleep is erratic—at times very noisy and fast, at times very quiet. The newborn baby breathes through his nose and finds it almost impossible to breathe through his mouth. This makes it possible for the newborn to feed and breathe at the same time, without ever removing the bottle or breast from his mouth.

The newborn keeps his hands tightly clenched most of the time and holds them close to his face. When he is picked up, his arms and legs may stiffen or make jerky movements. His hands and chin may tremble at times. These movements gradually disappear after the baby is a few weeks old.

At times, a young infant moves about in his crib, and goes from one end to the other. While the infant is lying on his back, he may kick, and when he is held erect, he may make stepping motions.

Babies are born with certain reflex actions. A noise or movement can set off flailing of the arms and legs, quivering of the chin, and loud crying. In the first month, the ringing of a bell can make the baby stop what he or she is doing. If you put your finger or an object against the baby's palm, he closes his hand and grips it, but then drops it. A soft touch of the finger or the nipple of mother's breast is enough to make him turn in that direction and start sucking.

During the first month of life, the baby has little control of his head. It lags when you lift him to a sitting position. It is for this reason you should keep a hand behind the baby's head when you pick him up.

Age 1 to 4 months

Between 1 and 2 months of age, the baby is able to raise his head up above a flat surface. As he continues to grow, he can hold his head up longer.

By 2 months of age, the baby usually stops crying on hearing mother speak, even though he is wet, hungry, or uncomfortable. At about four to six weeks of age, the baby smiles for the first time, generally in response to mother's voice. In the next few weeks, the baby begins smiling at all pleasant voices, then familiar faces.

At 3 months of age, the baby's head still bobs when he sits, but he is beginning to hold his head erect. When lying on his stomach, a baby 3 to 4 months old can raise his head and chest well above the mattress, supporting his weight on his forearms.

The 3-month-old may spend long periods of time looking at his hands and watching his fingers move. The baby plays with his hands as with a toy. Near four months of age, the baby can bring his hands together in front of him, and before long may actively suck his thumb.

Although at about 3 months he still cannot reach out and grasp an object, the baby does have an ever increasing amount of arm and hand movements. The hands are no longer tight little fists. The baby holds objects that are placed in them. By the age of 4 months, the baby can hold and shake a rattle.

At about 4 months of age, a baby's eyes can focus on an object and follow it through a full 180 degrees. He can also focus on objects that he is holding. The eyes may cross, particularly if he stares at objects for a long time. Do not let this concern you unless the baby's eyes persistently remain crossed.

When the baby is about 4 or 5 months old, he will probably roll over for the first time, usually from the belly to the back. So do not leave the baby alone on a table or bed.

Before long, if you put the baby on his back, he may roll over on his stomach and get onto his hands and knees, as though ready to creep. While lying on his back, he may lift his head and shoulders as though he is trying to sit up.

During this period, the baby begins to imitate sounds that he hears, almost to the point of carrying on a conversation. This is the beginning of language. At about 4 months, your baby may also laugh aloud, with a deep belly laugh. The first time he does, the sound may surprise him and scare him into a short period of crying. But soon, the infant laughs in response to almost any pleasant sound or smiling face.

At this age, the baby will begin to anticipate feeding. As soon as he recognizes his bottle, he may begin to wave his arms and legs excitedly and make sucking movements with his mouth.

Age 5 to 8 months

At this time, the baby is able to pull himself to a sitting position when someone lifts his hands, and he can sit alone for about half an hour if he is well propped. Some more placid infants, particularly if they are plump, lie on their backs a little longer and do not sit alone with support until the seventh month or so.

During these months, your baby is busy exploring his own body and all things around him. Everything seems to go into his mouth —not only his thumb and his hands, but also his toys, his toes, his rattles, and the ribbons on his nightshirts. As can be expected, he also drools a lot.

One of the biggest enjoyments of watching your baby grow is seeing the first tooth come in. Preceded by weeks of drooling, and followed by more of the same, the first tooth produces pride that is a forerunner of what you will feel when baby takes that first step.

The first tooth generally breaks through the gums when the baby is 6 or 7 months old. But if it does not come until several months later, do not be concerned. As you will be told over and over again, every child is an individual. (For more information about the teeth, see TEETH AND TEETHING in the Medical Guide.)

At some time in this period, usually at 6

Most parents eagerly look forward to the appearance of teeth in their baby's mouth. First teeth usually start to break through the gums when the baby is 6 or 7 months old.

Major milestones of motor development

Age in months	Activity
1-2	Lifts head when lying on stomach
3-4	Lifts chest when lying on stomach
4-5	Reaches out and grasps objects; Rolls over
5-6	Sits up if propped
6-7	Transfers objects hand to hand
7-8	Sits without support
8-9	Grasps small objects with thumb and index finger
9-10	Crawls; Creeps on hands and knees; Stands with support
11-12	Walks with support of one hand
13-15	Walks alone; Climbs onto furniture; Turns the pages of a book
16-18	Runs stiffly; Feeds self

Usually, the skills of motor development come one after another in orderly fashion. In some instances, the achievement of one skill depends on successful achievement of a previous one—for example, a baby learns to take hold of an object voluntarily before he learns how to pass it from one hand to the other. Sometimes, however, children skip milestones. For example, although most infants crawl and then creep before walking, others may skip the crawling and creeping stages completely. Every child is different. No two infants, even in the same family, develop at exactly the same rate.

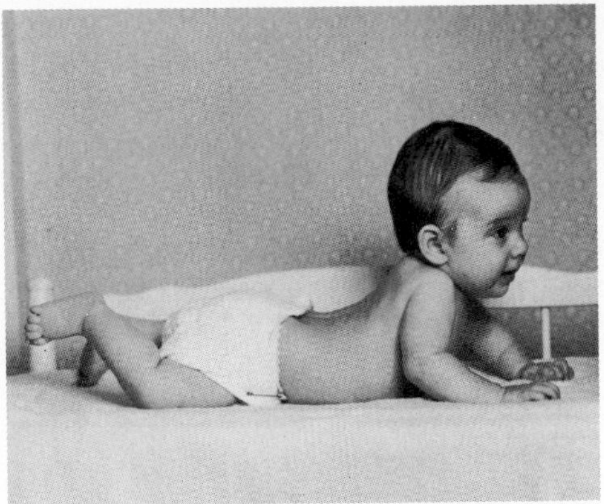

3-4 months: usually lifts chest

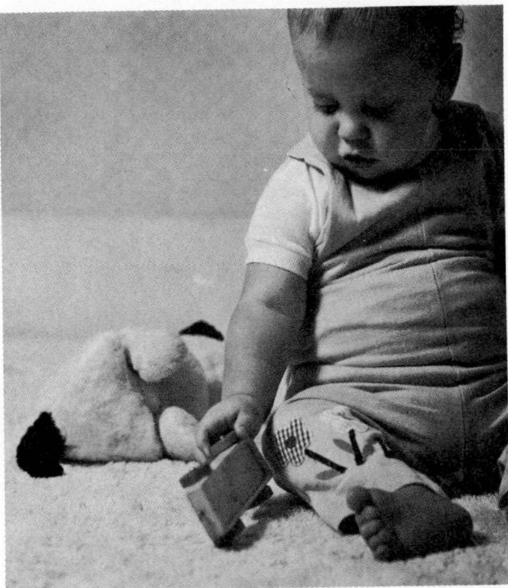

7-8 months: usually sits without support

9-10 months: usually creeps on hands and knees

13-15 months: usually walks alone

Babies love the shine, noise, and texture of pots and pans.

months, the baby may develop a fear of strangers. In all likelihood, this represents an increasing ability to tell familiar faces from unfamiliar ones.

At 6 or 7 months of age, the baby develops the ability to pass objects from one hand to the other. The infant can grasp an object, move it over to the opposite hand, and take hold of it with that hand.

By about 8 or 9 months of age, the baby usually starts to develop the ability to use his thumb and index finger for grasping small objects. And he uses both hands simultaneously—feeding himself a cookie with one hand while he bangs his cup or plate with a toy held in the other hand.

Age 9 to 12 months

At this age, the baby reaches out into his environment, not only with the hands but with the whole body. He can sit, lie on his back, and then sit again. By 9 or 10 months, an infant can crawl on his stomach and creep on his hands and knees. And he can support his weight by holding onto the sides of his crib or playpen.

Most babies of this age can pull themselves to a standing position without any help. You may put your baby down in the crib or playpen, only to find the child standing by the time you turn around. In the beginning, however, he may not know how to sit down again. About this time, cruising from one piece of furniture to another becomes an exciting event. By the end of the first year, most babies can walk with one hand supported, and some can walk without any support at all.

During this period, the baby learns to do many things with hands and fingers—poke, point, touch, lift, twist, squeeze, pick up, and drop. Simple items such as spoons, pots, and pans can keep a child busy for hours. The baby becomes adept at repeatedly dropping toys, utensils, or food from the high chair or over the side of the playpen. This can be quite upsetting, especially when cereal is dropped to the kitchen floor or when dropped glasses shatter. Console yourself with the fact that this is all part of your baby's normal development. He is learning that if he drops something, it will fall. He is also learning a new way to get attention.

He uses his spoon more at mealtime—but less to feed himself than to splash it in his food. He can drink from a cup by the end of the first year, although this is usually pretty messy. To save on breakage, and for safety, you might want to use plastic cups.

Age 13 to 15 months

During this period your baby will probably begin to walk alone, providing a new degree of independence and leading to considerable exploring. He climbs onto and off furniture. Since an infant does not know the difference between dangerous and safe situations, you should set limits on his activity.

The child of 15 months gets joy from dumping items out of a bottle or a box, and may practice this skill by emptying wastebaskets and pouring liquids out of bottles. Be certain that medicines, household cleaners, and other poisons are out of reach. A simple chain lock keeps kitchen closets closed. If one closet can be filled with pots, pans, plastic jars, and other favorite toys, let your baby open that one and play with its contents. This should divert him from locked closets.

Besides being so active, the baby will sit for long periods of time, turning the pages of a magazine or picture book, or playing with blocks and toys. He assists in dressing and undressing himself, although his "help" may lengthen the process.

Some children of this age virtually quit talking so that they can spend more time learning other skills. It is as though they can concentrate on the development of only one major skill at a time.

It is also at about this time that children understand a number of verbal commands, particularly "no." A child of this age usually understands "no" so well that he starts using it for his own purposes. He pushes toys or food that he does not want away from him. He may not want to give up a toy or stop an enjoyable game just when you want him to. And it becomes increasingly hard to substitute one activity for another.

Age 16 to 18 months

At this age, the child's motor activity is reaching such a fine level of control that he starts to run instead of walk. In fact, it may

A baby about a year and a half old can walk up and down stairs with help.

seem that he is on the run constantly, going from room to room with frustrating speed. And he can walk up and down stairs while holding your hand.

Feeding time is somewhat neater because the infant has better control of the spoon. Now he scribbles on paper with a crayon, and—when unsupervised—he is just as capable of doing so on a wall or on the floor. He enjoys building towers of two or three blocks and then knocking them down. At around 18 months, you may be able to determine whether your child will be left-handed or right-handed, but this is a trait that is seldom strongly demonstrated before the end of the second year.

By the time he is 18 months old, your child should know the names of many household items. He may not be able to call them by name, but he understands what they are and can associate the names with pictures, as well as with the objects themselves.

The 16-to-18-month-old is a conflict between dependence and independence. He sets out on his own to explore the environment—climbing, walking, opening doors, trying to dress himself, and helping to feed himself. But he still must be helped down from the steps he has climbed, given the proper foods to eat, protected from accidents, and cuddled and cooed over when he scrapes a knee.

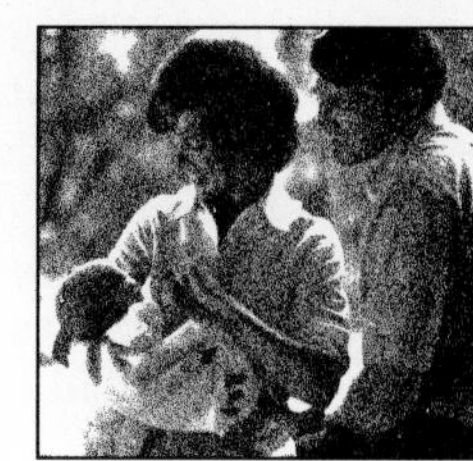

Health and safety

One of the best ways to keep your baby healthy is to take him to a physician who can regularly check the progress of the child's development and immunize him against many infectious diseases. The doctor may help prevent problems from occurring, or he may catch a minor problem early and deal with it before it worsens. He may discover any medical quirks the baby has, such as an allergy to a specific medicine.

Since the infant grows at such a rapid rate, and since he is continually developing

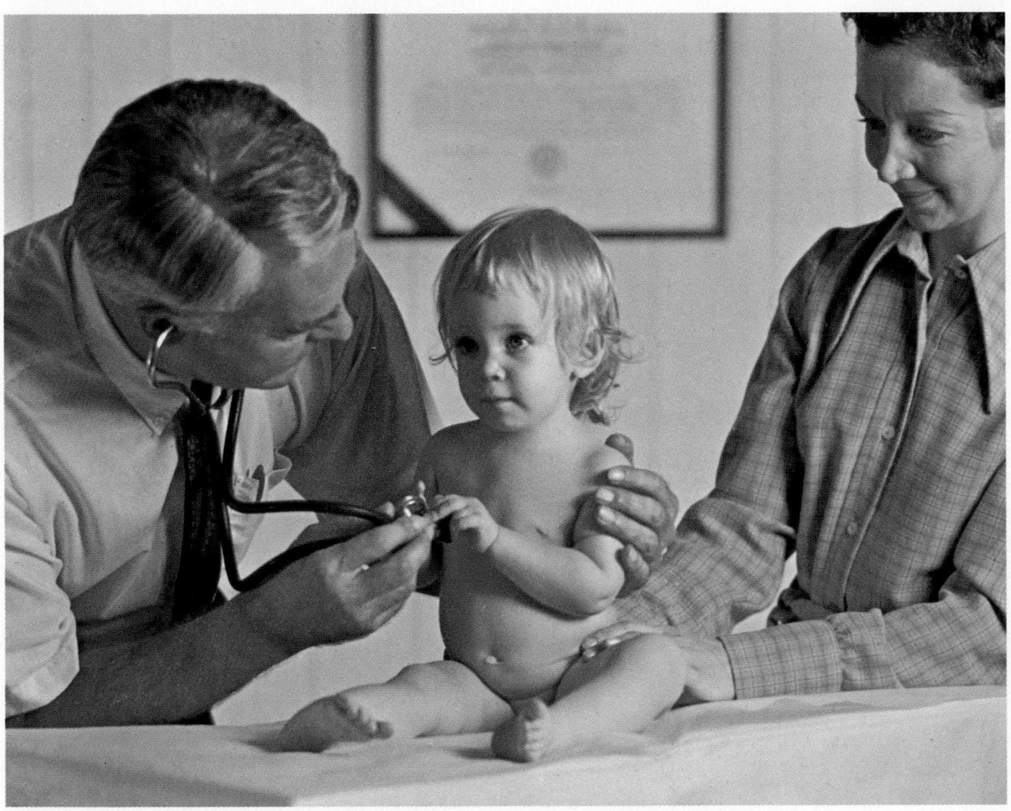

A doctor tries to ease a child's fears by his friendly, interested manner. Regular visits help build a trusting relationship between the doctor and child.

new skills, you should take him to the doctor almost monthly during the first six months of the baby's life. As the baby grows older, you can lengthen the time between visits to every two months in the last half of the first year, and to every three or four months in the second year.

Shots

Your baby should be immunized against diphtheria, tetanus, whooping cough (pertussis), polio, measles, German measles (rubella), and mumps. Except for oral polio vaccine, which is given by drops, the other vaccines are given by injection. The MMR vaccines—measles, mumps, and rubella—usually require only a single shot to give adequate protection. The DTP vaccines—diphtheria, tetanus, and whooping cough—are also usually given in a single shot, but at three different times. Oral polio vaccine is usually given at the same time as the DTP shots.

Your baby should be immunized as early in his life as possible, because most of the infectious diseases can be contracted then, and some (such as whooping cough) are more severe in young children than in older ones. Also, the younger the child is when he gets his shots, the less likely he is to remember them as unpleasant experiences.

(For more information on immunization, see the following articles in the Medical Guide: DIPHTHERIA, GERMAN MEASLES, IMMUNIZATION, MEASLES, POLIOMYELITIS, SHOTS, SMALLPOX, and TETANUS.)

Common illnesses and conditions

Here are a few of the common illnesses and conditions you may encounter during your baby's first 18 months. Each illness or condition is discussed in detail in a separate article in the Medical Guide.

Illness	Symptoms
Colds	Trouble eating, stuffy nose
Colic	Crying; hard, flat abdomen; gas
Cradle cap	Whitish scales on the scalp; yellow, greasy crust on the scalp
Diaper rash	Red pimples and irritation in the diaper area
Earache	Fever, irritability, pulling or rubbing at ears, crying when moved, turning head from side to side
Eczema	Itching rash, usually on the inside of the elbows and on the back of the knees
Hernia	A bulge in lower abdomen
Prickly heat	Pink rash, most noticeable in the folds of the skin
Roseola Infantum	Fever, faint rash

In the first years of your baby's life, his stomach and intestines may be very sensitive to any change in his health. Some infants vomit or have diarrhea with almost every illness—colds, earaches, intestinal infections, or more serious illnesses. The younger the infant, the more serious vomiting and diarrhea may be. Rapid losses of body fluids by vomiting and diarrhea can cause dehydration, which, if severe enough, may require hospitalization and intravenous feedings to restore fluids.

Most infants have between 3 and 8 small bowel movements a day of soft, pasty stool. This is not diarrhea. Diarrhea is an intestinal disorder marked by frequent, loose, watery bowel movements. Sometimes, diarrhea develops from too much sugar, too much liquid, or too concentrated a formula. Too little sugar, too dilute a formula, or too little liquid can cause dry, hard stools (constipation). If you breast-feed, be cautious of your diet. Foods which cause diarrhea in the mother are likely to have the same effect on the baby.

If diarrhea occurs without vomiting, follow these measures.

Do not feed the baby any fruits, meats, or vegetables.

If you are breast-feeding, try to find out what food in your diet is causing the diarrhea, and stop eating that food.

If you are bottle-feeding, substitute boiled skimmed milk, diluted with equal parts of water so that the baby's formula will be one-half of each.

Give the baby diluted weak tea, broth or clear soups, liquid gelatin, flat ginger ale, or other clear fluids alternately with the special milk feedings.

If your baby is still hungry, give him rice cereal, mashed bananas, and applesauce. You may add cottage cheese, mashed potatoes, and soft-boiled eggs to this menu for an older child who has diarrhea.

If vomiting occurs alone or complicates the diarrhea, limit feedings to less than an ounce at a time. If vomiting or diarrhea lasts beyond 6 to 12 hours, call your doctor.

(For more information on diarrhea, vomiting, and dehydration, see the separate articles on each in the Medical Guide.)

Accidents

In the United States alone, about 15,000 children under the age of 15 die each year because of accidents. That is more than the next three leading causes of death combined.

One of your biggest jobs as a parent is to be alert to dangers of which your child cannot possibly be aware. Never leave a young child alone in a bathtub. He can drown in very shallow water, or he may turn on the hot water and scald himself severely. Burns in the kitchen can occur from boiling hot water, hot plates, and the oven itself. The crawling baby can pull himself to a standing position and pull a pot off the stove, spilling the contents on himself. Use gates to prevent falls down a flight of stairs. Take precautions to prevent the young child from running into the street, and from accidentally drowning in a back-yard pool.

Medicines are the most common poisonous substances accidentally taken by children, and aspirin is the most common of all. Following this comes a whole series of cleaners and sanitizing agents (most often found in the bathroom); cosmetics (generally in or on nightstands in the bedroom); paint and furniture polishes; and insecticides, gasoline, and charcoal lighter fluids.

Here are some ways to "poison-proof" your home.

Find out which of your common household items are poisonous.

Keep all drugs, poisons, and household chemicals out of a child's reach.

Put medicines back in their usual storage place immediately after using them.

Discard medicines after you have recovered from the illness for which they were prescribed.

Never store poisonous or inflammable substances in food or beverage containers. They may be mistakenly consumed.

Toys

Since anything your baby plays with is bound to be put into his mouth, his toys should have smooth surfaces, and they should be easy to wash and keep clean. There should be no sharp edges or detachable parts such as glass eyes, buttons, pompons, and bells.

Even though loving relatives and friends shower your baby with elaborate rattles, and gadgets to be suspended over carriage or crib, you have to select and offer him only those playthings that are safe and appropriate for his age. And, if you ever decide to repaint a toy, never use a lead-base paint because it can cause lead poisoning.

Simple toys are best, especially for babies: rattles that cannot be broken or chewed into small pieces; teething rings; dolls and animals made of cloth, plastic, or rubber; spoons and cups; spools strung together; cereal boxes; and, of course, something that floats in the bathtub.

Cabinets under a sink are easily opened by children. Check to be sure nothing poisonous is stored there.

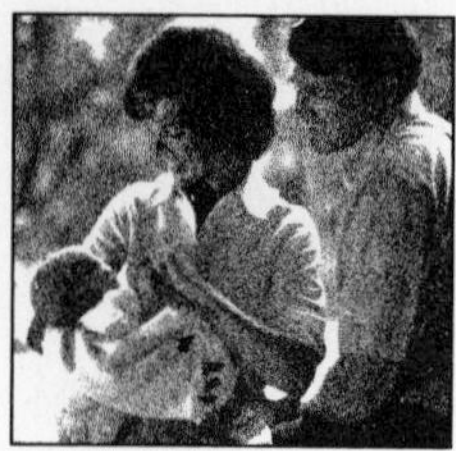

Common concerns

Spoiling

A young infant cannot be spoiled by too much love and attention. He learns to feel secure and develops good relationships with his parents by their response to his needs. The notion that it is good for a baby to cry just for the sake of crying is not a sound one.

It is perfectly natural for the new baby to be the center of attention in the family. During the first two years, he is dependent on his parents. He is held, carried, fed, bathed, changed, and dressed. As he grows, this physical dependence tapers off. Parents gradually give up controls as the child performs tasks independently. The 9-month-old is carried or pushed in a stroller. At one year, he begins to walk, but he is still carried or pushed in a stroller much of the time. But when he is 18 months or 2 years, he does not want to be carried at all. This natural progression is repeated over and over with feeding, bathing, and dressing.

A parent who is spoiling his child has a hard time "letting go." He is not willing to let the child do things for himself, even though the child is quite ready to do so.

Setting limits

Setting limits means setting up guidelines, which all children need. As a parent, it is your responsibility to set reasonable limits. Often a child's negativism is merely his way of testing you to see if you are being consistent in the limits you are setting.

Certain limits are obvious. Do not let your child crawl or walk onto the street. Do not let him pound on a glass door. Do not let him near a hot stove. These are limits that protect the child against danger.

Other limits are less easy to set, but just as important. A good example that deals with the very young child is setting a time for going to sleep. Establish a bedtime hour —not too early while the baby is still playful and alert, and not too late when he is irritable and overtired. But do not be overrigid about the time. If the child has had a longer nap than usual, he may not be ready for sleep at his regular hour.

If successful, the guidelines you set can serve as a basis for the child's behavior throughout childhood.

Toilet training

Many parents want to know how early they can begin toilet training. There is a natural desire to want the child "out of diapers." However, attempts at training too early can do more harm than good. They merely set the stage for confrontations between parent and child, and for a series of mutual frustrations and anxieties.

In general, wait until the child has mastered walking before attempting training. This usually occurs after 18 months. Bowel control most often is attained before bladder control. Daytime bladder control is generally attained before nighttime control. Girls are usually toilet-trained earlier than boys. Since each child is different, no single schedule should be expected to hold for any two children.

You will find further information on toilet training in THE TODDLER section.

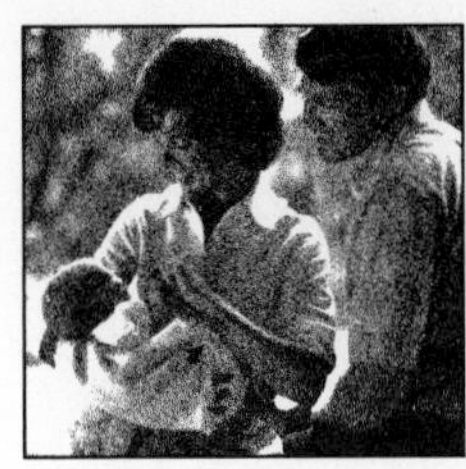

You and your baby

The coming of a baby into a home is bound to cause a certain amount of conflict. From time to time, mixed feelings are aroused in parents as well as in brothers and sisters.

Most fathers of first babies have their moments of wondering if their wives will be as considerate and understanding as they were before the baby's arrival. New mothers have their bad times, too, when they feel resentful or depressed about being so "tied down"—or about what seems to them lack of consideration from their husbands. And if the new baby is not a first one, the children in the family will inevitably feel, on occasion, that life was better before the baby came. These feelings are universal. They are nothing to be ashamed of.

The relationship between father, mother, and the baby is very important. The baby learns and develops skills, to a considerable degree, in response to the stimulation and love provided by you, his parents. You, in turn, become sensitive to your baby's needs—both physical and emotional. Only then can you respond to them appropriately.

Every baby develops a different relationship with his parents, different from any other set of parents and child. Even children in the same family react differently to their parents. Each child should be viewed as an individual. It often is necessary to modify an approach which has been successful in dealing with one child in the family, when the same situation comes up with another child. Certainly, what works for a neighbor may not be appropriate for you.

Magazines, television programs, and books like this are full of general advice for parents. What is more important is the development of confidence in *your* own abilities to deal with *your* child. Despite all the advice and pressures, you are still the one responsible and the one best able to solve day-to-day problems. Try to anticipate the needs of your children. Meet the needs with love, not overprotection. And help provide the environment for each child to grow and develop to his full potential.

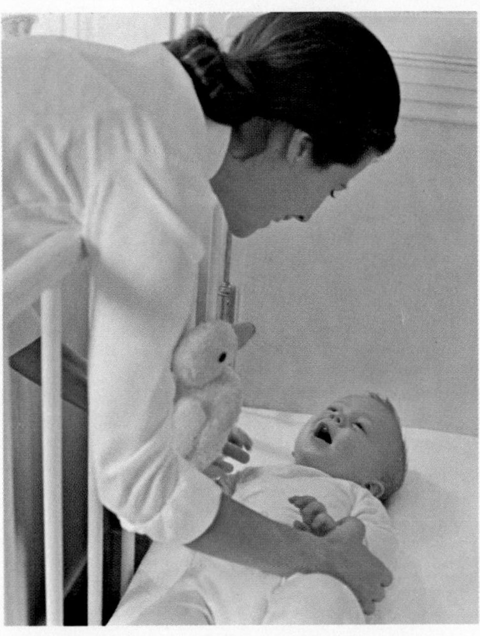

Bedtime should be a happy time—a time for lullabies and talking.

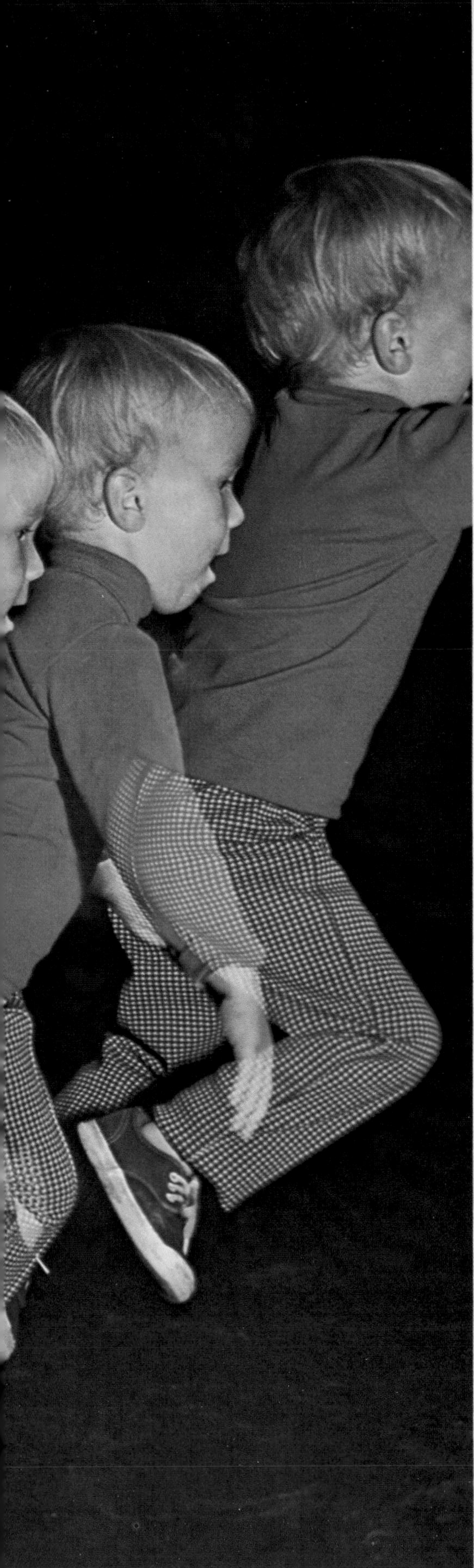

The Toddler: 18 months to 3 years

For months you have been saying, "I can't wait until my baby can walk." "I can't wait until my baby can talk." And suddenly—your baby can! Suddenly, your baby is a toddler—a walking, talking, jumping, grabbing, pot-bellied, knock-kneed toddler, who always seems to have a runny nose. What a difference from the baby you brought home from the hospital! Now the toddler stands, and has a new outlook. How sure, how cocky, how independent! Every object seen is a new challenge. And yet, the toddler is still very dependent on you—for love, for physical needs, for the setting of limits on aggressive behavior, for praise when it is earned. The toddler is a paradox, loudly proclaiming independence one minute; then seeking to be hugged and cuddled the next.

By Lendon Smith, M.D.

Portrait of the toddler

The toddler "toddles" for only a few weeks. By the time he is 18 months old, he is running, dashing, plummeting headlong into his environment—testing, tasting, clawing, groping, eyeballing, listening, poking, probing, stamping. He acts as if he must analyze the entire world and has only one day in which to do it.

There are times during this period that the child seems determined to conquer or even to destroy the environment. Actually, the toddler is trying out big muscles used for running, jumping, climbing, pounding, and hitting. The child's nervous system and attention span are not developed well enough to settle down to quiet work. You are doomed to fail if you try to force silent, stationary activity. A certain amount of time and energy must be channeled into big-muscle activity before the toddler can go to the next level.

Motor abilities and development

Keep in mind that no child can perform a task until sufficient development of that part of the nervous system responsible for its performance. Pushing a child beyond his physical and mental capacities only frustrates both parent and child. Every new activity the toddler performs indicates that nerves and muscles have developed sufficiently to allow him to perform it. He must acquire the ability for task A before going to task B. He sits before he stands. He stands before he walks. He walks before he runs.

The age at which a child is able to perform a specific task is largely determined by heredity. But it is also influenced by such variables as nerve and brain damage, environmental encouragement, nutrition, sickness, and availability of toys.

Yet even though each child is different, children master abilities at fairly predictable times and in a fairly predictable order. An average 18-month-old toddler generally can eat without help, drink from a cup, use a spoon, use five words accurately, walk well, stack a few blocks, and pretend to do housework. At 2, toddlers run well, throw a ball, scribble, turn pages, combine a few words, listen to stories, and know their first name. Toilet training may begin. (For more information, see TOILET TRAINING on pages 44 and 45.)

At 3, toddlers walk upstairs alternating feet, ride a tricycle, jump in place, copy a circle and a cross, and know their age and full name.

Growth

A toddler grows more slowly than a new baby. Most girls at 18 months have acquired about half of their adult height. Boys at age 2 are about halfway there. Body length increases in the second year by 3 to 4 inches (7.5 to 10 centimeters), and in the third year by 2 to 3 inches (5 to 7.5 centimeters). See GROWTH, page 133.

A toddler's appetite usually diminishes. The 2-year-old eats to live. When he was 2 months old, he was living only to eat. This appetite loss upsets most mothers. They feel that their child must be sick if he does not eat. The real reason for the child's loss of

The average 18-month-old toddler can eat with a spoon and drink from a cup.

By about 18 months of age, a toddler can usually build a tower of two or three blocks.

By the age of 2, most toddlers can throw a ball with some skill, and are able to run well.

A 2-year-old toddler may become fascinated with copying a circle that you draw.

appetite is that he is so busy exploring that food becomes less important. By the time he is 18 to 24 months old, his motor skills allow him to feed himself as much as he needs.

Mother vs. toddler

Toddlers constantly play games in which they test the physical properties of their environment. They confirm the law of gravity, the stickiness of juice, the wetness of water, and the heat of flame. They also discover mother's distress when they have gone too far. They learn that if they hurt a younger baby, they may get spanked. If they throw toys out the window, they may get scolded. If they say a bad word, they may get sent to their room. In other words, they learn that they must control their anger and impulsive behavior, or they temporarily lose mother's love. And this love is about the only real defense they have against a big, hostile world. In this way, mothers teach their toddlers, by example and discipline, respect for living things and dangerous objects.

Typical day

All toddlers seem to be early risers. It may be because of wet diapers, a full bladder, hunger, or just because they want to get on with the joyful business of living.

Some children can undress themselves at 2, but dressing themselves is another story. They stand and lift one leg after the other to have pants put on. But it takes much longer to figure out which arm goes into which sleeve of a shirt or blouse. And even a bright child of 2 cannot master putting on stockings properly. It may seem to take forever, but let the child dress without too much help from you. This adds to the child's self-esteem.

Most toddlers adapt to three meals a day. But some prefer several light meals. If so, you might serve small amounts of fresh fruits and vegetables, cheese, and peanut butter—all good, nutritional foods.

Off to breakfast

Breakfast for toddlers should include fresh fruit or juice, an egg or other food high in protein content, along with some wholegrain cereal or bread.

After breakfast

Now the toddler is ready for action. Try a walk through the neighborhood or a stroll in the park. This will give the toddler a chance to see, feel, and hear new things, as well as to run and shout.

Back home again, let the toddler listen to music or watch a carefully selected television program. This will give you both a breather before lunch.

Lunch

For lunch, you might offer your toddler a peanut-butter sandwich and a glass of milk or vegetable juice. This could be alternated with bean or lentil soup, cheese, or a frankfurter. Skip luncheon meats with

Outdoors, a toddler has the chance to run and shout and use up tremendous energy.

nitrates, or soups and canned pasta with MSG (monosodium glutamate). Nitrates and MSG are both unnecessary salts.

For dessert, offer fruit or a cookie made with honey rather than one made with sugar.

Nap

Then comes blessed nap time. Naps are often sanity savers for the mothers of toddlers. The nap should be long enough to be a real break for both mother and toddler, but not so long that the child will not go to bed at a reasonable time at night.

Some self-winding children cannot relax and sleep. They suspect that when mother wants them to nap, something big is going to happen that they will miss. They know that shutting their eyes and relaxing leads to sleep. To avoid this pitfall, they sing, talk, toss, pick their noses, pace the floor, gaze out the window—anything to prevent sleep. After two hours, when nap time is just about over, they fall asleep and—if not awakened—will sleep until 8 P.M. and then not sleep again until 1 A.M.

However, even if the toddler does not sleep during his nap time, the period has some value. Mother and child can confront each other afterwards with a fresh approach. After the toddler's nap, a cracker and some juice might provide just enough energy to hold him until supper.

Dinner

The ideal evening meal should be a relaxed, happy time that the whole family—father, mother, toddler—can enjoy together. However, what often happens is far from ideal.

Commuting problems and the toddler's early bedtime often make it impractical to hold dinner until father gets home. In such cases, let the toddler eat his dinner early but have dessert with father. Save those ideal family dinners for the less hectic weekend.

Bath and bed

The full stomach, some time playing with dad, then a hot bath and a change into night clothes usually drains enough energy from the toddler so that he is easily put to bed after a story or two (or three or four). Most

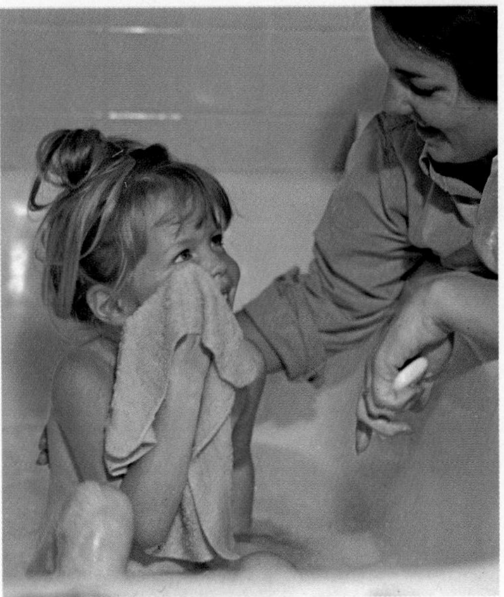

After an activity-filled day, a relaxing, warm bath helps prepare a toddler for bed.

children have a ritual they have to perform before calling it a day: brush teeth, say prayers, adjust toys and dolls, check for scary things under the bed, and so on. Almost all children of this age go through a period when they are reluctant to go to sleep at night. They try to extend nighttime rituals by asking for another story, another drink of water, another trip to the bathroom, and still another drink of water. Somehow parents put up with it.

Around the age of 2 years, the toddler has learned how to climb over the side of his crib and come out into the living room, where he suspects the action is. You know that he is tired, but he just refuses to go to sleep. Be firm. Put him back to bed. Keep his room free from stimulating toys. Leave a night light on for him if he is afraid of the dark. Shut the door firmly, but do not lock it. Hopefully, the toddler will fall asleep—from boredom if nothing else.

Most children need and want rules. They like to break them, but that is no reason for not having them. A reasonable bedtime should be gently insisted upon. Parents should back each other up on a mutually agreed-upon time.

For more information, see SLEEP in the Medical Guide.

The toddler's education

The role of play

The toddler at play is really at work coping with his environment. He thought he had complete control, but he learns that many things in his environment are immovable (walks, trees, cement). He also learns that some things are taboo (hurting pets, hurting other children) and that some things are painful (a hot stove, falling).

When he is with children of his own age, he usually tries to dominate. But, depending on his sex, genetic, and neurological makeup, he may sit mute as a passive observer or tearfully withdraw to thumb-sucking. Or, he may ignore a "playmate" for a ball or blocks. Children rarely play "together" until they are close to 3 years old.

"Playing" with mother is not merely play. It is an important way the toddler learns.

Because humans want and need love from other humans, the child learns to control his impulsive, aggressive, domineering attitude when his onslaughts bring tears, withdrawal, or counterattacks from his playmates. The mother or father usually acts as a referee when toddlers are romping together. It is not fair to expect toddlers to behave like perfect ladies and gentlemen. This is a period when they just have to run roughshod over their environment. A hellion at home may be an angel at nursery school. This is a good sign that he has some ability at self-control. By age 3, the child should be able to play with another child sometimes, or at least play alongside another child.

Toys

When toddlers play, they imitate things they have experienced themselves and activities they see adults doing. The toddler cuddles and feeds a doll or stuffed animal. He follows mother and "helps" her with the cleaning. He enjoys clambering under tables and chairs to dust furniture legs. Using a toy carpet sweeper, he, too, cleans the rugs. He probably will not stay with the job very long, but he gets a sense of belonging and he actually develops manual skill crawling in and out of small places.

Educational toys for toddlers have simple parts that fit together. Some of these toys have big bolts and locks, gears and wheels. Some come apart in several pieces and re-

Toddlers are talkers. And although they are not very good at first, they improve day by day. The best thing you can do is be a good listener.

quire dexterity to reassemble—dexterity a child gains only through practice.

Here are some other playthings the toddler will enjoy.

Toys with handles so that he can push and pull them along the floor

A large ball that he can throw and chase

Objects that he can load and unload in a toy truck

Boxes that fit together, and into which he can put things

Baby dolls and stuffed animals

A sandbox or dirt pile for digging in

A bathtub or small pool for splashing and kicking in, with sponges to squeeze, boats or animals that float, and a plastic pitcher to fill up and empty

A broom or other housekeeping toy to "help" mother

Learning to talk

Speech is one indication that we are intelligent animals. It is also a more highly civilized way to communicate personal needs than kicking and shoving. When the toddler begins to talk, he cries less. When he learns how to swear, his temper tantrums decrease. He spends so much of his time imitating others that his speech and vocabulary, in general, will reflect the verbal skills of those around him. Sentences and messages directed to him should be stated directly and clearly. Do not give him too many choices. To get him to bed, say "Do you want to say your prayers now or after you get into bed?" To get him to eat some peas, say "Do you want six peas or seven peas?"

Listen to your toddler when he speaks. A smile or a nod will encourage his speech struggles. Stammering at age 3 is considered a normal stage in speech development. Overzealous attempts to correct the toddler's speech may make him self-conscious and frustrated. Just keep smiling and nodding. For more information, see STUTTERING in the Medical Guide.

Storytelling

Educators know that children who come from homes where reading and books are

Toddlers like to imitate their parents, and often enjoy helping with some of the work around the house, such as washing windows and gathering leaves in the yard.

valued are more likely to succeed academically than those from homes without this interest. A toddler can be encouraged to read and listen and enjoy literature if his parents read to him from books written with his age and attention span in mind.

Story time can be a rich twenty minutes for parent and child and long cherished by both. It may be the only time during the day that nagging and whining are absent. It forces new thoughts and feelings on the participants. As a result, the child will often break in with a question or an observation. Stop reading for a moment and let him talk. He wants to learn something or share something with you.

Sometimes, a child wants to hear the same story every night. You cannot skip a word or two without loud protest: "You didn't say rabbit!" It is difficult to say why some children want or need to have one favorite story read over and over again. It is probably just part of the child's nightly ritual. Do not be concerned about it. This stage, too, will pass.

Learning by imitation

A wise philosopher once stated that children force parents to become more mature. Parents sense the responsibility they have in civilizing the animal inside every child before he can be pushed out of the nest. Parents who love their children will feed love into, and provide limits for, their children. Then these children, when they become parents themselves, will be able to imitate these methods. Some of the most disorganized teen-agers become the most efficient housekeepers when away from their mothers and confronted with the challenge of their own children.

Sometimes it is difficult, but parents should let their children know the joys and rewards of being parents and responsible breadwinners. Toddlers need to experiment with these roles by imitating them. They also need to feel the variety and range of human emotions—love, fear, anger, grief—and learn when these are appropriately expressed. For example, a toddler should not be sheltered from the fact of a loved one's death, but be allowed to experience the sorrow of the loss.

Health and safety

Accidents

One function of the parents is to prevent their child from hurting himself in a dangerous world. The toddler's all-embracing habit of getting into everything needs its rightful outlets, but it also calls for strong checks and a defining of limits. The toddler is surrounded by many dangers, so he must necessarily be surrounded by many safeguards.

A toddler needs to be both hemmed in and kept out. A closed door is not enough, because he soon learns to turn the knob. Lock doors to keep him out of potentially dangerous places. An accordion gate also provides restraint in dangerous places, such as the top or bottom of stairs.

Bathrooms especially need to be safe. The contents of a medicine cabinet fascinate

Gates at the top and bottom of stairs can prevent many toddler accidents. These safeguards may make your toddler unhappy, but they are necessary.

the toddler. The shapes and colors of bottles draw the child to this cabinet. As the toddler becomes adept at unscrewing or removing bottle tops, he is more likely to sample the contents. To protect the child, try to buy medicines and drugs with child-resistant caps. Even so, keep medicines locked up. Be sure to return them to the cabinet after use. If the pretty pills are out of sight, your toddler will not be tempted to taste or eat them. The major cause of child poisonings is an overdose of aspirin, so aspirin should be bought in small amounts.

Added hazards arise as the toddler learns to climb. He does not confine himself to the usual climbing, like stairs. He is all too often after things out of reach. He quickly learns where the cooky jar is kept. And, he will most likely have a special interest in climbing on top of radiators or furniture to get to window ledges.

A toddler also has a great desire to poke and pry. This often leads him to probing electric outlets with a hairpin or bobby pin. You can buy covers for outlets from a hardware store.

To further accident-proof your home, kneel down on the floor and pretend you are a toddler bent on exploring everything within reach. Is the cord for the coffeepot still plugged into the wall? Is a purse with pills in it within his reach? Does the coffee table have sharp edges? Are ant paste, paints, cleansers, and soaps within reach? Look at your stove. Are pot handles pointing into the room?

Common illnesses and conditions

The common cold seems to be the favorite illness of this age group. It usually begins with a fever and ends with a watery, drippy nose and a night cough that lasts about seven days. Most toddlers have a cold on an average of every six to eight weeks during the "cold season." If the colds are too frequent, or if they all end up with bronchitis or ear infections, consult your doctor.

Here are some other common illnesses and conditions that you may encounter while your child is a toddler.

Constipation is common among toddlers because a mother often urges the child to consume too much milk and other dairy products. Consequently, the child does not eat enough meat, fruit, and vegetables which have more roughage than milk and bread.

Anemia because of iron deficiency is common for the same reason that causes constipation. The mother encourages her child to eat large quantities of dairy products at the expense of other foods. Iron deficiency results because white foods have relatively little iron in them.

Probably the first disease you should suspect when your toddler has a rash is roseola infantum. Roseola is a virus infection which starts with a high fever that lasts three days. Then a rash appears on the child's face and trunk. It is not a serious illness.

Each of these illnesses and conditions is discussed more completely in separate articles in the Medical Guide.

Shots and tests

Most doctors give a DTP shot—diphtheria, tetanus (lockjaw), pertussis (whooping cough)—when the child is 18 months old. A DTP booster is given when the child enters school. If a preschooler is injured, your doctor may give a tetanus vaccine booster to protect against lockjaw.

The toddler has usually been routinely tested for tuberculosis earlier. But if contact is made with anyone who has the disease, the child should be tested again.

Chicken pox is another contagious disease that toddlers may catch. However, there is no shot to prevent chicken pox.

For more information, see the following articles in the Medical Guide: CHICKEN POX, DIPHTHERIA, TETANUS, TUBERCULOSIS, and WHOOPING COUGH.

Teeth, feet, eyes, and ears

"Toothbrush at 2, the dentist at 3" is a rule that encourages good dental habits. When your toddler nears 2, he will probably watch with fascination while you brush your teeth. Because of his passion to imitate things other people do, he will probably want to brush his teeth, too. This is a great time to hand him his own toothbrush and let him try. He will not brush well at first, but with a little help, he will catch on.

The best time to have him brush is after each meal. This means three times a day, which in most homes is nearly impossible. The most important brushing time is after supper. This brushing cleans teeth for the long night ahead. If brushing three times a day fails, aim for two times—after breakfast and after supper.

A fluoride is a compound that helps make teeth strong and reduces tooth decay. In many areas children receive fluoride from the water they drink. If fluoride is not available in the water, they should receive it as a supplement prescribed by their doctor or dentist.

If your toddler walks with his toes pointing inward and his heels pointing outward, he is pigeon-toed. This condition is common before walking is well established, and corrective measures should be taken early.

The lazy eye begins in this age group. The muscles of the lazy eye are weak and, if they are untreated, they may cause the eye to cross. Usually, a doctor puts a patch over the child's good eye so that the lazy eye has to work harder.

If your child has not imitated any words by the time he is 2 years old, he may have a hearing loss. Consult your pediatrician. He will probably suggest that you take the child to a doctor who specializes in hearing problems, so that the child's hearing can be evaluated. For more information, see DEAFNESS in the Medical Guide.

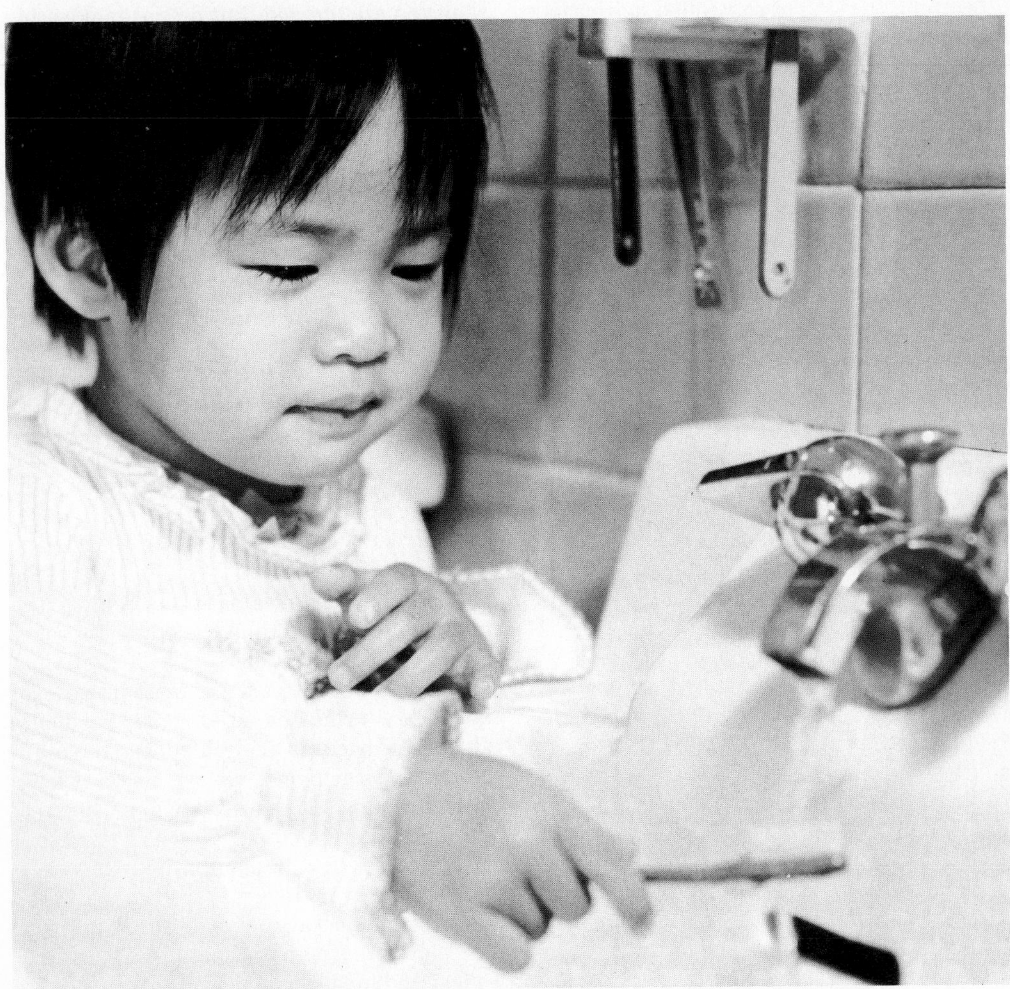

As awkward as toddlers may be when they first brush their teeth, they soon learn the proper way with your help and example.

Common concerns

Toilet training

Learning the skill of controlled defecation and urination must await development of the nerves and muscles involved. A child should be able to sit and to walk before you start to toilet-train him. The unfortunate paradox is that when the lower end of the child becomes ready, the upper end becomes unwilling. The stubborn child resorts to passive aggression when he detects his mother's interest in his body functions. If parents accept a child's social indifference toward the functions of his bowels and bladder, toilet training can be accomplished with ease and naturalness.

Bowel training

Training can be accomplished, and is being accomplished every day—but only with the cooperation of the child. True cooperation rarely comes before a child is 18 months old. An 18-month-older has his own way of letting you know when he is going to have a bowel movement. He may grunt. He may squirm. He may grow red in the face. You can begin your training then, or you can be smart and wait another six months.

When you notice that your toddler is going to have a bowel movement, calmly place him on a baby's toilet seat or a potty chair on the floor. Use words he can understand to tell him that this is the place to have a bowel movement and to urinate. Do not ask him to sit there more than five minutes. And at the start of training, one or two sessions a day are enough. When he has success, let him know he has done well and that you are pleased, but do not make a big fuss about this very normal function. Do not bribe him to have a bowel movement. And do not scold him when he does not succeed.

Successful training is not accomplished all at once. It is a matter of trial and error, usually, for both the child and his parents. Never force or punish or coax too much. And never discuss the child's success or failure in his presence. You may make it sound like something special with which he can tease or challenge you.

As a rule, most toddlers learn to control their bowels naturally. This usually happens when they are 2 to 3 years of age. Besides voluntary muscle control, toddlers must also be able to speak—to let you know their needs in time.

Bladder training

Partly because it is natural to empty the bladder more often than the bowels, it takes longer to teach toddlers to control urination. By about 18 months, most babies can hold their urine for as long as two hours at a time because their bladders have enlarged and their nervous systems are more fully developed. If your toddler can stay dry through a nap, chances are good that your child is ready for bladder training.

The best way to get your child to stop wetting the bed at night is to let him work out his own rhythm of holding his urine for longer and longer periods. If you take him to the bathroom too often in order to catch him before he wets, you run the risk of conditioning him to hold his urine for a very short time. As a child learns to hold his urine when he is awake, his bladder becomes conditioned to contain its urine automatically for longer periods so that he eventually sleeps through the night without wetting. This process is normal and natural in the growth and development of every child, but it usually is not accomplished entirely until he is around 5 years old.

A parting word: Time is on everyone's side. If a mother can be consoled by the "monkey see, monkey do" rule, training will soon be accomplished. If parents use the toilet, the child will also.

Temper tantrums

Temper tantrums seem to be so typical of the child who is about 18 months old that it is more realistic to worry if your child is not having them than if he is. The toddler wants to do dangerous, unsanitary, and "wicked" things. Mother says "No." The toddler reacts with rage.

Until the toddler can engage in a verbal rebuttal, he becomes physically violent—he cries, he screams, he lies on the floor, he kicks, he jumps up and down. And what should you do while all this goes on? No single piece of advice will do, but here are some suggestions.

Do not abandon the child.

Do not scold the child.

Do not spank the child.

Do not hold a grudge once the tantrum is over.

Just stand by, or go about what you are doing, and wait for the tantrum to pass—as difficult as that may sound. Once the child realizes that he has no audience for his tantrums, and once he realizes that he will not get his way by throwing tantrums, he will discontinue them. In their place, the toddler will sharpen his verbal skills and use the word "no" almost as expressively as he did the tantrum.

A temper tantrum is common and easy to handle. Just keep calm and wait it out.

"No! No! No!"

A child's first word may be "Mamma" and his second may be "Daddy." Or, he may say "Daddy" first and "Mamma" second. Here the language controversy usually ends because it is almost universally accepted that a child's third word will be "No." Why? Because he hears it so much from his parents.

A normally developing child who is between the ages of 18 and 24 months will shake his head, say "No," and look at his mother while touching "taboo" objects like a hot stove, television knobs, or the garbage. He is learning self-control, but someone has to teach it to him. And you are the one. Discipline your toddler because he is doing dangerous things—there is time for the social niceties later on. At this stage in your child's life, your main responsibility is to keep him whole.

Do not frustrate yourself by setting up occasions for discipline. Remove valuable and dangerous things from view. This means you will have to keep your favorite bric-a-brac out of reach for a few months. Do not offer a toddler a large, fat, slippery glass of juice. He will most likely spill it and you will find yourself saying "No! No! No!"

And by all means, there should be a good number of "Yes" situations about—some

All toddlers need a place where they can make a mess with their toys. It's a "Yes" situation in a world where they hear "No" so often.

corner where the toddler can make a mess with clay or blocks, some toy he can pull apart, some paper he can rip up. A child who hears too many "No's" may develop a poor self-image. He may go through life thinking that he cannot do anything right.

Jealousy toward a new baby

No matter what a child is told about the joys of having a brother or a sister, he nonetheless feels jealous of the new baby. A toddler is no exception. He feels dethroned from the central and exclusive position he formerly enjoyed in the affection of his parents. Even though they try to reassure him of their continuing love, he sees that it is now no longer his monopoly but obviously shared with the baby. Because of the child's dependence on this love, he sees the baby as a rival who threatens his status.

Jealousy assumes many forms. Each of these has a double purpose: to express hostility and to attract greater amounts of parental attention, though not necessarily love. Some youngsters come right out with their resentment. "I hate my brother! You don't love me any more!" What is called for is patient reassurance that feeling angry because of the baby is understandable—that the lot of an older child is indeed difficult at times. Also point out that there are compensations, too. Given this kind of sympathy, your youngster will usually return to his former good disposition. This might also be a good time to step up compensations; give special privileges, such as staying up later at night, being read to more, and having more outings with one or both parents.

Other children show their distress in a more roundabout fashion. They may pretend that the baby belongs to another family and has only come to visit. Or they may hug him so strenuously that he cries. Frequently they regress to other ways of coping with the world: thumb-sucking, clinging to mother, insisting on having a bottle just like their new brother or sister. A child who has been toilet-trained for some time may begin to wet his bed again at night or have daytime accidents. Deal with the child's anxieties by reassuring him rather than reprimanding him. Give him a bottle if he asks for it. Devote more time to him. Look for enjoyable activities in keeping with his age and status that will make him feel that being more grown up is fun.

You and your toddler

The parents of a toddler must act as the grand marshals of a parade. A violent, noisy exhibition of exuberant fury must somehow be channelled and controlled. A toddler needs rules to follow, just as marching bands need a route and a cadence to follow. The toddler is more secure if he knows his limits, and he frequently needs to be told he has gone too far. When the parade is over, someone has to tell him to stop.

The toddler needs:

Freedom to explore in a nondangerous environment;

Consistent limits set on his aggressive acts, especially hurting others;

Recognition of his accomplishments by love and praise;

More "yeses" than "noes"; and

Expectations based on his developing neuromuscular abilities.

With an impulsive toddler about the house, there is little time or need for a "significant dialogue." Do what you have to do at the time when it is needed. His behavior may make you scream with rage at times. But, if you loved him when he was born, and if you adored him when he smiled at you at 4 months of age, you will somehow keep him intact until you can get your breath again at age 3.

Ideally, you should be equipped with:

A sense of humor;

Energy;

Strength;

A sympathetic spouse, in-laws, and doctor;

The ability to nap;

The conviction that you are winning more often than you are losing; and

A map of the parade route.

Many toddlers like to arrange their toys before they are ready to go to sleep.

The Preschooler: 3 to 5 years

At about age 3, youngsters enter what are called the preschool years. These are truly formative years, marked by both intellectual growth and rapidly developing motor skills.

Most 3-year-olds are able to use or understand about a thousand words. During the next two years, they will more than double their effective vocabularies. And, as their curiosity grows, they will want to know more and more about everything.

By the age of 3, most children are able to ride a tricycle, but are still learning to use their hands. But by the time they are 5, these youngsters will be able walkers, runners, and climbers who can handle things with dexterity.

These are the years when children are ready and eager to learn. It is up to parents to keep this sense of curiosity and wonder alive.

Except for "Health and safety," this article was written by James L. Hymes, Jr., Ed.D. "Health and safety" was written by Eugene F. Diamond, M.D.

Portrait of the preschooler

The way a child uses a tricycle says a lot about how his motor skills are developing during this age span. When the child is 3, he is almost surely a beginner on his trike. He may be content merely to sit on it. Then he starts to experiment with the pedals. In the beginning, he may not quite have the hang of them. Sometimes he wants to move forward, but the trike goes backward. Then for a while, he rides along rather deliberately, proud of his movement, proud of his control, and proud of his steering. Soon, he sees how fast he can make the trike go. If he comes to a turn, he doesn't even slow down—he takes

Even though preschoolers may be together, they may not be playing together. Two may make sand cakes, while a third plays alone.

it as fast as he can. If people get in the way, he comes as close to them as he can. If he has to stop, he waits until the very last second and then puts on the brakes hard. Every bit of this hard pumping, daring turning, smart steering, and skilled stopping is accompanied by noises—motor noises of "brrr-brr," horn noises of "honk-honk."

You can also see progress in motor development as the preschooler gradually acquires greater skill in dressing himself. At 3, he can unbutton the front and side buttons of his clothes, but he has a hard time buttoning them. He cannot tell the back of his clothes from the front. He often puts his pants on backward. He may still need some help in putting on shirts, sweaters, and other articles of clothing.

When he is 4, the preschooler dresses himself with little assistance from his mother, but the process may seem to take forever. He can now both button and unbutton side and front buttons on his clothes. He is also able to distinguish between the front and the back of his clothes, and he puts them on correctly.

Social development

The way two preschoolers play together on their trikes shows changes in social growth as well as motor development. Two 3-year-olds may simply like to be near each other on their trikes. They may bump each other experimentally with little, testing, hardly touching bumps. A little laughter, a little giggling often go along with the bumps and touches, but there is seldom any great flow of words. One of the youngsters may decide to head off somewhere on his trike, to some near destination because pumping and steering are not yet automatic. The other will probably follow, but not always right away. A little thought has to go on first. The social response is not yet quick, sure, and certain.

As they near their fifth birthday, these same two youngsters are very different. There is almost no "just sitting." They are sure to be on the go. There are almost no quiet times.

The 3-year-old business of one child's going off on some venture of his own while the other tentatively follows is out. Now they play together. They have plans and they talk about them, sometimes with a few spats and brief fallings-out. Once they cook up an idea, each one is likely to carry it out with modifications that make the plan his own. These older preschoolers have grown into social creatures who get thrills from being with each other.

The pleasure of each other's company, the excitement of what they are doing together sometimes becomes so overwhelming that toilet-trained children "forget" and come home wet. In their own list of priorities, these preschoolers have put first things first. Anyone can stay dry. But being with a friend, playing with a friend—now that is something new.

Language development

Intermingled closely with social development is another major advance of the preschool years—the development of language. By the time the child is about 4, his mother complains that her child has become a chatterbox who never shuts up.

The preschooler does not simply chatter, however. His talking involves all the parts of speech, gradually longer sentences, and a

It takes time, but preschoolers eventually learn how to dress themselves—shoes and all.

Preschoolers like to imitate their parents with adult-type work, such as washing the family car. Imitation is one way a preschooler learns.

greater clarity. Language development and social development aid one another. Preschool children still fight at times, of course. If they are greatly provoked, they may even bite and kick. But they gradually learn to use words to settle their differences and their disputes.

The great growth in a preschooler's speech can trouble adults. Preschoolers seem to talk too much. They frequently interrupt because what they have to say is still the most important thing in the world to them. They often talk too loudly. Commonly, around the age of 4, they go on a spree of name-calling and experimenting with nonsensical singsongs.

One other occasionally annoying characteristic of the preschool child's language is his never-ending stream of questions. His inquiries become more complex from about 3 years of age on. The questions *Why?* and *How come?* increase as he tries to understand relationships, how things work and what things are for.

The preschooler's education

The child's constant questions reflect another side of preschool development—his intense curiosity and deep thirst for knowledge. One of the outstanding characteristics of the preschooler is that he is so completely ready to learn. He is ready to learn as much as he can about the world around him, about himself as a part of that world, about other children, and about adults. The preschooler is an eagerly curious child. He is open, and he is responsive. His eyes go out to all that is around him. His ears pick up what is around him. His fingers and hands are tools for fascinated exploration.

One of the most important tasks for parents is to keep this burning curiosity and this charmed sense of wonder alive. A child will go far with curiosity and wonder. Without them, now and in the school years, a child has to be pushed or pulled or lured.

Trips to a fire station or other nearby places are treats for a preschooler.

Most parents appreciate curiosity and do not realize that they sometimes discourage it. A curious child may trouble and frighten his parents. They worry about his safety. When their irritations or their worries mount, the danger is that the child will hear too steady a diet of *No* and *Don't* and *Be careful* and *Watch out.* Parents must take precautions, of course. But, at the same time, they should make sure that the world does not seem like a "bad" or "dangerous" or "not nice" place to the child. Curiosity cannot stand a never-ending stream of discouragement.

Parents must also be careful not to let their child's curiosity wither from lack of feeding. A child desperately wants to know more and to understand his world.

Trips

Trips are one of the best ways of bringing new, stimulating, mind-stretching experiences to the young child. A preschooler is basically ignorant—he simply does not know much yet because he has not lived long enough, nor experienced enough. No one can really "tell" this child much—words alone do not do the job. The child does not yet have the background or knowledge to which the words can attach themselves and take on meaning. He has to see things first—he needs firsthand experiences. Later, words can build on these experiences. Trips, now, are a perfect solution to learning for him.

Trips for preschoolers should be short. Young children tire easily, and a tired, fussy child learns little. The destination does not have to be spectacular either. To a young child, the filling station, the supermarket, the florist shop, the post office, the barn, the stream, the airport, and other ordinary, everyday locations are a treat.

Time transforms an everyday "trip to mail a letter" or "trip to get a quart of milk" into an educational experience. A good trip for a child has a slow, relaxed pace with time for talking en route, both coming and going. There ought to be time, too, for several short stops along the way. Unexpected side explorations can sometimes be better than the main trip itself. And at any stop, en route or at your destination, your preschooler needs time to stand and watch, time to touch, time to explore. Preschoolers cannot take in all they want to know at a glance. On trips, there are countless opportunities to point out sights your child might otherwise miss. And there are countless opportunities to ask provocative questions that might not otherwise occur to the child.

Stories

Good story books, like good trips, stimulate a child. They bring a part of the world closer to him so that he can take a better look at it and come to understand it more fully. Stories may be make-believe or about real people and events. They may involve animals that seem almost human. They may include more adventure than most people have in their everyday lives. But fiction or nonfiction, children's books help this beginner get a better handle on the people, the events, and the objects in the real life that exists around him.

Story time is a time for companionship and conversation. Try to make it a daily event.

The trick in reading a story well to your child is the same trick as in taking him on a successful trip. Take your time. Do not rush to the end of the story. Let your child interrupt to ask a question, even if it takes you both off on a tangent. Story time should be a daily event—a time for companionship and conversation between you and your preschool child.

Enriching your child's play

Language and social development, increased knowledge, a longer attention span, and vastly improved physical coordination all combine to produce the most distinctive characteristic of the preschool child. He is highly imaginative. He has a special capacity to make believe and to pretend. He can take on any role that suits his fancy. He can pretend any object is what he plays it is. The child himself can become a baby or a cowboy. A chair can become a horse or a plane or a prison. To the adult looking on, the preschool child seems to spend all his time "just playing." The play of the preschool child is far from a waste of time, however. It is highly significant activity that teaches important emotional, intellectual, and social lessons.

The child at play draws on what he knows. Young children play house, for example, mostly because home-living is what they know best of all. The play is imaginative, but it is firmly grounded in reality. The more a child knows—the more places he has been, the more things he has seen—the richer his play will be. All your child's trips to the store, the post office, the airport, the bus terminal, the truck depot, the boatyard —wherever he has been—enrich his imagination and give him the content for his childlike thinking.

Preschoolers need toys and materials, too, with which to carry out their play. Toys for this age should be simple, to allow the child room to use his imagination. Good pre-

Boxes are toys that stretch a child's imagination. They can be whatever the child wants them to be—a car, a rocket, a grocery store, a house.

school toys set up rough outlines, and give the child's fertile mind freedom to fill in the details. A tricycle, for example, is obviously some kind of moving vehicle, but the child decides whether it is a horse, ambulance, police car, ship, rocket, plane, bus, truck, fire engine, or tank. Among the best playthings are boards, boxes, blankets, sand, cartons, wagons, chairs, dolls, simple cars and boats, and other materials that can be used in various ways. They let the richness come from a child's own flow of images.

One kind of imaginative activity is special to this age—creating an imaginary playmate. Youngsters without many real agemates, and youngsters who have no brothers or sisters, are most apt to make up an imaginary friend. But even youngsters with many real-life pals add one more; their own, personal, not-seen-by-adults child. The imaginary playmate can be someone to boss or someone who gives support and comfort. This unseen friend is important to a child. Try to make the few adjustments needed to fit this new member into your home. He seldom stays for long.

Television and the preschooler

The fascination television holds for preschoolers is an indication of their thirst for stimulation. TV's fast-moving pictures and continuous sound lure many young children into watching contentedly for hours. For better or for worse, television is a teacher. In addition, in many homes TV is a welcome "baby sitter."

Television viewing does affect children's language and their awareness of the world around them. It also provides relaxation and entertainment.

However, television viewing presents many hazards. There is reason to worry about the impact of TV's violence on the feelings and morals of youngsters, to be concerned about the impact of commercials on their taste, and the effect of long hours of passive watching on their personality. One must also be concerned because too much television viewing can rob a family of time for talk and for shared activities, and can deprive children of creative play with their age mates.

Some families react to these concerns by having no TV set. These families usually feel that their preschoolers are not being deprived of anything of value. But most families do have one or more TV sets. When TV is available, it is important for parents to make thoughtful decisions about what programs may be seen, and to set reasonable but firm limits on how long a child may watch television. Children may complain, but they will respond to books, games, projects, and other interesting alternatives.

It is also wise to watch television often enough with your children so that you can discuss with them the ideas, feelings, and values the programs may generate. You may also wish to consider becoming involved with groups working to improve television for preschoolers. If more good programs are available, and if viewing hours are wisely regulated, television can be a positive educational force.

Schools for the preschooler

It may be hard for some adults to imagine a "school" for children only 3 or 4 years old. "School" to these adults means a teacher in front of the classroom, the children seated at desks, books as the major tool for teaching, and the children hushed and quiet with no moving about. Obviously, this is not the style of 3- and 4-year-olds.

The ways of the nursery school fit the children who come. A nursery school group is more like a workshop than a lecture hall. The youngsters move about. They spend most of their time in small groups of two or three or four. They begin to learn to live, work, and play together. They learn to take turns, to settle disputes fairly, and to cooperate. The nursery school program is also planned to let children use their bodies well. A good nursery school has both indoor and outdoor facilities and gives ample time for climbing, balancing, swinging, and other activities that build muscle coordination in preschoolers.

Nursery-school children hear stories and music. They sing songs and take many short, educational trips. They are surrounded by informative and challenging pictures and exhibits. There is ample time for them to ask many questions of their teacher and of their friends. Their knowledge, their language, their awareness of the world around them is always growing.

The children also have the opportunity to express themselves through block play, sand play, art work of many kinds, and working with carpentry tools and wood. Outdoors, they use such equipment as boards, boxes, big blocks, tricycles, climbing apparatus, wheelbarrows, and wagons. The children are almost constantly involved in make-believe play—play that gives them the chance to use their initiative, to think, to plan, to develop their attention span, and to build their capacity for problem solving.

Spend a morning visiting a nursery school before choosing it for your child. Your personal judgment—Does it feel right to you for your youngster? Do you like the teacher?—is an excellent guide. A nursery school should not be a stuffy, shushed, sitting place. Nursery school is school for noisy, active 3- and 4-year-olds.

If the school welcomes your visit, that is a good sign. That can mean they like parents—one indication of a good school. On your visit, you can look into some objective standards at the same time: 1) The teacher should have college training in nursery or early childhood education; 2) The teacher should have an adult aide at all times, not necessarily highly trained, but a pleasing, sensible human; 3) Fifteen 3- or 4-year-olds should be the maximum class size for these two adults; 4) The indoor room should be clean and attractive, of course, but also large enough so the children have room to move about, so several different activities can go on at once; 5) There should be an outdoor play space, fenced and well-equipped; 6) *And* something indoors or outdoors should catch your eye and excite you: an animal, an activity, something. If you are lured to it, that can mean your child's curiosity will also be stirred—and that is what you want in a nursery school.

Common concerns

The preschool period can be a happy time in family life, free from overwhelming problems. One reason for this is that the preschool child can do so much more for himself. He can be quite independent in feeding himself, in dressing, and in using the toilet. He is no longer such a physical drain on his mother. Another great help is the child's delight in the world and in the people around him. His eagerness, openness, and good feeling about being alive can be quite contagious. No age, however, is completely angelic. There are always some rough spots.

Dawdling

The conflict between a young child's time schedule and that of his parents is often a trouble area. Most adults have watches on their wrists. They are going somewhere and know exactly how many minutes they need to get there. The young child loafs along and dreams along, undriven and unpressured. Adults call his pace "dawdling." The child, of course, has no special name for what he does—he is simply himself. This slower pace is the way he acts. It can take him what seems like ages to finish eating, to get dressed, or to "come along." He tends to stop and fascinatedly watch the world go by. This special pace is a part of being a 3-year-old or a 4-year-old. It is a part of the newness of being able to do things for one's self—a part of the wonder at the world.

The best approach for coping with dawdling is a whole series of minor adjustments. For example, with eating and dressing, allow your child as much time as possible so he has leeway in which to do his dreaming. But if something pressing lies ahead, pitch in with a helping hand to speed up the eating or dressing process. Do not nag or pester. Angry words seldom produce a speed-up. There are times, too, when reality demands that the meal be ended—the available time has simply run out. There is no great harm in a child's experiencing this. The harm comes only when—as the food is taken away—adult anger, nagging, and complaining come to take its place.

It may help you to keep your balance if you remember that this slow pace does not go on forever. The time is not far distant when you may worry more because your child bolts his food and jumps into whatever clothes are left around.

Fears

Some problems arise, too, because it is so easy to forget that the 3-year-olds in particular, but also the 4-year-olds, are still little, dependent children. They have grown so much. They can do so much more for themselves. But they have many moments when they feel like the "little babies" that they, in part, still are. When parents forget this, they often are harsher than they should be. This is especially true when these children get frightened. And a wide, unpredictable range of events and sounds and sights can scare them. Preschoolers are still new to this world. And every day, their greater mobility opens up more and more of the world. The loud, the unexpected, the new, the big, the fast-moving, the dark—it is hard to know what will take their breath away next, but a great many events can.

The quick, easy response is the pep talk: "You're not afraid of a little thing like that, are you?" Parents are not afraid, but parents are old-timers. The child's only reply, and he often screams it with his whole body, is to say in effect: "I certainly am afraid . . . that's what this fuss is about."

Worse than the pep talk is unsympathetic scoffing and shaming: "Don't be a little baby . . . Don't be a scaredy cat . . . You're supposed to be a big boy (or girl)." When a child is afraid of a dog, of thunder and lightning, or of the dark, it hardly helps him feel stronger to have the added fear of losing his parent's love and respect.

A much more effective way to deal with fright is to accept the fact that your child is frightened. Give him support and comfort so that he feels strong enough to face the frightening event. Sometimes just moving over to stand by his side is all the support he needs. Sometimes this, plus a comforting word or two, does the trick. Sometimes a youngster who is deeply upset has to be held and patted and comforted. The goal is to give enough support so that he feels better, without doing so much for him that he feels pushed back into babyhood.

Accept the fact that your child has fears. Then give the support and comfort needed.

Then, when your child has calmed down a bit, try to teach him how to cope with the experience the next time it happens. The more competence he has, the less he will fear. Explain to him the causes of thunder and lightning, or why it gets dark. Or teach him a skill—where to pat the dog, how to hold the hamster—so that he can manage better by himself the next time. Once he understands, he is less apt to worry.

The most upsetting fear of all, of course, occurs when a child thinks his parents do not love him. Any one of a wide variety of happenings can start this unhappy train of thought. Being left alone in a strange new setting like a hospital, a doctor's office, Sunday school, or nursery school can start it. The hazard is separation. Young children can easily translate "Separation . . . they are leaving me" into "Separation . . . they don't love me for some reason." Harshness, coldness, and busyness can have the same effect. The child feels little and alone, unprotected and unsafe.

Sometimes the events parents think ought to make a child feel big have the opposite effect. A new baby in the family and starting school are two examples. The wise approach is the same as with all fears. Give support to the child and talk with him so that he feels he can cope with the problem.

Toilet-talk

Some troubles come along in these years because preschoolers are still young children. But other difficulties pop up because these are such "big-feeling" children. Much of the time these youngsters want to feel big, and much of the time parents are glad about this feeling. But there are moments when almost every parent wants to say, "Slow down . . . Not THAT big!"

Because of his increasingly good control of language, the preschool child does not have to use gross, physical ways to prove his bigness—as he did when he was only 2. Tantrums are rarities, almost a thing of the past. But the more refined ways can be as irritating and as troubling as the grosser ways.

Three-year-olds, and especially 4-year-olds, are apt to use toilet-talk because they

Reasoning is the best approach to discipline. But, it is a slow method requiring patience.

sense it is "shocking language" and a means of seeming big, tough, and clearly independent. Words like "do-do" and "grunt-grunt" and "wee-wee" become, for a while, standard adjectives to describe anything. Some families simply live with these sounds. The "shocking" noises run down after a while as children find other, more "improved" and "mature" ways of making the same point. Some families let the noises go on for a period and then, when they think the youngster feels he has made his point, say "That's enough of that." Or they give the child some funny-sounding substitute word.

Discipline

Developing good discipline in children is one of the most important jobs of parenthood. But this vital task takes time, patience, and understanding.

Many parents believe that discipline and punishment are the same thing. But punishment is only one of several ways to teach discipline. It is not the only way, nor is it the best. It is, in fact, the most difficult to use wisely, and often produces the very opposite of the result parents want.

Many parents also believe that children resent discipline. These parents not only hesitate to punish their children, but seldom use any of the better methods to build discipline. They want to be good to their child —and end up by being too lenient. Undisciplined children are almost always unhappy children. They never know what the limits are. They often feel unloved. No one seems to care enough to teach them what is right and what is wrong, and why.

Wise parents do not shrink from disciplining their children. But instead of using one method all the time, they seek, instead, to puzzle out why their children misbehave, and then to take whatever action best fits the situation. For example, young children often misbehave because *they simply do not know any better*. When this is the problem, one appropriate method of discipline is to patiently explain what the rules are and why rules are important. But be sure your child understands what you are saying.

Teaching is effective only if parents believe in what they are saying. Their way of talking must convey that the lesson is important. And the process must never be one of "talking to the wind"—to a child who pays no attention, or listens with only half an ear. When you say, "Stop," and tell the child why, the action must stop—at least for that moment.

For example, if your child is beating on a window with a stick, say very firmly:

"Stop that. Windows are made of glass, and glass breaks easily. So don't hit the window with your stick. The window may break."

Take the stick away, and move the child away from the window.

Reasoning is a slow method. You cannot expect a child to learn because you talk over an incident just once. But in the long run, reasoning is the best method because it helps children to learn values that they can act on when they are on their own. It is also a method that respects the child's growing independence.

Besides explaining and giving reasons, you should praise your children when they act well. Praise, especially when it directly follows good behavior, is a booster to learning. For example, if your child comes to the table with clean hands, or acts in a way you expect, offer immediate praise. You might say, "That's good!" or "I like to see that!" or whatever honest words of praise fit the situation. Your welcome approval reinforces the child's good behavior, making it more apt to be repeated.

"Not knowing any better" is only one reason for misbehavior, just as reasoning is only one method for teaching discipline. At times children do the wrong thing because of the *setting* they are in. When this seems to be the case, the way to discipline is not by talking, but by action. Change the setting to make it easier for the child to be good. This approach is especially useful with children too young to really understand words, but it also works with older children. For example, things that a toddler should not touch should be put out of reach. Older children who have to sit for a long time on a car ride or while waiting in a doctor's or dentist's office will behave much better if you give them a book to read or color, or a game to play.

Another reason for misbehavior lies in children's *feelings*. Children have to feel right to act right. Some boys and girls are driven to bad behavior because they desperately need more love, or more attention, or a feeling of importance. They do things they know they should not do. A jealous child, for example, may hurt a baby sister or brother. Of course the baby must be protected and the behavior must of course be stopped. The temptation is to punish children driven by upset feelings, but the surest way to help jealous children is to give them the love their behavior shows they need.

Parents have to be thoughtful in choosing an approach to discipline, one that fits the child and the situation. This sensitive process of deciding what action to take itself contributes to discipline. It is an expression of love, and the foundation of all good behavior is a child's sense of being loved. Children unconsciously identify with parents who show their love. Slowly but steadily, they will take on the attitudes and values of their parents. What is learned through this process of identification does not show up immediately, but the lessons are instilled in the child. Good behavior will evolve in time.

Health and safety

For information on growth in height and weight during these years, see GROWTH on page 133.

Dental care

During the preschool period, your child should visit the dentist. Arrange with your dentist to take your preschooler with you on one of your routine visits. Then, your child can sit in the dentist's chair, examine some of the dentist's instruments, and become acquainted with the dentist. This helps prepare the child for his own first visit. (See TEETH AND TEETHING in the Medical Guide.)

Accidents

The preschooler is shifting from a need for absolute protection to a need for protection plus education toward self-reliance. Discipline is a protection for the child and an efficient, workable safety tool for a parent. The undisciplined, impulse-controlled child is constantly at a greater risk than the disciplined child.

Rules for the child also imply rules for the parent. Here are a few suggestions on how to protect your preschooler from accidents.

Give as few negative commands as possible. Instead, teach him how to do things. For example, do not always say "Don't" when he tries to cross a street. When you are with him, teach him how to cross safely—to cross only at the corner, to cross only when the light is green, and to look both ways before crossing. And remember that most children do what they see their parents do. You are the best model for what you want to teach your child.

Let your child know when he has done the right thing. After he has safely crossed the street following the procedures you taught him, tell him that he has done well, and that you are proud of him.

Both parents should agree upon and be consistent about rules. This agreement does not come easily. Mothers and fathers fre-

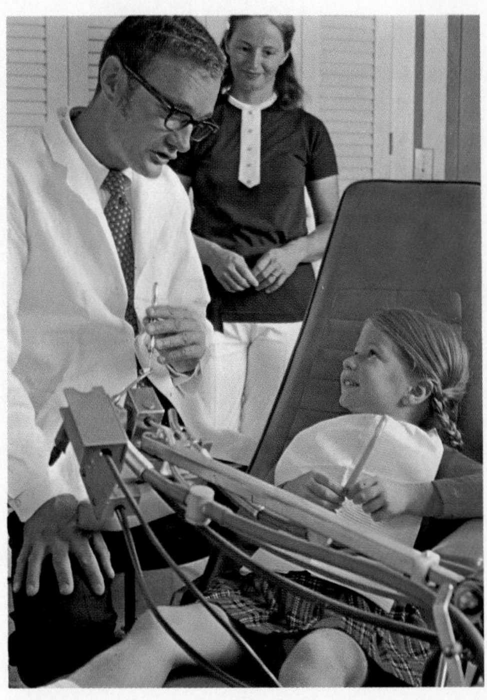

Age 3 is a good time for the preschooler to make the first visit to the dentist.

quently see matters through different eyes. But the talking through to agreement pays dividends in a child's sense of security.

The expanding curiosity and developing skills of preschoolers make them vulnerable to such accidents as falls, drowning, poisoning, and burns. By now, they are probably able to open doors and gates. You may have to use locks and secure latches to confine the area in which they can roam. Be sure that windows are kept screened.

Climbing, whether it is a tree or monkey bars, has great appeal to preschoolers. Let them climb. But teach them how to climb safely, and keep a watchful eye on them.

More drownings occur during the preschool period than at any other time in life. One of the best precautions you can take is to teach your preschooler how to float and swim. Also, make certain that backyard pools and pools of water in excavations are fenced or covered. Do not let preschoolers swim anywhere unless someone is there to constantly supervise them. Life jackets are a necessary precaution in boats, and life preservers should be available at swimming pools.

Continue taking precautions to prevent poisoning. Keep all drugs, including aspirin, locked up. Keep furniture polish, silver polish, bleaches, drain and toilet bowl cleaners, and other household cleaning agents out of the reach of children.

Burns in the home are most likely to come from tipping over containers of hot liquids. Keep panhandles, coffeepots, and vaporizers out of the preschooler's reach.

For more information on accidents, see ACCIDENTS and POISONINGS AND POISONS in the Medical Guide.

Preschoolers should learn to float and swim. Teach them yourself or put them into a swimming class run by professional instructors.

You and your preschooler

The preschool years can be a delightful time for a family. The child is now beyond the age when his physical care was a wearisome chore. And he has not yet reached the age when he will be so wrapped up in school demands and friends that you feel squeezed out of his life. A mother and father are lucky—and obviously a child is lucky—when the family can find time to enjoy these years together.

The preschool years are a time for companionship—a time for walks together and for short trips. They are a time for shared experiences at home. Youngsters have their moments of wanting to work along with a parent, helping in their own way with cooking, cleaning, and other household chores.

The preschool years are a time for words, for stories and for music. They are the years for listening to children and for talking with children. Children's questions ask all about the ins and outs of our world, and give parents the most magnificent teaching-time for explaining and interpreting. The preschooler's behavior gives parents opportunities to talk about values and about discipline. The words may have to be said over and over. Words take a long time to sink in. But be patient. Reasonable words eventually become a part of the child.

These years are a time for the shared awe and delight in the charming, never-ending variety of our world of bugs and nuts and bolts, of clam shells and cars, snakeskins, leaves, the birth of baby kittens, and the hot, smoky smell of a truck engine.

Lucky parents and lucky preschoolers enjoy these precious times together. But wise parents know that even at this early age children need more than their parents. These are wonderful years for youngsters to come to know well their wider family of grandparents, uncles, aunts, and cousins. These are the years when parents can help their children find friends in the family doctor and dentist. It is also the time for them to discover the librarian in the public library.

Equally important, children need friends their own age in these years. Their increasingly strong social drive is one of the reasons for nursery schools. But there are many other ways in which parents can satisfy their child's yearning for child companionship. Some parents work out informal play groups, taking turns with friends and neighbors in providing supervision while two or three children play together. Some invite a child's special friend to come for lunch or to join the family on a short excursion, or simply to come to the house to play.

Preschoolers are in an in-between age—not totally dependent, not totally independent—a mixture of both, sometimes all in a few minutes. It is easy to overestimate what these children can do and to expect too much. It is also easy to underestimate them and to open up too little physical challenge and too little social and intellectual stimulation. Your best safeguard and guide is to keep your eye on your child, to judge from his behavior how he is feeling at the moment—big and brave and bold, or like your little baby—and to enjoy him as he is.

The School-Age Child: 5 to 8 years

Children between 5 and 8 years of age tell you exactly what they feel and think. They inform you readily if they are sick, happy, or miserable. They flaunt their skills proudly and proclaim their thrills and horrors loudly.

School-age children are high-spirited. They laugh easily. They are full of ideas and questions. Yet, they will withdraw into themselves and reflect.

In school, most 5- to 8-year-olds are wide-awake mentally and uncomplicated emotionally. These are crucial years for children—probably the most important years of their education. Adults at home and school must make sure that children get the best possible start in their school careers.

Except for "Health and safety," this article was written by Minnie P. Berson, Ed.D. "Health and safety" was written by Eugene F. Diamond, M.D.

Portrait of the school-age child

It is simple, when looking at an 8-year-old, to see how much he has changed since he was 5. It is not so easy, looking at him when he is 5, to realize how much he will have changed by the time he is 8. But it is important that the parents of a child entering school be able to look ahead. They should be aware of the many changes that will occur in their child during the early school years; and they should understand the child's physical, mental, emotional, and social needs so that they will be better able to meet them.

Social development

At this age, for the most part, boys play with boys and girls play with girls. When friends of the same sex are not available in the neighborhood, a child usually finds playmates in school and asks them to come to his home to play, to eat, or to stay overnight.

Between the ages of 5 and 8, girls usually play only with other girls, and boys with other boys. A favorite game of school-age girls is jumping rope.

The child between 5 and 8 years old has lots of initiative. He is interested in accomplishments and wants to do things well. He needs encouragement and respect.

A school-age child likes a feeling of responsibility—of doing something needed to make the home operate smoothly. Parents may have a difficult time finding something for the child to do. Garbage disposals may eliminate the need to take out the garbage. Automatic dishwashers may eliminate the need to wash and dry dishes. Power lawn mowers are too dangerous for a school-age child to use, so he may not be able to cut the grass. However, it is extremely important that school-age children have some household chores for which they alone are responsible. These tasks, of course, should be ones children of this age are capable of handling—such as making their own beds, cleaning their rooms, setting the table, or putting groceries away.

When children start school, an important person enters their lives—their teacher. The teacher is often the first adult friend children make on their own. If they like their teacher, they want their parents to feel the same way. Most children are aware of every detail of their teacher's appearance. They respond to every shade of meaning in their teacher's voice, every shrug of the shoulder, and every smile or frown.

Imitation

During these years, it is only natural for girls to imitate and want to be like their mothers, other women, and older girls. Similarly, boys imitate and want to be like their fathers, other men, and older boys.

At one time, little girls were expected to be interested only in activities labeled as feminine, such as playing with dolls and jumping rope. Little boys were expected to be interested only in activities labeled as masculine, such as playing baseball and football.

Today, girls and boys, as well as their parents, are comparatively free of the stereotype roles that society once demanded of them. Now the choice is up to the individual. Games and other activities no longer bear sexist labels. This can be noted in everything from the advertising and packaging of games, toys, and play materials to the clothes children wear.

A factor contributing to the diminishing of sexism, especially in the United States, is the number of mothers of school-age children working outside the home in full-time or part-time jobs. Children in these families see both parents go off to work. And when the parents come home, their children see them share household duties as well as the responsibilities for their youngsters.

The increase in the number of households with a single parent has also added to the changes in the duties and responsibilities of parents.

Inevitably, little girls become women and little boys become men. Meanwhile, children are being increasingly encouraged to make highly personal choices, without sexist labels. These choices will help children to develop interests and competencies that will lead to fuller, more satisfying lives.

Fathers and school-age children

The quality of the relationship between a father and his school-age child is important. There is danger that both boys and girls will have almost all their important dealings with women until they reach the secondary schools. This overly effeminate world is not good for boys. Boys need as many experiences with men as possible. They need men, especially a father whom they admire, to set a pattern for them. Boys grow into manhood in part through their physiological maturing, but also through seeing how men act and talk and work and plan, how they react to each other, and how they interact with women. The companionship of men, of a good father in particular, is an essential ingredient in a boy's growth to manhood.

Girls, too, need the companionship of their fathers. An overly effeminate world is not good for them either. Fathers help girls to know what men are like and how men respond to different situations.

Visits away from home

Through visits away from home, a school-age child gradually develops social graces and independence. He tries out new foods and becomes accustomed to unfamiliar routines. He learns new skills by doing family chores with children in other households. He makes friends with children in the community where he visits. The child also can test and develop skills in relating to people away from home. He learns that all mothers are not alike, nor are all fathers, big brothers, or little sisters. A visit to the home of a friend for playing, eating a meal, or spending the night all add to a child's social development.

Before allowing a brief or extended visit away from home, parents should consider their child, his needs, and his hosts. Do his hosts like and want him? Is the host family reasonable and flexible? Will they be patient as he tries to fit into their situation? Have they been told of his special needs and possible idiosyncrasies? If the child is on special medication, are they willing to supervise the dosage? Is he a bedwetter—a condition that would be acceptable in some households and rejected in others? Does he have occasional nightmares? Is he allergic to certain foods or materials? Before a child is given permission to visit, the adults who will be responsible for him should know about his unusual characteristics, and have a chance to say "no" if the needs seem too great for them to meet.

Making choices

During the school-age years, a child learns to make choices—within limits. For example, a child may have pronounced preferences in food and the way the food is prepared and served. Some children eat vegetables only when they are raw. Some children prefer fruit juice rather than fresh fruit. So long as it is reasonably convenient and the child is eating nutritionally balanced meals, allow him to make choices. The experience adds to his personal development.

Clothing presents more opportunities to learn how to make intelligent choices—within limits. At bedtime, for example, allow

Visits away from home—for a day or overnight—help the school-age child develop socially. First visits are often with a grandparent or other relative.

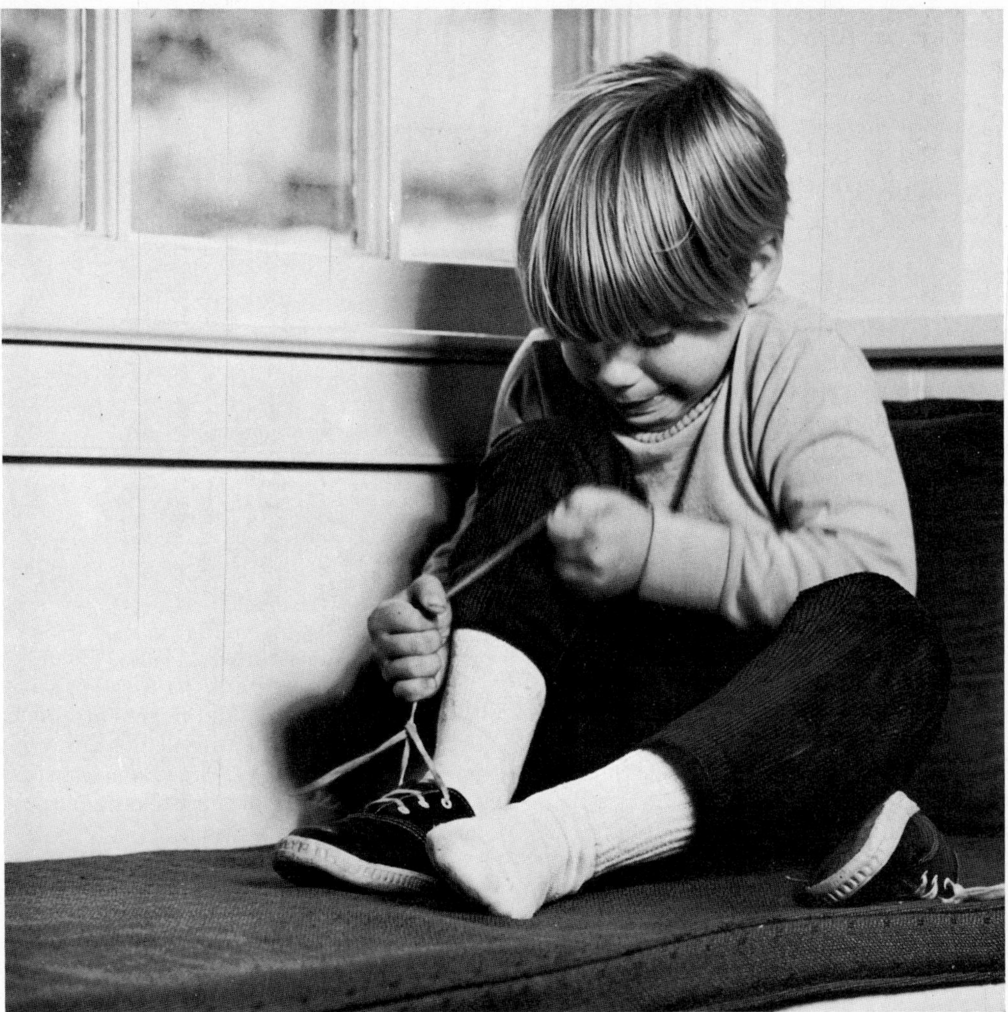

Sneakers may mean more to children than just something to cover feet. Often, they are a status symbol of their group. They must have them at any cost.

the child to decide what he will wear the next day. You may also want to let him pick out some new clothes at the store. At this age, the child may start to be caught up in fads. Sometimes, tennis shoes are the important symbol. For a girl, "hair things"—like bows, barrettes, or yarn ties—may be the "in" symbol. Again, respect the child's choice, within reason.

Allowances

Giving a regular allowance is one of the most worthwhile educational experiences parents can provide children. An allowance gives a child a realistic, firsthand experience in planning how to spend his money and how to get full value for what he spends. It provides a natural opportunity to learn arithmetic and an area in which he begins to develop a sense of logic.

The child may make mistakes or buy unwisely at first. He may rush to spend all his money the minute he gets it, forgetting that no more will be forthcoming for several days. From such unwise haste he may learn to be selective in his purchases and prudent in his spending, because an allowance also involves the necessity of choices.

Parental guidance may help a child learn that he can have two balloons this week, or he can save his allowance for two weeks and buy a toy airplane. But he cannot have both the balloons and the airplane. You may wish to start your child on a 10-cents-a-week allowance and give the same sum on the same day of each week. As he learns the possibilities and limitations of his allowance, and as his needs multiply, increase the amount of the allowance. He will become ready to take on the additional responsibility of managing money he will need for school expenses—bus fare, school supplies, or milk money. As you increase the amount of the allowance, you may want to discuss ways of budgeting the allowance with your child. Help him figure out how much he must spend each week on essential expenses. You may also want to talk about ways of spending any extra money.

An allowance should be considered a child's share of the family income, and therefore should be no more than the family can afford. An allowance should be considered the child's, to do with as he pleases. Do not control your child's buying. Let him make mistakes, for in this way he learns. Do not *insist* that a young child save something out of his allowance. A savings program will appeal to him when he has something special to save for. Never withhold an allowance because of disobedience, poor grades, or unwise spending. An allowance is not a bargaining tool to guarantee a child's good behavior, nor should it be considered a bribe.

Motor development

"Slow but steady" characterizes the development of motor skills during the school-age years. For example, a 5-year-old is usually not ready for writing. The small muscles that control his fingers and hands are not developed well enough. Writing also requires that the eye and hand work together. This eye-hand coordination is not well developed in a 5-year-old. Even 6-year-olds still find writing difficult because these small muscles and eye-hand coordination are not yet completely developed.

A 7-year-old usually concentrates hard when writing. He grips his pencil tightly and usually holds it close to the point. His letters are uneven in size. By the time he is 8 years old, his eye-hand coordination and the small

Primary-grade classrooms can often be identified by rows of toothless smiles.

muscles in his hands and fingers are much better developed. As a result, he can write more evenly and easily. Physical maturation and the ability to concentrate on a purpose also aid the child's writing.

The child's large muscles are also still developing. Girls at this stage are better coordinated than boys. Both boys and girls are physically active—they run, climb, skip, hop, and jump. Too long a time assigned to a chair and desk without a break can lead to restlessness and boredom.

Other physical characteristics

Growth in height and weight during the years from age 5 to age 8 is also slow but steady. The average child adds about 3 inches (7.5 centimeters) in height and 5 or 6 pounds (2 or 3 kilograms) in weight each year. See GROWTH, page 133.

A distinguishing characteristic of the school-age child is his smile—and the wide-open spaces that show where his primary teeth have fallen out to make room for the permanent teeth. Six-year molars are breaking through, and permanent incisors are beginning to appear. For more information, see TEETH AND TEETHING in the Medical Guide.

School days

Starting school

Starting school is a major adventure and a dramatic change from past living for all children. Most children can hardly wait to start school. They take this challenge comfortably and easily in their stride. A child's normal growth—in language, in attention span, in wider social interests, in curiosity, and in independence—enables him to welcome school without strain. There are, however, a few ways you can make it even easier for your child to move into school life without emotional upsets.

Adjusting to school will be easier if a child has had the experience of being away from home without his parents. Children who have gone to the store with a neighbor, who have eaten lunch at a friend's house, who have visited nearby relatives, or who have attended nursery school usually have no problem in leaving home to move into a classroom environment.

School adjustment will also be easier if a child has experienced accepting people other than his parents as authorities. A child who has been in the care of good baby sitters, for example, will probably have less trouble accepting a teacher. Children who have played with their friends in a neighborhood back yard or a house down the street, responding to whatever mother was in charge of the play, have a foundation for working with a teacher.

Most children beginning kindergarten or first grade know other youngsters in their neighborhood who will be their classmates. Seeing familiar faces helps a child adjust. If a child has no friends in his class, invite one or two future classmates to your house to play, or for lunch, so that your child can begin school knowing some of the children.

Most schools set aside one or more days in May or June for the registration of children who will enter kindergarten the following fall. At registration, the mother may have to present the child's birth or baptismal certificate. At a typical registration, a child is brought into his prospective classroom for a short time to become acquainted with his future classmates. A few typical daily kindergarten activities may be carried out, to give the children a brief taste of what kindergarten will be like.

Learning in the kindergarten-primary grades

Some school-age children approach learning (and life) in a systematic manner. They calmly and carefully assess the situation, moving in logical, methodical ways. Others are cautious. They move forward only when they are sure of themselves. Still others blunder in. They dive in and then look around. Both parents and schools must recognize, understand, and accommodate the child's unique way of learning.

Practically speaking, the child in the kindergarten-primary grades is taught to read, write, and work with numbers. The curriculum includes language arts, social sciences, mathematics, science, music, and art. These subjects generally are not taught as separate courses, though. They are integrated into a total experience for the child.

Hesitation, anxiety, anticipation, and fear are all a normal part of a child's behavior on the first day of school.

Then the learning process begins. Numbers must be mastered and objects identified. Letters must be drawn and words formed.

But there is time, too, for laughing and playing—for making new friends in an environment completely unlike home.

At the end of the school day, children are happy to share with their parents the work done and the many things learned.

The child learns best through firsthand experiences—seeing, hearing, touching, smelling, and, above all, doing. A child needs these firsthand experiences before he can learn to read. Some children arrive at school able to print, to identify letters, or even to read a little. Others are almost totally illiterate—no great tragedy at age 5. By the end of the second grade, most children are reading—anywhere from preprimer to fourth-grade level. Most understand the basics of phonics. They are learning to associate the sounds in words with written letters, and they are able to spell many words by applying some simple phonetic rules.

Social studies, in these early school years, generally means learning about people and the world about them. A group of kindergarten children studying their town may take trips to important places. They may lay out a model of the town's streets and roads, hills, waterways, and landmarks in a sandbox. Children may convert various sizes of boxes into houses, stores, post offices, and schools. Trucks, cars, and buses are placed on roads. People are made with modeling materials. And there is much, much talk from the children—discussing observations, asking questions, and checking impressions. Actually, what started out as a study of "our community" moves into geography, economics, consumer education, ecology, science, safety, history, map making, and map reading.

Science is experienced firsthand, too. For example, a child may prove that a magnet will only attract things made of iron by conducting experiments with a magnet and nails, paper clips, erasers, paper, and fabric. Then he may make his own magnets—a simple one from an ordinary needle or even an electromagnet from a nail, a piece of wire, and a battery. Next, he may make a compass or a buzzer to discover how magnets are used in different objects. By making the items himself, he understands better how they work.

School-age children enjoy music and art. Most of them love to sing, and some even make up their own songs. They use rhythm instruments—drums, cymbals, tambourines—alone or to accompany a song or a record. They like moving, dancing, and dramatizing or marching to music. Most school-age children like to paint, to work with clay, and to draw with crayons and pencils. They will often cut, bend, or paste paper to produce a three-dimensional object.

Imaginative children can create a city of their own with sand and cardboard boxes.

A calendar is an aid for teaching a child about many things—time, holidays, seasons.

School-age children also like stories and poetry. They enjoy being read to. When given the opportunity to use their imagination, they compose delightful stories and often write interesting poems.

The monthly calendar, displayed in jumbo size in many kindergarten classrooms, is also a learning device. At first, the calendar does not mean too much to the children. But as days go by, the children begin to identify the days of the week, dates in sequence, weekdays from weekend days, and the meaning of time and its components. The children have experiences with words, letters, numbers, holidays, seasons, and changes in the outdoors.

The parent and the school

During these years, the basis for the home-school relationship is formed. Conferences during the early years should serve both the teacher and the parents by identifying and discussing the unique needs and interests of the child.

Before your child starts school, try to meet his teacher. At this meeting, talk about your child openly. Then, when the teacher meets your child, she will already know something about him, and be able to accept him, respect him, and help him develop on the basis of her knowledge of him.

Most schools provide time for conferences between a child's parents and his teacher. At a conference, the teacher can give you samples of your child's work, descriptions of his behavior around other students and teachers, and observations of his habits, attitudes, capabilities, strengths, and weaknesses. A conference gives the parent a chance to raise questions that cannot be answered adequately by a mark on the child's report card. Similarly, it gives the teacher an opportunity to discover more about the child's home life. After a conference, you and the teacher can decide together where the child is, where he should be going, and in what way you can help.

You also should meet other parents whose children are in your child's classroom. These meetings can be informal—a coffee hour or an evening meeting that includes fathers as well as mothers. Or, teacher, children, and parents may get together after a class play or other special occasion.

Inquisitive school-age children learn best when they can study things firsthand.

Health and safety

It is important that children have a physical examination before entering school. Many schools require boosters for diphtheria, tetanus, pertussis, and polio. Many experts object to requirements for pre-school chest X rays, since any type of X ray is potentially harmful to a growing child. Eye, ear, and teeth examinations are encouraged. If any problems are found and corrected in these areas before the child enters school, the child will live and learn with greater zest than the child with eye, ear, or teeth defects.

Safety

Getting to school is one of the most important events of the school-age child's day. Before your child starts school, you or an older child should walk with him from home to school so that he can learn the route and what entrance of the school to use. Whenever you are with the child, emphasize the correct way of crossing streets—crossing only at corners, obeying patrol boys and crossing guards, observing traffic signals, and watching for traffic.

Teach your child to go directly to and from school without stops or side trips. Also, teach him never to accept rides from strangers and never even to stop to talk with strangers. Do not give these instructions in a frightening manner, but give them matter-of-factly—as part of your child's learning about his new role and his new responsibilities. A 5-year-old child should also be able to say his full name and street address before he goes to school—in case he gets lost.

Some parents prefer to walk with the child during the first days of kindergarten, to make certain that he knows the way. Some children are fortunate to have a classmate and walking companion on the same block. But even if two reliable 5-year-olds go together, it is reassuring to send them with an older child as an escort.

Even then, there can be complications. An older child who is escorting a younger one may regard the younger as a burden or a misfortune and make the journey an unhappy one. An older brother or sister may look on the younger child as a special possession and become so bossy and domineering that the younger child protests bitterly. Check carefully on any such arrangement rather than taking for granted that all is the way you want it to be.

In some communities, children in kindergarten and the primary grades regularly ride to school on the school bus. Generally, children are picked up by these buses at designated corners along the route. Check to see that someone on board is responsible for helping the younger children board and exit. It is also important to know whether the school vehicle is in good condition, whether the driver is reputable and qualified, and whether the roads traveled are safe from unusual hazards. If you have any doubts, talk them over with a school official.

Children of this age are particularly in danger from traffic when it is dark outside. They do not realize as they walk along dimly lit roadways that motorists have difficulty seeing them. You can purchase retroreflec-

Safety rules for walking to school include learning how to cross streets.

tive materials that make the child easier to see. Such materials reflect the headlights of approaching automobiles. Retroreflective materials come as tape or tags that can be attached to clothing or bicycles.

Common illnesses and conditions

Communicable diseases are quite common during the school-age years. Some of these illnesses can be avoided by vaccination, but the parents of school-age children must learn to take in stride the usual run of colds, sore throats, and coughs.

If your child has been exposed to a communicable disease, his teacher or the school nurse will probably send a note home informing you of the fact and telling you what symptoms to look for. If the child develops the symptoms, keep him home from school and call your doctor.

Here are some common illnesses you may encounter with your school-age child. Each illness is discussed in a separate article in the Medical Guide.

Illness	Symptoms
Chicken pox	Fever; blistering rash
German measles	Fever; rose-colored rash
Impetigo	Blisterlike sores which form a crust
Measles	Five to seven days of high fever, cough, runny nose, and watery eyes; rash
Mumps	Swelling of glands on top of jawbone and in front of earlobe
Scarlet fever	Rash with a rough "goosebump" feel; scarlet flush over face and trunk
Strep throat	Sore throat; fever

Common concerns

During the early school years, a child is presented with a new social environment and a series of social challenges unlike any he has had before. At home he was usually in an atmosphere in which it was taken for granted that he belonged and was accepted. This gave him a natural security. Certainly at home he has had to adapt to his parents and to brothers and sisters. But the home situation is unlike the challenge and interaction provided by contact with 25 or 30 classmates. Because of these new conditions, differences related to sex and age may become apparent and certain problems may appear in your child's life.

Differences among children starting school

Sex differences

Girls, when they start school, appear more mature than boys—and they are, because they have a more rapid maturation rate than boys do during these years. Physically and emotionally, girls are more apt to become organized and ready to work with symbolic and abstract tasks sooner than boys.

Patty can print her name correctly when she enters kindergarten, while Peter, who is the same age, may only recognize the first letter of his name. This does not mean that Patty is the brighter of the two. It may mean merely that someone took the time to teach her what she knows and that she may have been eager to learn this. Peter, on the other hand, may already know about many other things. Having classmates who can print their names and a teacher who can be helpful may encourage him to learn. It may also encourage him to share his knowledge with others.

Boys do indeed have much intellectual curiosity, but they more often focus their curiosity on physical, biological, and mechanical areas. They like to take things apart—like flashlights, old clocks, old radios—to find out what the component parts are and how they work. They discover and explore things by poking around. They are liable to walk in the kitchen with wet feet and ask the question, "Where does the water go after it goes down the sewer?"

This is not to say girls do not show these interests. Many do. And many go on to become scientists.

Age differences

No matter how bright a child may be, it makes an immense difference whether he has lived less than five years, or almost six years when he enters kindergarten. The younger child is less mature than his classmates and less experienced. He is often at a disadvantage from the first day he walks into the classroom.

Suppose December 1 is the cut-off date for kindergarten entrance in a school district. This means that a child who became 5 years old on December 2 of the previous school year is in the same class with the child who will be 5 on December 1 of the current year. The child entering kindergarten aged 69 months has a decided advantage over a classmate aged 57 months. The older child is better coordinated, more able to

Age differences may lead to problems in social adjustment as well as learning problems.

control his impulses, and more able to concentrate upon a learning task. If the younger child is a boy, he may find it doubly hard to compete with his classmates.

Regardless of intellectual ability, many kindergarten children cannot bridge the age-maturity gap between themselves and their older, more mature classmates. They also cannot conform to the arbitrary learning timetable of many schools. While a kindergarten teacher may be able to accommodate the youngest and least mature children, this accommodation may only be temporary. The real test comes in first grade when most schools require children to begin reading. As one boy sadly commiserated, "I always get a stomach-ache before I go to school. I go anyhow and I feel sicker because I don't catch on. And everybody knows I don't catch on. It's no fun."

Teachers often anticipate this problem and ask that the child continue kindergarten or another grade for a second year so that he may "catch up" with older classmates. Unfortunately, many parents who agree with the teacher's advice still insist that the child be put into the next grade.

Masculinity, femininity

This is the age when the child with a problem in sex identification becomes evident. The child, especially a boy, may be ridiculed by his classmates. The child may also appear to be confused and pained among classmates, even at the kindergarten or first-grade level.

Do not leap to the conclusion that a child has a problem in sex identification because of a few surface traits—merely because a girl is skilled in athletics, for example, or because

School-age children enjoy all kinds of boisterous, bustling activities.

a boy helps his mother by dusting furniture. However, if a girl deeply resents being a girl or if a boy deeply resents being a boy, then a problem may exist.

If a problem in sex identification is handled during these kindergarten-primary years, chances of improvement are far greater than if parents wait. When the child's problem is viewed as something he will "outgrow," complexities multiply and eventually the child becomes enmeshed in the web of added preadolescent and adolescent problems. The original problem is then submerged, and the child's life may become increasingly bewildering and lonely. If parents believe that their child has a problem in sex identification, they should seek professional help. The child's doctor or

Some boys meet with academic failure in the primary grades because they are more interested in such things as dismantling a radio, or taking apart a flashlight.

teacher may be able to provide the names of agencies and specialists who can help the child and his parents.

School problems

School is such an important part of a child's life that inevitably all youngsters face some problems in the course of the many years that they spend there. Therefore, parents and teachers must stay in close communication with each other.

Problems that have their origin in school may show up only at home. For example, a youngster who operates under tension all day long at school may seem like an earnest, conscientious child to his teacher. The parents may be the only ones to see the outbursts which reflect the strain the child is feeling. Similarly, a youngster may appear at home to be working smoothly. The teacher, watching him in a different setting and in comparison with other children his own age, may be the one who first becomes aware that a problem exists. The two sets of responsible adults—parents and teachers—must have some means of sharing their insights. Only in this way can problems be spotted before they become too severe, and solutions be developed.

Unwillingness to go to school

The first sign of a school problem may be a child's unwillingness to go to school. This unwillingness is the way in which some kindergarten and first-grade children show their fear of school openly. They cry, say that they hate school, and are unwilling to leave home. Sometimes this unwillingness to go to school shows in disguised form through frequent complaints of illness when it is time to leave for school or through prolonged dawdling and other delaying tactics. A fear or dislike of school can be a troubling problem. All the "legal" arguments parents are apt to use carry little weight in a young child's mind.

There are, of course, no pat solutions to this or any other problem. The causes can be many, and they vary from child to child. The only good solution is the one that gets to the root of the difficulty with each particular child. One youngster may hesitate because he has not had sufficient experience in being away from home; another because his group at school is too large for him to cope with; another because he has some specific fear, perhaps of the toilets at school, or the bus ride.

When parents and the teacher begin to talk together and to pool what information they have, they usually can uncover the difficulty and make some plan that enables a child to identify his problem, cope with it, and possibly solve it. The parents' attitude is important while this search is going on. On the one hand, they must feel sympathetic to the child who has the problem. Life can be uncomfortable when something is going wrong, whether the trouble is real or imaginary, whether it looks big or small to others. On the other hand, parents must have a broad, basic confidence that problems can be licked. A child catches the attitude of his parents. The child can easily give up if the adults feel that the problem is overwhelming. The steady sureness that a solution will be found and that life can go on is often one of the most helpful ways of building self-confidence and security in a child.

Problems related to success and failure

As a child moves further into his school career, more of his difficulties are apt to stem from his success or failure in academic work, and from his relationships with his classmates and teachers. Children are like the rest of us: They cannot go through day after day of failure, of not liking their assigned tasks, and of not enjoying people with whom they associate without feeling some dissatisfaction. Adults change their jobs when they feel this way. Children cannot leave school physically. Their only alternative is to leave mentally—to daydream, to give up in despair, to become rebellious.

Again, there is no single answer to every child's trouble. A patient, mutual search by parents and teacher is the only wise procedure. A physical difficulty, with vision or hearing in particular, may be the cause in some cases. Academic work puts the first great strain on hearing and vision. A complete physical examination is often a wise first step in seeking solutions.

Children, of course, vary greatly in their ability to do schoolwork. They vary in their native intelligence, in their rates of growing, in their ability to handle specific kinds of subject matter. There is always the possibility that, without meaning to, either home or school may be asking more of a child than he is able to do. When goals and expectations are set too high, the result almost always is that children do not succeed as well as they could. The school's solution is sometimes to readjust its program, aiming more realistically at goals a youngster can achieve. Sometimes the home must make the adjustment so that a child feels he is a good human being and not a constant failure.

Some youngsters face a problem because they are "underachievers." They have more ability than they use. They glide through their days, operating on only a small part of their ability. On the face of it, this may not seem like a problem but a joy. However, youngsters are more contented when they work up to their ability. Unchallenged, they can move quite easily into various forms of misbehavior that reflect their discontent.

It is easier for both home and school to overlook the child who is underachieving than the child who daily meets failure. The failing child quickly calls himself to adult attention. The underachiever can slide by unnoticed. Parents and teachers need not search for problems that do not exist, but it is important for both to talk together so that real problems are not ignored. A parent's account, for example, of a child's unusual persistence and success with a hobby or an out-of-school activity may be the tip-off to a teacher that the youngster has more ability than the school has tapped.

Family problems and school

The demands of schoolwork sometimes uncover tension a youngster is feeling in his out-of-school life. The child who worries about his place in the family, or about his relations with his brothers and sisters, cannot concentrate and meet the rigors of academic work. These difficulties, probably not new in the child's life, may well have gone unnoticed during his simpler, less demanding living before the school years. Many school systems have psychologists who are trained to spot and treat such problems. Many communities have child guidance centers or family service societies which can help you with your problems.

Social problems

School, of course, is not all academic work. A school is a social center too. Conflicts and achievements in getting along with classmates take place daily. A child's social acceptance or rejection is important in itself and often has repercussions on how well he learns. The lonely child frequently adds academic difficulties to his other miseries.

Problems in a child's social life are perhaps the hardest of all for adults to solve. Adults cannot force one child to like another. But they can sometimes help a child to be more likable. Teaching the isolated child some skills that other youngsters value is one useful approach. Inviting classmates home after school is another way. Teachers can lay a basis for friendships through their seating arrangements or through school activities which bring together children who may learn to like each other.

Solutions to school problems

Parents and teachers both must realize that it takes time, patience, and wisdom to solve all human problems. It is so easy to believe that there are quick solutions—the teacher should assign more work in school; the parents should take away privileges until a child's work improves. In individual instances these may be useful approaches, but they are not cures in every case. In some instances, a final cure may take a long time to achieve. Some of the factors that can be involved—for example, large class size, a teacher's long-established way of teaching, or a home's way of treating a child—do not lend themselves to modification overnight.

Parents and teachers both must feel good will and be patient in working together if answers are to be found. No one wants a child to face a problem needlessly. Everyone wants the best for a child. But school and family life both center around humans, and humans change slowly. It is important to recognize, too, that there are some problems a child has to solve himself. There are other problems which have no solution, but a child can be taught to live with them and even gain strength from the experience.

You and your school-age child

Between the ages of 5 and 8, most children are open, energetic, and easy to get along with. Perhaps that is why some parents and teachers tend to coast along with them. Some mothers and fathers—frustrated and exasperated with older children in the family—take refuge in these easy-to-manage children. These parents lose sight of the fact that the early school years can serve as a foundation for good preteen and teen-age behavior. Here are some suggestions on how to make the most of the early school years.

Develop expectations to fit your child's abilities. Then he will be encouraged to go on learning. He will not become discouraged because he cannot meet unrealistic goals.

Emphasize the positive. Stress the things the child can do. Do not overemphasize the importance of achievement, especially in school. Do not tell the child that he has to *be* the best. Instead, tell him he should try to *do* his best.

Do not give rewards for grades. This makes the child believe he must always be compensated for doing well. If you think your child has the ability to do better work in school than he is doing, discuss this problem with his teacher. She can help you determine ways of gently helping him.

Continue to read to your child. A school-age child likes stories and enjoys being read to. Reading by parents builds up a relationship which helps make communication easier as the child grows older.

Remember, also, that good communication requires that you be a good listener. If your child has something to say, take the time to hear him out, even if what he has to say seems of little importance at the time.

Help your child develop a sense of responsibility. Assign him some chores—drying dishes, taking the garbage out, making his bed, keeping his room clean. Also, recognize and encourage responsible behavior by praise. And, remember that responsible behavior also includes such everyday events as getting up and going to school and coming home promptly after school.

Give the child choices in his hobbies or extra activities. Do not make him do such things as taking dancing or music lessons solely because the other children his age are taking these lessons. Respect the uniqueness and individuality of your child.

Give the child the right kind of help. He needs help that allows him to develop his own abilities. Too much help may lead to overdependency. Too little help may result in feelings of inadequacy or frustration. For example, if the child writes a letter, he may ask for help in spelling certain words. When he does, help him with those words. But, do not rewrite, correct, or criticize the letter. Let the child be free to say what he likes.

The most important way to help your school-age child be successful is to accept him as he is and to inspire him to become what he wants to be. And what do most children want? They want to be liked, to have interesting work to do, and to be respected. This is human and universal, and highly possible during the kindergarten-primary years when the home and the school work together to achieve this end.

The Preteen: 8 to 13 years

The preteen is a volatile, changing individual who is beginning to be free of dominant adults. The preteen is extremely interested in, and influenced by, peers, better known as "the gang." The gang has a code to follow and secrets to keep. This gang phase and other preteen behavior may be hard on you. However, it is just as important that your child go through these phases as it was to go through the crawling, creeping, and toddling phases. You can deal with the preteen period if you try to understand what is going on, and if you remind yourself that a child's growing up usually costs a lot in adult comfort.

Except for "Health and safety," this article was written by Fritz Redl, Ph.D. "Health and safety" was written by Eugene F. Diamond, M.D.

Portrait of the preteen

Your preteen is not quite the child he was. And yet, he is not quite the teen-ager he will become. He is in a transitional period—a period of preparation. Something new is going to be added, and for this reason he is changing. He is something like a department store that is undergoing renovation while still conducting business.

Preteen change and preparation may shake your child's personality. He used to be fairly easy to get along with and eager to please. Suddenly he becomes reluctant and defiant. Boys who used to pride themselves on keeping a neat room drop their clothes on the floor as they make their way to the bathroom for the nightly shower. Girls who depended on you for the choice of their clothes suddenly break down in tears when you make the slightest comment on their appearance. Reluctance, defiance, and tears—all are signs of the preteen.

Preteens often avoid shows of affection.

When he was younger, your child usually relied on your judgment. He felt safe and secure and had a pleasant personality. But during the preteen years, he picks up new ideas. He makes more of his own judgments. And he is not always confident that his judgments are correct. He becomes less secure, and as a result his personality may become a little less likable. But this is necessary. It is a part of loosening up his childish personality to make room for his independent adolescent personality.

The body itself—especially a girl's—is preparing for the changes and additions brought on by puberty. And, of course, your preteen is preparing himself to move away from family ties—a move that will be his major task during the teen-age years.

This time of preparation and change begins around the end of the fifth or sixth grade and usually lasts into the seventh or the beginning of eighth grade. As in all developmental stages, exact ages cannot be given. Individual differences in physical, intellectual, and emotional growth are as varied as are the circumstances under which youngsters go through such a phase. Also, not every child gets hit by this change in the same way, nor in all areas of his life at the same time. To make matters even harder to predict, girls usually get the phase over with earlier and with less fuss than boys.

Restlessness

Perhaps the most striking quality of the preteen is a sudden upswing in physical restlessness. For example, "sitting" hardly describes what preteens do with a table and chair while they are supposed to be doing their homework. They are constantly on the move. They need to handle things and people—like some highly overstrung adult who almost tears the buttons off your coat while talking to you.

If your preteen reaches for gadgets on your desk while you try to have a serious talk with him, do not think he is being disrespectful. If he fiddles with everything in sight while supposedly doing homework, it does not mean he wants to play instead of work. He literally cannot help it. Any gadget in sight must be handled. His "manipulative restlessness" is enormous. His workbooks look as though they had been fished from last year's trash can. His pencil tops are chewed up long before the writing part is even slightly used. And if no gadgets are around, then body parts are acceptable substitutes. He may pull at his ears; he may drum his fingers; he may scratch at his elbows or twist his hair.

The preteen's restlessness also shows up in a short activity span. Most preteens cannot stick to anything for long, even if it is something they enjoy—an experience for which they have been longing.

Try to allow for your preteen's restlessness. When you have to interfere with his normal urges, do so in a reasonable and friendly way, without showing indignation or excitement. Try to provide opportunities for him to rid himself of his restlessness with as little disturbance to others as possible. For instance, break up periods of quiet work with some activity—giving him a chance to move around, stretch, sing, talk, and yell. Preteens just cannot be forced to spend most of the day sitting and writing, reading, or listening. If you or his teacher can suggest ways for the child to satisfy his need for activity and manipulation, he will probably find it easier to remain quiet when he must

The restless preteen is almost always in motion—in the playground or in the classroom.

Even when seriously at work, a preteen may be biting a lip or chewing a pencil end.

Talking, laughing, shifting in a chair—the restless preteen finds it hard to do "nothing."

Almost every preteen indulges in daydreams—fantasies that help the child deal with new feelings or feelings that are not easily expressed.

study or do other things that require that he be sitting still.

Also, remember that he cannot easily change preteen habits and behavior patterns, even on the command of an adult. He has to go through this stage. He does not purposely do these things to annoy you. Avoid constant nagging and reminders that make him embarrassed and self-conscious.

Forgetfulness

A preteen forgets. And, there seems to be no excuse—especially since he can remember things his parents *wish* he would forget. For example, a teacher assigns homework on Friday to be turned in Monday. She writes the assignment on the board. She makes half the class repeat it. Yet on Monday, when the assignment is due, a third of the class has forgotten all about it.

Obviously, children sometimes use forgetting as an alibi. The amazing thing is that half of those who said they forgot were telling the truth. They *really* forgot. Preteens block out things that interfere with their pursuit of happiness. These memory blocks save them from unpleasant guilt feelings. A person who really forgets obviously cannot help it. Remind your preteen of obligations, but try to do so without nagging at him.

Daydreaming

An otherwise alert preteen may stare into space in the middle of a class, even when the subject is one he is good at and interested in. Youngsters of other ages can tell you, if they are so inclined, what they daydream about. However, if you ask a preteen what he was thinking about he usually answers, "Nothing." This may not be an evasion. Preteens have an extraordinary ability to think of nothing—or at least nothing that they can describe or name. Frequently, their daydreams are not organized at all. One picture after another flits rapidly through their minds. You might compare this to your own thoughts just before falling asleep.

When there is content in the daydreams, this varies as widely as do the preteens themselves. However, two basic kinds of daydreams dominate preteen fantasies.

One is a "technological" daydream. Many technically inventive and gifted children spend a lot of time looking at such things as a speck on the wall or a piece of string or wire. In their minds, such spots of color or pieces of metal or wood combine in the widest range of possibilities; they see "gadgets." Children may come out of such technical daydreams with imaginative, demonstrable products.

The other trend in daydreams concerns extreme power, cruel victory, destruction, fear of destruction, rebellion, mourning, and so on. They include the whole range of emotional relationships the preteen lives through, moves away from, or contemplates moving into. Many people worry that comic books and television create these daydreams. Indeed, such things may at one time or another be the cause. But if comic books and television were not available, children would still daydream about unpleasant things.

Daydreams fill a need of the youngster who is leaving one world (his childhood) and wondering about entering another (the teenage years). He must deal with puzzling and unpredictable themes, and he cannot deal with some of them directly because he would be punished by shame, guilt, terror, panic, fury, or rage. So he daydreams.

For example, if a boy dreams of cruelly killing a wild monster, it may not mean that he has such wild needs troubling his soul. It may simply mean that he was terribly embarrassed the day before when his father scolded him in front of his buddies. The child cannot consciously direct rage against his father, because he loves his father and knows his father was right. However, the shame still burns. How can he deal with it? He does so in the same way he deals with otherwise unmentionable pain—he projects it into the future or the past. He makes familiar persons into strange ogres or powerful enemies. He destroys with vehemence something that obviously cannot have anything to do with his real life. Only then can he let out the total force of his anger or panic or guilt or shame or rage.

Success and praise

For a young child, a reward that is "deserved" is especially gratifying. Something he gets only by "chance," while pleasant, is not a source of pride. Not doing one's job or assignment is shameful and embarrassing, while "working hard at it" is something to be proud of.

During the preteens, this view of success and failure may suddenly reverse, at least in part. A preteen is often especially proud not so much of what he did, but what he got away with. The fact that he worked hard on an assignment may be embarrassing, and he may even try to hide what he did from his group. To get something undeservedly ("This stupid teacher doesn't even know I haven't done any work at all!") seems to be the height of glory. Argument against this attitude is not effective. Actually, many youngsters pretend this attitude, though they do not mean it. But the group code demands that a preteen make light of his virtues, brag about shrewd evasion of the normal consequences of his actions, and glory in the luck or skill that brought him ill-gotten and undeserved gain.

It is easy to see, then, why youngsters of this age often react irrationally when praised. For the preteen, open praise makes him think he is being treated like a baby or teacher's pet. It may be more painful to him than the praising adult can imagine. If a preteen is told that he has acted like a "little gentleman," or that she has acted like a "little lady," chances are the child will be insulted rather than complimented.

Even the type of argument used with preteens needs examination. A boy may well accept the fact that you want him to come to dinner with clean fingernails. But arguing that a "nice little boy" would not want to appear with dirty fingernails is like throwing gasoline on a burning fire. Anything that makes the preteen feel that you are treating him "like a kid," no matter how well meant, hits the youngster the wrong way. This does not mean that you should not interfere. But, try to treat your child as the maturing person he is.

The preteen and "the gang"

Ever since your child entered school he has been learning that the group is something to be reckoned with. Always, part of his concern was to be accepted according to the group standards set by the neighborhood play group or his schoolmates. In the preteen period, however, what was perhaps a marginal problem suddenly becomes an essential adjustment.

The most important part of the world used to be the child's family. Suddenly, the "kid culture" of the neighborhood takes over. Now the important thing in the child's life is to be in line with the code of his peers, even at the cost of considerable open conflict with the family.

During the preteen period, the gang may become more important than the family.

Parents become "The Adults"

Many parents report that what hurts most during the preteen period is the peculiar way in which preteens cut off whatever relationships have existed between them and their parents by suddenly making their parents "The Adults." You know that they know better, that they love you, but—especially in public—they treat even your fair demands as angrily barked insults from an enemy. In fact, once your child has shifted you from the role of parent to the role of "The Adult," nothing personal may remain. You may become two power agents in battle.

You may happily suggest to your daughter that she have some of her friends over for a party. Her comment: "Where will you be?" You stammer something about being somewhere in the house and assure your offspring that you will not intrude on her fun. You get the rejoinder, "But we don't want any *Adults* around." It is hard to accept the fact that to your own child you are suddenly an archenemy. Of course, you should take consolation in the fact that not all preteens react so dramatically.

Your child's attitude is normal. In fact, the more a youngster is "attached" to you, the heavier is his need to defend himself against you—or his attachment to you. It is often the very loving and beloved parent,

Experimenting with lipstick is normal for a preteen girl but may cause conflict with parents.

the very cordial teacher, who bears the brunt of this puzzling behavior. And although it is easier to understand than to bear, do not take it personally. The battle stance between your child and you as "the authority to be challenged" does not mean that his relationship with you deteriorates permanently. It only means that, in certain moments of his life, he perceives himself as a member of the preteens. And that leaves you in the role of "The Adult."

Most preteens experience such moments frequently. There is no reason for concern unless the experiences become so all-inclusive that no personal relationship remains between parent and child.

Secrecy

Another way the preteen may try to cut you out of things is to have secrets. Girls, especially, may tease you by mentioning something somebody said or did, and then clam up if you want details. The youngster who previously ran to you with every little concern now cuts you off. Inquiries about what happened at school are met with a curt "Nothing."

This secrecy has reasons, though, and is part of the normal preteen trend. Partly, it is the preteen's need to have a domain safe from adult invasion. The content of a secret may be irrelevant. It is the fact of having one that counts.

Even some of the preteen's need to collect things and keep these things in his pockets or dresser drawers is part of that need to have his own domain. For example, if you try to get his stamp or coin collection quickly transformed into a well-organized enterprise, you may find that he loses interest in the hobby. It has become family domain instead of something he can deal with in his own way.

Related to the need for secrets is the fact that at this age communication often comes easier with other adults than with parents. This does not mean that your child has lost confidence in you. It is simply typical.

Picking up the dare

During the preteens and teens, even the most wonderful youngster may become extremely vulnerable to the compelling illogic of a dare. Under certain conditions a preteen must pick up a dare, no matter how silly, dangerous, disgusting, or obnoxious it is. If he does not pick up the dare, he loses honor in the eyes of the group.

Picking up the dare is seen most clearly in the older teen-ager. In the preteens, the kind of dare children are exposed to is not so easy to recognize, but plays as heavy a role. A preteen may, for example, accept a dare to put thumbtacks on the teacher's chair, talk dirty in public, thumb his nose at an adult, or talk back to an adult.

Dare situations may develop even when the gang is not around. Psychologically, the preteen may feel that the gang is looking over his shoulder. If the way you scold him or demand compliance seems to constitute an unwritten dare, he may suddenly become silly, stubborn, fresh, or defiant. He then becomes an actor in a show put on for the benefit of the absent group. He has to accept the dare or he will violate the code that governs his actions.

In dealing with a dare, avoid "extraneous reasoning." Do not resort to, "Your cousin Janice doesn't wear lipstick," or "When I was a boy, I never would have done that."

Preteens must pick up a dare. If they do not, they lose honor in the eyes of the gang.

Many preteen girls want to get a boy friend, and many preteen boys want a girl friend. But this is only a game that seldom develops into anything serious.

Fortunately, only a few situations at a time become loaded with this dare-vulnerability. In all other areas the child remains as reasonable, or at least as easy to influence, as he was before. For one youngster, being asked to put on galoshes or warm underwear may be an unbearable demand; for another, an anxious admonition to be sure he does not climb a tree or talk back to his teacher is an unbearable challenge. For another, mother's concern about lipstick, table manners, or language may be it. And what is "it" also changes from time to time.

These dares, although changeable, are fairly easy to identify. A more important concern, and one that is not easy to satisfy, is just what constitutes a dare when your preteen is alone with his gang. For if he shows signs of disturbing behavior, or if he is having unusual trouble at school, you will want to know if he is acting out of response to a dare or if he has a basic problem. Your child's teacher or school counselor may help you answer this difficult question.

If your youngster is heavily dependent on what you consider the bad standards of his group, the worst thing you can do is preach against them. This is considered an additional dare to show his loyalty to his friends, in spite of knowing better and being sure that you are right. Strengthening your child's own judgment and awareness is the only safe way to help him along, but this is a long-time job. Remember that success is not achieved overnight.

Face-saving

Many minor issues of daily life, such as schedules or your suggestions about what clothing to wear, may put a youngster into a situation where he is afraid of surrendering too openly to adult demands. Immediate and easy acceptance of adult orders somehow reminds him too much of early childhood years. Even though he realizes that your demands are perfectly reasonable, he still has to fight before surrendering. It is honorable to surrender after battle, but simply giving in is cowardly and childish. This has nothing to do with the question of your youngster's love for you and respect for your values. He needs to maintain pride in his own decision-making powers.

In fact, just to have the proud feeling of doing the right thing, your youngster may do what you suggested "on his own." He can only achieve this feat if he first refuses to do it, and then does what you want because he himself "decided" to do it on his own.

Any mother who has ever sponsored a Cub Scout meeting may remember that her own child behaved the most poorly. The reason for his bad behavior was simply that obeying mother in public can be construed

When preteens gather, they may not want "The Adults" intruding at their parties.

by the gang as childish. The only way to show that he is no longer hanging onto mother's apron strings is to defy her openly. Stop your child's behavior or tolerate it—but do not discuss it in front of his friends.

The need to show up well in the group does not end with the preteen period. The preteens merely start practicing it. In many cases it will be with them, and you, all through the teen-age years. And, sorry to say, it is likely to get worse.

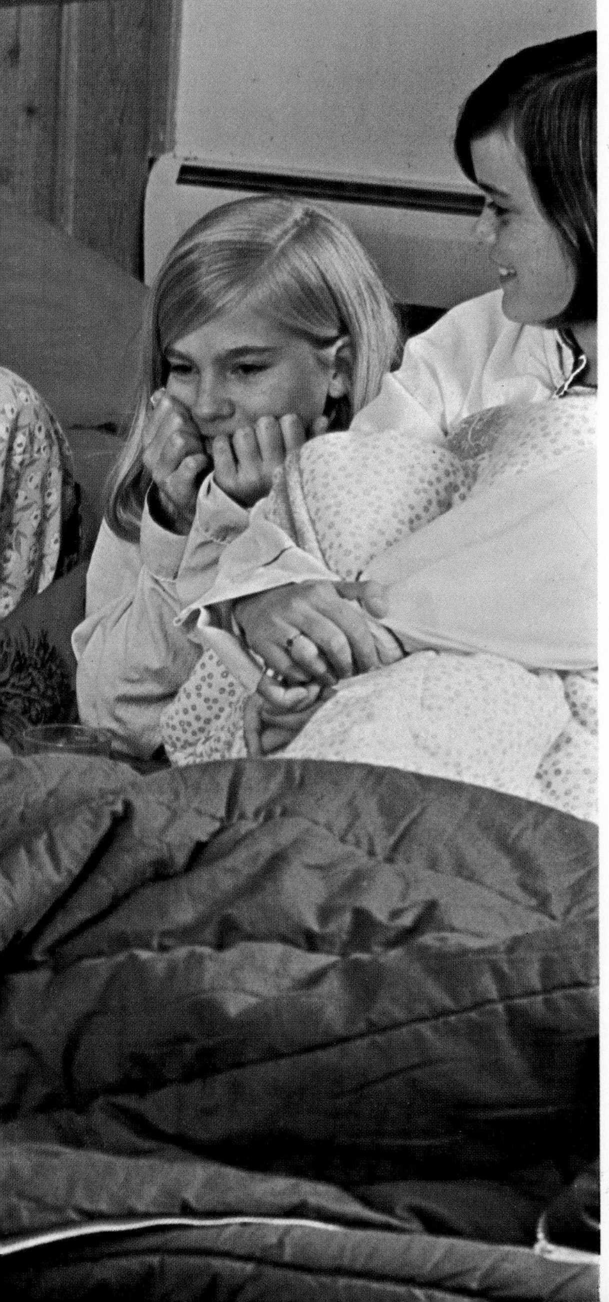

Toughness

A young child, when having a problem, seeks refuge in a friendly adult apron. If a serious problem hits a teen-ager, he longs for the friendly shoulder of an understanding adult. Most preteens want neither. Or if they do, they would rather be "caught dead" than admit it.

The informal preteen group code views any friendly talk with an adult as childish, sissyish, and cowardly. Also, according to preteen philosophy, trouble is a source of pride, not shame. You do not have problems as a preteen. You cause problems for others. Then they cause problems for you, so you fight back or take it. It may be hard to take, but it is better to go under in glory than to ask for help or advice.

Preteen love

Love in the preteen years is like a game. And it is a game that almost every preteen in the group plays. Preteen girls spend much time trying to get a "boy friend," and many preteen boys are busy trying to find a "girl friend." But these friendships seldom blossom into love.

Most preteen boys and girls do not see the person of the other sex as a love object in the way that will become apparent in adolescence. There are, however, many exceptions to this, and a semblance of being in love may become apparent from time to time. But preteen boys generally consider girls merely as members of the other sex. Girls are acceptable, or not, primarily on the basis of the same criteria by which anybody else is acceptable to the group. Girls operate in the same way, but they quickly tire of boys their own age and develop "crushes" on older boys in higher grades.

During these years, boys and girls still consider each other "closed groups." The importance of getting a girl friend or a boy friend is in winning the game. Then a girl can tell her less fortunate girl friends that she has a steady, that she is in love. And the boy can go bragging to his buddies. Probably all the boy does is carry the girl's books home from school, or go skating with her—accompanied by the group. Left alone they might well have a hard time carrying on a five-minute conversation.

Organized groups and school

Most preteens want to be as far away from the family as possible. For some, it may mean only the basement—where somehow family rules and regulations do not apply so strongly. Or it may be a tree house, a shack, or even nomadic wandering around the neighborhood.

Organized groups

Many preteens join organized group activities—the Boy Scouts, the Girl Scouts, the Camp Fire Girls, church groups, camping groups, cycling groups. These groups give preteens a chance to satisfy two of their great needs—being out of the house and doing something. Because of these two needs, you should take care when looking at preteen clubs or organizations. No organization should use as bait the child's yearning to belong to a group, while hiding actual motives. Some organizations use the time simply to stress table manners, obedience, fingernail cleanup, language mouthwash, and such other things as lofty ideals of character and education.

This does not, of course, mean that these characteristics cannot be part of the preteen curriculum. But the main thing is that preteens need a place where they can be what they are—rambunctious, out-of-step with what you may think is best for them—free to express the feelings and the thoughts of being a preteen.

Outside the home, the preteen is on the way to becoming his own person. Look to see that the organization your child joins is flexible enough to make room for preteen development. Be sure that the atmosphere a healthy preteen needs to grow in does not get lost among more marketable demands.

The preteen and school

Teachers find that many students who have been models for getting things done on time suddenly become fidgety and unreliable when they become preteens. This is a passing thing, and teachers usually allow for it. But what are *parents* to do when their preteen seems to lose interest in school, neglects his homework, and receives grades that are lower than what they know is possible?

Attitude toward school

Most preteens "gripe" about school. "This teacher hates me." "They give us too much homework." Griping about school is common among preteens and usually can be ignored. It is much like the eternal griping about boarding school food or being in the army.

But be careful not to add to your child's seeming negativeness. What you say about schools in general may easily affect his attitude toward school. Preteens are always ready for an argument to hide behind, something that will get them "off the hook." If you criticize collectively the schools and the educational system of your neighborhood, your preteen may find it easy to develop a stereotyped concept of school.

Homework

Preteens generally consider homework an undesirable thing. Unfortunately, many

Group activities are important because they give preteens a chance to be out of their homes and doing something—both basic needs of the preteen.

adults figure that things that are undesirable but necessary should be done first, before pleasurable activities are pursued. For this reason, parents often say "Complete your homework first; then go skating." The trouble with this reasoning is that preteens seldom study hard when they are thinking of somebody else already skating. A better plan might be to suggest that your preteen do 20 minutes of homework first, go skating for 45 minutes, and then come back home to finish his homework. This allows for the child's short attention span by breaking up the work into two periods. It also reduces the number of unavoidable head-on confrontations between parent and child.

Be sure that homework gets done, but be flexible enough to make allowances for preteen behavior that affects the way in which it gets done.

Report cards

Most parents worry when their child brings home grades that are lower than what his normal abilities indicate they should be. Low marks usually call for more supervision to ensure that homework is being done and that the child is properly motivated.

If trouble persists, however, this may be a good time to look for a tutor. A tutor can give the child the one-to-one attention he needs to stick to his work. And a good tutor can interest a child in a subject which until then has bored him.

Your child's teacher can help you decide if a tutor is needed, and for how long. The time will vary according to your child's needs. The important thing to remember is that using a tutor when your child is a preteen may help set up better study habits for the important adolescent years.

The preteen's health

Height and weight

Usually during the period from 8 to 13, major physical changes start to occur in a child's body. The most obvious change is a rapid increase in height and weight. In girls, this growth spurt usually begins between the ages of 11 and 14. Girls may continue growing until they are 17 or 18 years old. Boys start their rapid increase in height and weight somewhat later, usually between 12 and 16 years of age. Since their growth spurt is usually greater, and since it continues until their early 20's, most of them catch up and pass the girls in size by the end of high school. For more information, see GROWTH, page 133.

Other signs of maturity

Other signs of maturation usually accompany the increase in height and weight. There are changes in body contours and development of secondary sex characteristics. In girls, the leggy, straight-up-and-down appearance changes to a more rounded figure. This change in body contour is due to the settling of body fat over the hips, thighs, and chest; widening of the pelvis; and development of the breasts.

The changes in the body contour of a boy are due to an increase in muscle strength in his arms and legs, broadening of his shoulders, and an increase in the size and structure of his skeleton.

Sex development in girls

Secondary sex development in girls usually begins with the development of the breasts, starting with an enlarging of the nipples and then a gradual increase in the size of the breasts. At this time your daughter may become interested in brassieres—not so much for their function but because "everyone else is wearing one." If your daughter is an early developer, or if she is a late developer—the best rule of thumb to follow in this matter is, "Are her girl friends wearing them?" If they are and she is not, she will most likely feel left out and have more reason to cry.

Girls hit their growth spurt earlier than boys, a fact that shows up at school dances.

Soft, downy pubic hair—which later darkens and coarsens—is the next stage of sex development. Growth of hair under the arms follows the growth of pubic hair.

The first menstrual period usually occurs about the time of underarm hair growth. This may be preceded by several months of vaginal discharge, which may be blood-tinged. For the first year or two, periods may be irregular because the development of the ovum (egg) and ovulation (the release of eggs) occur irregularly. Almost all girls have their first period between ages 11 and 15.

Menstruation occurs because of interaction between the ovaries and the pituitary gland. When menstrual bleeding stops, the ovaries release hormones called estrogen into the blood stream. Estrogen causes rapid growth of the inner lining of the uterus. When estrogen is released, the pituitary gland releases hormones called FSH.

FSH increases the production of estrogen and also causes an egg to begin ripening in an ovary. As the egg ripens, the ovaries secrete other hormones called progesterone, which also help build the lining of the uterus. When progesterone is released, the pituitary gland releases hormones called LH. When the ratio of FSH to LH reaches a certain point, the egg is released. If the egg is not fertilized, the ovaries stop making estrogen and progesterone. Without these hormones, the lining of the uterus breaks down, causing menstrual bleeding. (For more information, see MENSTRUATION and VAGINAL DISCHARGE in the Medical Guide.)

Sex development in boys

Secondary sex development in boys begins with an increase in the size of the penis and testicles, accompanied by a growth of pubic hair. Hair appears next under the arms, and then on the face. About the time hair starts to grow under the boy's arms, there is a change in the tone of his voice. First the voice may break, alternating between high and low tones. Then it gradually deepens.

When the pubic hair becomes coarse and curly, the boy usually begins to produce sperm. Sperm are produced continuously in the testicles. Sometimes, the accumulated sperm and other secretions are discharged in a nocturnal emission (a wet dream). Explain

The unpredictable growth spurt of the preteens results in children of many sizes and shapes.

to a boy that this may happen. Otherwise its occurrence may frighten him, or—since it is usually accompanied by sexual fantasies during sleep—it may leave him with undeserved guilt feelings.

Dental care

The primary-grade child was conspicuous when he smiled because of the spaces in his mouth where his primary teeth had fallen out. Many preteens who smile are conspicuous because of the braces they wear to help straighten their permanent teeth.

After the six-year molars have fully erupted, your dentist should examine your child's teeth for irregularities. Some irregularities—protruding front teeth, too much space between teeth—cannot be corrected without braces. Your dentist will probably suggest an orthodontist (a dentist who specializes in correcting irregularities of the teeth) to apply this treatment.

Although many children dislike wearing braces, the results are well worth the relatively short time of inconvenience and possible embarrassment that may accompany them—and the cost to you. (For more on this subject, see BRACES, DENTAL and MALOCCLUSION in the Medical Guide.)

Common concerns

When he is about 8 or 9, the preteen is no special worry. Sure, he is noisy, forgetful, and restless; but he is also frank, loyal, and friendly.

Then, around 10 or 11, the problems start. Body image and personal appearance become matters of concern for many preteens. Some boys become sensitive about being shorter than girls their own age. And, just as often, those girls who have hit their spurt in height early may feel embarrassed and walk hunched over to appear shorter.

Both boys and girls may take pride in looking sloppy. Sweat shirts, brother's or father's shirts with the tails hanging out, bare feet, and bleached-out jeans may be just the thing for girls. Boys cut the sleeves off their sweat shirts. Some let their hair grow long. Corners of their bedrooms accumulate dirty clothes daily.

Do not be dismayed. This is a stage they will outgrow. Just keep the lines of communication between you and the child open. And do not nag.

Problems such as acne, overweight, and underweight arise. (See separate articles on each of these subjects in the Medical Guide.) The whole movement away from the influence of family, and toward that of friends, increases. Everything, it seems, is a "special problem." One potential problem deserves extra attention.

Preteens want to know more about sex than they did previously. And it is important that they know as much as the other members of their group. A child who is much less informed than his playmates runs the risk of being ridiculed. He may become afraid to open his mouth when sex is mentioned. Or he may exaggerate the importance of sex knowledge he does not possess to such a degree that the whole matter is unduly emphasized.

The preteen should already know the basic facts about where babies come from. Now he starts to ask for more specific facts concerning human reproduction. This is not wrong. Ideally, a child should feel free to come to his parents first for this kind of information. Give it to him accurately. Do not talk about sex in general terms. Do not give him vague ideas about how babies begin and where they grow.

Talk about your child's body, how it functions, and what is going to happen to it in the next few years. This is important even though the developments may actually be a year or so off. It is important that the child be prepared emotionally for what is happening and is going to happen to him before he enters adolescence, so that fear, anxiety, or abnormal curiosity can be avoided.

It is especially important that children be put at ease about new body sensations and observations of growth in their own body organs. Girls should know about menstruation before it occurs. Boys, also, should know something about this process. (For information on how to explain this process, see MENSTRUATION in the Medical Guide.)

One subject worries parents needlessly—masturbation. Most developing boys and girls masturbate. Do not be concerned about it. Masturbation is entirely normal.

You and your preteen

During their preteen years, boys and girls go through so many changes that growth seems to disorganize them rather than to improve them. The preteen period is one in which children grow "away from" more than they grow "into." They lose most of the characteristics with which you were familiar when they were children. Yet they neither look nor act as they will when they are older, when they are teen-agers.

Perhaps no other period of childhood development offers so many chances for parents to lose their tempers or become alarmed, sensitive, or indignant. But parents should try to figure out the best approach to each problem as it arises and to separate their own emotional attitudes from the problem. They should try to be the voice of authority without becoming authoritarians.

Some parents correct their child continuously and in his weakest moments. They give a moralistic speech each time their preteen daughter is five minutes late for dinner. They tell their preteen son that he will never amount to anything because he shows such irresponsible behavior at school.

Paying so much attention to surface behavior is unwise, especially if parents make more of the situation than the occasion demands. If you feel there is an issue in which you should interfere, plan your strategy wisely. Do not start a campaign of daily scolding and nagging. Let the misbehavior crystallize itself into definite incidents that can be well demonstrated and interpreted. Accompany this interpretation with a happy and secure personal relationship, and follow it up with a period of special interest in and companionship with your child. You may win more in the end if you do not insist on coming out on top in each little situation along the way.

Remember, few children show all the problems of the preteen period, and few of them go through all the difficulties at the same time. Life with your child from 8 to 13 should be fun. The basic test is not whether you have problems with your preteen, but whether you can enjoy your preteen child in spite of whatever problems may arise, and help him through a period that is as difficult for him as it is for you.

Keep lines of communication open between you and your changing preteen.

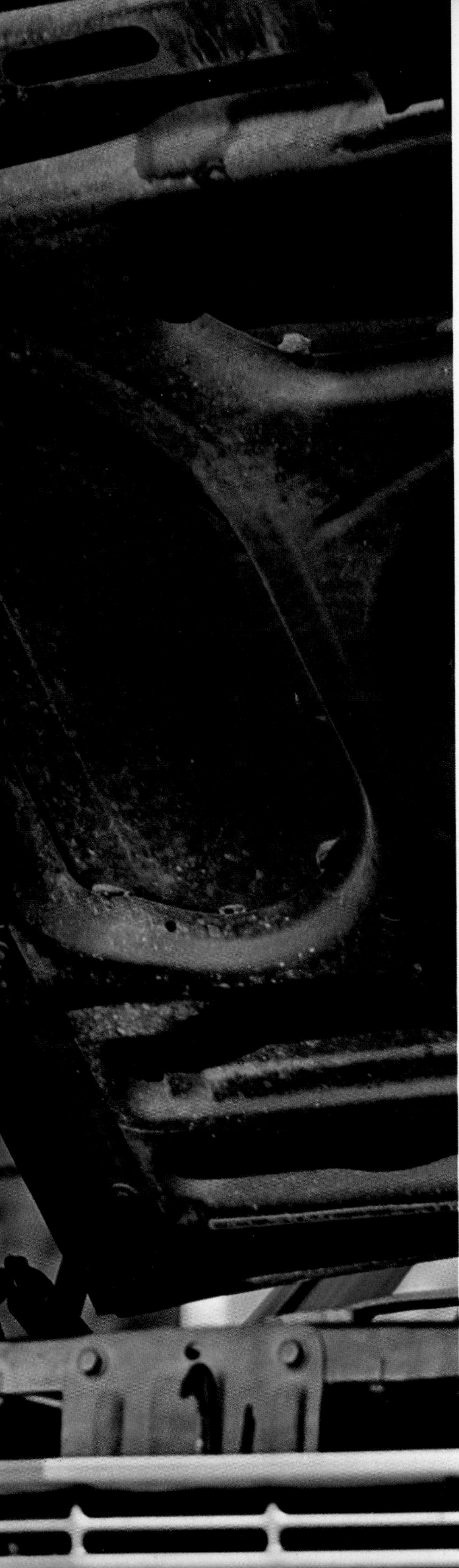

Looking to the Future

For the past dozen years you've watched over your child, worrying through childhood illnesses and giving comfort when it was needed. You've talked—and listened—to your child. You've offered praise when it was deserved, and discipline when it was necessary. You've shared secrets and sentiments, good times and bad times. You are sure you know your child as well as one human can ever know another.

Then—it seems overnight—the child, who until now has accepted your actions and opinions without question, begins to challenge just about all that you say and do. The child's moods change constantly—defiant one moment, dependent the next. Puzzled and provoked, you may begin to question your ability as a parent. Take heart. Your child is now a "teen-ager," an "adolescent," a "young adult."

By Graham B. Blaine, Jr., M.D.

The adolescent years

Your child begins his final step toward adulthood when he reaches the age of puberty. His body continues to grow and change. At the same time, he adds new values, opinions, attitudes, and ways of expressing himself to all that he had developed during his childhood. The old and the new are combined and modified, and eventually crystallize into an individual personality unlike that of anyone else. This physical and psychological process takes place in an uneven way over a lengthy period of time.

The child who was predictable during the first 12 or 13 years of life may become an adolescent who baffles you. He says one thing when, really, he means something quite different. Sometimes he is completely independent. Other times he is almost childishly dependent on you. He becomes involved in situations he cannot handle and expects you to get him out of his difficulty. Then he becomes upset with himself and hostile toward you because he feels that he has given you added reason to continue to treat him like a child. Usually, he tries to make up for his feelings of dependence by rebelling against you and other adults. He may ridicule all that you stand for.

Often, parents reinforce adolescent confusion by making inconsistent demands regarding the amount of responsibility an adolescent should have. For example, a 16-year-old may be asked to baby-sit with his little sister for a few days while parents are away. However, he may not be allowed to take a trip alone because he is not "responsible enough to stay out of trouble."

The search for identity

Perhaps the strongest force behind adolescent behavior is the search for identity—the adolescent's desire to find out who he is and where he is going. The teen-ager rebels against parental authority because he needs to prove that he is an independent human being and not simply an extension of his parents. He wants to be able to separate his life goals from those set by his parents.

Parents must allow an adolescent the freedom to experiment within the limits of safety so that he can learn for himself what is right for him. At the same time, parents should be aware that their child is watching them closely and that what they say and do makes a difference to him.

Some adolescents go to extraordinary lengths to provoke parental disapproval to see if their parents care enough about them. Some parents are inclined to be overly tolerant in the belief that their child will regard them as understanding. Usually, such parents get the opposite response. The child concludes that his parents let him do as he pleases because they do not love him and do not care about him.

Some parents go to the other extreme. They try to stifle all rebellious behavior by inflicting punishment that is much too severe. The child who is punished too severely also concludes that his parents do not love him. He may even decide to make his behavior fit the punishment.

Parents must learn to accept nondestructive rebellious behavior without being overly tolerant or overly punitive. But, they must keep in mind that adolescents feel strongly that parents and others in authority should be consistent in their beliefs and actions, sure of themselves, and courageous enough to stand up for what they believe in.

An adolescent needs to have a close association with adults he respects. This gives him the opportunity to choose and incorporate into his own identity the traits he most admires in them. Although the adolescent does not consciously imitate such adults, he absorbs these admirable traits. Eventually they crystallize into the core of his being and become part of his personality. He feels independent of the people he admires, but he now has values and ideals similar to theirs. He begins to identify with them, and his own sense of identity grows.

Some adolescents find it easier to talk to adults who are not their parents.

In the process of achieving his identity, the adolescent may go through a kind of delayed-action period. During this time, he feels uncomfortably neutral. He discovers that many well-respected individuals have values that differ from those of his parents. Until now he has considered his parents' word infallible. Suddenly, he may become confused. He may wonder whose values are the right ones. Were the many things he was afraid to do in the past really wrong? This prompts him to examine his own values. Are they really his, or are they borrowed and expressed without change to please his parents? What are *his* values?

If he cannot find an answer, he may be afraid to move in any direction. He can no longer consider his parents' values as absolute, but as yet he has found no substitutes of his own. This may cause him to become apathetic, depressed, and uncertain about his future.

Some adolescents feel compelled to drop out of school to spend time in contemplation or traveling. Others may take unchallenging jobs while they try to "find themselves." After a time, most adolescents who have gone through this period of growth find that much of what they had thought was dull and pointless takes on new meaning and importance. Education becomes a more meaningful part of the adolescent's plan for the future—one that he believes is his own, not one conceived by his parents.

Nondestructive rebellion

Some adolescents fill the gap between parental expectations and their own ambitions by rebelling in ways that are nondestructive, but nevertheless irritating to parents and other adults. The adolescent may be attracted to fads in dress or to hero worship. He may tie himself to a group with a nonconforming life style. He enjoys the feeling of independence he gets from belonging to a group that looks and acts different from the average. Loyalty to the group—seen earlier, during the preadolescent years—grows stronger. At the same time, being part of the group gives the adolescent the sense of belonging that takes the place of former family closeness—a closeness that now seems constricting and even hostile.

Dress fads are a form of nondestructive rebellion.

Parents are upset by this rejection. They feel they have worked hard to give their child the best they could, only to find him ungrateful and disdainful.

If parents would try to understand that such seeming ingratitude and disdain are only expressions of a healthy striving toward independence and eventual maturity, they would find this temporary withdrawal easier for all concerned.

Usually, a healthy conscience developed during early childhood keeps an adolescent from moving too far out of line. But parents, teachers, and other adults who have children in their care must take the major responsibility for helping young people channel natural rebelliousness into constructive outlets. Adults must set guidelines clearly, provide good examples, and be willing to allow their values and opinions to be challenged by adolescents without becoming either loudly angry or sullenly silent. Quiet discussion is the best way to keep communication open—even when opinions differ strongly.

Destructive rebellion

If an adolescent's conscience has not developed adequately, it is difficult to help him gain the self-control needed to curb rebellious behavior that is damaging and that may be fatal to him and to those around him. Drug abuse, abnormal or promiscuous sexual activity, and stealing are examples of destructive rebellious behavior.

Drug abuse

The fact that certain drugs are illegal makes their use an attractive way for adolescents to express rebellion against parents and others in authority. In addition, drugs such as marijuana, heroin, and alcohol provide a temporary sensation of ease and well-being. Amphetamines provide a temporary sensation of competence. Adolescents who take drugs prefer not to think of the damage drugs cause. When adolescents are asked why they use drugs, three reasons given are boredom, pressure, and family problems. (See THE DRUG PROBLEM, page 121.)

Abnormal or promiscuous sexual behavior

Another form of adolescent rebellion is sexual activity to gratify nonsexual needs. Some adolescents feel that no matter how hard they try, they are unable to gain their parents' love. To punish parents for such rejection, adolescents may engage in abnormal sexual activity such as Peeping Tomism, indecent exposure, and sexual promiscuity. Because pregnancy outside of marriage is usually a source of shame to the parents of adolescents, it may be used as a weapon in adolescent rebellion.

Most people consider premarital sex to be both immoral and potentially psychologically damaging for adolescents. But many young people challenge this belief in both word and action. This makes it important that adolescents learn about sex accurately. Parents, teachers, and religious organizations share the responsibility of transmitting information about reproduction, birth control, and venereal disease to young people. This is wiser than having youngsters pick up possibly distorted or unreliable information from street-corner gossip or myth.

One of the greatest contributions parents can make to their child's sex education is through the example of their relationship with each other. Appropriate physical expressions of tenderness between parents—a kiss before father goes to work, a pat on the arm—show a child the normal and loving relationship between the sexes. Similarly, when parents express disapproval and discuss the unfortunate results of abnormal sexual behavior, the child is encouraged to gain a healthy attitude toward sex.

Stealing

Adolescents, unlike preschoolers, know that stealing is morally wrong. Yet, it is not unusual for children who have been taught socially acceptable values to steal during adolescence. An adolescent may steal what he neither needs nor wants because it gives him an emotional uplift or "kick." To him, the act of stealing is a kind of game where the

A loving relationship between parents helps an adolescent form a healthy attitude toward sex.

Some teen-agers steal just for "kicks."

player tests his ability to avoid getting caught. It is a way of showing off to friends. Also, stealing may be a way of gaining the admiration of the group by having something no one else in the group has. Some adolescents steal because they feel unloved. Acquiring things gives them a feeling of security. But the most frequent motivation for adolescent pilfering is to express rebellion against authority. Each time an adolescent steals without getting caught, he feels he has played a trick against authority.

The child who steals occasionally is not headed for a life of crime. But persistent stealing, no matter what the motivation, may be the symptom of a deep-seated emotional problem. Parents who become aware that their child has a compulsion to steal should consult a psychiatrist.

You and your adolescent

In general, parents must let the adolescent experiment within limits of safety while serving as respected adults with whom the child can identify. They must continue to set an example for the child, and they must strive to keep lines of communication open.

Perhaps the best slogan for the parents of an adolescent to keep in mind is "Learn to tolerate temporary dislike if you want to gain permanent respect."

The adolescent is in the process of transition from child to adult. Parents must keep their faith in him. They must realize that often their child is suffering along with them, but in a different way. His irritating behavior, his arrogance, and his rebellious behavior are temporary. They must be borne with patience and understanding.

Section Two

For Special Consideration

Adoption

By Eda LeShan, B.S., M.A.

A couple considering adoption should be as clear as possible about why they're doing it and how they feel about it. Many childless couples feel they have failed as men and women. In addition to feeling frustrated and disappointed, they may even feel guilty or angry. Sometimes they feel their marriage is threatened or become ashamed, afraid they are "losing face" with friends and relatives. Some couples think that adopting a child will help them fulfill their own unrealized ambitions. None of these reasons is a good one for adopting a child.

A couple should adopt a child primarily because they want the joys and challenge of being parents—not because the child may be the means of correcting an unsuccessful marriage, or of giving them status with friends and relatives. A couple are ready to adopt a child only when they respect themselves as human beings worthy and ready to offer love and understanding, and when they can accept what every parent must accept—the fact that there is no way of knowing exactly what a child will be like.

Social agencies can help

Because motives and feelings are so important when adopting, it is wise to consult legally recognized social agencies about adoption. Carefully trained, experienced workers can help a couple explore their motivations, give them advice and guidance, and explain the importance of legal protection. A couple who adopt a child through sources that are neither recognized nor licensed cannot always be sure that the child is legally available for adoption. There is always the possibility that the natural parents may change their minds and want the child returned to them. Also, independent sources are usually unable to provide the kind of information and advice that agencies can provide through the experienced study that is done to make the adoption most satisfying for the child and the adopting parents.

A social agency is the best source for insuring maximum help and continued assistance. Information about recognized public and private agencies is available through state welfare authorities such as the state de-

Parents should adopt a child only through a licensed agency.

partment of public welfare, the department of public assistance, or the state department of social welfare.

Because of advances in child psychology, as well as changing circumstances, many agencies now have more flexible adoption rules and regulations. Factors such as race, religion, age, and background are not as restrictive as they used to be. In general, there is increasing awareness of the importance of family experience in every child's life. However, fewer babies are available for adoption than ever before. Many people use some form of birth control, and more unmarried mothers keep their babies. But older children, and those with special problems are available. Many couples thinking of adoption consider one of these children.

How it feels to be the parents of an adopted child

Parents of an adopted child experience all the joys and satisfactions of natural parents. They also experience all the normal problems, challenges, and stresses. But having an adopted child is not exactly the same as having a child of your own—mainly because parents who adopt tend to be too hard on themselves.

All parents sometimes wonder whether they are doing a good job when their child is unhappy, naughty, angry, fearful, shy, bossy, or jealous. But parents who adopt are likely to be extrasensitive to such behavior. When their child misbehaves, they often jump to the conclusion that somehow they are inadequate as parents.

If parents employ love, support, and guidance as the basic ingredients for helping the child to grow, and if they can anticipate the unfolding of their child's unique qualities with interest and joy, they need have no fear about their ability to be good parents.

Telling your child he is adopted

Tell your child he is adopted. Sooner or later he will find out anyway. Some parents find the easiest way to introduce the word "adoption" to their child is to tell him about himself as a tiny baby. All children love to hear stories about their babyhood. Sometimes the opportunity may come through looking at pictures in an album, or in telling or reading a story about an adopted child. It is wise to postpone any detailed discussion until the child is 6 or 7 years old. Before then, when the child asks for details about the adoption, it is possible for you to say with complete honesty, "There are things you cannot understand until you are older. I will tell you then."

Usually, it is a good idea to explain to close friends and relatives how you are interpreting the fact of his adoption to the child. If the groundwork has been properly prepared, it will not matter if someone says something to the child that represents a different point of view.

The child's questions about adoption will change as he grows older. First, he will be interested only in the circumstances that brought him to you. At 7 or 8, he may begin to ask questions about his natural parents. When answering such questions, try to keep lines of communication open so that the child will feel free to ask questions whenever he is confused or troubled. If questions are brushed aside, the child might find it difficult to share important feelings with you. The information the child asks for is secondary to sharing his feelings with you.

Do not sentimentalize or romanticize the facts of the child's adoption. You can tell him that there were good reasons for the adoption, that his natural parents were concerned for his welfare, and that giving him up was an act of responsible caring.

Yet, no matter how good the reasons for the adoption, the child may feel that his natural parents gave him away because there was something wrong with him. Even when you tell him that he was an adorable, beautiful child, and show him pictures of himself as a baby, he may still have this feeling of rejection. To a young child, it is incredible that parents would give away their baby unless there was something wrong with him. Such feelings of rejection may leave an emotional scar, especially in a child who is particularly sensitive. But this is true of many life experiences. It is true of the child who is lame, or sickly, or slower to learn than other children his age. Every child has some feelings of being different. But, in general, children are strong enough to face almost any reality if it is shared with loving parents.

Some special problems

Even though all parents face similar problems with their children, adoptive parents may encounter special problems that arise because of the fact that they have adopted. Here are three of them.

Brothers and sisters

In any family, children will at times resent or be jealous of each other. They will quarrel, bully each other, and fight. But they will also enjoy each other's companionship, fight for each other when threatened by outsiders, and on occasion even team up against their parents.

In a family made up of both natural and adopted children, parents may sometimes create a problem by singling out the adopted child for special attention. Often this is done in the mistaken belief that the adopted child will feel more secure. Usually the result is just the opposite. The adopted child is made aware that somehow he really is different from the others. He may even think he is being given favored treatment because he is not as capable as the other children in the family. At the same time, the natural children may feel a growing resentment against the adopted child because they feel cheated. Parents must take care to make it quite clear that each one of their children—natural or adopted—is loved.

Adopting an older child

Adopting an older child may involve problems of another kind. The older child may remember his natural family, or he may have a history of complicated adjustments in other settings—such as orphanages or foster homes. His new adjustment will be made easier if he is helped to share his memories and feelings with his new family. An older child needs a bridge between the past and the present to face the future. If a child has had unfortunate experiences which have deprived him of love and acceptance, adopting parents may have to face the fact that the child will be constantly testing them, trying to see if indeed they love him and will keep him, even when he misbehaves. During such adjustment, which is hard on both parents and child, an adoption agency can play an important part in guiding the family toward a solution. Patience, compassion, and the

When a family has an adopted child and a natural child, a parent must make it clear that each of the children is loved.

Adopting an older child may present special problems as well as pleasures. Contact the adoption agency if you have any problems.

readiness to ask for expert help when it is needed are some of the basics necessary for the successful adoption of an older child.

The search

Instances of extreme curiosity about his natural parents rarely occur to the adopted child. Usually, he feels so close to his adoptive parents, the idea that once he was part of another family seems unreal. But should the child raise the question of a search for his natural parents, the adoptive parents should understand the child's curiosity without letting it lead to any action. Usually, the child is not truly concerned in searching for his natural parents. In raising the question of a search, he may just be testing his adoptive parents. He may be saying, "Prove that you are more my parents than those who brought me into the world." If the child persists in the search, it should be pointed out that the natural parents' decision to give up their child must be respected; that whatever the circumstances, it was a difficult decision for them to make and it must have been necessary for the child's well-being.

According to adoption laws, search for parents is not desirable. Every state has laws requiring that a court order be obtained before adoption records can be seen, and the order is issued only under the most unusual and special circumstances.

If an adopted child continues to insist on the search, it may mean that he is having a difficult time adjusting to his present life. When this happens, it is wise for parents to seek professional help to find out what the real problem is. The adoption agency is usually a reliable source to consult. Also, the agency can help by referring parents to other sources of help.

Adoption and the law

Usually, an adoption decree ends all rights and duties between the child and his natural parents, and makes him the legal child of the parents who adopt him. The adopting parents become responsible for the child's education, care, and support. Each state and territory has its own adoption laws. When adopting parents and the child they seek to adopt live in different states, the adoption is governed by the law of the state where the adoption proceedings are brought, and the adopting parents must comply with the law of that state if the adoption is to be legally binding.

Almost all states issue a new birth certificate for the adopted child. This bears no information relating to the natural parents. It does not indicate in any way that the child is adopted. The new birth certificate carries the child's new name and the names of the adopting parents. Also, most states have laws or statutes making all proceedings in an adoption secret. The old birth certificate is sealed and filed. It may be obtained only under court order.

In matters of inheritance, the adopted child is entitled to inherit property from his adoptive parents except when a will states that inheritance is restricted to "heirs of the body." Some states bar an adopted child from inheriting property from his natural parents or other blood relatives. But other states prohibit the adopted child from "being debarred from inheriting" from his natural parents or other blood relatives.

Laws pertaining to inheritance by adopted children vary from state to state. Information about inheritance as well as any laws governing adoption may be obtained from the state welfare authority in your state or from the social agency that handled your child's adoption.

Behavioral disorders in children

By Jerome L. Schulman, M.D.

At times, all children behave in ways that puzzle or worry their parents. Many children may even show what seem to be symptoms of a behavioral disorder. Symptoms such as extreme aggressiveness, fears, and compulsions indicate a behavioral disorder only when they are severe or occur frequently. Be careful not to let your concern about your child's behavior exaggerate the significance of a symptom. Fortunately, most children are mentally healthy.

Behavioral disorders and mental retardation are different from one another, but sometimes it is hard to tell them apart. Emotional problems may make learning so difficult that even a normally bright child will appear to be mentally retarded. (See THE MENTALLY RETARDED CHILD, page 137).

The importance of physical health

Before concluding that a behavior problem is the result of emotional disturbance, you should be certain that your child does not have some physical illness. Many symptoms of behavioral disorder can be created or made worse by a physical illness. Regular medical checkups are important. They become even more important if your child is having an emotional problem.

Where emotional problems may occur

A child may be thought of as living in four worlds, and is expected to behave in certain ways in each of these worlds. If the child's behavior is frequently very different from what is thought of as normal, there may be a behavioral disorder.

Family and home—the first world

A child's first world is the family and the home. One's attitude toward oneself, toward other people, and toward life in general begins here. In a normal situation, there is a bond of affection between the parents, and between the child and each parent. They enjoy each other's company, but each has other interests. Gradually, the child moves from almost total dependence in infancy to almost total independence toward the end of adolescence. Throughout these years, the child is expected to pay a reasonable amount of attention to family rules, and to perform tasks that are reasonable in terms of age and ability.

A child may have a behavioral disorder if there is not a good relationship with parents, if independence proceeds either too slowly or too rapidly, or if family rules and assigned tasks are ignored. Attitudes toward other children in the family are hard to classify because quarreling and jealousy are a normal part of the brother-sister relationship. Such behavior seldom indicates a behavioral disorder.

School—the second world

A child lives in this second world about 1,000 hours a year during childhood. A child's tasks in school are fairly clear-cut. The child is expected, within reasonable limits, to perform well and to conform socially, to be interested in studies, see learning as an opportunity for a full and productive life, and to become interested and involved in extracurricular activity.

All parents have ambitions for their children. A problem may occur if the child's ability does not match the parents' expectations. The child's attitude toward school may become bad, or achievement may fall below ability. Also, if behavior at school is such that frequent discipline is necessary, it may indicate a behavioral disorder and that help is needed.

Friendships—the third world

As children move from infancy into childhood, they encounter a third world—the world of friendships. This world becomes increasingly important as children grow older. Childhood associations are extremely important. Children begin to learn social customs and patterns of behavior by imitating adults and by influencing and being influenced by other children. Much of the ability to be good at adult relationships grows gradually out of a good childhood beginning. Normally, the child should want to be with friends and should feel wanted by them. They should participate in pleasurable activities together.

Parents should be concerned about the child who is always alone, the child who tries to buy friendships with bribes, the child who acts the fool to get other children to laugh at him rather than with him, and the child who prefers to play with children who are much younger or much older, when children of his or her own age are available. And certainly parents should be concerned about the older child whose friendships lead to antisocial behavior such as vandalism or stealing.

The inner world—the fourth world

The child's inner world is in some ways the most important and the most difficult to understand. It is the world of thoughts, fears, hopes, attitudes, and ambitions. Children see themselves in many ways. They may think of themselves as smart or stupid, lovable or unlovable, ugly or good-looking, good or bad. Together, these self-evaluations make up what is known as the *self-concept*. When a child has a strong and continuous feeling of not measuring up to other children, it is reasonable to assume that there is an emotional problem.

Everyone has to face problems of one kind or another throughout life. In spite of this, the well-adjusted person continues to find life a source of satisfaction. No matter how bad the problem happens to be, such a person is usually optimistic about the future. If this feeling of optimism never occurs, then there is an emotional problem.

Specific symptoms

The most serious symptoms of behavioral disorder may be referred to as thinking disorders. They may occur singly or in combination. A child has a thinking disorder if he or she seems unable to respond to people or surroundings, or if completely without a sense of time. The child may hear voices or see things that do not exist. This should not be confused with the behavior of the normal child who may sometimes play with and talk to an invisible friend.

Obsessions are thoughts that occur repeatedly until they reach a point where they interfere with normal thought processes. At times a normal child may have an experience which is similar to an obsession, such as when the same tune keeps running through the mind. This is short-lived and does not interfere much with normal thought processes.

Compulsions are urges to repeat certain acts even though there is no reason to do so. An example of a compulsion is the uncontrollable urge to repeatedly wash the hands. This is not the same as a child's urge to avoid stepping on cracks in a sidewalk, which is more a game than a compulsion.

A phobia is a fear so terrifying that it prevents the child from carrying on normal activities. A phobia is one symptom of a behavioral disorder that gives parents much concern. This is not to be confused with the normal child's dislike of school at a given time, or with the temporary fear some small children show on first entering school.

Anxiety is a nameless dread not related to anything specific. Anxiety is harder to understand than a phobia because the cause of the child's fear is hard to pinpoint.

Extreme aggressiveness, such as a compulsion to hurt others or to be cruel, must also be considered a symptom of a behavioral disorder if it is a frequent occurrence.

Some symptoms of behavioral disorders

interfere with the normal body functions. Among these are tics, hysteria, enuresis (regular bed-wetting), and encopresis (the constant inability of the child to control bowel movements).

Tics, or habit spasms, are sudden repeated movements of muscle groups. Generally these occur in the muscles of the face, but they may involve any muscle group. The child has no control over a tic.

Hysteria is best described as the loss of a physical or sense function because of emotion. Hysteria may cause blindness or the loss of the sense of touch. It may also cause paralysis of arms or legs.

Enuresis and encopresis may be considered symptoms of a behavioral disorder if they persist after the child has reached school age.

What to do about behavioral disorders

If your child frequently shows symptoms of a behavior disorder, do not ignore the symptoms and hope they will disappear in time. Your child is too important for you to rely on chance.

Parents should discuss the problem together. It is extremely important that the discussion take place during a time of calm and good feeling. It must not take place when parents are upset and angry because the child has behaved badly.

During the discussion, parents must decide how the family as a group, and how each member individually, behaves differently from the average. Do not hesitate to admit that your own behavior may be different. In a variety of ways, everyone is likely to be on one side or the other of the average.

Also, you must be able to admit that while the ways in which you differ from the average may work well with some children, and may even be necessary, they have not been successful with the disturbed child. This admission calls for a willingness to accept the fact that your behavior is related to child's difficulty, and that a change in your approach to the child may be a solution to the problem.

Parents may have problems

The *perfectionist parent* believes there is a place for everything and that everything must be in its place at all times. As a result, demands on the child are often unreasonable. The child's room is never kept neat enough to please the perfectionist parent. If the child gets a "B" on an otherwise straight "A" report card, the child is criticized and made to feel inadequate. The child is constantly compared to others, but no matter how hard he or she tries, the perfectionist parent is never quite pleased. Emotional problems the child has can often be related to this abnormal demand for perfection. The perfectionist parent should try to be less rigid to relax rules, and to praise more than criticize.

The *inconsistent parent* creates an uncertain environment by changing rules so often that the child cannot know what is expected. Most parents are inconsistent at times, but when they constantly change rules relating to the child's behavior in the home, in school, at play, and in other areas of life, it is damaging to the child and should be corrected.

The *overprotective parent* shields the child excessively, either because the parent cannot bear the thought that the child is growing up, or because of undue concern for dangers in the world outside the home. This attitude may contribute to the development of emotional problems. The parent who recognizes that overprotection is the cause of a problem can find a reasonable guideline for correcting it by studying the behavior of parents with well-adjusted children.

The *indulgent parent* buys the child's affection by never setting any limits. This may also be the source of the child's behavioral disorder. Children are much more comfortable when they have rules to follow. Rules prepare a child to face the many situations where individual desires must be put aside in favor of group needs.

Quarreling parents may also contribute to a child's emotional problems, if the quarreling is constant. The obvious solution is for parents to avoid quarreling in the child's presence and to compromise their differences.

The *uninvolved parent* has little to do with the child. Such a parent will be unable to convince the child of love, interest, and a concern for the child's welfare. Children need models after which they can pattern their own behavior. To be effective, models must be available and interested in the child.

The *punishing parent* tends to deal with problems by thinking up new and unusual punishments. Although punishment may be essential on some occasions, it should not be excessive, and there should be sufficient praise to counterbalance it. Punishment must be considered a failure if it does not produce the desired result. If a child shows symptoms of a behavioral disorder, and has been punished a great deal, it is reasonable to assume that more punishment will only tend to aggravate the condition.

Changing tactics

When parents recognize that previous methods of handling their child have been unsuccessful, and even harmful, they should plan a new program. If the child is old enough to reason with, the process will be made easier by a frank discussion when all are feeling friendly. The parents should tell the child how concerned they are about the difficulty, and how much they want to help. They should indicate to the child how they plan to change their behavior toward him. They should agree to meet on a regular basis at a prearranged time to discuss progress. The child should be allowed to speak freely during the discussions, and nothing the child says should be held against him or her.

If the child's behavior has become a problem at school, it is important that both parents meet and discuss the problem with the child's teacher and other appropriate persons such as the principal, the school psychologist, a social worker, or the school nurse. These people are interested in the child and can offer the parents advice and guidance. This may be extremely valuable in helping parents understand why their child is behaving badly.

When to seek professional help

Usually, it is difficult for parents to admit, even to themselves, that their child may need psychiatric treatment. And it is reasonable for parents to assume that they can work on some of their child's problems without outside help. If there is any improvement, they should continue. But if at the end of a reasonable length of time there is no improvement, then it is time to seek professional help.

If the child's problem is in the category discussed under "Specific symptoms," parents should consult their pediatrician or the family doctor. If necessary, the parents will be referred to a psychiatrist. If a psychiatrist is not available for consultation, the doctor may refer parents to a clinical psychologist or to the local mental health clinic. Often it is easier for an outsider, especially one with specialized training, to approach the problem with greater objectivity or from a different point of view.

When parents consult a psychiatrist, they must be prepared to accept the fact that they may be partly responsible for causing their child's emotional problem. Parents should want to know how they have contributed to the problem, and they should be willing to work along with the doctor to produce good results.

Children with behavioral disorders tend to respond favorably to treatment, especially when all members of the family are involved in the effort to help. The treatment of an emotionally disturbed child often requires a great deal of time and patience on the part of parents and child guidance specialists.

For one thing, a disturbed child is, as a rule, completely unaware that anything is the matter. For another, disturbed children seldom want to change their ways. The professional working with the child may need time to bring the child to the point where the child wants to do something about the behavioral disorder.

Parents should not be discouraged if psychiatric treatment or treatment in a child guidance clinic fails to produce immediate results. Diagnosis and treatment take time and the results may be slow in coming. A severe behavioral disorder usually takes a long time to develop. It follows that as long a time may be required to correct it.

Fortunately, many of the emotional illnesses of children can now be treated successfully. Ongoing research in the important field of mental health should offer even more help in the future.

Choosing a baby sitter

By Stella Chess, M.D.

Parents and children should occasionally spend time apart from each other. Parents should be able to enjoy an evening out, or a few days away from home, free from the demands made on them by their child. And a young child needs to learn to accept the temporary absences of his parents without fear that he is being rejected or deserted. But this is possible only when you are completely at ease, confident that your child is being looked after by a friendly, efficient, and trustworthy sitter.

When you place your child in the care of a baby sitter, you should be as certain as possible that she (or he) is fully able to assume responsibility for the safety and needs of your child. Whether the baby sitter is an adult or a teen-ager, whether she is needed for a few hours or a few days at a time, it is important that you choose her carefully.

A friendly, efficient baby sitter can make parents and children feel at ease.

If you do not already know your prospective baby sitter, you should be certain that she comes to you well recommended by someone whose judgment you trust. Depending on your child's age and the length of time you expect to be away, you will expect the baby sitter to have special qualifications. There are many things you will want to know about any baby sitter you engage.

- Does she like and understand children?
- Do children like and respect her?
- How much experience does she have?
- How will she react to an emergency?
- Is she physically and mentally healthy?
- Is she clean and neat?
- Are her morals and conduct acceptable?
- Does she have a sense of humor?
- Does she refrain from gossiping?

A competent sitter should have little or no difficulty making your child feel at ease. But no child, with the possible exception of a tiny infant, should be expected to accept the care of a complete stranger without some objection. It is, therefore, a good idea to invite the sitter to your home so that you and your child can get to know her. While she is in your home, perform some activity in your child's daily routine such as playing with him, feeding him, or dressing him, so that you and the child can begin to establish a friendly, personal relationship with the sitter.

If such an opportunity is not possible, arrange to have the sitter arrive early for her first job. If you show that you like and trust her, your child will be quick to sense this. Usually, he can be counted on to relax and enjoy the quiet, pleasant atmosphere created by friendly conversation. Hurried, last-minute warnings and instructions to the sitter are likely to leave the child less relaxed.

During the sitter's first visit to your home, point out all exits, and special hazards such as electric heaters, electric outlets, open stairs, or swinging doors. Show her where thermostats and other temperature regulators are and how to operate them. Tell her where she can find a flashlight if there is an electric power failure. Also, instruct her in the use of any appliances she may need to know about while she is in your home.

Show her where extra supplies of food, clothing, bed linen, and diapers are kept; where she can find first-aid supplies; and where you keep your permanent list of names and telephone numbers of people to call in an emergency. This list should include the name and telephone number of your family doctor (as well as the name of an alternate doctor to call if your family doctor is not available), the names and telephone numbers of several close neighbors, and the telephone numbers of the police and fire departments. Be sure to give her the name and telephone number where you can be reached during the time you are away from home.

A baby sitter will do a much better job of caring for your child if you tell her about any special habits and problems your child has. Is he normally a restless sleeper? Does he often cry in his sleep? Does he have to be awakened at a certain time to go to the toilet? Does he always fall asleep clutching his favorite toy or blanket?

It is helpful for your sitter to know which books, stories, and records are your child's favorites. Sometimes a familiar song or story will comfort a child who misses his mother.

When a sitter is to supervise bedtime for children of varying ages, you should tell her when each is to be in bed. You should also tell her what your child may have to eat or drink before bedtime. If the child is an infant, be sure to make enough formula to last the time you are away, and show the sitter how to heat and feed it to the baby.

Also, your sitter will feel more at ease if you tell her what foods she may help herself to, and what other privileges she may take while she is in your home.

When a sitter is to take over your household for several days, you should leave her a detailed list of your child's activities, duties, and privileges. The sitter should know whether you permit your child to have friends in after school, how many may visit at a time, and where they may play. If your child is required to wear special clothing when outdoors, the sitter should be informed. Also, tell the sitter if certain television programs are not permitted and what rules you expect your child to follow.

If you choose a baby sitter with care, and if parents and baby sitters respect the obligations and responsibilities each has to the other and to the child, then everyone concerned can be sure of a pleasant, satisfying relationship.

What your baby sitter should know

- Telephone number where you can be reached
- Family doctor's name and telephone number, and a substitute doctor's name and telephone number
- Telephone number and name of nearest neighbor
- How to operate any appliance that may have to be used
- How to set the thermostat
- Where extra food, clothing, and bedding are kept
- Where flashlights or candles are kept if there is a power failure
- Telephone numbers for the police and fire departments
- Whether your child sleeps with a night light on
- Where first-aid supplies are kept
- Any special problems or habits your child may have
- Television programs your child is allowed to watch
- Privileges the sitter may take

Divorce

By Stella Chess, M.D.

Divorce is an upsetting experience for everyone involved. It is especially difficult for a child to accept a threat to the security that comes from living with a united and loving mother and father. But a divorce need not permanently damage your child's emotional development if you learn to handle the problems that may arise from this major change in his life.

Telling your child about divorce

When divorce becomes inevitable, tell your child about it. By the time parents have reached the point where living together is no longer possible, even a young child will be aware of the tensions. If he is not aware of what is going to happen, he may be upset, believing the truth is too terrible to know.

It is not unusual for a child to think that he is responsible for the split between his parents. He may remember times when he was the cause of a disagreement between them. Or he may think of times he wished his mother or father would leave and never come back. Suddenly he sees his wish coming true, and he feels guilty and ashamed.

How to explain the reasons for a divorce depends on your child's age and his ability to understand. Above all, make him understand that he is not to blame. A 3-year-old will probably be satisfied with, "Daddy is not going to live with us any more." An older child may want to know why. You can tell him, "Your father (or mother) and I are not happy together so we are going to try living in different houses to see if we will be happier that way. If we are, we will get a divorce. We will tell you about it as soon as we are sure." When you take the child into your confidence and let him know what is happening each step of the way, he feels less bewildered and shut out. At the same time, try to make him understand that parents, even if divorced, do not stop loving and being responsible for their children.

Break the news to your child as calmly as you can. No matter how bitter or angry you may be, try not to speak of the other parent in an unfavorable way. There is no harm in explaining why you and the other parent could not get along, but do not burden your child with details that he cannot understand. Never put him in a position where he has to take sides. It is unfair, especially when he needs to know that even though his parents no longer love each other, they still love him.

If a parent deserts the family, do not hold out false hopes that he will return. Waiting for a thing that may not happen is harder on the child than being told the truth.

Sharing feelings

No one who has been through the emotional shock of a divorce can act as though nothing has happened. Do not weep on your child's shoulder, but if you are unhappy at times, there is no reason why you should not share your feelings with him. If you can convince yourself and him that you will be happier as time passes, both you and he will adjust to the situation more easily.

Now and then every child is angry with his parents, even where there is no divorce. But divorce may bring out an unusual amount of resentment. Let your child express his anger. No matter how understanding of the divorce he seems to be, he may secretly feel that if you had tried harder you could have kept his world intact. Sometimes a child will not voice his resentment because he thinks you may "divorce" him, too. Instead, he may act out his resentment. He may refuse to eat. He may bite his fingernails. He may lie.

Let your child know that you understand how he feels, and assure him that no matter how angry you may become with each other, it is not the same kind of anger that led to the divorce. Children need to be able to act out their "bad" feelings and to know that it is safe for them to be angry.

Visiting the other parent

Unless it is impossible, your child needs to be able to visit the other parent. There are no set rules regarding the amount of time to be spent with each parent, but it is generally believed that an equal division of time may confuse the child. He will feel more secure if he has one home where the greater part of his life is spent—a place where he knows he belongs. He should be able to say, "This is where I live," and "This is where I visit."

In most cases, it is best to have the court set up visiting arrangements. Visits should be regular, and parents should try to keep to the schedule. For the child under 4, daytime visits are usually more satisfactory. As he grows older, he may want to spend the night with the other parent. This may be good, if the experience is a happy one and does not increase strain between the parents.

As a child grows older, the legal arrangements concerning visits—and possibly custody—may well be reviewed and revised to fit the child's changing circumstances, interests, and needs.

A parent shouldn't compete for a child's love by giving him expensive presents and making every visit a holiday. This is unfair to the "stay-with" parent. It is obviously easier for a parent to make a child feel that the child is more fun to be with when the parent is not bothered by the responsibilities of living with the child daily.

If after visits your child makes unfavorable comparisons between you and his other parent, perhaps you are taking the weight of your responsibilities too heavily. Perhaps you should spend a little more time enjoying your child and less time trying to improve him. Both parents must keep in mind that down-to-earth caring, understanding, and discipline when needed are more valuable gifts than anything that can be bought.

When a parent remarries

A parent's remarriage is another change in the child's life. If you plan to remarry, share the fact with your child. Let the child know what to expect.

Some children adapt easily to suddenly having a new parent, relatives, and perhaps brothers and sisters. Other children feel that the change means being left out or taking second place in a parent's affections. It is important for your child to know that the change will not affect your love for him.

When visiting a parent who has remarried, the child needs to spend time when just the two of them can talk, read, and enjoy things together. He also needs time to get to know his stepparent. It is not unusual for a child to resent the stepparent at first. But if the stepparent is patient and loving, the resentment will disappear.

When a new baby arrives in any family there is bound to be some jealousy and bad feeling. Half brothers and half sisters are no more immune to rivalry than full brothers and sisters. Allow your child to express his bad feelings about the baby. He may say, "You spend all your time with the baby and every time we go anywhere you take him with us. I liked it better before. I'm going to stay with my daddy." Don't scold or lecture the child. The storm will blow over if you do not make him feel ashamed. Help him find new interests and friends so that he will feel less dependent on you and less left out.

Each parent of a divorce must help the child adjust to changing circumstances, but neither parent should dictate to the other how the child is to be treated. If there are problems, and if both parents are willing, they may get together to discuss them. Both parents must try to give their child the certain knowledge that they love him and that he can be happy and comfortable no matter which parent he happens to be with.

The drug problem

By Thomas E. Cone, Jr., M.D.

The misuse of drugs, including alcohol, by young children is a grave concern for parents. The drug problem, once confined largely to city slums, has spread to all parts of cities, as well as to suburban and rural towns. The misuse of marijuana, PCP (phencyclidine), and alcohol appears to be on the increase among children in elementary school and junior high school. Some of these children are now committed to these drugs, and to the unreal world the misuse of drugs helps to create.

Why children misuse drugs

There is no single reason why young people turn to drugs. Some try drugs out of curiosity, for "kicks," or because it is considered the "in" thing to do. Many children feel isolated from their families and from a society that they believe has distorted values, is hypocritical, and materialistic. To these youngsters, drugs provide an escape from a fast-moving world where they feel insecure and confused. They feel unable to cope with the problems and pressures of everyday living. The misuse of drugs is also a way to rebel against parents and other authority figures. Some teen-agers experiment with drugs because adolescence is the time to live dangerously.

Studies among young teen-agers show that a small but constantly increasing number drink alcohol, not only for social reasons but also to relieve boredom and anxiety. The "shift to alcohol" among adolescents may represent a trend toward reconciliation with society's "drug of choice."

There is no *good* reason to misuse drugs. But in a world where pills and other drugs are available for the relief of many ills, and alcohol is socially acceptable, teen-age experimentation with drugs is understandable, though not justifiable.

Habit-forming and addictive drugs

Marijuana, PCP, LSD, amphetamines, cocaine, and certain substances found in aerosol sprays, glue, gasoline, and lighter fluid are *habit-forming.* This means that if used at regular intervals, they can cause psychological dependence on them. Users develop a mental or emotional need for the drug, even though their bodies can do without it.

Heroin, barbiturates, nicotine, and alcohol are *addictive* drugs. They create both a psychological *and* a physical dependence on them. Addicts actually become physically ill if they cannot get the drug to which they are addicted. Furthermore, the body gets so used to the drug that doses must be increased to get the desired effect.

Sudden withdrawal from addictive drugs is painful and dangerous. On an average of about 18 hours after taking a last dose of heroin, an addict may have severe leg and stomach cramps, chills, nausea, and diarrhea. The body may shake uncontrollably and perspire a great deal. Sudden withdrawal from barbiturates is extremely dangerous. It can cause convulsions, mental disturbance, and even death. Withdrawal from barbiturates should be gradual, and done under a doctor's supervision. A chronic drinker's withdrawal from alcohol may cause tremors, convulsions, hallucinations, and delirium. The symptoms develop after a period of relative or absolute abstinence from alcohol.

Experimentation does not necessarily lead to drug dependence. Alcohol is one example of this. Most people who try alcohol do not become dependent on it. It would be untrue to say that one or even a few tries of a habit-forming drug will "hook" a child. Yet, all experimentation must be regarded as risky. The drugs to which children are most commonly exposed can lead to psychological dependence or addiction. Parents must make sure that children understand the dangers involved.

Commonly misused habit-forming drugs

Marijuana, also known as "pot" and "grass" among other slang terms, is most often smoked in a homemade cigarette called a "stick," "joint," or "reefer." Heavy doses can alter perception, impair judgment, and release inhibitions that normally regulate acceptable behavior.

PCP (phencyclidine), known as "angel dust" and "hog," is an animal tranquilizer. It can be inhaled, injected, or swallowed. Most often it is dusted over cigarettes, marijuana, mint leaves, or parsley and smoked. A small amount can produce a state similar to drunkenness, ranging from euphoria to depression and hallucinations. Larger doses can cause convulsions, psychosis, rage, coma, and death.

PCP is so punishing that the rate of misusers who quit using it is very high. Usually, its use flares up in a given area and attracts large groups of experimenters. Many suffer so severely that they soon quit, but they may then move on to other drugs.

LSD (lysergic acid diethylamide), also known as "acid," is a psychedelic drug. If unadulterated, it is colorless, tasteless, and odorless, and so powerful that a very tiny amount (0.2 mg) can cause strange mental images and distort hearing, sight, smell, and touch. Greater doses may induce an anxiety or rage so strong as to lead to suicide or homicide. LSD may remain in the body for weeks, and persistent adverse reactions may recur long after the initial dose is taken.

Amphetamines, also known as "uppers" and "speed," are stimulants. They are sometimes prescribed by doctors for obesity, to relieve mild depression, or to reduce fatigue. Large doses can make users see and hear things that do not exist (hallucinations). The person becomes more talkative, and also often more irritable. Amphetamines can also make users act in dangerous, unpredictable ways.

Cocaine, also known as "snow" and "coke," is usually sniffed, but it is also injected or swallowed. It produces a feeling of well-being, depression of appetite, a deceptive feeling of unbounded energy, rapid heartbeat, and increased blood pressure. Chronic use causes emaciation, insomnia, tremors, and convulsions.

Cocaine is not addictive in the sense that a narcotic is. If its use is stopped, physical withdrawal symptoms are rarely encountered. There is, however, a marked psychological dependence on this drug, and its use tends to become compulsive. Like the amphetamine abuser, the individual abusing cocaine is likely to develop paranoia and to hallucinate.

Acetone, carbon tetrachloride, ethyl acetate, and toluene are found in many common products such as the glue or plastic cement used in making airplane models, nail polish, nail polish remover, gasoline, lighter fluid, cleaning fluid, and many paints, lacquers, and thinners. Drug misusers inhale the fumes to get a feeling of intoxication, or until they hallucinate.

Glue sniffing, as this is called, often leads to unconsciousness, and may affect the brain, liver, kidneys, and bone marrow. It may cause death by asphyxiation. Glue sniffing is most common among children from 8 to 14 years of age.

Aerosol sniffing is a fad among some pre-teens and younger adolescents. Various common aerosol products, such as hair sprays and deodorants, are sprayed into a paper or plastic bag. The contents are then sniffed in hope of achieving a "high." The active chemical ingredient in aerosol sprays can be extremely toxic. Many deaths by suffocation or cardiac arrest have been reported following the inhalation of aerosol propellants.

Commonly misused addictive drugs

Heroin, also known as "snow" and "horse," is a narcotic. It is related to morphine, but is far more addictive. Usually, it is mixed with lactose (milk sugar) or quinine. Heroin addicts are always in danger of death from an overdose because they can never be sure how much heroin there is in the mixture "bag" they buy. Most heroin addicts inject the drug into their veins. Often, unsterile needles cause hepatitis. Heroin addicts usually suffer from chronic liver infections and malnutrition.

Barbiturates, also known as "downers" and "barbs," are depressants and sedatives. Doctors prescribe them to induce sleep and to relieve nervous tension. Barbiturates are extremely dangerous when misused. Large doses of barbiturates distort vision and slow down reactions. The effect of a large dose of barbiturates is similar to intoxication. Users lose the ability to think and to concentrate. They stagger and their speech is slurred. An overdose, or a mixture of barbiturates and alcohol, may cause death.

Alcohol is a depressant. Studies done in the United States and Canada report a precipitous increase in the use of alcohol by young teen-agers. Alcohol has been "rediscovered" by some adolescents as an alternative to marijuana. Further, the social acceptance of alcohol among adults has lessened the anxiety of parents toward drinking by their children. Many adults tend to be far more permissive in their attitude toward alcohol than they are toward a similar use of marijuana. Thus, the use of marijuana is often considered drug abuse, while the use of alcohol is ignored. Yet, alcohol continues to be the most dangerous and most abused drug in the United States and Canada.

Signs to look for

The sooner parents and teachers act when they suspect a youngster of experimenting with drugs, the better the chances are of preventing addiction.

It is not easy to tell when children are misusing drugs. Those who do so become adept at hiding the fact. But there are a number of telltale signs, none of which is absolutely conclusive, that should alert parents and teachers to the possibility that a youngster may be taking drugs and in need of help.

- Change in school attendance (frequently absent or late)
- Change in work habits (sloppy homework, apathy)
- Unusual flare-up of temper
- Furtive behavior
- Poor physical appearance
- Associating with known drug misusers
- Stealing or borrowing money
- Wearing sunglasses at inappropriate times (to hide the pupils of the eyes)
- Hiding in closets and other secluded places (to take drugs)
- Refusal to wear short-sleeved shirts (because needle marks would be seen)
- Unusual aggressiveness
- Unusual sluggishness

Where to get more information and help

As soon as parents suspect that a child is misusing drugs, they should get in touch with the family doctor. The doctor, if unable to deal with the problem, will refer them to someone who is qualified in the treatment of drug misuse. The family doctor may refer the child to an established Adolescents' Unit, a residential treatment center staffed by physicians who are specially trained in the management of drug misuse, including alcohol.

You can obtain the hot lines to drug information and treatment centers by dialing Directory Assistance for the telephone number of the local Poison Control or Poison Information centers.

For help with alcohol abuse, Alcoholics Anonymous (AA) provides dedicated assistance and guidance 24 hours a day. Many AA chapters have teen-age members. Local chapters are listed in telephone directories.

If you suspect that your child is misusing drugs, keep calm and act intelligently. Remember, the problem is yours as much as it is the child's.

Explaining death to a child

By Stella Chess, M.D.

Even when there is no direct contact with death, it is not unusual for a child to ask, "What does it mean when you're dead?" or, "Will I die too?" He may want to know why and how a pet or a flower dies. He may have seen a funeral procession or heard about the death of a well-known person.

Many parents who are willing and able to discuss almost any subject with their children become evasive and ill at ease when questioned about death. Perhaps it is because most of us would rather not think about death. But death does occur. And when a loved one dies, it is especially important that parents be prepared to talk about it. A child usually has mixed emotions about death. He may have feelings of sorrow, fear, resentment, and even guilt. He may become confused and bewildered. How parents explain death, and how they answer their child's questions about death are important. Parents should be aware that a child's concept of death changes as he gets older.

All children do not react to death in the same way. However, research into how children view death has shown that the following concepts were common at specific ages.

Between 3 and 5, children tend to think of death as a kind of journey from which a person will soon return. Or, they may think that death is a kind of going to sleep, and then waking up. When told of a death, a child in this age group may express sorrow and then seem to forget about it soon afterward. Parents who are unaware of this common reaction may worry that their child is self-centered and heartless.

Between the ages of 5 and 9, most children accept the idea that death is irreversible, but they believe that death happens only to certain people and that it cannot happen to them. Around the ages of 9 or 10, children begin to understand that death happens to all living things, and that they, too, will die eventually.

Some ways to answer questions

No matter how difficult it may be for you, a direct, honest answer about death is the best one. Evasive answers may make a child's feelings of grief, fear, and resentment stronger and longer lasting. Children are not nearly as afraid of what they can understand as they are of things that are cloaked in mystery. Even death can be less terrifying if it is discussed openly and calmly.

In explaining death, you usually have to deal with such facts as illness, accident, or old age. The amount of detail you include in your explanation should relate to the child's capacity for understanding. For instance, if a 3-year-old wants to know why a grandparent has died, it is usually enough to say, "She was very old and very tired." A 6-year-old might be told that his grandmother was very old and tired, and that eventually everyone grows old and tired and can no longer go on living.

Some parents evade an honest answer in the mistaken belief that they are guarding their child against the pain that may be caused by the truth. But a child cannot go through life constantly protected from pain and grief. Sometimes, evasive answers may even be dangerous. A 6-year-old may be told when his beloved grandfather dies that the old man has "gone to sleep." But the child sees that the "sleep" is one from which his grandfather never wakes. What will be the child's reaction? It may happen, and it has happened, that the child becomes afraid to go to bed. He begins to fear that he, too, will never wake up.

Even the religious explanation, which seems desirable to many adults, is not always helpful to a child. Few children find comfort in such explanations as "God took him" or "He has gone to heaven to be with the angels." Such explanations may build feelings of resentment, fear, and even hatred against the God who can strike without warning someone for whom the child cares deeply.

Naturally, children are more deeply affected by some deaths than they are by others. When a playmate dies, a child needs more reassurance. He suddenly realizes that a person need not be old to die. He may, therefore, see himself threatened. It is important that parents answer the child's questions about such deaths so that he understands that because someone his age has died of an illness or an accident, it does not mean that he, too, will share a similar fate.

When a playmate's father or mother dies, children are likely to think that they might also lose a parent. Such fear can be lessened by stressing the fact that very few young parents die. Parents might also add that should anything happen to them, they have made arrangements for the children to be cared for.

The death of a parent is especially difficult for a child to face. For not only does he suffer grief but, understandably, he also feels the loss of security. He may even feel deserted. Sometimes the surviving parent is in no condition to comfort the child, and this may reinforce his sense of rejection.

Sometimes, in the hope that the child will feel needed and, therefore, more secure, the child may be mistakenly told, "Now you are the man of the family," or "Now you must take your mother's place." No child, no matter how willing, can take the place of the lost parent. Such a responsibility should not be thrust on him.

This is a time when an adult relative or close friend of the family can be a source of strength to the child by reassuring him about his future.

Guilt feelings

Children often feel that in some way or other they may be responsible for the death of a member of the family or a playmate. If a sick grandparent has lived with the family, it is quite likely that the child was constantly "shushed" during the illness. Understandably, he has not always been completely quiet. This in itself may make a child feel guilty when the grandparent dies. If the child is overly sensitive, such feelings can be most disturbing. Should a brother or sister die, some of the natural feelings of hostility that are found among brothers and sisters may haunt the child. It is as though something he did or thought contributed to the death. Parents can help their child overcome such feelings of guilt if they are aware that they may occur.

Mourning

There are differences of opinion and practice about children's participation in family gatherings of mourning relatives and in funeral ceremonies. A common practice is to send the children to stay with friends. This is done in the belief that children will be spared the upsetting effects of grief. In some instances, this may be wise. But usually this procedure tends to make the child feel alone and shut out. It may add to his confusion about death and even deepen any feelings of fear that he has. To be with the family, yet to be protected against some of the more extreme demonstrations of grief that may occur, is often more reassuring for the child than being spared the experience.

If, then, you find yourself facing the necessity of helping your child understand death in the family or the death of a close friend, be honest. Help him to realize that life holds sorrow as well as joy for everyone. And recognize that the child is in special need of love, affection, and understanding to help him through the experience in a positive way. The value of the feeling of belonging, in sorrow as well as in joy, cannot be overestimated.

The gifted child

By E. Paul Torrance, Ph.D.

For many years, the term "gifted child" usually meant a child with a high intelligence quotient (IQ). But a few leaders in the field of education for gifted children thought otherwise. They insisted that the term should apply to any child who performs much better than others in any field of endeavor highly prized by society.

This definition is now widely accepted by educators, and six types of giftedness are generally recognized.

- Generally intellectual ability
- Specific academic aptitude, as in science, mathematics, or languages
- Creative or productive thinking
- Leadership ability
- Visual and performing arts ability, as in music, drama, painting, or sculpture
- Psychomotor ability, such as mechanical or manipulative skills

Educators are finding new ways to identify gifted children in each of these areas, and developing specialized programs for them. Many states require that school systems provide programs for all gifted children. Some schools still provide only for the academically gifted—children identified on the basis of intelligence tests and grades. In some states, provisions are also made for the creatively gifted, using tests of creative thinking ability, the production of creative products, or solutions to problems.

A few school systems have developed excellent programs for gifted children in the visual and performing arts. Identification for inclusion in these programs is usually through auditions or other performances, portfolios of products, and the like. Sometimes tests are used that may make teachers and parents aware of outstanding talents which might otherwise go unnoticed.

School programs for gifted children vary greatly. In sparsely populated areas, the program may consist of an itinerant teacher in a bus filled with resource materials. In large cities, there may be separate schools for children gifted in different ways. In most special programs, however, gifted children spend part of their time in regular classes and the balance in separate classes with specially trained teachers. In some programs, gifted children remain in the regular classroom and the teacher adjusts some part of the program for them.

Intelligence tests are often used to identify the academically gifted. There is, however, no standard score. Some programs require an IQ of 120, while others require 130 or 140. Some academically gifted children are also creatively gifted. But not all creatively gifted children are academically gifted.

Characteristics of gifted children

People once thought of most gifted children as small, sickly, and wearing eyeglasses. Obviously, this is not true. Just as some academically gifted children are also highly creative, others are gifted in social leadership. Some are also outstanding in athletics, dance, or the like. The following characteristics of the intellectually or academically gifted child are generally accepted:

- Early and accurate use of a larger vocabulary than that of the average child

- Early use of sentences
- Early interest in calendars and in telling time
- Keen observation and unusual retention of facts
- Insatiable curiosity
- Early attraction to picture books
- A long attention span
- Early discovery of an interest in cause and effect relationships
- Early interest and skill in reading

Creatively gifted children may also have some of these characteristics. These children are also noted for their high energy level, questioning, experimenting, manipulating, and insistence in discovering the truth.

While gifted children have a great deal of energy, and may even be hyperkinetic, they are also able to sit still longer than the average child. Their absorption in what they are doing may be intense. The creative child insists upon examining things closely and seems to have an irresistible tendency to manipulate and explore objects.

Parents' role

Although gifted children tend to be superior to the average in social development, they are by no means as advanced socially as they are mentally. There may be a marked gap between the child's mental ability and his or her social, emotional, and physical development. The child may know the meaning of such words as *loyalty* and *cooperation,* but not be loyal or cooperative. Patient understanding and guidance are needed to help the child translate language into deeds.

Like all children, the gifted child needs security, affection, encouragement, recognition, and praise from sympathetic parents. Parental insight is needed to nourish a child's gifts and to help the child to develop harmoniously. Some children never fully develop their gifts because strong emotions or a feeling of insecurity at home block expression of growth.

Parents of a gifted child should encourage their child's gifts, not exploit them. A good way to encourage the child is by reading aloud before the child learns to read independently. Some gifted children learn to read before they start school and should be encouraged to read when ready. Even so, parents should continue to read aloud to some extent. As the child's interests expand with age, parents can help the child satisfy these interests.

If your child shows an interest in the arts, encourage participation. Only through performance can a child gifted with creativity and imagination be recognized.

At age 8 or 9, an intellectually gifted child usually reads many books and makes use of encyclopedias and dictionaries. The child may read about special subjects or pursue hobbies. Provide related books and magazines. Encourage the use of school and public libraries. Discuss the child's favorite books and the discoveries made in them. Some discoveries will be about one's self; some about other people.

The gifted child constantly asks questions. If you do not know the answer, say so. Then, help the child find the answer. Occasionally, instead of answering a question, encourage the child to find the answer independently.

Parents need to give special attention to helping the gifted child learn problem-solving skills. Many gifted children actually lag behind less gifted classmates in problem-solving skills because they remember solutions and are not challenged to solve problems for which there are no learned solutions.

Parents can provide opportunities for creative problem solving and constructive responses to change and stress. They should prepare their children for and develop creative ways of coping with new experiences. Above all, the family should offer purpose, commitment, and courage. Without these, giftedness is likely to wither or turn in wasteful directions.

Growth

By Nancy Bayley, Ph.D.

Healthy children may show wide variations from the average in all aspects of growth. Some are naturally tall, some short, some heavy-set, some slender; some are long-legged, some long-bodied. Some grow and develop at a fast rate; others are slower than the average. There are individual differences in the degree to which a girl's build becomes feminine or a boy's build becomes masculine.

Growth rates

An individual's growth starts with the fertilized egg. And the most rapid growth and development takes place during the nine months before birth. From a single original cell, there is a rapid multiplication of cells. Soon several different types of cells develop and, from these, the characteristic human form emerges.

The heart in the fetus starts to beat about four weeks after conception. The earliest body movements occur at about eight weeks. By 25 weeks, the body structures are well defined and most of the reflexes necessary for postnatal life are present.

Birth normally occurs when the fetus is 40 weeks old, but an infant may live if born as young as 28 weeks or as old as 50 weeks. So infants, even at birth, may be at different stages of maturity. The average newborn is skinny. His arms and legs are short, and his head is larger around than his chest. He is about 20 inches (50 centimeters) long and weighs about 7½ pounds (3.5 kilograms).

Through the first year, most of the child's growth occurs in the torso of his body, with a generally increasing chubbiness. By 6 months of age, the baby has more than doubled his weight to an average of 16½ pounds (7.5 kilograms), and increased his length to about 26 inches (65 centimeters).

The growth in height and weight for different ages of boys and girls is shown on the accompanying growth charts. Typical growth in height and weight is shown by the heavy center line *A*. If a boy or girl has a bone age that is one or two years beyond the average, the height curves for that child will look more like line *B*. If the bone age is a year or two slower, the height curves will be more like line *C*. The weight curves of these same children tend to follow the corresponding lines in the weight charts.

The broken-line curves on each chart, lines *D* and *E*, indicate approximately the normal limits of height and weight. About 98 per cent of children are at least as large as the lower line *E* and are no larger than the upper line *D*.

The curves on the height and weight charts show that there are periods of rapid and slow growth. After the fast growth of the first year, the changes are more and more gradual, becoming fairly steady between about 6 and 10 years. Then, there is a spurt of rapid growth before slowing down and stopping.

Changing body proportions

The child's proportions are constantly changing as he grows because different parts of the body grow at different rates. From the big-headed, skinny newborn, he changes to

Boys: Growth curves of height by age, maturing at average, fast, and slow rates

Age in years	Average growers	Fast growers	Slow growers
	Per cents of mature height		
Birth	28.6	—	—
1.0	42.2	44.5	40.4
2.0	49.5	51.3	47.0
3.0	53.8	55.6	51.6
4.0	58.0	60.0	58.0
5.0	61.8	64.0	59.7
6.0	65.2	67.8	63.8
7.0	69.0	70.5	66.8
8.0	72.0	73.5	69.8
9.0	75.0	76.5	73.2
10.0	78.0	79.7	76.4
11.0	81.1	83.4	79.5
12.0	84.2	87.2	82.2
13.0	87.3	91.3	84.6
14.0	91.5	95.8	87.6
15.0	96.1	98.3	91.6
16.0	98.3	99.4	95.7
17.0	99.3	99.9	98.2
17.5	—	100.0	—
18.0	99.8	—	99.2
18.5	100.0	—	—

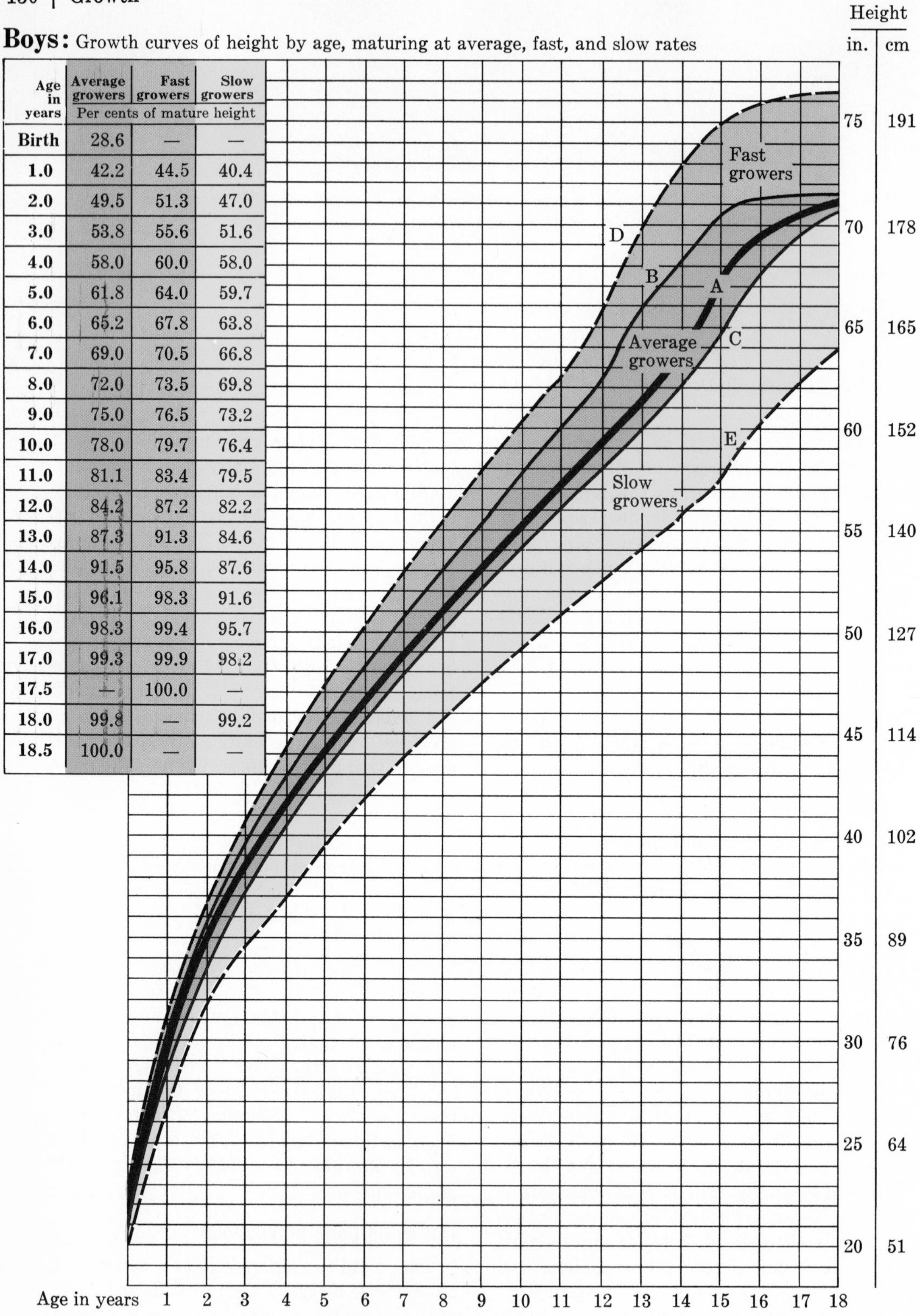

Figure 1

Adapted from Bayley, Nancy: Growth Curves of Height and Weight By Age for Boys and Girls, Scaled According to Physical Maturity, *Journal of Pediatrics*, 48:187-194, 1956.

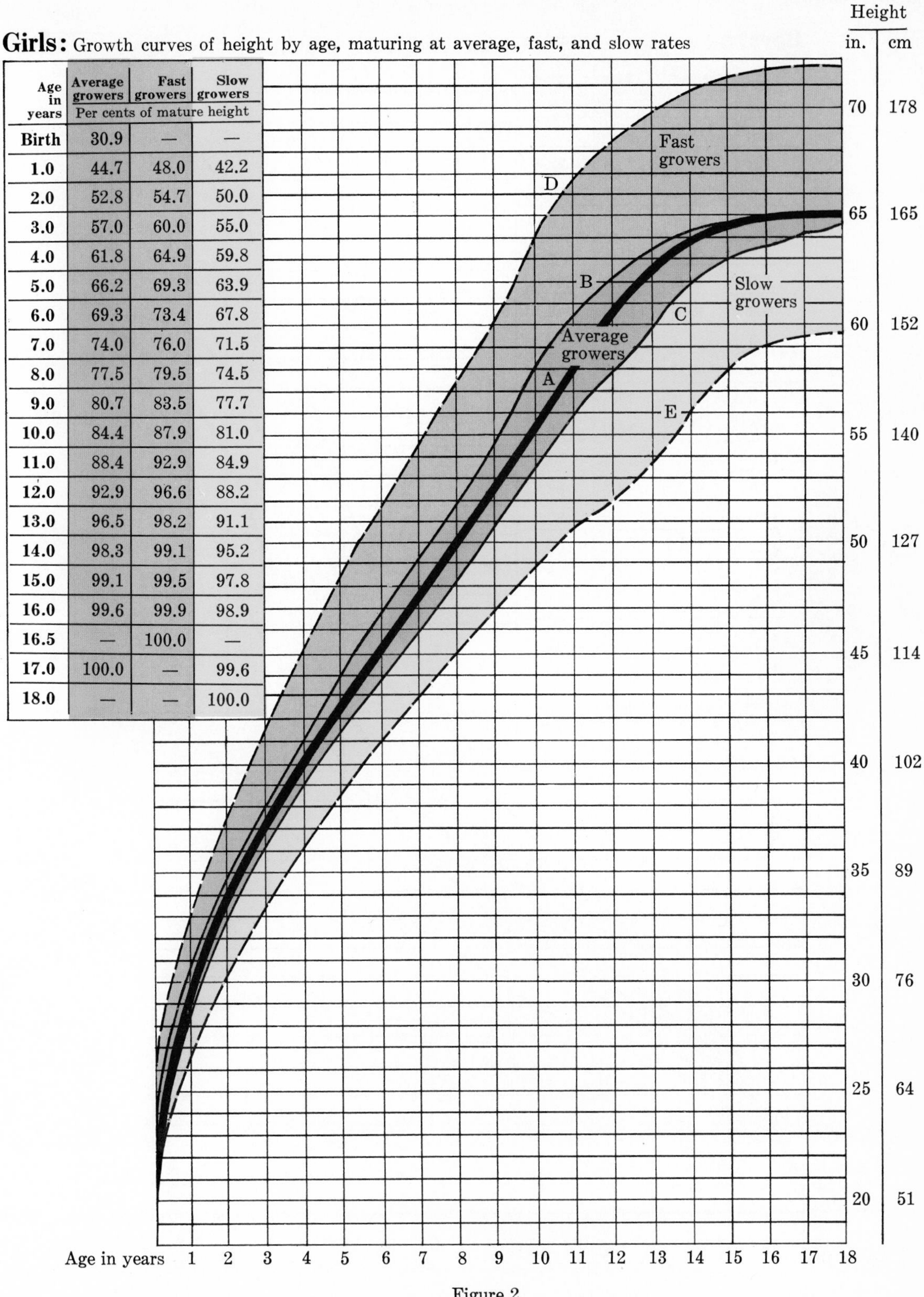

Girls: Growth curves of height by age, maturing at average, fast, and slow rates

Age in years	Average growers	Fast growers	Slow growers
	Per cents of mature height		
Birth	30.9	—	—
1.0	44.7	48.0	42.2
2.0	52.8	54.7	50.0
3.0	57.0	60.0	55.0
4.0	61.8	64.9	59.8
5.0	66.2	69.3	63.9
6.0	69.3	73.4	67.8
7.0	74.0	76.0	71.5
8.0	77.5	79.5	74.5
9.0	80.7	83.5	77.7
10.0	84.4	87.9	81.0
11.0	88.4	92.9	84.9
12.0	92.9	96.6	88.2
13.0	96.5	98.2	91.1
14.0	98.3	99.1	95.2
15.0	99.1	99.5	97.8
16.0	99.6	99.9	98.9
16.5	—	100.0	—
17.0	100.0	—	99.6
18.0	—	—	100.0

Figure 2

Adapted from Bayley, Nancy: Growth Curves of Height and Weight By Age for Boys and Girls, Scaled According to Physical Maturity, *Journal of Pediatrics*, 48:187-194, 1956.

Boys: Growth curves of weight by age, maturing at average, fast, and slow rates

Age in years	Average growers	Fast growers	Slow growers
	Weight in pounds		
Birth	8.4	—	—
1.0	22.9	23.8	22.4
2.0	29.3	31.1	27.3
3.0	34.6	35.5	30.6
4.0	39.0	41.4	35.7
5.0	42.8	45.9	40.3
6.0	47.6	51.8	44.1
7.0	52.9	56.9	48.5
8.0	58.2	65.0	54.7
9.0	66.8	74.5	60.2
10.0	74.1	86.0	66.1
11.0	82.2	97.2	73.4
12.0	91.3	109.8	80.7
13.0	101.4	124.8	90.2
14.0	116.0	134.5	100.1
15.0	133.8	147.9	112.2
16.0	142.6	154.1	131.0
17.0	149.7	155.9	143.1
18.0	154.1	—	150.8

See the weight scale on the graph for the approximate weight in kilograms.

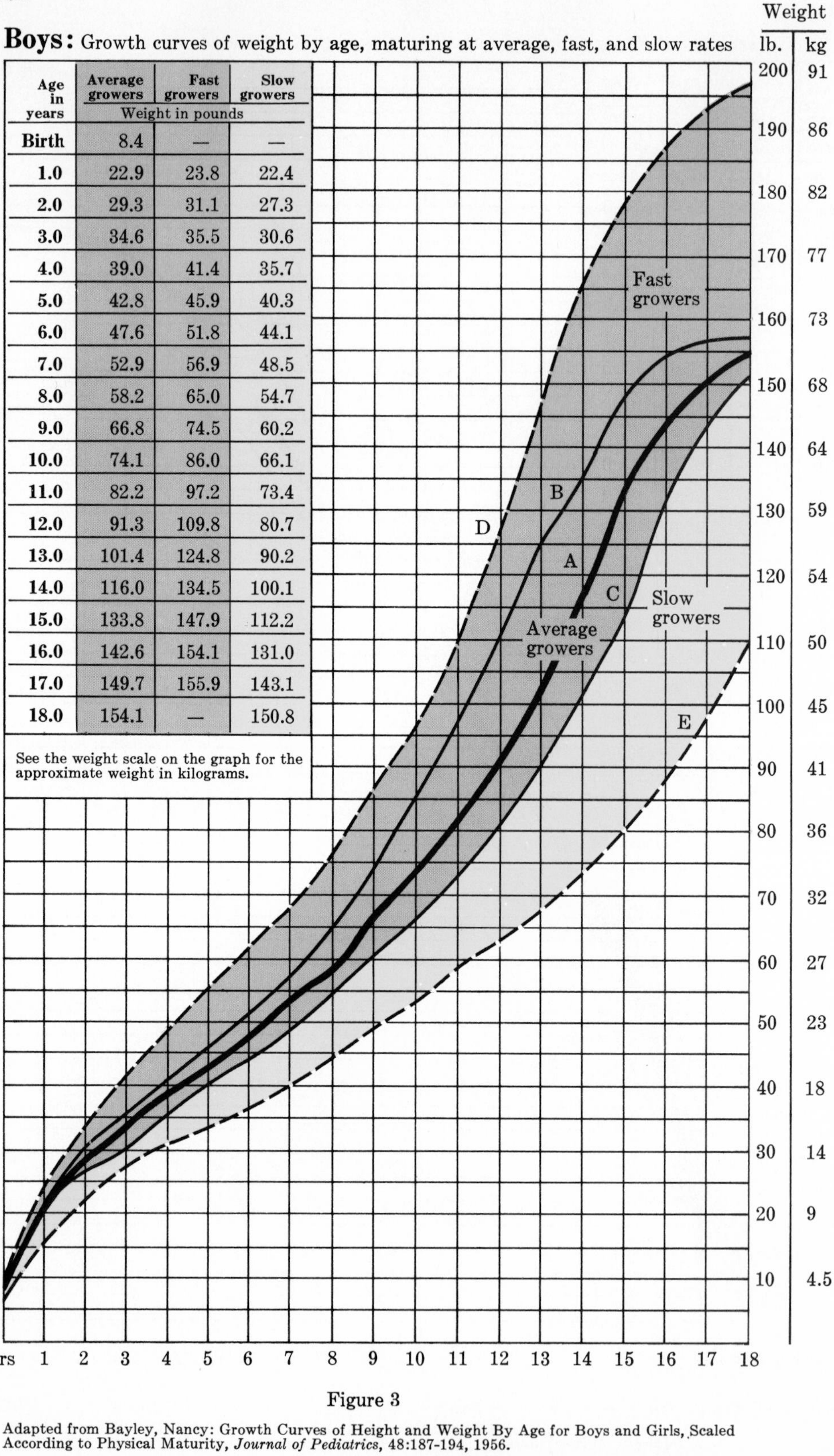

Figure 3

Adapted from Bayley, Nancy: Growth Curves of Height and Weight By Age for Boys and Girls, Scaled According to Physical Maturity, *Journal of Pediatrics*, 48:187-194, 1956.

Girls: Growth curves of weight by age, maturing at average, fast, and slow rates

Age in years	Average growers	Fast growers	Slow growers
	Weight in pounds		
Birth	7.5	—	—
1.0	21.5	24.0	21.2
2.0	28.0	30.2	25.9
3.0	32.4	34.7	30.6
4.0	37.5	42.1	33.7
5.0	41.2	48.1	37.9
6.0	46.7	53.2	43.0
7.0	52.9	57.3	47.6
8.0	60.0	66.8	51.1
9.0	66.4	78.5	59.7
10.0	76.1	92.2	64.8
11.0	86.6	108.9	69.9
12.0	99.2	124.8	78.0
13.0	112.4	131.2	86.9
14.0	121.0	135.0	99.0
15.0	128.8	138.7	108.5
16.0	131.6	139.3	114.6
17.0	132.3	137.6	119.3

See the weight scale on the graph for the approximate weight in kilograms.

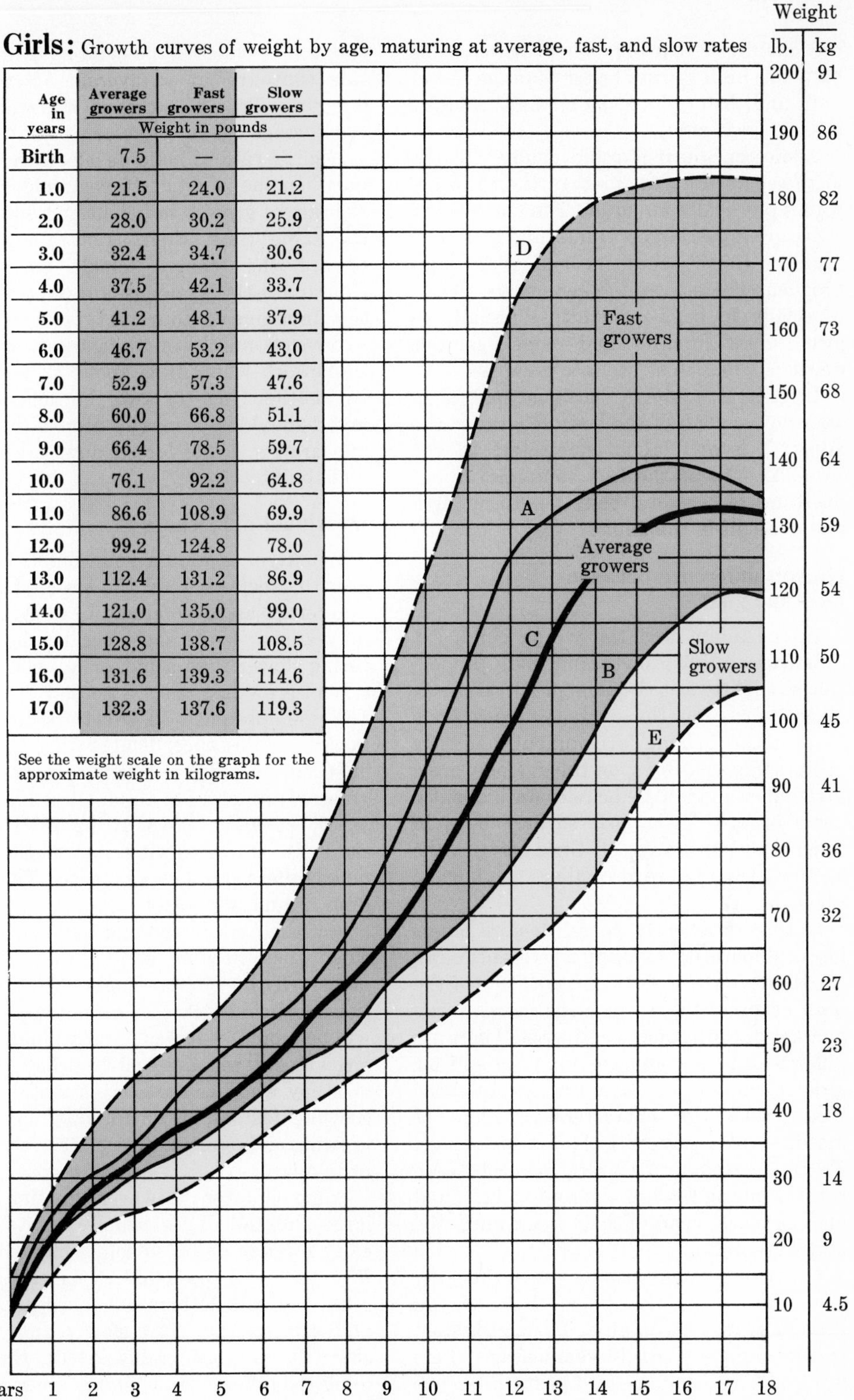

Figure 4

Adapted from Bayley, Nancy: Growth Curves of Height and Weight By Age for Boys and Girls, Scaled According to Physical Maturity, *Journal of Pediatrics*, 48:187-194, 1956.

the chubby 1-year-old. Then he loses his baby fat; his legs grow faster than the rest of him; and, before long, he emerges a lanky 9- to 11-year-old.

Adolescence brings rapid changes. Often in the span of a year or two, the child becomes physically an adult. The entire bony structure grows larger. Hands and feet grow rapidly. Boys' shoulders and girls' hips broaden. There is an increase in muscles—especially in boys—and fat—especially in girls. Girls' breasts and boys' genitals develop. The size of the face enlarges.

In general, at birth the head makes up about one-fourth of the body length. In the adult, it is only about one-eighth of the total. Length of the legs comprises about one-third of the total body length at birth and one-half in the adult.

Growth difference between boys and girls

In the infant and the young child, sex differences affect growth and body proportion so slightly as to be of no practical significance. Girls, on the average, are a little more mature in bone development than boys of the same age. Boys, on the average, are a little taller and a little heavier until about 6 years of age. Then girls surpass boys in weight until about age 14. Girls between the ages of 10 and 13 are also taller than boys of the same age.

During these early years, doctors assess physical maturity by using a series of X-ray standards for bone development. One of the most useful of these standards shows X-ray pictures of the left hand and wrist. There are different sets of standards for boys and for girls. Each picture in a series shows the bones with the characteristic stage of maturity of a boy or girl of a given age. There is a standard picture for each three months during the first year and a half, and one for each year or half year until the bones are mature.

For the first eight or nine years, the bony contours consistently appear to be only a little more mature for girls. Then, girls start maturing rapidly. By 13 years of age, there is a two to two and one-half years difference in degree of skeletal maturity between boys and girls of the same age. Girls reach adult status (the bones in the hand have fully mature contours) at an average of 16 years, 3 months. Boys do not reach this stage until the average age of 18 years, 9 months.

A girl's rate of bone development speeds up when she is about 10 years old. So does her rate of growth in height and weight. At the same time, there is a rapid change toward the mature female body form. Characteristic fat deposits form, giving her soft, feminine contours. A typical boy starts to develop muscles on his fast-growing, bony framework when he is about 12 years old. In another year or two, he achieves the broad-shouldered, narrow-hipped, muscular appearance that foreshadows the adult male build.

Individual differences

When you evaluate your child's build or growth, keep in mind the extent to which differences are normal and healthy. A child may appear to be short because he is maturing slower than usual, or tall because his rate of growth is fast.

These differences in growth occur mostly in early adolescence. That is when the starting time of rapid growth and maturing varies greatly from child to child. Girls at 10 or 11 years, or some boys at 12 or 13, may suddenly start growing fast and become much taller than their age-mates. These children are usually early maturers. They will attain their adult size and build early. But when they become adults, they will not necessarily be outstandingly tall. The relation of their heights to others of their sex will be more like it was in early childhood. A girl who still remains a little girl at 13 or 14, or a boy who has not started maturing and growing fast at 15 or 16, may soon start growing and overtake age-mates only a year or two later.

Some children, however, are inherently large and tall. They usually are tall from early infancy and also somewhat advanced in bone age. These children usually remain relatively tall. Others are inherently short and consistently grow slowly and remain short. To a considerable extent, these are inherited differences. Children are much like their parents or other family members in their sizes and their rates of growth.

Learning disabilities in children

By Helmer R. Myklebust, Ph.D.

For many years, handicaps in children were thought to be of only five types: blindness, deafness, emotional disturbance, mental retardation, or physical disability.

Then, psychologists began to describe children who had none of these handicaps, yet were unable to learn as other children do. Our awareness of such children was late, perhaps because these children appear normal. True, some may be easily upset, use their hands awkwardly, or walk awkwardly. But they are not primarily emotionally disturbed, and have no other physical disability.

The issue is not how these children appear, but how they *learn.* This is why we call their problem a learning disability. Often, the learning disability is so subtle it goes unnoticed. But it is important to recognize a learning disability before other problems arise. The earlier it is identified, the more the child can be helped.

There are two types of learning disabilities—*verbal* and *nonverbal.* Verbal learning disabilities affect the way a child learns to speak, read, and write. The deficit in learning may affect one or more of these ways of communicating with others.

Nonverbal learning disabilities are those that do not involve language. Such disabilities may affect memory, behavior, or sense of orientation.

Verbal learning disabilities

Perhaps the most common verbal learning disability is *dyslexia,* which affects learning to read. It can be either auditory or visual. *Auditory dyslexia* interferes with learning the sounds of letters. *Visual dyslexia* interferes with learning what the letters themselves look like.

When most children begin to read, they match the way a word looks with how it sounds because they have already learned spoken language. But dyslexic children cannot do this. Their ability to mentally process information is disturbed.

If children know the sounds of the letters but cannot remember how the words look, they go by sound. They write words phonetically. For example, they may write the word *chair* as *chr,* and *people* as *pepl.* Conversely, if children know what the letters look like but cannot associate the correct sounds with them, they leave out the sounds. They may write the word *mother* as *gmehs.*

When the difficulty is learning to speak, it is called an *aphasia.* This is not a speech defect. The children know what they want to say, but they may be unable to understand what is said to them or to get words out. Sometimes they are able to understand speech and to talk, but garble syntax, grammar, and sentence structure.

Nonverbal learning disabilities

A learning disability does not always involve language. Some children can speak, read, and write. But they cannot learn to find their clothes and get dressed, to tell time, or the days of the week. They may not know how to get from one place to another. They may also have difficulty in mathematics—learning how to judge size and the meaning of measurements.

Nonverbal learning disabilities are not well-recognized and may be more common than suspected. There are many children whose lives are unusually difficult because they are not getting the help they need.

Causes of learning disabilities

Parents of a child with a learning disability often feel they did something wrong. But a child does not have a learning problem because of something the parents did or did not do.

The primary cause of a learning disability is *minimal cerebral dysfunction.* This means that the child has a mild disturbance that affects the way the brain functions. Learning-disabled children cannot properly organize and integrate the information they get through their eyes, ears, and hands. Because the information cannot be learned, it cannot be understood and given meaning. When the disturbance is on the left half of the brain, the learning disability is of the verbal type; if on the right half of the brain, the nonverbal type.

It is the brain that learns, and the efficiency with which it learns can be affected in various ways. Disturbances often result from childhood diseases, problems of blood type, or insufficient oxygen during birth. In studying causes of learning disabilities, the family pattern is also considered. The genetic influence of both parents affects a child's brain, just as genetic influence affects the color of a child's eyes. If a parent has dyslexia, one or more of the children may have it, too, even though in other respects all family members are highly competent. When inherited, the learning disability most often appears in a son rather than a daughter.

What parents can do

Parents are in the best position to discover and meet the needs of a learning-disabled child. They see early in life that the child cannot understand what is heard, cannot utter words, or cannot get dressed. Parents see the child's awkwardness, or dizzy spells, falls, or stares. They are also the first to see that the child does not play with others, that he or she is unable to understand "taking turns," cannot clap hands in rhythm, and is confused by simple rules.

If any of these signs appear in your child, consult your pediatrician. Arrangements may be made for a study by a child psychologist whom you can contact through the local school superintendent, a nearby university, a medical center, or a local chapter of the Association for Children with Learning Disabilities.

The pediatrician and psychologist can assist in obtaining other valuable studies to understand the complex nature of your child's problem. For example, an examination, including a brain-wave test, by a neurologist can clarify whether or not medication can help. Some children learn more effectively through proper and controlled use of medication, as well as through specialized teaching and instruction.

After the learning disability has been evaluated, parents have a major role in working with the teacher and the psychologist to bring about more efficient learning.

Attention is the key to learning. Being able to hear is not the same as being able to listen. Being able to see is not the same as being able to look. One way you can help is to play "listening" and "looking" games that help your child to organize experiences so that they become meaningful.

A learning-disabled child often tires more easily than other children. This usually makes the child more, not less, active. Learn to recognize overactivity as a possible sign of fatigue and arrange for needed rest periods. Organize the child's schedule to control demands made on him or her. This will establish the child's *tolerance level.* This control, or routine, is often essential to avoid outbursts at inappropriate moments or at times of stress.

With patience and understanding, you have every reason to feel confident of your child's future. All the aspects of the learning disability may not be overcome, but your child will adjust and become more competent. Learning-disabled children do succeed. Year by year, we achieve more progress. Your learning-disabled child is a challenge, as is the help that you can give to others who have a child with a learning disability.

The mentally retarded child

By Laura Dittmann, Ph.D.

About 30 of every 1,000 children born in the United States are diagnosed during infancy or later as mentally retarded. The most severely retarded are often discovered in infancy. Some are identified in their early formative years. Others are found after they enter school.

The term *mental retardation* covers a wide range of children with subnormal mental ability—from nearly normal to totally dependent. In general, children are considered mentally retarded if they perform far below average, both intellectually and behaviorally. More simply stated, they do not think, reason, remember, and learn as well as other children of the same age.

A number of other terms have been used to describe this condition, such as mental deficiency, learning impairment, subnormal intelligence and incompetence. They all mean the same thing. But mental retardation and mental illness are *not* the same. Mental retardation means that a person has subnormal mental ability, usually because the higher centers of the brain are damaged. Mental illness means that a severe emotional disturbance prevents a person with normal mental ability from using the higher centers of the brain in a normal way. (See BEHAVIORAL DISORDERS IN CHILDREN, page 114.)

A mentally retarded child who is neglected, treated badly, or forced into unmanageable situations, may develop emotional problems and become mentally ill.

Mentally retarded children are not just "slow learners." They can never catch up to the average child. In fact, they fall farther behind as they grow older. But, except in cases of extreme retardation, parents and teachers can help mentally retarded children develop limited mental ability so that they need not be totally dependent on others to survive. The way the family and others treat a mentally retarded child has a lot to do with whether or not the child can remain emotionally healthy and well adjusted.

What causes mental retardation?

Many causes of mental retardation have been discovered. A child may be mentally retarded as the result of heredity, birth defects, illness, or accident.

For example, if a child inherits certain defective genes from one or both parents, the brain may not develop completely. Brain damage may also be caused by an infection of the central nervous system before birth, during infancy, or in early childhood. If a pregnant woman contracts German measles or if she experiences severe malnutrition, her baby's development may be seriously damaged. Extensive injury to the baby's brain during an extremely difficult birth may also cause mental retardation.

Even a child who has a healthy start in life may, in the formative years, have an illness that produces a high, long-lasting fever or a brain injury that interferes with mental development.

Some experts in the field of mental retardation believe that neglect, malnutrition, surroundings that are dull and monotonous, and lack of love and attention may also retard a child's normal ability to learn. In some instances, when these abnormal life conditions are improved, the child's mental development also improves.

Types of mental retardation

Mental retardation is classified as severe, moderate, or mild.

Severe retardation can often be detected in infancy, possibly at birth. The severely retarded infant may have difficulty learning to suck and to swallow. The child may be slow to hold up the head, roll over, and sit up. Some degree of independence in eating, toilet habits, dressing, and self-care may be achieved. But usually, the severely retarded remains dependent throughout life. Sometimes, blindness, impaired hearing, heart disease, epilepsy, or malformation of limbs are also present.

Moderate retardation causes a child to develop more slowly than normal. A few moderately retarded children may seem normal, except that they are much slower to learn to speak, or their speech may be unintelligible. Generally, they can learn to take care of their personal needs. But they may never learn to read or write. They can be trained to do simple work.

Mild retardation may not be recognized until a child begins to have difficulty at school. The child may not be able to pay attention as well as other children. Simple directions may be impossible to follow. The child may be unable to use scissors, crayons, pencils, and other materials the way normal children do. But a mildly retarded child can learn enough to become a self-supporting adult in any of a variety of jobs.

What parents can do

Whenever parents are puzzled by their child's development, they should seek professional help. The family doctor or pediatrician can refer parents to a special clinic where they can take the child for a detailed diagnosis and evaluation of the condition. As a rule, a good diagnosis will include a thorough study of physical, psychological, and social factors involved in the child's behavior. When a thorough study has been made, parents feel less compelled to go from one doctor to another in the hope of finding an easy cure for the condition.

Retarded children, like normal children, should get good medical care and attention. They need nourishing food, plenty of sleep, scheduled immunization shots, correction of any physical defects that can be corrected, and careful nursing during illness. A periodic reassessment of the child's condition is important.

Few parents adjust easily to the idea that their child is mentally retarded, but some react more extremely than others. Many parents find that talking to others in the same situation can be a great comfort. The National Association for Retarded Citizens has parents' organizations in most cities. Parents and others who are interested in retarded children meet to exchange ideas, discuss problems, set up camps or schools, and promote understanding of mental retardation. The local health and welfare council or the department of health will supply information about such groups in the community. (See AGENCIES AND ORGANIZATIONS INTERESTED IN THE WELFARE OF CHILDREN, page 150.)

Living with the retarded child

The retarded child, like all children, needs to begin life with parental love in family surroundings. Today there is greater understanding of retardation and more help available in the community. So most experts recommend keeping the child at home rather than in an institution. If parents can help the child do more and more alone, they will begin to see the child as a learning individual rather than a family burden.

The mentally retarded child's day should be kept simple and orderly. Let the child know what is expected from day to day. Patient teaching is required to help the retarded child learn what the average child of that age learns quickly. You may have to repeat the same instructions, activities, and simple lessons many times before a simple idea is grasped. Do not push the child beyond ability. If overloaded, the child may become confused and any efforts to learn will be blocked.

To determine ability, watch the child's behavior and concentrate on whether or not the child is ready to do certain things. When the child is physically and mentally able to do one task, think of a related or slightly more complex task that you can teach next. Does the baby reach for the bottle when it is offered? Then try to teach him or her to hold the bottle. Can the child take off shoes and socks? Then maybe he or she can learn to put them on. If a hand can move to the mouth, chances are the child can learn to eat unaided. Begin with small bits of food and don't discourage the use of fingers. The child can be taught to manage a cup if there is only a small amount of liquid in it and the cup is easy to hold. In time, increase the amount of liquid and change the type of container. Tell the child what you want in clear and specific terms. But remember to ask the child to do only one thing at a time.

After a while, most parents come to accept the fact that their retarded child will never have normal mental ability. They begin to find satisfaction with their child's progress, even if it seems slow and the accomplishments are small. They no longer make comparisons with other children in the family. They judge progress by what the retarded child can do today compared to last month or last year. In some cases, however, there may be no progress at all.

Parents need patience to discipline the retarded child. The child needs to learn rules, but what is expected should be based on the child's ability and development. Sometimes, parents demand better behavior from the mentally retarded child than from the other children in the family. They do not want the retarded child to "act" retarded. They expect far more in the way of control and cooperation than the child can possibly offer. As with any other aspect of learning, the demand for more than the child is capable of giving will hinder rather than help.

The retarded child's effect on the family

All retarded children are not alike. Some are easy to care for. Others cannot be trusted out of sight for a minute. Some need special care and equipment from the time they are born. Others seem normal at birth, and do not show retardation until later. One child may be attractive and physically healthy. Another may have physical as well as mental handicaps.

While it is not always the case, the severity of the retardation may determine its effect on the rest of the family. If the retardation is severe, it may be necessary to leave the child in the care of a sitter occasionally so that the rest of the family can get out. The other children may become resentful if their activities are curtailed by the retarded sibling.

It is a good idea to train a special caretaker, and to keep the same one if possible. Students enrolled in special education courses at nearby colleges are often eager to experience caring for a retarded child.

Usually the brothers and sisters reflect the attitudes and behavior of their parents toward the retarded child. The child can become the scapegoat for any problems that arise, even those the family would have encountered were the child not present.

On the other hand, the retarded child can become a valued member of the family around whose needs the others can rally and become united more strongly than ever.

Schools and institutions

Many people have been long concerned about the educational needs of mentally retarded children. In 1975, the United States took a major step forward in this area when a new public law was passed. The law protects the rights of these children and their parents or guardians. What's more, through federal aid to the states, the law assures that all handicapped children—regardless of how they are categorized—have a free public education available to them to meet their individual needs.

This law makes it possible for more retarded children to attend nursery and regular schools in their own neighborhoods. Nevertheless, there are some children and some families for whom a special school or institution for retarded children is a better choice.

In deciding what is best for all concerned, parents of a retarded child may find it worthwhile to talk with a family counselor, a pediatrician, a public health nurse, or school personnel.

Moving

By Gladys Gardner Jenkins, M.A.

Moving can be an exciting adventure or an uncomfortable disruption in your child's life. But since children usually follow the lead of their parents, the degree of excitement or uneasiness that your child feels will depend largely on your attitude toward the move and how you explain it to him.

Most children, especially those who have close friends or who have formed strong ties to people, places, and the routines of the old neighborhood, will feel sad at leaving. But beyond such normal regrets, how you act can give your child either a dread of the unknown or an eagerness to tackle a new and interesting life experience.

A move can be a valuable educational benefit. It can help your child learn to meet new situations and adapt to new ways of doing things. The challenge of adjusting to a new situation is probably better preparation for life than the false sense of security that often results from a lack of change.

Preparing your child for the move

If your child is old enough to understand, you should explain why the family is making the move. Perhaps it is necessary because father has a new job, or is being transferred by his company to another city. Maybe someone in the family is ill and must have a change of climate. Or maybe you are just moving to a different neighborhood. Whatever the reason, your child will probably be better able to accept the fact that he will be leaving much that is familiar and dear to him if he understands the reasons that make it necessary for the family to move.

If it is possible, both parents, or at least one of them, should visit the new community. After you have seen the house or apartment, neighborhood, school facilities, and perhaps talked to some of the people among whom you will be living, you can give your child a clear picture of the advantages or disadvantages he can expect to find in his new neighborhood. Whether or not this procedure is possible, it is a good idea to find out all you can about your future home. If you are planning to move to another part of the country or to another country, it will be helpful for the family to get together to study maps, and to read stories and articles about the area where you are going to live.

Also, you should discuss any aspects of the move that you feel may present problems, such as difference in climate, differences in attitudes and customs of the people living in the new neighborhood, or a lack of the kind of facilities to which your child may have become accustomed. Whenever possible, you should explain unfamiliar local customs so that your child will become interested in the many different ways people do things, and will learn to respect rather than scorn such differences.

If you are moving to an area where you anticipate real hardships because of climate, inadequate housing, or inadequate schools, you should give your child some idea of what they are likely to be. At the same time you should make him understand that as a family in which each member helps, there is no reason why you will not be able to cope with any difficulty you may encounter.

Problems you may meet

Even with the best preparation, your child still may have some deep emotional reaction to moving. Often, anxiety over the welfare of a pet that cannot be taken along may precipitate an emotional crisis. You can relieve your child's anxiety by letting him help you find a home for his pet where he knows it will be well cared for.

Your child's attachment to his friends may be so genuine and intense that he will be distressed by leaving them. You can help lessen this distress by suggesting that an exchange of letters and postcards will keep the friendships going, and that later on perhaps there can be visits.

Leaving friends may be especially hard on a teen-age child to whom a close friend or membership in a club, special group, or an athletic team has meant the security that goes with the sense of really belonging. The child in his last year of elementary or high school may be quite upset by the move. He has probably been looking forward to this last year in the old school, to the graduation and the fun that are part of the senior year. In the new school, he may feel strange. Also, he may have difficulty becoming part of already formed groups. Membership in some of the smaller community, church, or synagogue groups which usually welcome newcomers may help him feel more at home.

Usually, social groups in an elementary school are not so exclusive or as tightly knit as they are in a high school. In general, a child who is good at games or who is friendly and outgoing will be accepted into a group almost casually. Also, it is easier for mothers of younger children to get to know each other through informal neighborhood meetings or through the PTA. It is a rare community where neighbors will not welcome you. Most people have had some experience with moving and establishing their families in a new community, and they expect to welcome newcomers. The friendly atmosphere makes it easier for your child to meet other boys and girls and to develop new friendships and interests.

If your child is shy or timid or if he shows much uneasiness in the new situation, he will need your support when he is ready to enter the new school. Take him to school before he is to begin classes, and introduce him to the principal, his teacher, and if possible, to some of his classmates. If he has difficulty with schoolwork, or if he has physical problems such as poor coordination, vision, or hearing, the school should know about them. The school should also know about any special abilities he has. Most teachers want to be helpful, but they can do their best only when they are aware of your child's special needs.

Sometimes a child appears to have adjusted to the move without any difficulty. But after the initial excitement has worn off, he seems to go into an emotional slump. You can help your child by encouraging him to tell you what is causing his unhappiness. It may be that school is not as challenging or as stimulating as it was in the old community. It also may be that the new school is quite a bit more challenging than the previous one, so that he is having trouble keeping up with his new classmates. Or it could be that he has trouble finding compatible new friends. In any case you can agree that the situation is for him less than ideal. But do not sympathize too much. Instead, help him to make the best of circumstances. Talk to his teachers. They might be able to help the child find more interests to occupy him, or they might be able to help him find more congenial friends. If the school is inadequate, provide him with books and materials he can use at home. Encourage him in personal hobbies, and increase family trips to places of interest.

It is not unusual for a well-adjusted child to feel lonely, restless, and moody after a move. But if your child was already unhappy within himself, the move may increase his anxiety. You may have to turn to someone trained to help you understand the basic causes of your youngster's unhappiness.

Most youngsters, however, settle into the new community within a period of months. Their adjustment is helped considerably if the experience of the move has given the secure feeling that, "Wherever we live we are a family. We can make a home and meet all kinds of circumstances." This is a fine way to establish the emotional security that will support a child throughout the rest of his life.

The physically handicapped child

By Edward F. Lis, M.D.

Most physically handicapped children with normal intelligence have a good chance for a useful and satisfying life, within limits. But their parents must love and accept them, and help them develop self-confidence by concentrating on what they *can* do rather than on what they *cannot* do.

Many parents of handicapped children are overwhelmed by the responsibility of caring for their child. When problems become acute, they may even begin to resent him. Some parents feel guilty. Some, ashamed of their handicapped child's looks, make him feel unloved. Feelings of guilt and resentment may cause parents to treat their child in ways that are harmful to his growth and development.

Some parents try to shield their handicapped child from any situation that they think might hurt his feelings. The result of this shielding is that the parents do things for the child that he can do for himself. Such treatment can make the child dependent and self-conscious.

Some parents go to the other extreme. They ignore their child's disability and push him beyond his limits. If he fails too often, he may be afraid to try anything, since he may not readily succeed.

The child who feels unloved because of his parents' attitude toward him may become emotionally as well as physically handicapped.

Causes of some common physical defects

Parents of a handicapped child should have as much reliable information as possible about their child's condition so that they know how to deal with his capabilities and his limitations.

Physical defects may result from many causes and may involve any part of the body. A child may be born with defects that stem from abnormal genes passed on to the child from either or both parents at the time of conception. Such hereditary defects may include cleft lip and cleft palate, congenital heart disorders, improper closure of the spinal canal, and various bone and joint disorders.

A child may be born with a physical defect if his mother had an infection such as German measles during pregnancy, if she misused drugs, or if she had toxemia (blood poisoning) of pregnancy.

Some physical defects result from premature birth or complications during delivery. Such abnormal births do not always result in defects, but they can cause cerebral palsy, epilepsy, hearing and seeing difficulties, and mental retardation.

Many children who are born with one or more physical defects may develop further disabilities. For example, a child with a cleft lip and a cleft palate may also have trouble with his teeth and ears. A child with a hearing defect may also have visual problems. Similarly, a child with defective vision may also be hard of hearing.

Infection, an accident, or poor nutrition may produce physical disability. For example, meningitis or encephalitis may cause brain damage. A streptococcic infection may cause rheumatic fever and rheumatic heart.

Many physically handicapped children are able to attend school.

An accident may cause loss of limb or paralysis. A burn may cause disfigurement, and insufficient vitamin D may cause rickets.

Treatment

Severe birth defects and acquired disabilities require the services of a specialist experienced in treating the particular defect. The family doctor or pediatrician can best determine the appropriate specialist for treatment and for continuing child care.

Clubfoot and other bone and joint defects are treated by an orthopedist. Facial defects, such as cleft lip and cleft palate, are treated by a plastic surgeon. Brain and spinal cord defects are treated by a neurosurgeon. Physical medicine helps habilitate persons with neurological and muscular disorders. It includes physical therapy, occupational therapy, special braces, and other means of improving disorders without the use of drugs or surgery.

Caring for the handicapped child at home

The physically handicapped child has needs that go beyond special medical attention to his defects. A handicapped child, like a normal child, needs good nutrition and immunization against disease. He needs periodic visits to the family doctor or the pediatrician. A handicapped baby needs the same amount of cuddling and attention as a normal baby. A handicapped toddler needs to explore, and the preschool child who is handicapped should be stimulated with new experiences.

A handicapped child, like a normal child, must be allowed responsibilities and tasks in keeping with his age and his ability. This gives him the feeling that he is trusted and needed. A handicapped child also needs discipline—neither more nor less than that needed by all children—to learn the limits of socially acceptable behavior. A handicapped child feels more secure if he knows that he is expected to be as well behaved as a normal child.

Parents should refrain from rushing to help their handicapped child do things he can do for himself. But there is no harm in making things easier for him. For instance, parents can alter clothes so that the child can dress or undress himself with as little difficulty as possible. They can arrange furniture so that he can get around the house more easily.

Depending on the nature of the handicap, the child may need additional attention in the home. His parents may have to learn special skills and techniques to carry out treatment prescribed by the doctor. At times, they may have to make changes in the home to accommodate a wheel chair or other necessary equipment. Parents should not hesitate to inform their doctor when problems arise in treating the child at home. He may be able to suggest ways to ease or correct the problems.

Educating the handicapped child

Medical treatment and special education given during early childhood help many physically handicapped children to lessen or even overcome a handicap. For example, special education can give the child with cerebral palsy a chance to improve his coordination and his speech defects. It also provides the opportunity for a physically handicapped child to better relate to people outside the family, and to learn to handle reactions to his condition.

Some physically handicapped children can attend regular classes in a private or a public school. Some public schools have classrooms adapted to the special needs of handicapped children, and trained teachers to instruct them. Some communities provide bus service for the handicapped child who needs a wheel chair, braces, or other equipment to get around.

When a child is too severely handicapped to attend school, the public school may send a teacher to his home or it may provide electronic or other types of teaching equipment. Residential schools may provide medical and educational services in those cases where parents are unable to cope with the handicapped child at home, or where local facilities are either inadequate or nonexistent. Such schools are similar to boarding schools in that the child may return home for holidays and other school vacation periods.

Parents who want information about special educational services should write or call the office of their school district or the office of the division of special education in their state.

Help for parents

The cost of providing treatment and special education for the handicapped child may become a financial burden. Each state has an official department that serves the handicapped and that has federal and state funds to help parents in financial need or those who require help in planning a program of education for their child.

Many agencies and groups that deal with handicapped children have parent-education programs to help parents face problems and better understand their own attitudes. Lectures help parents better understand the nature of their child's disability and its cause. And perhaps most important, parents learn they are not alone. They have an opportunity to share experiences with other parents of handicapped children.

Parent-education programs are led by qualified people in the fields of medicine and special education. Discussions, lectures, visual aids, and trips to schools and institutions for the handicapped supply parents with information on health care, discipline, and physical and psychological adjustments necessary in caring for the handicapped child.

In areas where such groups do not exist, some agencies have mobile units to provide parents of handicapped children with guidance and counseling.

A child like all others

In time, parents become aware that their handicapped child is in most ways like all other children. They also learn that there are other children with handicaps similar to his and that he needs the medical treatment and the educational services available to such children. Finally, the parents of the handicapped child discover that he is an individual in his own right.

Sex and your child

By James Walters, Ph.D., and Lynda Walters, Ph.D.

All children want to be accepted and loved. But if this means they are not to think about sex, or to act sexually, an important part of their lives will be kept a secret from you.

Increasingly, parents want their children to develop the attitude that sex is a normal, natural part of life, and that sexual feelings are healthy and desirable. Sexual behavior, however, requires responsibility, not only because it can result in pregnancy or social disease, but because it can result in guilt feelings that are damaging to sexual functioning in adulthood.

Infants spend a considerable amount of time touching and exploring their bodies. We smile at the sight of a baby chewing on a toe, but our response may be less accepting if the infant rubs his or her genitals. It is important for parents to understand that rubbing the genital area—masturbation—is natural, and does not reflect precocious sexuality.

Having pride in one's body contributes to a healthy self-concept. If children are taught that nudity is shameful, they may conclude that the body is something to be ashamed of. This feeling may be carried into adulthood.

Discussing sex with your child

Sex should be talked about. Many people believe that if they avoid discussing sex, their children will not become sexually active. But not discussing sex only means that parents will not know about their children's sexual values and behavior. A wall of silence between parents and children is particularly unfortunate in the light of research indicating the misconceptions children and youth have about sex.

For one thing, many young people believe that they are more sexual than their parents. Because they think their parents do not understand their feelings, young people often find it difficult to discuss their sexuality. Part of the problem is that many adults have learned to keep their sexual feelings hidden, and convey this idea to their children.

Another problem is that we tend to live with a number of myths. For example, many people believe that sex education for children may lead to less responsible sexual behavior. There is no evidence to support this belief. For another, some fathers believe that an open show of affection toward a son is unmanly and may cause the boy to grow up preferring sexual responses from persons of his own sex. Again, there is no evidence to support this belief. But these myths persist, and actually prevent us from creating the kind of environment that will contribute toward the healthy sexual development of our children.

People have different values about sex. Children will understand your values only if you clearly indicate *what* they are and *why* you hold them. Of course, for very young children you'll need to keep your explanations simple. Older children, however, will profit from an explanation.

Parents who do discuss sex with their children are often too serious. They label and describe body parts and functions without communicating the most important message of all: sex is a means by which grown people share their love.

Other parents teach about the birds and flowers in order to avoid talking about human sexual intercourse. Yet, describing sexual intercourse isn't all that difficult. You can do it.

With the thumb and index finger of one hand, form the letter "O." Say to your preschooler, "This is the mother's vagina." Holding up the index finger of your other hand, say, "This is the father's penis. He slips his penis into the mother's vagina." Then slowly insert your index finger into the letter "O."

Your child may ask, "Where is your vagina?" or "Where is your penis?" Simply say, "My vagina (or penis) is right here," and place your hand there.

Remember, the exact words you use aren't as important as the feelings you convey. If you reflect embarrassment, your child will think that sex is something to be embarrassed about. If you reflect shock, your child will think that there is something shocking about sex.

Specific details about menstruation can be left to preadolescence, at which time both boys and girls need to be informed.

Helping a child accept his or her sexuality, and so grow into a sexually responsible adult, is not only possible, it is an important responsibility of parents. The philosophy of letting someone else do it will not ensure a satisfactory result.

Sexual influences of the media

Children learn a great deal about sexual behavior from television, motion pictures, magazines, comic books, and newspapers. But it is difficult for them to sort out the facts. Some of what they learn is likely to be in error. Even if the information is not wrong, the values communicated may violate those of parents.

Parents can guide movie and television viewing by setting rules. Make a point of knowing what movies or television programs your child wants to see. When you believe that something is objectionable, a simple explanation is often best: "This is an adult film (or program). It isn't meant for children."

You may discover that your children have magazines with highly explicit sexual material to which you object. Explain how you feel: "This magazine really bothers me. I feel that love is an important part of sex. This magazine leaves out the most important part of all."

Guidance should lead to increasing self-direction. If you attach too much importance to what you forbid, you may inadvertently stimulate your children's curiosity. And, in so doing, you may lead them to satisfy their curiosity behind your back.

Sexual problems in our society

In the course of growing up, children learn that some forms of sexual expression are more acceptable than others. But, without some guidelines from their parents, children may respond with naiveté, fear, or disgust.

Realistically, children must be taught some caution in their interactions with strangers. However, not all child molesters are strangers. Frequently, children are acquainted with persons who make sexual advances toward them. Teach your child to say, "Leave me alone or I will tell my parents!" In many cases, fear of exposure will deter the offender.

If the offender is a stranger, fear of exposure may not be so great. Tell your child to scream, and to run to the nearest adult. In every case, children should report such incidents to their parents. They should never be made to feel guilty if overtures are made to them.

A thought to remember

The most important thing to remember in educating our children sexually is that we do not have to convey to them many of the negative messages we may have learned as children.

There *are* better ways. Hiding sex, or pretending it doesn't exist in children, doesn't contribute to the development of responsible sexual behavior. Recognizing that sex is important, and preparing your children for it, does.

The working mother

By Eda LeShan, B.S., M.A.

Some mothers feel worried and guilty if they hold jobs that take them away from their families. Others, who find personal fulfillment in homemaking and motherhood, are made to feel like second-class citizens. Neither of these negative attitudes is valid. The truth is that women can find personal fulfillment whether they are full-time homemakers or have a job outside the home.

Some preschool children thrive on group experience in a first-rate nursery school.

The young mother who considers working away from home is most likely to be influenced by four major factors:

- She is concerned about the psychological effect on her children, especially if they are quite young.
- She is experiencing a new consciousness of her needs and rights as a woman because of the growing influence of the Women's Liberation Movement.
- She is aware that she is living in a climate that discourages large families, and may have to think seriously of other avenues of personal fulfillment.
- Finally, today's young mother can expect to have better health and to live longer than did her mother. Even if she finds complete fulfillment as a mother and homemaker, she may want to prepare herself for the years when her children are grown and no longer require as much of her time and energy.

Whatever social forces influence the young mother, going to work will create many special and practical problems.

Concerns of all working mothers

The question that occurs most often among working mothers is whether or not they are short-changing their children. In general, the working mother is consciously concerned about the *quality* of the time she spends with her children because she knows how limited the *quantity* of time is. Mothers who stay at home are less likely to worry about this. And, sometimes, a mother's mere physical presence at home may become a substitute for genuine emotional involvement in her children's lives.

Often, the working mother is so conscious of the pitfalls of psychological neglect of her children she may go overboard in the other direction. For example, mothers who feel guilty about working, tend to read most often to their children, to "play house" when their feet are killing them, or to play endless games with a sick child.

Children do not need constant attention to know they are loved. No child will grow up suffering from nervous and mental damage because his mother sometimes says, "Darling, I can't play with you now, I'm too tired." Mothers who stay home say the same thing after cleaning a stove or waxing a floor. What children need most of all is the abiding sense that they count most when the chips are down.

Of course, there are times when a mother should recognize that her own needs must be set aside—that her greatest responsibility is to her child. A mother's job may be very important to her, but when her child is in real trouble, priorities become very clear.

Another serious concern for all working mothers is the fact that there are so few satisfactory resources for the care of young children, as well as planned and properly supervised after-school play programs for older children. Fine nurseries and day-care centers are in short supply. There are a great many that are inadequate at best and may be damaging at worst. At present, many working mothers are involved in trying to get their communities to provide better child-care facilities for children of all ages.

Some preschool children thrive on early group experience in a first-rate nursery school. Some are not ready for such an experience until they are 4 or 5 years old. Most young children catch many colds and childhood illnesses during the first year at school. Then they begin to build up better immunity. Some 2-year-olds thrive on an eight-hour day in a group setting, but some become overtired and cranky after an hour and a half.

Children differ greatly in how early they can be separated from their mothers, or from a mother substitute in the home. This means that the working mother needs time to evaluate her child's needs and possible reactions so that she can make the best arrangements for his care. She also needs a list of reliable baby sitters of various types. She may need an experienced grandmother with free morning hours who can be called on when a child is sick, or an energetic teenager who is willing to play outdoors with a child after school.

There is no way of knowing in advance when a child will need his mother's attention most. Sometimes a young child is quite happy with a baby sitter, or attending a nursery school or day-care center, then begins having learning problems when he starts school. Some mothers work until their children are teen-agers, then quit because they feel this is the most crucial time—the time their children need them most.

The single working mother

Single mothers are mothers without partners to help share the burden of supporting and caring for their children. They may be widowed, separated, divorced, or unmarried.

The single working mother is less likely to feel guilty about working because in most cases she has no choice. But her concern for her children's welfare is usually very intense. The single working mother is isolated and more responsible for her children's welfare. She may not feel guilty about working, but when her children are ill, or when she is exhausted at the end of a day, she has no one to whom she can turn for help at all times.

The single working mother needs to think of ways to provide loving father substitutes for her children—a favorite uncle to babysit on a Saturday afternoon; a retired grandpa who can take a child to an after-school dental appointment; a neighbor father who is willing to include her children in the backyard games he plays with his own children.

Because she has to work, the single mother tends to take less satisfying jobs than the mother who has a choice. This, combined with the burden of full parental responsibility, often results in what one mother called "a life that is never for me." The single working mother needs to devote thought to how she can nourish her own life. She cannot be a good mother to her children unless she cares about herself. Even though she may have to give up material things, an interesting job that pays less may be more rewarding in happiness for herself and her children.

The married working mother

Many married women also have little or no choice about taking an outside job. A husband may be working part time while studying for a profession. He may be unemployed for a long period, or have a long illness. When there is no choice about the wife's working, both parents need to explore ways to help each other with child care and household chores.

However, couples should do some genuine soul-searching about the phrase *have to work*. Sometimes a woman who *wants* to work for her own fulfillment feels guilty. She may feel that she is selfish and unfair to her family, yet at the same time she will convince herself and her husband that she *has* to work because the family income is inadequate even when it is not. If this is the case, she damages herself and her children by denying an important truth about her nature. She may also unnecessarily damage her husband's self-esteem.

The mother who has a real choice needs to take a hard look at the situation before she decides to take a job. Will the additional income really make a difference? Or will the cost of baby sitters, nurseries, additional taxes, extra clothes, lunches out, and transportation actually make taking a job a luxury? Is the cost too high in terms of neglect of her family's emotional needs at this particular time?

Husbands of working mothers

Husbands should not feel that their masculinity is threatened by changing a diaper, washing dishes, or cooking a meal. In a true marital partnership both parents can find ways to share in all areas of child care and household chores.

The mature woman will consider her husband's needs. Some men feel threatened by a wife who has a rich, rewarding life of her own. Husbands and wives need to keep lines of communication open between them at all times so that they can work out whatever conflicting feelings they may have, find acceptable compromises, and show continuing respect for each other's needs.

Time and changing roles

Women need a sense of perspective about time and changing roles. The period when children are truly dependent is short. It is wise to think in the broadest terms about how to plan one's life.

Women must accept the fact that no matter what their decision about working, there will be frustrations, fatigue, boredom, and uncertainty. A crowded subway at the rush hour, impatient demanding bosses, and TV dinners three nights in a row may be no less harrowing than colicky babies, sleepless nights, and lack of adult stimulation.

Indeed, having a job outside the home may sometimes seem mad, especially on the day your child cries because you can't get to the school play or you come home tired and realize you forgot to defrost the meat you were going to have for dinner.

Having two careers is not for everyone. There are talented and energetic women who enjoy their professions so much that to cut them off from this, even briefly, can play havoc with their lives. The woman who must follow her own star needs to understand that if she stifles her needs she may become an emotional cripple. And such a person cannot be a good influence on her children. No one can feel truly loving toward others unless, first of all, he cares about his own life.

If we care deeply about teaching our children those ethical values that will lead to good human relationships, the first lesson must be that it is only when we respect our own special talents and possibilities that we are capable of offering equal respect to others. To want to fulfill oneself is not selfish—on the contrary, the fulfilled person feels a deep joy in being alive and communicates it to everyone around him. If we want our children to search for their own best potentialities, to become truly individual and unique, then the best way to help them is to be this kind of person ourselves.

Agencies and organizations interested in the welfare of children

Hundreds of agencies and organizations in the United States and in Canada provide information and counseling to anyone seeking help with special problems relating to family and child health, welfare, and education. Some of these agencies and organizations are privately sponsored. Others are sponsored by city, state, or federal governments in the United States, or by provincial or territorial governments in Canada.

Telephone directories usually list local agencies and organizations and, where they exist, the local chapters of state, national, provincial, and territorial agencies and organizations. Whenever possible, get in touch with a local chapter or agency first.

The following list contains names of some of the major agencies and organizations in the United States and in Canada. The list also contains a brief description of what each does. To make it easier for you to find the one you think may be able to help you, the agencies and organizations are grouped under general headings.

United States

- Diseases
- Education and recreation
- Health
- Mental health
- Physically handicapped
  - *Birth defects*
  - *Blind*
  - *Cerebral palsy*
  - *Crippled*
  - *Cystic fibrosis*
  - *Deaf*
  - *Multiple sclerosis*
  - *Muscular dystrophy*
- Welfare and safety

Canada

- Diseases
- Education and recreation
- Health and welfare
- Mental health
- Physically handicapped
  - *Blind*
  - *Deaf*
  - *Disabled*
  - *Muscular dystrophy*

If this list does not include an agency or an organization that seems equipped to meet your special need, your doctor, the nearest hospital, the local health department, or your minister may be able to suggest others.

United States

Diseases

Asthma and Allergy Foundation of America
801 Second Avenue
New York, New York 10017

A national voluntary health agency that brings together the public, the medical profession, research scientists, and public health workers to help solve health problems related to allergic diseases. These diseases include allergic reaction to foods and drugs, insect bites, asthma, hay fever, and skin diseases. The foundation promotes facilities for research and clinical training; provides information to the public, the medical profession, and health workers; cooperates with hospitals, other medical institutions, and health organizations in the development of facilities to prevent and treat allergies. Publications available on request.

American Cancer Society, Inc.
777 Third Avenue
New York, New York 10017

Seeks to control cancer through research, education, and service. Filmstrip kits, pamphlets, and manuals are available.

American Diabetes Association, Inc.
600 Fifth Avenue
New York, New York 10020

Encourages education and research in diabetes. Seeks to educate the public in the early detection of diabetes. Helps the diabetic patient understand the condition better. Local affiliates sponsor meetings for diabetics and camps for diabetic children. Booklets, a bimonthly magazine, a cookbook, and a programmed course of instruction are available from the association.

American Heart Association
7320 Greenville Avenue
Dallas, Texas 75231

Seeks to control heart and blood vessel disorders. Promotes programs designed to improve counseling and rehabilitation of children with cardiac ailments. Local chapters offer information and educational services.

American Lung Association
1740 Broadway
New York, New York 10019

Seeks to help eradicate tuberculosis, control other respiratory diseases, discourage cigarette smoking, and eliminate air pollution through research, education, and service. Local affiliates help parents and teachers develop child-health programs. Booklets, films, and filmstrips are available from the local affiliates on request.

American Social Health Association
260 Sheridan Avenue, Suite 307
Palo Alto, California 94306

A national voluntary organization. Works with schools and communities on training programs in family life education, the eradication of venereal disease, and the drug problem.

Arthritis Foundation
3400 Peachtree Road NE
Suite 1101
Atlanta, Georgia 30326

Seeks to control arthritis and rheumatism through education, research, and service. Refers people to local treatment clinics. Answers questions pertaining to particular types of arthritis and rheumatism. Films and publications are available from the foundation.

Epilepsy Foundation of America
1828 L Street NW, Suite 406
Washington, D.C. 20036

The national agency concerned with the needs of Americans with epilepsy. Conducts programs in research, public and professional education, and patient services. Free literature available on request. Information and referral service. Local chapters in 38 states.

Leukemia Society of America, Inc.
211 East 43rd Street
New York, New York 10017

Seeks to control and check leukemia through research, education, and service. Local chapters offer counseling, guidance, and aid to patients and families affected by leukemia. Literature is available from the society.

The National Foundation for Asthma, Inc.
P.O. Box 50304
Tucson, Arizona 85703

Provides complete medical, educational, and recreational care for asthmatic children between ages 6 and 13. Accepts children from all areas of the United States. Children from low- and middle-income families are accepted with no cost to the family. Pamphlets are available from the foundation.

National Genetics Foundation, Inc.
9 West 57th Street
New York, New York 10019

Seeks to control and check hereditary diseases through research, treatment, and prevention and counseling in genetic disorders. The national headquarters is the referral office for a network of genetic counseling and treatment centers located at leading medical centers throughout the United States and Canada. (Formerly known as the National Foundation for Neuromuscular Diseases, Inc.)

National Kidney Foundation
Two Park Avenue
New York, New York 10016

Seeks to control and check kidney disease through research, education, and service. Local chapters provide drug banks and renal clinics. Literature is available from the foundation.

Education and recreation

American Camping Association, Inc.
Bradford Woods
Martinsville, Indiana 46151

Promotes the improvement and development of organized camping for children and adults. Furnishes information to parents about reputable camps for their children. A publications catalog is available on request.

American Friends Service Committee, Inc.
1501 Cherry Street
Philadelphia, Pennsylvania 19102

An international Quaker service agency. Programs include voluntary service projects and seminars for teen-agers, educational packets for children 6 to 12 describing projects to help children in countries where AFSC is at work. Packets include background material on each country. Catalog available upon request. Please send a stamped, self-addressed envelope with request for catalog.

Association for Children with Learning Disabilities
4156 Library Road
Pittsburgh, Pennsylvania 15234

A national association of professional people and parents of children with learning disabilities. Works to advance the education of children who are adequately intelligent but have learning disabilities because of coordinative problems, or perceptual or conceptual difficulties sometimes accompanied by behavioral problems. The association assists local affiliated groups which serve parents through schools, camps, parent education, recreation programs, information services, and publications. Some free publications available on request.

Boys' Clubs of America
771 First Avenue
New York, New York 10017

A national organization concerned with helping boys from 7 to 18. Local Boys' Clubs offer programs in physical fitness, hobbies, vocational skills, reading, music, drama, arts and crafts, and many other activities.

Day Care and Child Development Council of America, Inc.
805 15th Street NW. Suite 520
Washington, D.C. 20005

A national association of individuals, citizens' groups, and service agencies concerned with children. Works to promote broader public understanding and support of quality daytime services for young children. Serves as an information center for such services; offers counseling on program planning, organizational techniques, and fund-raising for day-care centers. Publications list available on request.

JWB, The Association of Jewish Community Centers and Camps
15 East 26th Street
New York, New York 10010

A national association of Jewish community centers and Young Men's and Young Women's Hebrew Associations (YM-YWHA). Local centers conduct nursery schools and educational programs for preschoolers; summer day camps, physical-education programs, and social work programs for school-age children.

The National Association for Creative Children and Adults
8080 Springvalley Drive
Cincinnati, Ohio 45236

A nonprofit organization with membership throughout the United States and abroad. The United States Department of Health, Education, and Welfare has designated the association as a major educational association of the nation. It conducts consulting services for children, adults, schools, agencies, and organizations. Surveys colleges and universities to encourage courses for the gifted. Works with the public to encourage understanding and support of the gifted.

National Catholic Youth Organization Federation
c/o United States Catholic Conference
1312 Massachusetts Avenue NW
Washington, D.C. 20005

A member of the Division of Youth Activities of the United States Catholic Conference. CYO promotes a program of spiritual, cultural, social, and physical activities.

The National Conference of Christians and Jews, Inc.
43 West 57th Street
New York, New York 10019

A national organization that educates people about racial, religious, and nationality prejudices. Conducts a five-part program to better human relations in the United States—workshops and institutes on community relations and the administration of justice, youth programs, courses in how to rear children without prejudice, human relations seminars and institutes for teachers, and interreligious programs for better interfaith understanding.

The Play Schools Association, Inc.
111 East 59th Street
New York, New York 10022

Holds workshops and discussion groups for parents, teachers, and volunteers concerned with recreational facilities for children. Pamphlets and films are available.

United States Department of Agriculture
SEA—Extension
Director of Information
Washington, D.C. 20250

Sponsors 4-H programs for boys and girls from 10 through 19 who "learn by doing" through projects in science, agriculture, home economics, personal development, community service, leadership, and citizenship. More information may be obtained from any county Extension office or the Extension Service of any state land-grant college.

United States Department of Health, Education, and Welfare
Administration for Children, Youth, and Families
P.O. Box 1182
Washington, D.C. 20013

Deals with all matters pertaining to the welfare of children. Plans programs for children and parents. Develops standards and guidelines. Provides technical assistance to states and public and private agencies for programs on child health; handicapped, retarded, and emotionally disturbed children; protective day-care services for children, and parent-child counseling; adoption, institutional, and foster care for children; service for unmarried mothers; and community programs for youth development. Directs the Community Coordinated Child Care Program which helps local public and private organizations involved in child-care to work together. Conducts research and evaluation of programs serving children, and provides information about services for children. Prepares Office of Child Development publications and the magazine, *Children.*

Health

American Academy of Pediatrics
1801 Hinman Avenue
Evanston, Illinois 60204

Works with physicians and health organizations on child-health problems. The academy also provides information and assistance on child-health problems to parents and teachers.

American Dental Association
211 East Chicago Avenue
Chicago, Illinois 60611

The national organization of members of the dental profession. Provides information on dental treatment, dental hygiene, and dental products. Is the accrediting agency for the nation's dental schools. Literature on dental health is available from the association.

American Medical Association
535 North Dearborn Street
Chicago, Illinois 60610

An organization of members of the medical profession which seeks to advance the practice of medicine and to better the public health. Services to the public include health-education materials, a question-and-answer service, a monthly bulletin for teachers, conferences on health subjects, as well as campaigns on health and safety problems.

American Podiatry Association
20 Chevy Chase Circle NW
Washington, D.C. 20015

A national association of podiatrists. It provides literature, filmstrips, films, and slides pertaining to the growth and care of the feet to parents, teachers, and children.

Mental health

The American Association of Psychiatric Services for Children
1725 K Street NW
Suite 1112
Washington, D.C. 20006

A standard-setting, nationwide membership organization of psychiatric clinics for children. Local approved clinics, which may be both inpatient and outpatient, vary as to age range and services. The association guides parents and teachers in the selection of an appropriate local clinic.

Mental Health Association
1800 North Kent Street
Rosslyn
Arlington, Virginia 22209

Works for the care and treatment of the mentally ill. Local chapters work for and give information about community-based services, special education, and hospitals for the treatment and education of mentally ill children. Local chapters sponsor parent-education programs. Pamphlets and films are available.

National Association for Retarded Citizens
2709 Avenue E East
Arlington, Texas 76011

A national organization with state and local affiliates dedicated to improved welfare, education, habilitation, and recreation for the mentally retarded of all ages. It sponsors research into the causes and prevention of mental retardation.

Physically handicapped

Birth defects

The National Foundation-March of Dimes
1275 Mamaroneck Avenue
White Plains, New York 10605

Provides information on scientific research, birth defects, centers, and professional and public education in the fields of birth defects and prenatal care.

Blind

National Society for the Prevention of Blindness, Inc.
79 Madison Avenue
New York, New York 10016

A national health agency concerned with the prevention of blindness and with eye health and eye safety. Offers program consultant services. Publications and films are available from the society.

Cerebral palsy

United Cerebral Palsy Associations, Inc.
66 East 34th Street
New York, New York 10016

Seek to control and check cerebral palsy through research, education, and service. Local affiliates offer therapy, medical, educational, recreational, vocational, social work, and other services. Help patients and their families with special problems.

Crippled

The National Easter Seal Society for Crippled Children and Adults
2023 West Ogden Avenue
Chicago, Illinois 60612

Assists parents and families of physically handicapped children through education and research. State and local affiliates conduct education and other service programs for the handicapped. Offers scholarships to personnel interested in working with the handicapped. Conducts national research program. Publications available from the society.

Cystic fibrosis

Cystic Fibrosis Foundation
3379 Peachtree Road NE
Atlanta, Georgia 30326

A voluntary health agency concerned with research, services, teaching, and the dissemination of information about cystic fibrosis and related pediatric disorders including asthma with lung damage, chronic bronchitis, bronchiectasis, childhood emphysema, and malabsorption problems. Local chapters arrange for the loan of therapy equipment and provide help in referring patients to regional Cystic Fibrosis centers, of which there are 110 nationwide. Professional literature and public information materials are available from the foundation.

Deaf

Alexander Graham Bell Association for the Deaf, Inc.
3417 Volta Place NW
Washington, D.C. 20007

Encourages the teaching of speech, lip-reading, and the use of residual hearing to deaf children. Helps parents and teachers understand the special problems of deaf children. Advocates improving the educational and vocational facilities available to deaf persons. Encourages people to become teachers of the deaf. Furnishes free information kits on speech, hearing, and education of the deaf to individual parents and teachers. Membership in the association includes subscription to *The Volta Review*, published monthly except June, July, and August.

John Tracy Clinic
806 West Adams Boulevard
Los Angeles, California 90007

An educational center for preschool deaf and hard-of-hearing children and their parents. The clinic's program consists of a consulting service that studies each child; hearing tests to determine what the child can hear; parent classes open to all parents of deaf or hard-of-hearing children; and a demonstration nursery school that operates throughout the school year. A correspondence course is available to parents of children 5 years old or less anywhere in the world. Parent-education films and records available to groups of 4 or more parents. Service to parents of deaf or hard-of-hearing children is free.

Multiple sclerosis

National Multiple Sclerosis Society
205 East 42nd Street
New York, New York 10017

Is concerned with research into the cause, prevention, and cure of multiple sclerosis. Local chapters provide patient services including special clinics, aids to daily living, and counseling and referral services. Public and professional educational materials are available from the society and its chapters.

Muscular dystrophy

Muscular Dystrophy Association
810 Seventh Avenue, 27th Floor
New York, New York 10019

Sponsors an international research program with the objective of finding effective treatment for muscular dystrophy and related neuromuscular disorders; maintains a nationwide network of clinics which provide differential diagnosis, expert medical care, and family counseling; provides, through chapter affiliates, direct and extensive services to patients, including the purchase of wheel chairs, lifts, braces, and other orthopedic aids, as well as educational and recreational programs adapted to their needs; carries out a broad program of professional and public health education. Literature is available from the association on request.

Welfare and safety

American Red Cross

A national organization charged by the Congress of the United States of America to assist members of the armed forces and their families and to provide for disaster preparedness and relief. Other health, safety, and welfare programs are carried on by local chapters. The work is supported by adult, junior, and high school volunteers. For a fee, publications on first aid, health, and safety are available from your local Red Cross chapter.

American Public Welfare Association
1155 Sixteenth Street NW, Suite 201
Washington, D.C. 20036

A national organization of public welfare employees, agencies, and others interested in public welfare. Provides information about public welfare programs and services for children and families. Does not provide financial assistance to families. Direct public welfare services such as financial assistance, foster care, or adoption planning are provided through state and local departments of public welfare.

Big Brothers/Big Sisters of America
117 South 17th Street
Philadelphia, Pennsylvania 19103

A national organization that helps youths between the ages of 8 and 18 who do not have parents. Supplies men and women with helpful information on how to be a needed friend to a boy or girl.

Child Welfare League of America, Inc.
67 Irving Place
New York, New York 10003

A national federation of private and public agencies serving children and their families. Sets standards, conducts research, surveys, and field consultation; provides leadership to the child welfare field through its regional conferences, information service, and publications (including the journal *Child Welfare*). Works with national and international organizations to improve conditions affecting the welfare of children.

Canada

Diseases

The Arthritis Society
920 Yonge Street, Suite 420
Toronto, Ontario M4W 3J7

A national voluntary health agency. Stimulates attack on arthritis and rheumatism through research, professional education, public information, and patient care. Provides physiotherapy, occupational therapy, and social and medical consultant services in a number of provinces.

The Canadian Cancer Society
77 Bloor Street West, Suite 401
Toronto, Ontario M5S 2V7

Seeks to control cancer through an educational program of considerable scope. Films, filmstrips, and pamphlets are available.

Canadian Cystic Fibrosis Foundation
51 Eglinton Avenue East
Toronto, Ontario M4P 1G7

Conducts research into the basic causes and treatment of cystic fibrosis, and aids those afflicted with cystic fibrosis. Films and literature are available from the foundation.

Canadian Heart Foundation
One Nicholas Street,
Suite 1200
Ottawa, Ontario K1N 7B7

A federation of provincial heart foundations throughout Canada. Information on the heart and its diseases is available to parents, teachers, and schools, either through the national office or the provincial foundation.

Canadian Tuberculosis and Respiratory
Disease Association
345 O'Connor Street
Ottawa, Ontario K2P 1V9

A national voluntary health organization aiding in the promotion of measures and facilities for the prevention, diagnosis, and treatment of tuberculosis and other respiratory diseases.

Education and recreation

Canadian Council of Christians and Jews
229 Yonge Street, Room 506-8
Toronto, Ontario M5B 1N9

A national organization seeking to educate people about racial, religious, and nationality prejudices. Among its many programs in the human relations field, it sponsors a project to promote better understanding between English-speaking and French-speaking youth. Books, pamphlets, and films are available.

Canadian Council on 4-H Clubs
185 Somerset Street West
Ottawa, Ontario K2P 0J2

A nonprofit organization that coordinates provincial 4-H programs. The 4-H Clubs program is a nationwide educational program for young people. It is concerned primarily with the personal development of rural youth.

The Canadian Education Association
252 Bloor Street West
Toronto, Ontario M5S 1V5

A national association whose membership is drawn from senior educational administrators but is mainly supported by tax funds. It maintains an information service that prepares and distributes reports on current education activities and projects. Publishes *Newsletter* and a quarterly magazine, *Education Canada*.

Canadian Home and School and
Parent-Teacher Federation
240 Eglinton Avenue East, Suite 204
Toronto, Ontario M4P 1K8

The federation of provincial and local associations. Publications on parent education are available from the federation.

Girl Guides of Canada-*Guides du Canada*
50 Merton Street
Toronto, Ontario M4S 1A3

Helps to prepare girls to become good homemakers and capable citizens through an educational-recreational program based on spiritual values. For girls 7 to 18.

Young Women's Christian Association of Canada
571 Jarvis Street
Toronto, Ontario M4Y 2J1

A national organization for women and girls. It seeks to provide opportunities for personal growth, to deepen concern for human needs, and to act responsibly in the world community through its training, social action, intercultural, educational, and physical activities programs. Major emphasis is on work with youth.

Health and welfare

Canadian Dental Association
1815 Alta Vista Drive
Ottawa, Ontario K1G 3Y6

A national organization of members of the dental profession in Canada. It seeks to advance the practice of dentistry and to improve public dental health. Services to the public include dental health pamphlets and booklets.

The Canadian Red Cross Society
95 Wellesley Street East
Toronto, Ontario M4Y 1H6

A national organization providing health and welfare programs and services. Notable among these is a free blood transfusion service for all Canadian hospitals. Other services cover outpost hospitals and nursing stations, emergency services, and water safety. Publications are available from national headquarters or local branches.

Department of National Health and Welfare
Information Services
1200 Brooke Claxton Building
Ottawa, Ontario K1A 0K9

Aids the provinces through grants for research. Provides advisory and consultative services. Prepares educational material—booklets, manuals, films, and filmstrips—for parents and professionals. Prominent among these is *The Canadian Mother and Child,* a handbook for mothers. Provincial departments distribute all materials.

Mental health

National Institute on Mental Retardation
Kinsmen NIMR Building
York University
4700 Keele Street
Downsview, Ontario M3J 1P3

A federation of groups working on behalf of the mentally retarded in Canada. Local associations operate classes, day schools, summer camps, and other recreational programs. Programs underway include home care, parent counseling, and mobile clinics.

Canadian Mental Health Association
2160 Yonge Street
Toronto, Ontario M4S 2Z3

Concerned with improving services for people with mental disorders. Conducts programs promoting prevention. Provides support through speakers, literature, and films for parents of children with emotional and learning disorders and for professional groups working with them.

Physically handicapped

Blind

The Canadian Council of the Blind
96 Ridout Street South
London, Ontario N6C 3X4

Seeks to aid the blind through legislation, education, and maintenance of places of meeting and recreation.

The Canadian National Institute for the Blind
1929 Bayview Avenue
Toronto, Ontario M4G 3E8

Seeks to improve the condition of the blind of Canada and to prevent blindness. Conducts a program of rehabilitation and prevention of blindness for children and adults. Aids parents of blind and partially sighted children with counseling and services designed to supplement the child's education. Provides guidance and counseling for those entering the labor force or planning a university education.

Deaf

The Canadian Hearing Society
60 Bedford Road
Toronto, Ontario M5R 2K2

A national organization serving the deaf and hard of hearing. Guides parents in the education of a deaf child, and other helpful services.

Disabled

Canadian Rehabilitation Council for the Disabled
1 Yonge Street, Suite 2110
Toronto, Ontario M5E 1E8

The result of a merger between the Canadian Council for Crippled Children and Adults, and the Canadian Foundation for Poliomyelitis and Rehabilitation. Works with all agencies to provide a unified approach to the problems and needs of the disabled.

Muscular dystrophy

The Muscular Dystrophy Association of Canada
74 Victoria Street, Suite 1014
Toronto, Ontario M5C 2A5

Finances and supervises research programs which include clinics for diagnosis and consultation. Local chapters conduct service programs for patients. Literature is available.

Books for parents

A great many people have had a great deal to say about child development and related subjects dealing with child guidance, family living, education, sex education, and health. The books listed here are but a small sampling of the wealth of interesting literature to help you in raising your child. The article AGENCIES AND ORGANIZATIONS INTERESTED IN THE WELFARE OF CHILDREN, page 150, lists some of the specialized sources that offer pamphlets and other literature.

The Adopted Family by Florence Rondell and Ruth Michaels. 2 vols. Rev. ed., Crown, 1965

Adoption and After by Louise Raymond. Rev. ed., Harper, 1974

Baby and Child Care by Benjamin Spock. Rev. ed., Hawthorn, 1976. Also in paperback from Pocket Books

Before You Were Three: How You Began to Walk, Talk, Explore and Have Feelings by Bobie H. Harris and Elizabeth Levy. Delacorte, 1977

Between Parent and Child by Haim G. Ginott. Macmillan, 1965. Also in paperback from Avon.

Between Parent and Teenager by Haim G. Ginott. Macmillan, 1969. Also in paperback from Avon.

Books and the Teen-Age Reader: A Guide for Teachers, Librarians, and Parents by G. Robert Carlsen. Rev. ed., Harper, 1971. Also in paperback from Bantam

Children at Risk: A Handbook of the Signs and Symptoms of Early Childhood Difficulties by Gary A. Crow. Schocken, 1978

A Child's Journey: Forces That Shape the Lives of Our Young by Julius Segal and Herbert Yahraes. McGraw, 1978

Child's Work: A Learning Guide to Joyful Play by Paul S. Shakesby. Running Press, 1974. Also in paperback from same publisher

The Conspiracy Against Childhood by Eda LeShan. Atheneum, 1967. Also in paperback from same publisher

Coping with Prolonged Health Impairment in Your Child by Audrey T. McCollum. Little, Brown, 1975

Crisis in the Classroom by Charles E. Silberman. Random House, 1970. Also in paperback from same publisher

Dare to Discipline by James Dobson. Tyndale, 1970. Also in paperback from same publisher, Bantam, and Regal

Dialogues with Mothers by Bruno Bettelheim. Free Press, 1962. Also in paperback from Avon

Dr. Spock Talks with Mothers by Benjamin Spock. Fawcett, 1974. Paperback

Don't Push Your Preschooler by Louise Bates Ames and Joan Ames Chase. Harper, 1974

Early Childhood: Behavior and Learning by Catherine Landreth. 2nd ed., Knopf, 1967

Early Education: Current Theory, Research, and Action edited by Robert D. Hess and Roberta Bear. Aldine, 1968

Education and Ecstasy by George B. Leonard. Delacorte, 1968. Also in paperback from Dell

The Family: From Traditional to Companionship by Ernest W. Burgess and others. 4th ed., Van Nostrand, 1971

The Games Children Play by A. H. Chapman. Berkley, 1972. Paperback

Good Schools for Young Children: A Guide for Working with Three-, Four-, and Five-Year-Old Children by Sarah H. Leeper and others. 3rd ed., Macmillan, 1974

Growing Up Handicapped: A Guide to Helping the Exceptional Child by Evelyn W. Ayrault. Seabury, 1977

Helping Children Overcome Learning Difficulties by Jerome Rosner. Walker, 1975

Helping Children with Problems: What Parents and Teachers Can Do by June Marie Schasre. Walker, 1978

Helping Parents Help Their Children by Eugene L. Arnold, M.D. Brunner-Mazel, 1978

Helping the Handicapped Teenager Mature by Evelyn West Ayrault. Association Press, 1971

Hide or Seek by James Dobson. Revell, 1974

How Children Fail by John Holt. Dell, 1972. Paperback

How Children Learn by John Holt. Dell, 1969. Paperback

How to Adopt a Child by Robert A. Farmer. 2nd ed., Arco, 1968

How to Influence Children: A Handbook of Practical Parenting Skills by Charles E. Schaefer. Reinhold, 1978

How to Live Through Junior High School by Eric W. Johnson. Rev. ed., Lippincott, 1975

How to Parent by Fitzhugh Dodson. Nash, 1970. Also in paperback from New American Library, 1973

Infant Culture by Jane Flannery Jackson and Joseph H. Jackson. Crowell, 1978

Intelligence Can Be Taught by Arthur Whimbey and Linda Shaw Whimbey. Dutton, 1975. Also in paperback from Bantam

The Intimate Environment: Exploring Marriage and the Family by Arlene Skolnick. Little, Brown, 1973

Living with a Mentally Retarded Child: A Primer for Parents by Beatrice Buckler. Hawthorn, 1971

Loving and Learning: Interacting With Your Child from Birth to Three by Norma J. McDiarmid and others. Harcourt, 1977

Mothers and Daughters: A Lifelong Relationship by Edith G. Neisser. Rev. Ed., Harper, 1973

Mothers, Fathers, and Children: Explorations in the Formation of Character in the First Seven Years by Sylvia Brody and Sidney Axelrod with Ethel Horn and others. International University Press, 1978

Oneness and Separateness: From Infant to Individual by Louise J. Kaplan. Simon & Schuster, 1978

Parenting: Principles and Politics of Parenthood by Sidney Cornelia Callahan. Penguin 1973. Paperback.

Parents and Children, Love & Discipline: A Positive Approach to Behavior Modification by Clifford K. Madsen and Charles J. Madsen. AHM Publishing, 1975. Paperback

A Parent's Guide to Children's Reading by Nancy Larrick. 4th ed., Doubleday, 1975. Also in paperback from Pocket Books and Bantam

The Parent Test: How to Measure and Develop Your Talent for Parenthood by Ellen Peck and William Granzig, M.D. Putnam, 1978

Race Awareness in Young Children by Mary Ellen Goodman. Macmillan, 1964. Paperback

Revolution in Learning: The Years from Birth to Six by Maya Pines. Harper, 1967. Also in paperback from same publisher

Secrets in the Family by Lily Pincus and Christopher Dare. Pantheon, 1978

Should the Children Know?: Encounters with Death in the Lives of Children by Marguerita Rudolph. Schocken, 1978

Signals: What Your Child Is Really Telling You by Paul Ackerman and others. Dial, 1973

Something's Wrong with My Child: A Parent's Book about Children with Learning Disabilities by Milton Brutten and others. Harcourt, 1973

The Special Child: A Parents' Guide to Mental Disabilities by Robin White. Little, 1978

Studies in Adolescence: A Book of Readings in Adolescent Development by Robert E. Grunder. 3rd ed., Macmillan, 1975

Teaching the Child Under Six by James L. Hymes, Jr. 2nd ed., Merrill, 1974. Paperback

These Are Your Children by Gladys Gardner Jenkins and Helen S. Shacter. 4th ed., Scott, Foresman, 1975. Paperback

Thinking Is Child's Play by Evelyn Sharp, Dutton, 1969. Also in paperback from Avon

Twins and Twin Relations by Helen L. Koch. Univ. of Chicago Press, 1966

Underachievers: How They Can Be Helped by Benjamin Fine. Dutton, 1967

Understanding Your Parents by Harold Rashkis, M.D. and Levon Tashjian, M. D. Stickley, 1978

The Vanishing Adolescent by Edgar Z. Friedenberg. Beacon Press, 1959. Also in paperback from Dell

Watching the New Baby by Joan Samson. Atheneum, 1974

What Every Child Would Like His Parents to Know: To Help Him with the Emotional Problems of His Everyday Life by Lee Salk. McKay, 1972. Also in paperback from Warner Books

What Is a Father? by Lee P. McGrath and Joan Scobey, eds. Simon and Schuster, 1969. Paperback

What You Can Do About Drugs and Your Child by Herman W. Land. Hart, 1970. Also in paperback from Pocket Books, 1971

Young Alcoholics by Tom Alibrandi. CompCare, 1978

Your Child's Self-esteem: The Key to His Life by Dorothy Briggs. Doubleday, 1970

Section Three

Medical Guide

It is always best to have a medical doctor on whom you can call if your child becomes ill. A continuing relationship with a doctor, a relationship that starts with the in-hospital examination of your baby at birth, has many advantages. By his periodic examinations and immunizations, the doctor gets to know your child intimately. He establishes a rapport with the child. He gains your confidence in his abilities to diagnose a condition and treat the child whenever necessary.

This guide is not meant to replace your family doctor. It is meant to help you recognize and treat symptoms that call for immediate first aid—as in the case of shock. It is meant to help you recognize symptoms that require diagnosis and treatment by the doctor—a rash and sore throat, high fever and lethargy. Above all, it is meant to make communications between you and the doctor clearer and more complete.

Caring for a sick child

By Morris Green, M.D.

All parents try to keep their children healthy. But in spite of all efforts, a child is bound to become ill occasionally. Suddenly, for no apparent reason, he has a high temperature, or he complains of a stomachache or an earache. He may catch chicken pox, mumps, German measles, or some other communicable disease.

When your child becomes ill, keep calm. Remember that most children quickly bounce back to normal after an ordinary illness. It is quite natural for a child to worry about not feeling well. He may be listless and irritable. Be sympathetic, but not overly so. If you look grim and anxious, he will react to your obvious anxiety by becoming even more upset.

Before you call your doctor, be prepared to answer his questions and to give him certain information about your child's condition. Take the child's temperature before calling the doctor, and tell him whether you used the thermometer orally or rectally. Tell him if the child has a rash, a sore throat, swollen glands, or aching muscles. Tell him if the child's breathing is irregular or if he has any other symptoms that you think are serious. Any clues you can give the doctor about your child's condition will help him in his diagnosis and prescription.

Try to convince your child that if he gets plenty of rest and does what the doctor tells him to, he will soon be well. If the child is seriously ill and must be confined to bed for a long time, usually it is a good idea to tell him just enough about his illness to lessen any fears he may have. Do not burden him with all the details, but do not lie to him.

Making a sick child comfortable. Ideally, the sickroom should be a room that is easily reached from any other part of the house and from which you can hear the child if he calls you. Keep the room uncluttered and softly lighted. In nursing your child back to health, arrange things so that he will be as comfortable as possible without overburdening yourself. Arrange his bed so that you can get around it easily. If possible, place it near a window so that he can look outside, but be careful to avoid drafts. If the bed is placed so that you can see him and he can see what others in the family are doing, he will feel less isolated. Be sure that the room is well ventilated. Ideally, room temperature should be kept between 68° and 72° F. (20° and 22° C). This will make it unnecessary to cover the child with heavy blankets to keep him warm, and he will be more comfortable.

When you bathe your child in bed, wash one part of his body at a time to avoid chilling him. Keep the rest of his body wrapped in a large bath towel and be sure to dry the skin thoroughly.

Use a drawsheet on the bed to save time and labor. To make a drawsheet, fold a bedsheet in half the long way. Lay it across the bottom sheet of the bed so that it reaches from the point where the child's knees rest, up to his shoulders. Tuck both ends securely under the mattress. If a rubber sheet is used, place it over the bottom sheet. Then put the drawsheet over both the rubber sheet and the bottom sheet. When necessary, the drawsheet can be replaced without having to remake the bed completely.

Giving medicine to the child. Your child may balk at taking his medicine, especially if you indicate by words or facial expression that it tastes bad. The best way to give medicine is in a matter-of-fact way. If he continues to fuss, mix the medicine with some fruit juice. But be sure the juice is not a regular part of his diet. If you put the medicine into a juice that he is accustomed to drinking, he may notice the difference and refuse to drink that kind of juice when he is well. If the medicine is a pill that does not dissolve easily, crush it before putting it into the juice. Also, you can mix medicine with a spoonful of jelly, honey, or syrup in order to make it easier for the child to take.

Always follow your doctor's instructions. If you have any questions, be sure he answers them so that you clearly understand what you are supposed to do. Write down the times you are to give your child his medicine, and any instructions about diet and special treatment. Keep all medicine away from your child's reach. Never give him medicine left over from a previous similar illness without consulting your doctor.

When the child goes to the hospital. Sometimes it is not possible to care for a sick child at home. He may need an operation, or the illness may be so serious that it requires hospitalization. Most children become concerned if they must go to the hospital. Usually, it is anticipation and uncertainty that worries a child—not the actual experience. Even when he does not seem to be concerned, he may have some strange ideas about being in the hospital.

It is wise for the parent to prepare the child for his hospitalization by telling him what he can expect from the time he enters the hospital to the time he is ready to return home. If you are not familiar with hospital procedure, take the time to find out. The child will accept the situation better if he is convinced that you know a great deal about the place where he is going and how he will be treated when he is there. Do not promise him that his hospital stay will be an enjoyable experience. On the other hand, do not stress the possibility that it may be unpleasant. Be as matter-of-fact as possible.

You need not go into great detail, but you can describe those parts of hospital procedure that are usually most reassuring to a child. For instance, you can tell him about the bracelet with his name on it that the nurse will put on his wrist. You can describe how a hospital bed can be cranked up and down to make him comfortable. You can tell him that when you are not with him, there will always be a nurse to take care of him and that all he has to do to call her is to press a button or pull a string. You can tell him about the special table that fits over his bed so that he can eat his meals without getting out of bed.

If he is going to have surgery, you can tell him how he will fall asleep before the operation, and about the recovery room where he will wake up without even remembering that he has had an operation.

If the school-age child is accustomed to spending time away from the family, and if he adjusts easily to new situations, he may look forward to his hospitalization as a new adventure. It may not be so simple for the preschooler. In spite of knowing what to expect, he may become frightened when the time comes for you to leave him at the hospital. He may feel that you are deserting him at a time when he needs you most. You may be upset by his tears. It will help you and your child if a member of the hospital staff is present just before your first leave-taking. The child will feel less abandoned if someone is at hand to comfort and cuddle him for a few moments after you leave. Do not linger after you tell him you must go. But never slip away without telling him that you are leaving and will come again.

While the child is in the hospital, he will probably spend much time alone. Let him take one or two favorite toys to play with, and bring him little surprises when you visit him. Visit him as often as you can so that he is confident that you love him and miss him.

When your child is recovering from an illness, whether after his return from the hospital, or from an illness at home, you can help make his recovery less tedious. See that he has enough suitable toys, games, and books to keep him quiet and occupied. If he has been missing classes at school, ask his teacher for work he can do at home. Then set aside time for study periods when you have the time to help and advise him. A long recovery period need not be tiresome or unproductive for your child. If you plan ahead, you can make it a time when he can profitably pursue old interests and happily discover new ones.

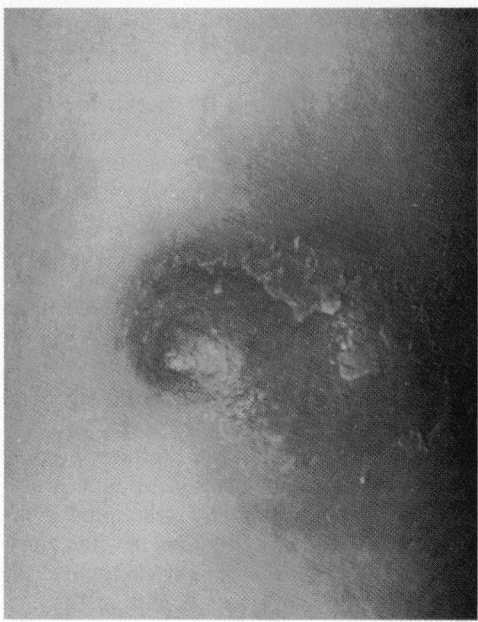

Abscesses of the skin are usually red, warm, swollen, and painful. Hot compresses often can be used to bring the abscesses to a head so that they open and drain.

Abscess is a collection of pus in any infected part of the body. Abscesses occur most commonly in the skin. They also may form around the appendix as a complication of appendicitis, or around a tooth. Perhaps the most common types of abscesses are pimples and boils.

Abscesses occur when bacteria infect body tissue. Blood flow to the area increases to fight the infection, and pus forms. Blood vessels expand to make room for the increased fluid, and the infected area swells.

Many abscesses open and drain naturally or with the application of hot compresses. Some have to be opened by a doctor. Some subside and do not have to be opened. Do not squeeze abscesses, because bacteria can get into the blood stream and cause infections elsewhere.

Keeping all parts of the body clean helps to prevent infections that can cause abscesses. Antibiotics may clear up an infection, but should be used only as a doctor directs. T.M.H.

See also **Acne**; **Boil**

Accidents. Every child gets his share of bruises, bumps, and scrapes. And minor injuries, although momentarily upsetting, may be educational in the long run. They teach the child valuable safety concepts. Of course, serious accidents are another matter.

Do all you reasonably can to protect your child from accidents. But be careful not to overprotect him and stunt his curiosity so that he gets the idea that the whole world is a dangerous place. Fit the precautions you take to the age of your child and the circumstances you live in. Certain precautions are especially necessary if you have a helpless infant or a curious toddler. Others are important if you live close to a busy traffic area, or if you have a lot of power machinery.

Protecting your baby. The younger your child, the more you must protect him. A baby, of course, requires almost total protection. Your baby's high chair and stroller should have straps to prevent his tumbling out. Do not leave him alone in an infant seat on a table, couch, bed, or car seat. The plastic seat may slide off and fall to the floor. His crib should have sturdy sides. As soon as he starts crawling, put portable gates at the tops and bottoms of stairways. And there is nothing better than a playpen to fence him in, and keep him out of mischief. However, do not pen a child in too much. Be sure that he has adequate "crawl and explore" time under your supervision.

Make sure his toys are safe. Do not give him beads or rattles that he can swallow. Avoid stuffed animals with tiny button eyes that he can pull off and swallow.

A very young baby who cannot raise his head should never sleep on a pillow. He could suffocate in it. Never cover your baby with heavy blankets or set his crib near heavy draperies that could cover his face. Thin plastic, such as that used by cleaners, is taboo in your baby's world. Never cover a crib mattress with it or leave it where your baby can grab it and pull it over his face.

Surprisingly, more children drown at home than in public pools. These are usually young children left alone in bathtubs, wading pools, or near swimming pools—sometimes for only a few minutes. Never leave your child alone in the bathtub, even to answer the phone or the door.

Curiosity and caution. As soon as your child can creep, he peeks into every corner and tries to stick his fingers and toys into electrical wall outlets. Eliminate this hazard by covering the sockets with caps that are available at most hardware stores.

To guard against electric shock, repair frayed cords and damaged appliances promptly. Have the washing machine, dryer, television set, power tools, and other large appliances equipped with ground wires that divert current harmlessly into the earth. Then, if a short circuit develops, there is no danger to a child who touches the faulty appliance. Do not allow electric appliances near water, especially at bath time. Your child may touch the appliance with his wet hands or pull it into the tub, electrocuting himself and perhaps others.

Street and automobile safety. An automobile accident is the greatest threat to your child. From the time he is able to understand, gradually teach him traffic safety—to look both ways for cars before crossing a street, to cross only with the green light or the "walk" sign, to obey patrol boys, and to walk on the left side of the road when there is no sidewalk. Point out the hazards of playing in the street and running into the road without first looking in both directions.

Your child should have a car seat, harness, or seat belt to restrain him in case of a sudden stop or an accident. These devices will greatly increase his chance of survival in a car accident. A car seat should be used for any child who weighs less than 40 pounds (18 kilograms). Do not buy a car seat that does not have a label stating that it meets federal safety standards.

Do not allow your child to stand on the seat, climb over seats, lean out of windows, or play in the rear of an open station wagon or truck. He could fall out of a window or plunge through the windshield in a quick stop. Special safety catches on doors are not necessary if the child is strapped in. Do not remove handles from the inside of doors. In an emergency, a child might be trapped inside the car.

Bicycle safety. A bicycle provides pleasure, exercise, and transportation. But it can be a hazard for your child if it is not right for his height, and if he does not know how to use it safely. Be sure your child's bicycle is sturdy, has good brakes and tires, and all the safety devices required by law.

Check the bicycle to be sure it is suitable for the child's height. Adjust the saddle so that it is parallel to the ground. Then, have your child sit on the bicycle with his thigh, leg, and heel extended down in a straight line. His foot should rest comfortably on the pedal at its lowest point. The handlebars should be about as wide as your child's shoulders. The handlebar grips should be at right angles to the handlebar stem and a little higher than the saddle.

Never buy a bicycle that is too big for your child in the hope that he will grow up to it. A bicycle that is either too big or too small is difficult to handle and may be the cause of an accident.

Your child should learn to ride his bicycle in the backyard or in a playground. Do not permit him to learn on the sidewalk, where he may run into a pedestrian, or in the street, where he may be hit by a car.

While learning the mechanics of handling a bicycle, your child should also learn the importance of courtesy and safety. He should be able to recognize traffic signs and signals. He should know and obey all traffic regulations and safety rules pertaining to the operation of bicycles in your city. No local program of bicycle safety will be successful if parents do not support it, and if they do not insist that their children obey all rules.

Caution your child against showing off on his bicycle by jumping curbs or riding without grasping the handlebar grips. Your child should not ride his bicycle at night. But if for any reason he must do so, it should be equipped with front and rear lights and he should wear light-colored clothing so that motorists can see him.

Teach your child to keep his bicycle in top condition. Check periodically to be sure the brakes are in good working order and that the handlebars are securely fastened. A well-cared-for bicycle is safer than a neglected one and will last longer.

Burns are a hazard. Fascinated by fire and sensing little danger, small children walk right up to flames. Never leave your child alone in a room with an open gas fire or a

Protect your child

Birth to 4 months
(Wriggles, rolls over)

Dangerous objects

Do not allow very small or sharp objects near your baby.

Fire

Be careful that cigarette ashes do not burn the baby. Do not buy baby clothing or blankets that are flammable.

Motor vehicles

Never park a buggy where it might roll into traffic. Your baby's safest spot in a car is strapped into a car bed on the rear seat.

Play areas

The best play areas are a padded playpen, a blanket on the floor, or a big bed.

Poisons

It is highly unlikely that a baby of this age can poison himself, but be careful that no one accidentally mixes poisonous substances in his formula. Avoid overdosage of aspirin. Check with your doctor before giving more than two doses.

Stairs, doors, windows

Do not put your baby near an open door or window that is so low that the baby could roll out. Do not park his buggy near an open stairway.

Toys

Give your baby only large, soft toys and sturdy rattles. Do not give him toys with sharp points or edges.

Water

Before your baby's bath, check the water temperature with your elbow. While bathing the baby, hold him securely. Never leave him alone in a bathtub.

Special hazards

Keep crib sides up so your baby cannot roll out. Do not leave him in an infant seat on a couch or bed when no one is with him. Do not put pillows on your baby's bed. Do not use filmy plastic sheets or coverings on his mattress.

4 to 7 months
(Begins to sit and crawl)

Dangerous objects

Keep buttons, pins, and beads out of your baby's reach. Check the floors and the playpen for small objects before letting him play there.

Fire

Never leave your baby alone in the house. Do not leave a cigarette, cigar, or pipe where your baby can reach it or knock it to the floor.

Motor vehicles

Keep your baby strapped in a bassinet or in a harness attached to a seat. Never leave him alone in a car.

Play areas

Your baby will love to play in the yard or on the porch, and possibly in a playpen. Keep these areas clean and free of things that might hurt him.

Poisons

Your baby is beginning to grab. Do not leave poisons, medicines, or other materials such as bleach, detergents, or kerosene within his reach.

Stairs, doors, windows

Put gates at stairways, porch steps, and seldom-used storage areas. Never leave your baby alone near an open stairway, door, or window that is not securely screened.

Toys

Give your baby only soft rubber and soft plastic toys. Beware of toys small enough to swallow. Do not put strings of beads across his crib.

Water

Follow the same bath routine. Never leave your baby alone near water. He can drown quickly in only a few inches of it.

Special hazards

Do not put pillows on your baby's bed or filmy plastic sheets or coverings on his mattress.

7 to 12 months

(Crawls, sits, stands, walks)

Dangerous objects

Put knives, scissors, and breakable objects high out of your baby's reach. Beware of dangling tablecloths and appliance cords. Do not use baby clothing that has bells, pompons, or loose buttons that he can swallow.

Fire

Empty ashtrays before your baby does. Never leave him in a room with an open, burning fireplace. Use a fireplace screen.

Motor vehicles

Encourage your baby to sit quietly in the car. Do not let him have suckers or ice cream on a stick while he is riding. At home, never leave him alone outside near driveways or traffic.

Play areas

The playpen is still the safest place for him.

Poisons

Lock up everything poisonous. Do not keep household chemicals under the sink. Do not leave medicine bottles or tins where your baby can get them, not even in your purse.

Stairs, doors, windows

Keep all gates closed. Keep screens locked or nailed in place. Keep dark stairs lighted.

Toys

Large blocks, a sandbox, and a wide-wheeled kiddy car are suitable toys. Never let your baby out alone on his kiddy car.

Water

Watch your baby in his bath or in a backyard pool. In a boat, every child should wear a life jacket.

Special hazards

Put safety caps on wall sockets. Prevent your baby from chewing on cords. Do not leave plastic bags lying around.

1 to 2 years

(Crawls, walks, runs, climbs)

Dangerous objects

Keep sharp tools and glass objects out of your child's reach. Do not let him eat popcorn, peanuts, or candy with nuts.

Fire

Keep matches and lighters out of his reach. Never let him near a trash burner or leaf fire. Teach him that fire is hot and will hurt him.

Motor vehicles

Teach your child not to stick his arms out of a car window and not to stand on the seat. Outfit him in a car safety harness. Teach him not to run into the street or play in the driveway or near the street.

Play areas

Fence the section of the yard where your child plays so he cannot wander into traffic. Keep an eye on him.

Poisons

Your child will eat anything and will climb great heights to get it. Lock up medicines (including aspirin), insecticides, and household chemicals (including kerosene and furniture polish). Never get your child to take pills by telling him they are candy.

Stairs, doors, windows

You may need taller gates now. Watch your child carefully. Lock gates. Do not use wax on stairs.

Toys

Everything your child picks up will go into his mouth. Avoid toys with removable parts (check the wheels on toy cars). Do not repaint toys with lead paint.

Water

Safety precautions are the same as for a younger child. Also, fence in ponds, pools, and cisterns.

Special hazards

Keep all hot appliances—toasters, irons—out of reach. Put a guard around heaters and radiators.

Protect your child

2 to 3 years
(Always investigating)

Dangerous objects

Turn in handles of pots on stove. Lock up power-operated tools. Do not allow your child near operating machinery.

Fire

Do not let your child play with matches. Never let him poke a fire. Beware of fluffy skirts around fire.

Motor vehicles

Never let your child touch the car controls. Teach him how to cross the street, but teach him not to cross it alone. Teach him the meaning of traffic lights and walk signs. Do not let him play near streets.

Play areas

Keep the play area in the yard free of dangerous debris. Check play equipment for slivers and loose bolts and nails.

Poisons

Keep all poisonous substances locked up. Never leave empty containers where your child can find them.

Stairs, doors, windows

Your child can now open doors and possibly windows. Lock those that may lead to a dangerous situation. Keep stairs clear.

Toys

Balls, blocks, and stuffed animals without bead eyes or other ornaments that can come loose and be swallowed are good toys for this age.

Water

Supervise your child's bath closely. Do not leave him alone in the bathroom. Begin to teach him how to float. Never leave him alone near a body of water.

Special hazards

Teach your child to play gently with pets and to avoid stray animals.

3 to 4 years
(Always in motion)

Dangerous objects

Same as for 2-year-old.

Fire

Same as for 2-year-old.

Motor vehicles

Teach your child never to chase a ball into the street. Make sure his seat belt is fastened before you start your car.

Play areas

Teach your child that a closed gate means he is to stay in the yard. Check his activities frequently. He is now good at climbing fences and opening locked gates.

Poisons

Same as for 2-year-old.

Stairs, doors, windows

Never let your child lean out open windows. Caution him about running up and down stairs. Tack down carpeting. Avoid using throw rugs that he might slip on.

Toys

Your child can use simple playground equipment. Check all his toys for sharp edges. Buy soft canvas swings rather than wooden ones.

Water

Start teaching your child to swim. Do not let him use an inner tube or inflated toys alone.

Special hazards

Never leave trunks or large picnic coolers where your child may crawl into them and suffocate. Warn him about the dangers of abandoned refrigerators. Do not keep such refrigerators around, or remove all their doors.

4 to 6 years
(Getting independent)

Dangerous objects

Caution your child about picking up sharp or rusty objects. Tell him to avoid broken glass.

Fire

Store flammables out of his reach. Begin to teach safety rules about fire: He should not go near brush fire. He should not turn on the stove.

Motor vehicles

Teach your child to obey traffic signals, patrol boys, and policemen. Remind him to be careful away from home.

Play areas

Take your child to park playgrounds. Teach him to use swings and slides. Supervise him carefully.

Poisons

Same as for 2-year-old.

Stairs, doors, windows

Teach your child never to lock the door to his room or the bathroom. Teach him not to pound glass. Protect the glass in storm doors with an adequate glass guard, or replace the glass with plexiglass.

Toys

Keep your child's toys in good repair, or discard them. The child can throw and catch a ball. Warn him not to dart into the street after the ball.

Water

Never let your child swim alone. Watch him closely.

Special hazards

Let your child participate in home fire drills and let him practice escaping out his bedroom window. For second floors, get a portable ladder that attaches to a window and teach him how to use it.

6 and older
(Goes to school)

Dangerous objects

Continue to lock up hazardous objects. Do not let your child use dangerous tools or power mowers. Stress that safety rules also apply away from home.

Fire

Teach your child first aid for burns, what to do if his clothes catch fire, and how to call the fire department.

Motor vehicles

Be sure your child looks both ways before crossing a street. Teach him the rules of bicycle safety.

Play areas

Warn your child about playing in construction areas, around large holes, in caves, and in abandoned or empty houses. Do not let him play in the car.

Poisons

After a child is 6 years old, he usually loses his appetite for distasteful substances that can poison him, but take no chances—tell him what substances around the house are poisonous.

Stairs, doors, windows

Tell your child to sleep with his bedroom door closed to keep out smoke in case of fire.

Toys

Games, puzzles, creative toys, sports equipment. Teach your child to handle balls and bats safely.

Water

Sign your child up for formal swimming lessons. Stress that he should "always swim with a buddy."

Special hazards

Be sure your child knows what to do if he is lost, never to go with strangers, and how to handle emergencies.

(**Accidents,** *continued*) burning fireplace. Make him keep his distance from burning trash, bonfires, and barbecues. Protect him from hot substances—turn the handles of pots and pans toward the back or center of the stove, and put the cords of electric appliances out of his reach.

Fire safety. What can you do about your child's fondness for fire? First, do not give him the chance to experiment on his own. Keep matches and cigarette lighters out of reach. As he gets old enough to understand, teach him about fire and its dangers. When you use matches, let him strike one or two while you watch. Under your supervision, let him help start the barbecue. This may erase some of the mystery of fire and keep him from secretly playing with matches.

Never leave your child alone in the house. He can kindle a fire, or a fire can spring up and trap him. A child panics easily in fire, and he may hide under a bed or in a closet. When he is old enough, teach your child how to escape from a fire, especially from his bedroom. If he sleeps on the second floor, buy him a rope ladder that fastens to a window so that he can climb down in case of fire. Encourage him to sleep with his bedroom door closed, because a door provides a barrier against fire and smoke. Teach him never to open the door if he suspects fire. He should first place his hand against the knob and panels. If the door is warm, he should not open it because there are flames and superheated air on the other side. One whiff of hot air could fell him in an instant.

Protection from poisons. Put locks on medicine cabinets, and keep other potentially dangerous materials safely out of reach. Until your child is about 6 years old, he will eat anything, including bleach, medicines, insecticides, and cosmetics. A crawler easily invades low spaces such as under-sink cabinets, so never keep household chemicals there. Older children often search for pills that they think are candy. Flavored aspirin for children is a great menace. A child can down a lethal dose of 30 to 40 tablets in minutes. Do not leave your child alone in a bedroom where a night stand holds drugs. Do not leave him alone with a purse containing drugs. Never encourage your child to take medicine by telling him it is candy.

A child of 6 is less likely to drink bad-tasting substances. But he develops new fascinations just as dangerous, such as guns, machinery, and fire. He is no longer idly curious. He is intensely serious about discovering how things work.

Guns are deadly. It is not enough just to hide a gun, no matter how secret the spot. Many a child has found not only the gun, but also the ammunition. Often he inserts the bullets, fires the gun, and kills a playmate or parent or himself. Lock up empty guns and the ammunition in separate places so your child cannot discover both at once. Never allow a loaded gun in the house.

Power machinery is treacherous. A young child should not be allowed around farm machinery, power tools, and power mowers unless he is carefully supervised. Do not allow your child near a power mower while it is being operated. The mower may throw off stones, wire, or even broken blades at tremendously high speeds. You can lessen the hazard by picking up such objects before mowing.

Do not let an older child operate a power mower, power tools, or other hazardous machines without close supervision. And remember that a child may sneak into a workshop and try his skill, to be "just like daddy." So equip stationary tools with key-operated switches or plugs, and lock portable tools in a cabinet.

Swimming safety. One of the most important lifesaving skills your child will learn is swimming. You can teach him yourself, or you can put him in a class run by professional instructors. Issue strict orders about swimming—that he should never swim alone, and never in quarries or other unsupervised areas. Teach him how to give artificial respiration and other elementary first aid.

Avoiding animal bites. In many instances, the child, and not the animal, is the cause of a bite. To protect your child from animal bites, teach him these safety precautions.

- Never touch a sick or injured animal.
- Never try manually to stop a fight between animals. Call an adult or use a stream of water from a hose.
- Never take food away from an animal.
- Never pet strange animals. M.G.

Acne is a condition in which the sebaceous (oil) glands become overactive and inflamed, causing a breakout of pimples on the skin. In severe acne, infections and abscesses form in the oil glands. The disease may leave scars if there are large abscesses.

Acne develops mainly on the face, but it may also appear on the chest and back. It can occur at any age, but it develops most often during adolescence. Doctors believe that during adolescence, hormones produced by the adrenal glands increase the activity of the oil glands. Doctors do not know why some children develop acne and other children do not.

Severe acne and consequent scarring can be reduced if the child carefully cares for his skin and watches his diet.

- The affected skin should be cleansed thoroughly at least three or four times a day with warm water and soap. This cleansing helps keep the openings of the oil glands from becoming clogged.
- The child should not squeeze or pinch pimples.
- He should keep his hair clean.
- He should not take any medicine unless the doctor advises it. For example, iodides and bromides should be avoided.

A balanced diet is also important. The child should not eat fatty foods, nuts, seafood, cola drinks, chocolate, and sweets such as pie, cake, candy, ice cream, or cookies. Milk should be kept to a minimum. The child should drink about one pint (0.5 liter), preferably skimmed, daily.

Encourage your child to follow his doctor's instructions. The doctor may advise antibiotics, astringent lotions, vitamins, special surgery, or exposure to sunlight or ultraviolet rays. A happy environment, proper exercise, and adequate rest are also important. With proper care, the child's acne should become less severe or disappear after a few years.

Many young people worry excessively about skin disorders and become discouraged while trying to clear them up. You can reassure them by pointing out that acne is a normal—although annoying—part of growing up. A.M.M.

See also **Abscess; Endocrine glands; Hair care; Nutrition; Vitamins**

Location of the adenoids

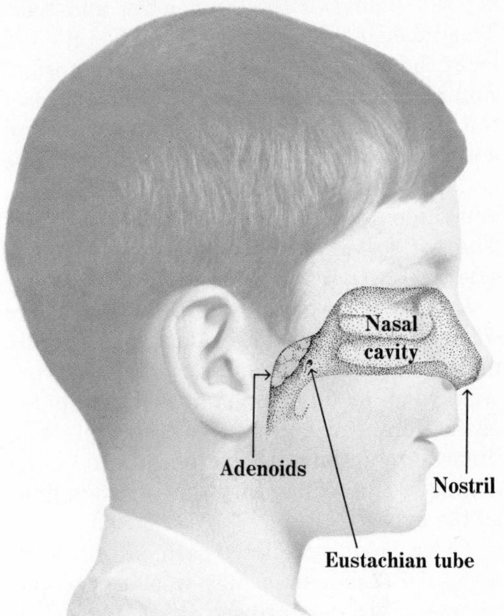

The adenoids are located in the back of the throat, behind the nasal cavity. They help fight infection.

Adenoids are clusters of lymphoid tissues which grow high up in the back part of the throat, directly behind the nasal cavity. Healthy adenoids may help to prevent or overcome infection.

If the adenoids swell (usually because of an infection), they may block the passage from a child's nose and force him to breathe through his mouth. Or they may block the opening to the Eustachian tube (the passage leading to each middle ear). This may cause ear infections or impair hearing. If a child has frequent nose and throat infections, the adenoids may become infected and cause fever.

The adenoids may have to be removed surgically if they obstruct nasal breathing, obstruct the Eustachian tube, cause recurring nasal or ear infections, or impair hearing. However, doctors can often successfully treat these conditions with medication to shrink the tissues and with antibiotics to treat the infection. C.F.F.

See also **Anesthetics; Earaches; Swollen glands; Tonsillitis**

Albinism is the absence of pigment (a coloring substance) in the skin, eyes, and hair. This inherited disorder results when a child lacks the enzyme needed to produce normal skin pigment. Albinism may be total or partial. In total albinism, the child's skin and hair are milk-white or platinum colored. The child's eyes are extremely sensitive to light, and the pupil and iris have a pinkish color. The eyes are weak and may also waver from side to side in a searching motion.

A child with partial albinism may have white skin patches. The patches are usually present at birth. The child might have a triangular- or diamond-shaped white patch on his forehead and a streak of white hair immediately above the forehead. In ocular albinism, the pigmentary defect is confined to the eyes.

There is no specific treatment for albinism. An albino child may wear tinted eyeglasses if his eyes are sensitive. He should wear the proper clothing to protect his skin and sunglasses to protect his eyes from excessive exposure to sunlight. M.G.

Allergy is an abnormal reaction to substances that are neither harmful nor infectious to most people. Children of parents who are allergic inherit the tendency to become allergic, but do not necessarily inherit the same allergy that the parents suffer.

Substances that cause allergic reactions are called allergens. They include foods, drugs, pollens, airborne mold spores, animal dander (particles from hair, feathers, or skin), household dust, bacteria, viruses, parasites, and other substances. Light, heat, and cold may also cause allergic reactions. Emotional factors aggravate allergies, and a doctor will take them into consideration when treating a child who suffers from such allergies as hives, eczema, or asthma.

Allergens may enter the body by being inhaled, eaten, drunk, touched, or injected. When they enter the body, the allergic person develops antibodies. The interaction of the allergens and the antibodies releases histamines and other chemical substances that circulate throughout the body and cause allergic symptoms.

Allergic symptoms may occur in any part of the body. When they occur in the respiratory tract, the child may appear to have a cold—he sneezes, his nose runs or is stopped up, or he wheezes, coughs, and has trouble breathing. When allergic symptoms appear in the skin, the child may have a rash or wheals (flat, hard ridges on the skin that usually itch). When symptoms occur in the central nervous system, the child may be irritable and have headaches or seizures. When they occur in the gastrointestinal tract, the child may have cramps, nausea, vomiting, or diarrhea. These reactions are often completely reversible so that no permanent damage results. Doctors often prescribe antihistamines and other drugs to relieve symptoms.

An allergy may develop at any time during a person's life. It usually develops gradually. At first, the body does not react to the substances. But, as exposure continues, an allergy results. Doctors do not know why one child develops an allergy to a substance that is harmless to another child.

Common allergies. Four common allergies that children develop are asthma, eczema, hay fever, and hives.

Asthma affects the bronchial tubes. Common symptoms are coughing, wheezing, and labored breathing. The coughing commonly occurs at night. In children older than 9 months, the wheezing usually occurs when they exhale. In infants, the labored breathing is rapid and the child seems short of breath. Children 3 years old or older also feel tightness in the chest, or breathlessness. Common causes of asthma are airborne allergens and respiratory infections.

Eczema is a rash that occurs in patches on the skin and itches intensely. The patches may be red and oozing or crusting. Or they may be thickened, dry, and scaly. Foods, drugs, inhalants, and allergens that touch the skin are common causes.

Symptoms of hay fever include sneezing, stuffiness or blockage of the nose, runny nose, watering of the eyes, and itching of the eyes, nose, ears, and the roof of the mouth. Pollens, airborne molds, and house dust are usually responsible for hay fever.

Hives are raised, whitish wheals with reddened edges. The wheals usually itch.

Foods, drugs, and insect bites are common causes of acute (sudden and severe) hives.

Some children outgrow their allergies. Others develop complications and become worse. About one half of all allergic adults developed allergies before they were 11 years old. If you think that your child has an allergy, consult your doctor. How much treatment is required depends on the severity of symptoms.

Determining allergies. A doctor begins the search for the cause of an allergy by compiling a detailed history of the illness, especially the events preceding the first attack. He tries to relate the symptoms to foods eaten, to substances inside and outside the home, to the time of day, to the season, and to other factors. Usually a doctor can determine the possible allergen through this history. He may prescribe removing the suspected allergen from the child's diet or his environment to determine if the substance is causing the reaction. For example, a child who coughs when he goes to bed at night, and for a short time in the morning, may stop coughing when his feather pillow is replaced with one to which he is not allergic.

Unfortunately, treatment is sometimes complex. Often allergic symptoms result from a combination of several allergens. Also, there may be persisting factors such as house dust, animal dander, or airborne molds. And, the attack may be triggered by infections, emotional upsets, weather changes, or simply an overload of allergens.

Skin tests help identify possible allergens. These tests are simple, not painful, and can usually be done in a few testing sessions.

- Using the scratch test, the doctor makes small, light scratches, usually on the child's arms or back. On each scratch, he places a small amount of a suspected allergen. If the child is allergic to the substance on one of the scratches, that area becomes red, swollen, and itchy.
- In another method of testing, the doctor injects a small amount of the possible allergen under the child's skin and waits about 10 to 20 minutes for a reaction.
- With an infant covered with eczema, or with a highly emotional older child, the doctor may use the indirect, or passive transfer, method. A blood sample is taken from the child and, after preparation, is injected into the skin of a nonallergic adult who then becomes temporarily sensitive to possible allergens. The following day, a suspected allergen is injected into the same skin site on the nonallergic adult. If there is no reaction in the adult, then the child is presumed not allergic to that particular substance. This test is limited in use because of the danger of transmitting serum hepatitis, and because the test can be neutralized by food eaten or drunk by the nonallergic adult.
- In the patch test, the doctor places the possible allergens on unbroken skin and covers them, usually for 48 hours, to determine what substances may produce an allergic reaction upon contact.

Skin tests, however, are limited in their usefulness. There is no correlation between the size of the reaction and the child's sensitivity. And, not every positive skin test is significant because irritants such as tobacco, cow hair, mustard, cottonseed oil, and spinach can cause false positive tests. Also, with few exceptions, food allergies are not reliably detected through skin testing. The food may cause an allergic reaction only after it has been altered by digestion. Consequently, foods are often tested through a controlled diet. Avoiding the suspected food allergen should bring relief from allergic symptoms. Including it again in the diet should produce the symptoms. Eggs, fish, nuts, beans (which include peanuts), pork, and milk are common food allergens.

Treatment. Doctors may treat allergic disorders such as hay fever and asthma by a series of shots over a period of years. Repeated injections of gradually increasing doses of the responsible inhalant allergens help build up resistance to these allergens.

Doctors usually treat an allergy by eliminating the allergen from the child's surroundings. For instance, it is easier to remove a dog or cat, feather pillows, or a wool rug from the child's home because immunization is generally ineffective.

When a particular food is the allergen, the doctor may suggest eliminating it from the child's diet. For example, if milk is the allergen, all foods that contain milk—such as ice cream, cheese, and butter—must be eliminated. Immunization against food

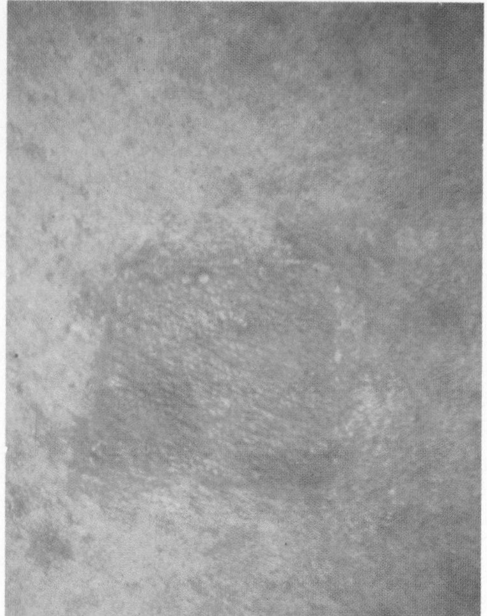

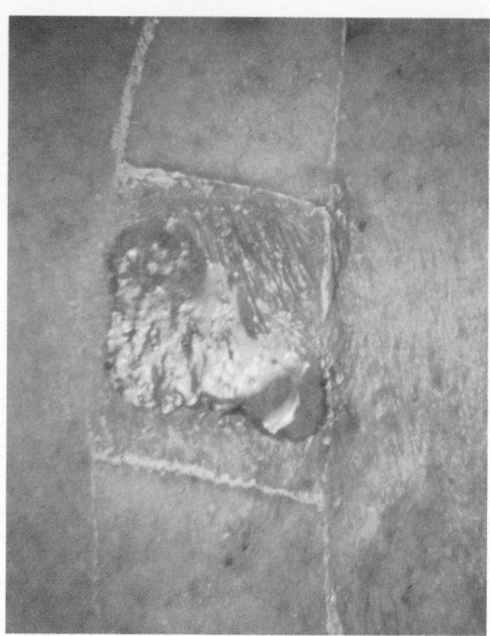

Doctors sometimes use patch tests to determine if a child is allergic to a substance upon contact. Possible allergens are placed on unbroken skin, covered, and left touching the skin. These pictures show two different reactions. The one on the left is moderately severe, the one on the right is very severe.

(**Allergy,** *continued*) allergens is not practicable, because there is no proof yet that it is effective.

In rare instances a child is so allergic to the venom of bees, wasps, yellow jackets, hornets, spiders, or ants that he may have a serious or fatal reaction. He should have a special medical kit for emergency treatment if he is bitten or stung. The doctor will probably advise shots to desensitize the child to stinging insects.

If your child suffers from a respiratory allergy, your doctor may also suggest some of the following procedures to help reduce airborne allergens in your home and make the child's bedroom as dust-free as possible.

- Use an air conditioner that filters out pollen.
- Eliminate woolen rugs and blankets, stuffed toys, and feather pillows from the child's room.
- Enclose the child's mattress and box spring in heavy plastic or latex muslin to prevent dust from escaping into the air.
- Do not keep pets that have fur or feathers.
- Do not use Venetian blinds, cotton draperies, curtains, bookcases, upholstered furniture, or other dust-collecting objects in the child's room.
- Avoid smoking in the house or automobile, because smoke irritates the mucous membranes in the respiratory tract.

Children who are extremely sensitive to certain foods or drugs should wear a warning bracelet or necklace bearing this information. A bracelet may be purchased from the Medic Alert Foundation, 1030 Sierra Drive, Turlock, California 95380.

Preventing allergic reactions. If you have a strong family history of allergy, consult your doctor to attempt to prevent allergies in your child. The doctor may recommend starting your infant on prepared milk formula or milk substitutes. He may also recommend that you slowly introduce new foods, and that you not give the baby foods of high allergy potential, such as uncooked cow's milk, eggs, and wheat, until he is from 10 to 12 months old. J.S.H.

See also **Asthma; Eczema; Hay fever; Hives**

Anemia is a condition that results from a reduction in the number of red blood cells, or a reduction in the amount of hemoglobin in the red blood cells. Hemoglobin is made up of iron and protein and gives the red color to red blood cells. The hemoglobin in the red blood cells picks up oxygen from the air that a child breathes into his body and carries this oxygen to all of his body tissue. When the number of red blood cells or the amount of hemoglobin in these cells is reduced by anemia, the child's body does not receive enough oxygen to function properly.

A child with anemia is usually pale, and he may not feel as energetic and playful as he usually does. If anemia is severe and comes on suddenly, the child may be without energy, short of breath, and critically ill. If you think that your child is anemic, consult your doctor. He will probably take a blood sample to determine if the child has anemia.

The most common cause of anemia is insufficient iron in the child's diet. Between the ages of 6 months and a year, a baby may become anemic if he receives only milk, because milk lacks iron. Meats, iron-fortified cereals, egg yolk, and vegetables are necessary and should be added to the diet. Your doctor may also prescribe iron tonic.

Sometimes, a child's diet contains plenty of iron, but the child's body does not absorb enough of it. During certain long-lasting diarrheas, iron is not absorbed by the intestines. The diarrhea must be controlled before the anemia can be corrected by iron tablets or tonic. In rare instances, injections of iron may be necessary.

Loss of blood from an injury, from an ulcer, from hemophilia, or from other bleeding diseases may also cause anemia. This anemia is cured by stopping the bleeding and, if necessary, by the giving of blood transfusions.

Some anemias, called hemolytic anemias, are caused by the destruction of red blood cells. Hemolytic anemias may be inherited or acquired. Sickle cell anemia is an inherited hemolytic anemia. Some acquired hemolytic anemias are caused by sensitivity to certain drugs or plants. F.O.

See also **Bleeding; Blood count; Hemophilia; Leukemia; Nutrition**

Anesthetics are most commonly used to eliminate the feeling of pain. Doctors usually give them to a child who is having an operation.

There are two kinds of anesthetics—local anesthetics and general anesthetics. Local anesthetics eliminate pain in a small area of the body but they do not cause unconsciousness. The anesthetic is usually given by injection. Doctors use local anesthetics for such operations as the stitching of a cut or the pulling of a tooth. This is the safest form of anesthetic, but it can seldom be used for large operations.

General anesthetics eliminate pain over the entire body. They cause partial or complete unconsciousness. General anesthetics affect the brain directly and block reception of pain. The most common way of administering a general anesthetic is to have the child breathe the drug, which is given in the form of a gas. Intravenous drugs such as sodium pentothal, while frequently used with older children and adults, are seldom used for infants and young children.

Before receiving a general anesthetic, a child is not given anything to eat or drink for several hours. This allows his stomach to empty so that while he is unconscious he will not vomit and possibly breathe the food into his lungs.

Preanesthetic medications are given by injection to the child an hour or two before the operation. They decrease the secretions in the child's air passages so that he can breathe easily during the operation. And they make him drowsy or unconscious before he reaches the operating room, to lessen chances of his being frightened.

Major operations, and in small children many minor operations, are carried out under general anesthesia. The administration of anesthesia is no more risky in children than in adults. Even premature, newborn infants can be safely anesthetized. The day before an operation, the person who will give the anesthetic usually explains to the child how it will be administered.

Parents can ease a child's apprehension before an operation by explaining the purpose of the surgery, the sequence of events before, during, and after the operation, and any discomfort involved. T.M.H.

Anorexia nervosa is an extreme form of very poor appetite or self-starvation. It occurs mainly in girls about 12 to 14 years of age. The cause is an emotional or cultural one.

The condition may begin when the child goes on an extreme diet because of a fear about being fat. This may lead to a refusal to eat or self-induced vomiting after eating. The amount of weight loss may not be appreciated by the parents until it is extreme. It may be accompanied by a failure to menstruate.

In spite of the loss of weight, the child may not only continue normal activities but may even exercise quite vigorously. Some children show signs of depression.

Although anorexia nervosa may be mild, it is generally a severe and chronic problem. It may even result in death. Children are usually hospitalized under the care of a physician and a psychiatrist. M.G.

See also **Appetite; Diets; Overweight; Underweight**

Location of the appendix

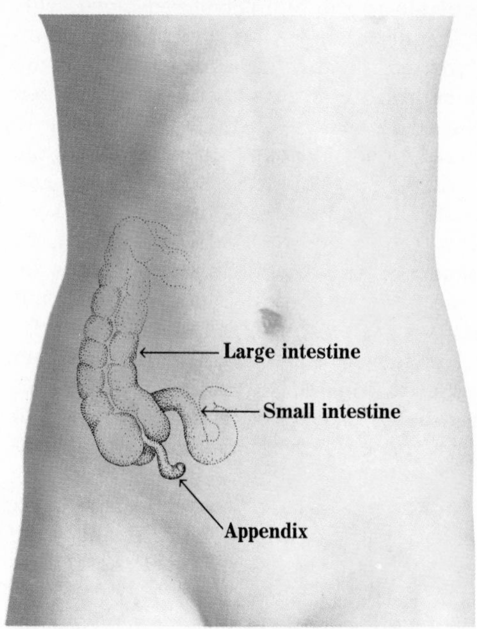

The appendix is a small sac in the lower right abdomen. One end of the appendix is attached to the large intestine.

Antibiotics. *See* **Drugs**

Antidote. *See* **Poisoning and poisons**

Antihistamine. *See* **Allergy**

Appendicitis is an inflammation of the appendix, a narrow tube in the lower right part of the abdomen. One end of the tube is closed. The open end of the tube is attached to the large intestine. If the appendix becomes infected, it becomes inflamed. It swells and fills with pus. If a surgeon does not remove the inflamed appendix within 24 to 48 hours, it may burst and cause peritonitis, an inflammation of the lining in the abdominal cavity.

Appendicitis occurs most commonly in school-age children and young adults, but it can occur in younger children, too.

Acute (sudden and severe) appendicitis usually begins with vague, general abdominal pain which localizes within four to eight hours in the right lower abdomen. The abdomen may become tender. The child may vomit, he may run a fever, and he may feel constipated. Laxatives may aggravate the dangers of appendicitis. Never give laxatives or cathartics (such as Epsom salts or castor oil) for abdominal pain unless advised to do so by a doctor.

Children complain of abdominal pain often, but the pain is usually caused by something other than appendicitis. For this reason, many parents wait dangerously long before seeking medical aid. If your child's abdominal pain lasts for more than an hour, call your doctor. Doctors estimate that about one-third of the small children with appendicitis have ruptured appendixes before they reach a hospital.

A child who has an unruptured appendix removed usually stays in the hospital for three to five days. Normally, he can return to school 7 to 10 days after the operation. A child who has a ruptured appendix removed stays in the hospital about 10 days. Normally, he can return to school a week or two after coming home. T.M.H.

See also **Anesthetics; Laxatives; Stomach-ache**

Appetite. Whether a child has a good or poor appetite depends mainly on his experiences with food. Of course, his appetite may be temporarily affected by an illness such as a cold or chicken pox, or by an emotional upset. But his day-to-day appetite is probably determined by his early experiences with food. From infancy on, he gradually forms impressions of food that are based on emotional reactions. A baby experiences hunger pains when he needs food. When he eats, the hunger pains stop. So his first reaction to food is pleasant. Gradually, he recognizes his mother as the giver of food. If his mother is loving and tender when she feeds him, he begins to associate food with love. But, if she fails to feed him when he is hungry, if she appears uninterested in him, or if she forces him to eat when he is not hungry, he may have mixed feelings.

How can you promote good appetite?

- Give food only to satisfy your child's hunger. Do not force him to eat. Do not use food as a reward (by giving him sweets when he is good) or as a punishment (by denying him sweets when he is bad).
- Respect your baby's appetite as the best indicator of how much food he needs. For several months after his first birthday, he generally needs less and eats less food. You may think that he is not eating enough because he is no longer growing at a tremendous rate. However, you may be surprised to discover that he is gaining weight.
- Respect your baby's continuing development in feeding practices. Let him feed himself when he wants to, even though he may be messy for a time.
- As your child gets older, do not let him drink milk at the expense of other food.
- When preparing food, make it as attractive as possible. Consider color, odor, texture, and arrangement on the plate. Children are sensitive to these factors.
- A child likes foods that he can handle easily—foods that he can eat with his fingers and foods that are cut into bite-size pieces.
- Present new foods in small quantities. And, be patient. It may take several times before a child gets used to the new food.
- And remember, mealtimes should be happy occasions, free of struggle. M.G.

See also **Nutrition; Vitamins**

Arthritis is an inflammation of body joints. A joint may swell and become painful, and the skin covering the joint may be red and feel warm. The joint becomes stiff and its movement limited. Arthritis can result from injury or infection. Usually, its exact cause is unknown. If you suspect that your child has arthritis, consult your doctor.

Rheumatoid arthritis is the most common form of arthritis in children, especially children between the ages of 2 and 6. Doctors do not yet know what causes rheumatoid arthritis. Usually, only one or two joints, such as the knee or ankle, are affected. However, the disease may affect many joints. The joints can become dislocated, deformed, or fused. Rheumatoid arthritis usually lasts for several years. Your doctor may prescribe drugs to reduce inflammation and relieve pain. He may also suggest exercises that concentrate on using the joints afflicted by arthritis.

Infectious arthritis, which also affects children, usually follows an infection somewhere in the body, often in the upper respiratory tract. Bacteria cause pus to form in joint cavities. Usually, only one or two of the larger joints, such as the hip, shoulder, or knee, are affected. The child may also have fever and chills. Doctors usually treat this condition with antibiotic drugs and by draining the pus from the affected joint.

Rheumatic fever is a serious childhood disease that may cause temporary arthritis. (This form of arthritis is not connected with rheumatoid arthritis, which usually lasts for several years and can cause permanent crippling.) Usually, the larger joints, such as the ankles, knees, hips, wrists, elbows, and shoulders, are affected. The arthritis tends to move from one joint to another, with any one joint being affected from a few days to several weeks. This type of arthritis is generally treated with drugs to relieve pain and reduce inflammation.

Other forms of temporary arthritis may also affect children. For example, a child may injure a joint—most commonly a knee joint—and develop arthritis in that joint. Occasionally, a young child develops a brief episode of arthritis of the hip from an unknown cause. M.G.

See also **Osteomyelitis; Rheumatic fever**

How to give mouth-to-mouth artificial respiration

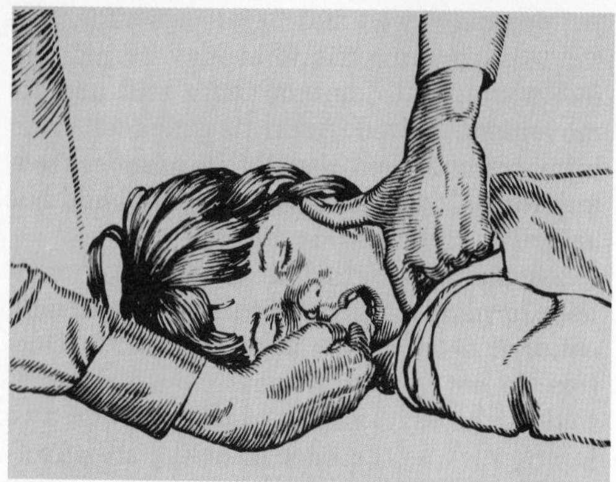

1. Place the victim on his back, on a firm surface, and turn his head to one side. Use your fingers to remove any foreign object, such as chewing gum, food, or vomit, from the child's mouth.

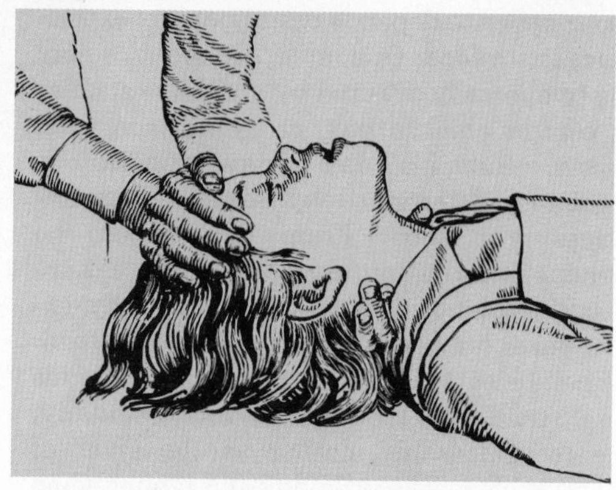

2. Place one hand under the victim's neck and the other hand on his forehead. Then tilt the head back. If the head is not tilted back, the tongue may block the throat.

3. If the victim is a small child or infant, take a shallow breath and cover both the nose and mouth of the victim with your mouth. Blow into the mouth and nose every three seconds.

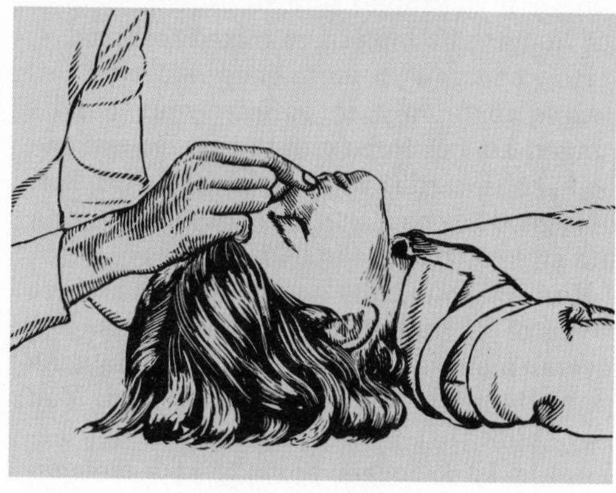

4. If the victim is a large child or adult, pinch the nostrils shut with the thumb and index finger of the hand pressing on the forehead. This will prevent any leakage of air.

5. Take a deep breath and cover the victim's mouth with your mouth. Blow into the victim's mouth. For a large child or adult, you should provide about one breath every five seconds.

6. Watch the victim's chest. When it rises, turn your head to the side and listen for a return rush of air. When the victim has finished breathing out, repeat step 3, or steps 4 and 5.

Artificial respiration. When a child's breathing stops for any reason, quickly apply artificial respiration while someone else calls for additional help. If the child's breathing has stopped because of drowning, lay him on his stomach, turn his head to the side, and press down on his back before you start artificial respiration. This clears water from his throat and trachea.

The aim of artificial respiration is to open the passage from the lungs to the mouth, and to move air in and out of the lungs by alternate expansion and contraction of the chest.

Mouth-to-mouth artificial respiration (also called mouth-to-mouth resuscitation) is the most effective type you can use with children. It provides positive pressure to inflate a child's lungs immediately. It also enables the person giving respiration to judge the volume, pressure, and timing needed to inflate the lungs. When giving artificial respiration to a child, take relatively shallow breaths to match the child's own small breaths—about one every three seconds.

When you blow into a child's mouth (or mouth and nose), his lungs should fill with air and make his chest expand. If the chest does not expand, something is probably still blocking the flow of air to the lungs. Check again to be sure there is nothing in the child's mouth. Also check to be sure you have his chin pointing upward and his lower jaw pulled forward.

If, after rechecking the child's mouth and his chin position, you still have been unable to get the child to breathe, quickly turn him on his side and slap or punch him sharply—several times—between the shoulder blades. This should dislodge any foreign matter that you may have overlooked in the upper throat. With a very small child, you may be able to clear the air passages by holding him upside down by the ankles for a moment, or by holding him head down over one arm, and giving him two or three sharp pats between the shoulder blades.

Continue artificial respiration until the child's normal breathing resumes or until professional help arrives. M.G.

Asphyxiation. *See* **Suffocation**

Aspirin poisoning. *See* **Poisonings and poisons**

Asthma is an allergy that affects the bronchial tubes. It causes coughing, wheezing, and labored breathing. Breathing is obstructed by the swelling of the mucous membranes of the bronchial passages, by muscle spasms in the walls of the bronchial tubes, and by the excessive secretion of a thick, sticky mucus. The onset of asthma may be abrupt or gradual. An attack may be mild, or it may be severe enough to require hospitalization.

Childhood asthma is usually caused by inhalants (substances that float in the air, such as house dust, molds, pollen, and animal dander—particles from animal skin, hair, and feathers) or respiratory infections. Less often, emotional problems or foods may bring on or aggravate an asthmatic attack. Air pollutants, barometric pressure, humidity, changes in temperature, and other factors may also provoke asthma.

Any child with asthma should be under a doctor's care. A child rarely outgrows asthma without treatment by a doctor. If asthma is neglected, it often recurs for many years, and it may permanently damage the child's lungs and chest wall.

In treating asthma, the doctor tries to determine the substance or substances causing the attack. He will want to know if the child has had previous or associated allergies. He will also want to know the frequency of the asthma attacks, circumstances surrounding the attack, foods the child eats, pets the child is exposed to, and other details of the child's life. He may also perform skin tests or have the child inhale possible allergens to determine what airborne substances the child is sensitive to.

The doctor may treat the symptoms of asthma with drugs to widen the bronchial tubes by relieving bronchial spasms and shrinking the mucous membranes. He may prescribe breathing and physical fitness exercises. He will probably suggest eliminating dust, feathers, pets, wool, or other substances from the child's surroundings. Immunization to build up a child's resistance to airborne substances is helpful. The child's adenoids and tonsils may be removed surgically if they obstruct breathing or if they are frequently infected. J.S.H.

See also **Allergy**

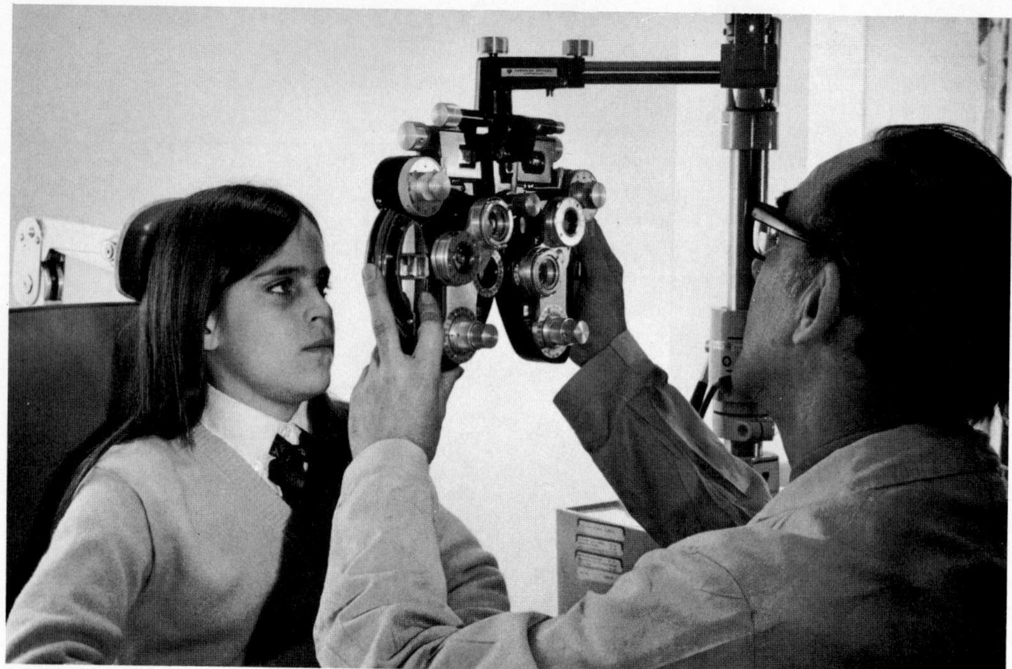

An eye examination is necessary to determine accurately whether or not a child has astigmatism. Astigmatism can be corrected by glasses or contact lenses.

Astigmatism is a defect of the eye that makes images appear distorted or blurred. It occurs when the lens or the cornea of an eye is improperly curved. Because of this defect, not all the rays of light from an object fall evenly on the retina. Some rays focus in front of the retina, some on it, and some behind it. Both near-sighted and far-sighted eyes can be astigmatic. The condition is a common one and seldom is a serious handicap. It can be corrected by glasses or contact lenses. Eight out of 10 children have some degree of astigmatism.

Astigmatism is difficult, if not impossible, to diagnose without a careful eye examination. But there are some signs that may indicate the condition. Occasionally, in more severe forms, a child may hold his head at an angle to make up for a blurred image. In milder forms, the constant effort of the eye to overcome the irregularly blurred images may result in headache, fatigue, irritability, or eyestrain. R.O.S.

See also **Eye health; Far-sightedness; Headache; Near-sightedness**

Ataxia is a lack of muscle coordination. A child with ataxia moves unsteadily and staggers when he stands or walks. He may turn awkwardly, and frequently he may bump into objects such as tables and chairs. All children have an ataxic gait when learning to walk, but a child who is developing normally should have a smooth gait by the time he is 3 years old. If you suspect that your child has ataxia, consult your doctor.

Ataxia usually indicates that the part of the nervous system that controls balance and coordination is not functioning properly.

Here are some causes of ataxia.

- Infection of the nervous system
- A tumor in the nervous system
- A hereditary disease that affects the nervous system
- Lead poisoning
- Hysteria
- Overdoses of sedatives, or of medicines that prevent convulsions or vomiting. A.G.S.

See also **Cerebral palsy; Hysteria**

Athlete's foot. *See* **Ringworm**

Bandage. *See* **Bleeding; Cuts and scratches; First aid**

Bed-wetting. *See* **Wetting**

Birthmark. Many children have birthmarks, but most birthmarks are small and do not impair a child's health in any way. Many disappear if they are let alone. Others last throughout a person's life. Some "birthmarks" do not appear until years after birth. If a new birthmark appears, or if an old one suddenly seems to be growing, consult your doctor. He will want to examine it to be sure it is not harmful to the child's health. For example, a birthmark that suddenly starts to grow may develop sores and may become infected.

Red birthmarks are the most common. They are caused by slightly enlarged or prominent blood vessels in the skin. Black or brown birthmarks, often called moles, occur because of increased amounts of pigment in the skin.

Salmon-patch birthmarks are light red or pink blotches commonly found on the back of the neck, on the forehead, and on the eyelids. They usually disappear by themselves during childhood.

Strawberry birthmarks are bright red, spongy in texture, and elevated from the skin surface. Most of these birthmarks disappear by the time the child reaches 3 to 5 years of age. But if one starts to grow rapidly, consult your doctor. He may treat small strawberry birthmarks by freezing them with carbon dioxide snow. Occasionally, he may remove the birthmarks surgically.

Port-wine birthmarks are flat and purplish-red. They are commonly found on the face or neck. A few may become lighter in time, but they rarely disappear. You may wish to use a special cosmetic to cover them.

Mongolian spots are blue marks on the buttocks or lower back. They usually disappear during childhood.

Some mothers of children with birthmarks wonder whether experiences or thoughts they may have had during pregnancy could have caused the marks. No evidence supports such a notion. A.M.M.

See also **Moles**

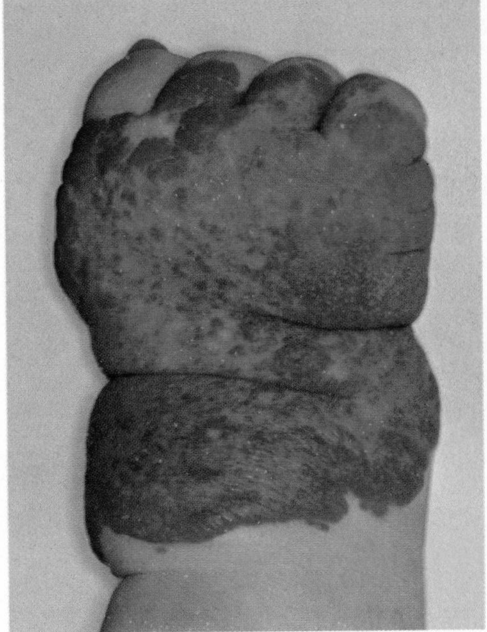

Some birthmarks disappear by themselves. The baby shown above was born with a birthmark on his hand and wrist.

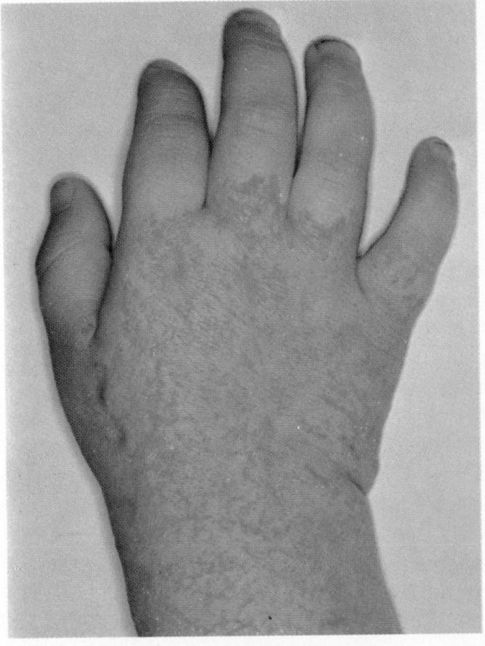

Three years later, the birthmark on the baby's hand and wrist had almost disappeared even though it was not treated in any way.

Bites and stings are common hazards of childhood. Some bites and stings require little treatment—nothing more than washing with soap and water. Others are serious injuries that call for treatment by a doctor.

Mammal bites. The mouths of animals contain a variety of germs that may cause infection or a serious disease. Rabies, one of the most serious diseases, destroys nerve cells in part of the brain and almost always results in death. The rabies virus lives in the saliva of many kinds of animals. The disease is most commonly transmitted by dogs, but it may also be spread by other mammals, including cats, bats, foxes, and skunks. To prevent rabies, have your pet dogs and cats vaccinated. Also, report all stray dogs and cats to the police or health authorities.

The circumstances surrounding the animal bite help determine the treatment. The child may be bitten by a family pet that has been vaccinated against rabies. For minor wounds that are no more than a scratch, wash with soap and plenty of warm water, and rinse thoroughly. Then cover the wound with a bandage strip or a sterilized gauze dressing. If the scratch becomes inflamed, call your doctor. If the bite is a puncture wound, wash the wound with soap and water, and call your doctor.

If your child is bitten by a stray mammal, wash the wound with soap and water, and call your doctor. If your child has a cut, scratch, or other wound on his skin and this wound comes in contact with the saliva of a stray mammal, follow the same procedure. If the animal can be captured, it is usually kept under observation by a veterinarian so he can find out if it has rabies. If your doctor suspects that it has rabies, he will start rabies inoculations for the child immediately. If the animal cannot be captured, he may give the injections as a precaution.

Ratbite fever is also transmitted through a bite. If your child is bitten by a rat, wash the wound with soap and water, then call your doctor or take the child to a hospital emergency room. The doctor may administer antibiotic and tetanus shots.

A human bite that breaks the skin can also cause a severe infection. Wash the area with soap and water. Then consult a doctor immediately.

Snakebites. If your child is bitten by a snake, it is important to know whether the snake is poisonous. A nonpoisonous snakebite is no more harmful than any other animal bite. Wash the bite with soap and water, then call your doctor.

Recognizing poisonous snakes. There are two types of poisonous snakes in the continental United States—coral snakes; and pit vipers, which include rattlesnakes, copperheads, and cottonmouths (water moccasins). Rattlesnakes are the only poisonous snakes found in Canada.

Poisonous snakes can often be identified by the following characteristics.

- Both pit vipers and coral snakes have two fangs along with their normal teeth.
- A pit viper has a pit on each side of its head, between its eye and its nostril.
- Most rattlesnakes have noise-making rattles on the end of their tails.
- Coral snakes have black snouts and fairly wide red and blackish-blue bands, separated by narrower yellow bands.

If you cannot find the snake that bit the child, you may be able to tell if the snake was poisonous by asking the child whether he is in pain, or by observing the bite area for swelling and discoloration.

The bite of a harmless snake may produce mild pain, but the pain rarely lasts and it does not spread. A child bitten by a poisonous snake almost always feels deep, burning pain. If the bite is that of a pit viper, the pain usually spreads. If the bite is that of a coral snake, the pain does not spread.

A nonpoisonous snakebite rarely produces swelling. If swelling does occur, it does not spread. The bite of a pit viper produces swelling within three to five minutes. The swelling usually spreads rapidly toward the trunk of the child's body. The bite of a coral snake does not cause swelling.

A perfect bite pattern of two fang marks generally indicates the snake is poisonous. However, the bite pattern is not always a reliable sign because it may be obscured by marks inflicted by the snake's other teeth.

Poisonous snakebites. If your child is bitten by a poisonous snake, he needs immediate medical attention. Call a doctor or take the child to a hospital. If possible, kill the snake and keep it for identification.

Common poisonous spiders and snakes

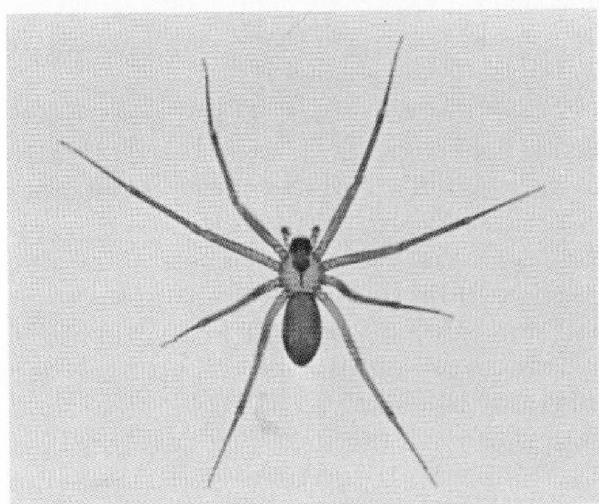

Both the brown recluse spider (*left*) and the black widow spider (*right*) have distinguishing marks. The brown recluse spider has a dark violin shape on its head. The black widow spider has a red or yellow hourglass shape on its abdomen.

The best way to identify a coral snake is to remember the distinctive color pattern— red bands touch yellow bands.

The body of the western diamondback rattlesnake has a pattern of brown diamonds, edged with a light-colored border.

The copperhead has broad, brown, X-shaped bands on its light-colored body. The top of its head is copper colored.

The eastern cottonmouth usually has broad dark bands on its body. This pattern may become obscure as the snake grows older.

(Bites and stings, *continued*) Activity causes the poison to spread more rapidly, so keep the child as still as possible until medical help arrives, or until you can get to a hospital. If the bite is on an arm or leg, tie a bandage above the wound, between it and the heart. Make sure that you can wedge a finger under the bandage. Release the bandage for 90 seconds every 10 minutes to prevent damage from lack of blood circulation. If possible, hold an ice pack over the bite to slow the spread of the poison and to reduce the pain. The doctor will remove venom from the wound and give the child antivenin, tetanus immunization, and, possibly, antibiotics.

If the child has symptoms of poisoning—pain, swelling, numbness, difficulty breathing—and you cannot get the child to a doctor or a hospital within 30 minutes, continue first aid. Sterilize a knife or razor blade and make an "I" shaped cut through—and slightly below—each fang mark. Make the cut no longer than ½ inch (12 millimeters). Cut through the skin, but not deep enough to sever muscles and nerves.

Apply suction to the cut or cuts with a suction or bulb syringe found in many first-aid kits. Or, if you have no cuts or open sores in your mouth, suck and spit out the poison. Rinse your mouth. Continue suction for 30 to 60 minutes, or until the swelling stops spreading. Take the child to a hospital.

Insect, spider, and tick bites. Most insect and spider bites are more annoying than serious. Put calamine lotion, an ice cube, a drop of household vinegar, or a thick paste of baking soda and water on the bitten area.

Two spiders dangerous to man are the brown recluse spider and the female black widow spider. The brown recluse spider is found in at least 17 states—Alabama, Arkansas, Colorado, Georgia, Illinois, Indiana, Kansas, Kentucky, Louisiana, Mississippi, Missouri, North Carolina, South Carolina, Ohio, Oklahoma, Tennessee, and Texas. Because it hides in dark places—wadded-up newspapers, bedding, clothes, or shoes—it can be easily transported by travelers to new areas. The black widow spider is found in nearly every state and in Canada.

Bites from either of these spiders produce a burning sensation, followed by severe cramps in the abdomen, chest, and legs. If you suspect that your child has been bitten by a brown recluse spider or a black widow spider, call your doctor.

Ticks are parasites that suck blood through a hooked beak that they fix tightly in their victim's skin. If your child has been in a tick-infested area, examine him carefully for ticks, especially along his hairline.

A few drops of turpentine or petrolatum will make a tick loosen its hold. Holding a hot match or lighted cigarette near the tick may also be effective. Working gently and slowly, remove the tick with tweezers or a piece of paper. If you tear the tick loose, its mouth or other body parts may stay in the skin and cause festering sores. Also avoid crushing the tick. Ticks often carry germs which they transfer to their victims. Scrub the area from which the tick is removed with soap and water for five minutes. If the bite becomes inflamed and swollen, or if the child runs a fever, becomes weak, or develops a rash, call your doctor. M.G.

See also **Allergy**

Bleeding, if excessive, must be controlled promptly because it can be fatal. Stop excessive bleeding before you take precautions against infection. An infection can be treated later with drugs and antibiotics, but profuse bleeding is an immediate threat.

You can control severe bleeding by firmly pressing a folded towel, handkerchief, or other cloth pad directly over the bleeding wound. Hold the pad of cloth in place with your hand until you can fasten it in place with a bandage. Do not remove the cloth. If blood seeps through, cover the first cloth with another pad of cloth. If bleeding is severe, and the blood is red and spurting, do not wait to find a bandage or pad. Use your hand. And try to remain calm—both to reassure your child, who will probably be frightened, and to ensure that the steps you take are the proper ones.

Bleeding of the foot, leg, hand, or arm will stop sooner if you elevate the limb. Have the child lie down, and place a pillow or a folded blanket or coat under the limb. Then, apply direct pressure to the wound and bandage it.

How to stop bleeding

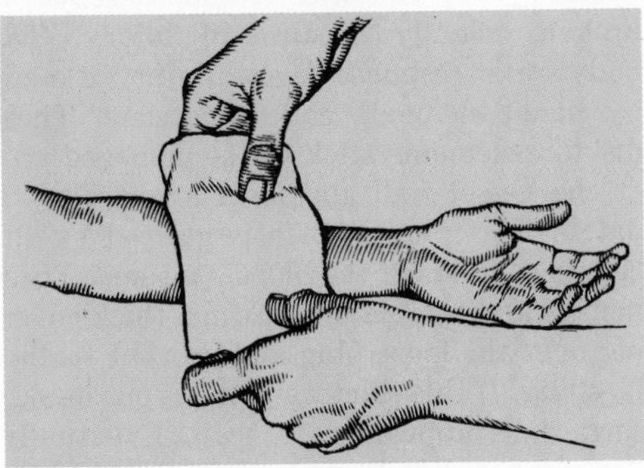

1. Fold a piece of cloth into a pad and place it on the bleeding wound.

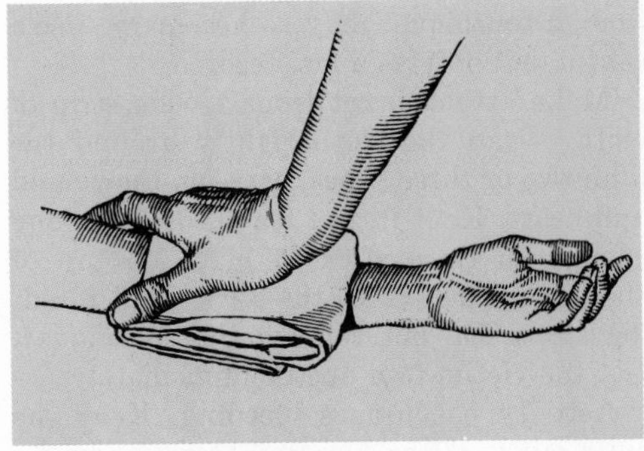

2. Then, press the cloth pad firmly against the bleeding wound.

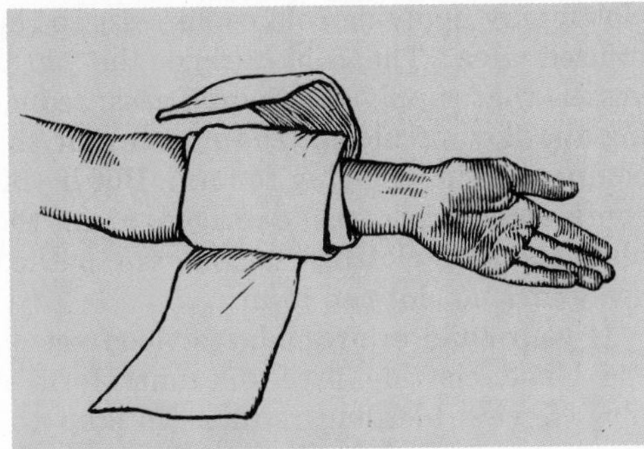

3. Wrap a strip of cloth around the pad and the injured part of the body.

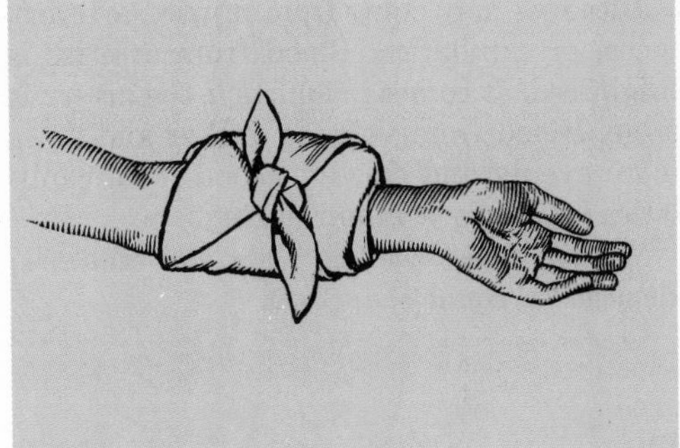

4. Tie the cloth strip to hold the pad in place over the wound.

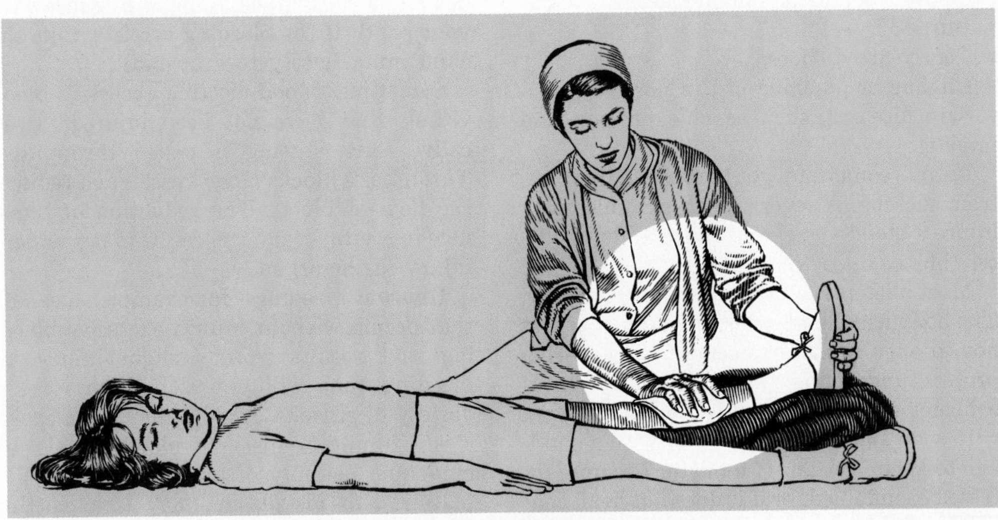

You can stop bleeding from a limb more quickly if you have the child lie down. Next, elevate the limb by placing a pillow, a folded coat, a folded blanket, or some other object under the injured limb. Then place a folded cloth pad over the wound and apply direct pressure.

(**Bleeding,** *continued*) If pressure does not control bleeding, and the bleeding is in a limb, a tourniquet may be necessary. Use a tourniquet only as a last resort.

Make a tourniquet from a wide strip of cloth. Wrap the cloth tightly around the limb two or three times, between the wound and heart. Knot it, but leave the ends long enough to tie a stick in place on top of the knot. Then twist the stick until bleeding stops. Do not remove the tourniquet. Get the victim to a doctor immediately.

Activity encourages bleeding. Keep the child quiet. If the bleeding seems to be severe or persistent, or to come from a large vessel, take the child immediately to a hospital emergency room.

Bleeding may come from injured arteries, veins, or capillaries. Blood from arteries is bright red. It comes in spurts if the artery is large. Blood from veins is darker and flows more evenly and slowly. Blood from capillaries is usually a minor oozing. M.G.

See also **Blood clotting; Cuts and scratches; Hemophilia; Nosebleed; Shock**

Blister is a collection of fluid under the skin which causes the top layer of skin to puff out. Blisters can be caused by many things. Here are the most common causes.

- Burns
- Poorly fitted shoes
- Chafing or pinching of the skin
- Skin diseases, such as chicken pox and impetigo

Infants sometimes get blisters on their lips from sucking. A severe pinch or bruise may injure a blood vessel and cause a blood blister (blister filled with blood).

Most blisters require no special treatment. The body usually absorbs the fluid. It is best not to open a blister, because the covering protects underlying tissues from infection. If a blister opens accidentally, wash the area with soap and water, and cover with a bandage to keep it clean. If a blister becomes infected or inflamed, or if it does not heal, consult your doctor. A.M.M.

See also **Burns; Chicken pox; Fever blisters; Frostbite; Impetigo; Poison ivy, oak, and sumac; Sunburn**

Blood clotting helps to stop bleeding. Bleeding starts when a blood vessel is broken, usually because of injury. The body's first response to such injury is made by blood elements called platelets. These disklike elements stick to the damaged area of the vessel wall and form a soft plug or patch. This plug is then reinforced by the clotting factors of the blood's plasma. These factors and the platelets form a thick covering over the loose plug and prevent further bleeding. If this thick covering is on the skin surface, it appears as a scab. Eventually, the plug is dissolved as the injured tissue heals.

Bleeding from small blood vessels usually stops within 5 to 10 minutes. You can help clotting by applying cold compresses to the injured area. The cold shrinks the blood vessels that supply the injured area, reducing the flow of blood. The pressure of the compress helps the plug to form. But if you continually wash the damaged area, the platelets and clotting factors are bathed away and no clot can form.

If your child injures a large blood vessel, the blood clotting process cannot form a plug. Severe bleeding results. To stop the bleeding, apply direct pressure to the wound. Fold a towel or handkerchief into a pad, and hold it on the wound. If you cannot find a cloth quickly, apply pressure with your hand. If the bleeding persists, take the child immediately to a hospital.

Sometimes blood clotting occurs in blood vessels that have not been injured physically. This clotting is called thrombosis. Thrombosis blocks blood vessels and reduces the flow of blood. The reduction of blood flow to a vital organ can result in permanent injury to the organ.

Unusual bleeding—for example, bleeding that occurs without injury, excessive bleeding that results from a slight injury, or bleeding that will not clot—occurs for a variety of reasons. A child may have excessively fragile or diseased blood vessels, an inadequate supply of platelets or defective platelets, or his plasma may lack clotting factors. The lack of clotting factors is known as hemophilia. F.O.

See also **Bleeding; Blood count; Hemophilia; Nosebleed**

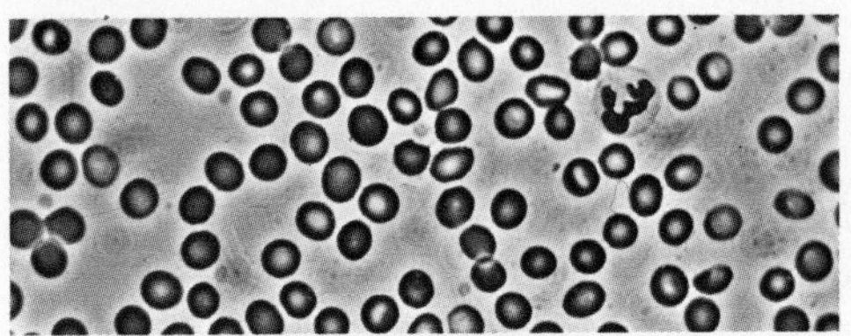

This blood sample is magnified and stained for examination. It is taken from a child who has a normal blood count. The red blood cells are doughnut shaped. The large cell in the upper right corner is a white blood cell. A normal blood count is one sign of good health.

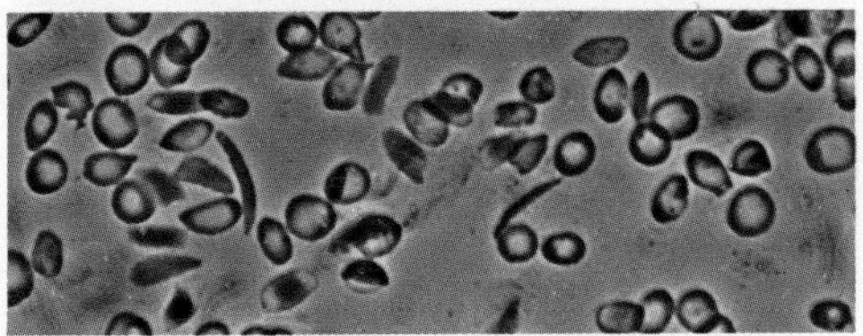

This magnified, stained blood sample is from a child with sickle cell anemia—a hereditary, permanent anemia. In this type of anemia, from 50 to 90 per cent of the red blood cells are shaped like sickles.

Blood poisoning is an infection of the blood stream caused by microbes such as bacteria, fungi, and protozoa. Although microbes may enter the blood stream directly at the time of an injury, they usually get into the blood by way of an infection that already exists in the body—for example, appendicitis, pneumonia, a boil or a pimple, a sore throat or tonsillitis, or an infected tooth.

A child with blood poisoning may run a fever and develop a skin infection. As the infection spreads through the body, a red streak may run up an arm or leg, and the lymph glands in the armpits or groin may become tender. This is an emergency. Call your doctor immediately, or take the child to the nearest hospital, where antibiotics can be administered to fight the infection.

Blood poisoning occurs more frequently in babies than in older children because babies seem less able to keep infections from spreading. In rare instances, a child's body cannot produce the antibodies needed to protect him against infection, and he has blood stream infections repeatedly. H.D.R., JR.

Blood count is an actual count of the cells in a precisely measured drop of blood. The blood sample is usually taken from one of the child's fingers or one of his earlobes. The count is done by examining the drop of blood under a microscope. Blood contains many different cells that perform special jobs in the body. The most important cells are the red cells, the white cells, and the platelets. Healthy blood contains these cells in certain proportions.

Red cells get their bright coloring from hemoglobin, which contains iron. Hemoglobin absorbs oxygen from the lungs and carries it to the body tissues. White cells attack germs to prevent infection. Platelets, which look like tiny disks, assist in blood clotting.

A blood count can give a doctor vital information. For instance, a low count of red blood cells may show that a child has anemia. An increase in white blood cells may indicate an infection. A normal blood count is one sign of good health. F.O.

See also **Anemia; Blood clotting; Blood type**

Blood type. Everyone's blood contains inherited chemical substances known as "blood factors." Various combinations of these factors determine a person's particular blood type. You should know your children's blood type.

One type of blood is just as healthy as another. But if a blood transfusion is necessary, it is important to know that the blood of patient and donor will mix without serious reaction. If they do not mix, certain combinations of factors may cause red blood cells to clump together. This clumping blocks small blood vessels and can cause serious illness or even death. Blood typing makes safe transfusion possible by ensuring that the blood of donor and patient will blend.

There are four major human blood groups —A, B, AB, and O—and many subdivisions. Blood is further classified as Rh-positive and Rh-negative. F.O.

See also **Rh factor**

Blue baby. *See* **Cyanosis**

Boil is a painful abscess under the skin that develops when a sweat gland, an oil gland, a small wound, or a hair follicle (the sac containing the hair root) becomes infected and fills with pus. If one boil develops, others often follow. Several boils formed close together constitute a carbuncle. The bacteria that cause boils are almost always present on the skin, but they cause infection only occasionally. Squeezing of pimples or failure to keep the skin clean may cause boils.

When a boil is developing, the area first is red and tender. Considerable swelling and pain may develop. Gradually, pus forms and the center of the boil becomes yellowish.

Moist heat helps keep the infection from spreading and draws the pus to a head so it will drain. Soak a towel in warm water and apply it to the boil for 20 to 30 minutes every 4 or 5 hours. Be careful that the towel is not so hot that it burns the child's skin. The boil may subside and not have to be opened or it may come to a head, erupt, and drain. If your child has boils frequently, have him examined by a physician. T.M.H.

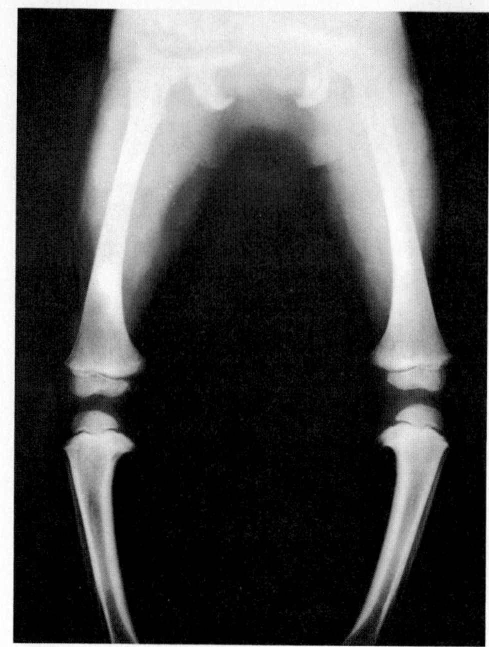

This X ray shows the leg bones of a child who was born with bowlegs. The child's knees turn out and his feet turn in.

Bowlegs. Almost every new baby appears to be bowlegged. The knees are held out and the feet are slightly turned in. Although the bones themselves are usually well formed and straight, the legs tend to remain in the position they were in before birth.

A baby does not lose his bowlegged appearance until he has been walking well for some time. He must first strengthen his ankle and foot muscles, and the muscles and ligaments of his legs and knees. As these muscles become stronger with walking, the legs gradually look straighter and the knees come closer together. Usually, a baby loses his bowlegged appearance when he is between 1 and 2 years old.

If you are concerned that your baby may be too bowlegged, or if his legs have not straightened by the time he is 2 years old, have your doctor check the position of the legs to make sure they are all right.

In some cases, bowlegs may result from rickets, caused by a vitamin D deficiency. A few cases of bowlegs require medical treatment of braces and surgery. J.J.G.

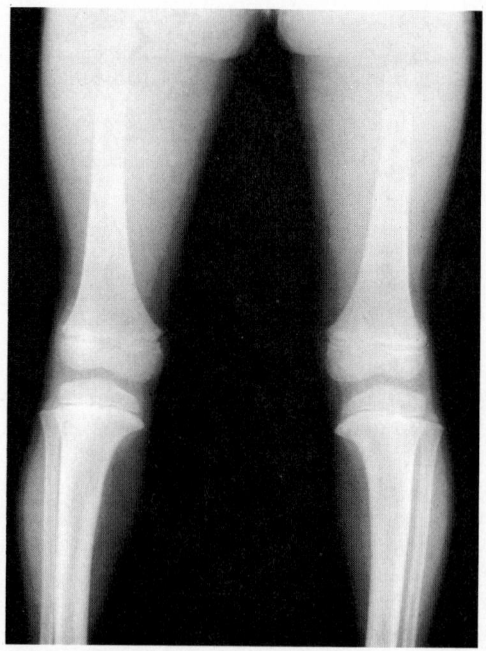

This X ray of the same child shows how much the legs were corrected after 4½ years of medical treatment.

Braces, dental. If your child has malocclusion (poor bite), his dentist will probably suggest that you take him to an orthodontist (a dentist who specializes in correcting irregularities of the teeth and jaws). Malocclusions are corrected with braces.

The orthodontist will X-ray the child's teeth and make study models of the mouth so that he can be sure of the irregularity that needs correction. He will make regular and thorough examinations, adjusting the braces as the teeth move into their proper positions. He will also give instructions on keeping the teeth and braces clean. For instance, he will tell you that a child wearing braces should not chew gum or eat sticky candy.

Many parents worry that their child will suffer severe pain during orthodontic treatment. A child may occasionally experience some discomfort, but at no time should there be severe pain. Some parents worry that continued use of braces may cause tooth decay. If the child practices good dental hygiene, this should not happen. M.G.

See also **Malocclusion**

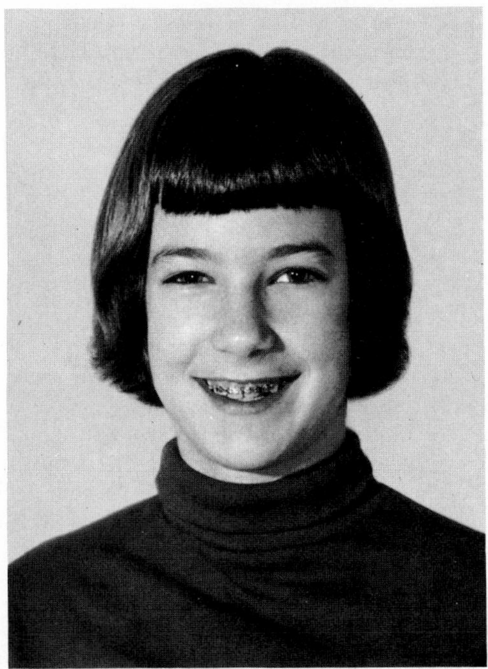

Dentists use braces to correct irregularities of a child's teeth.

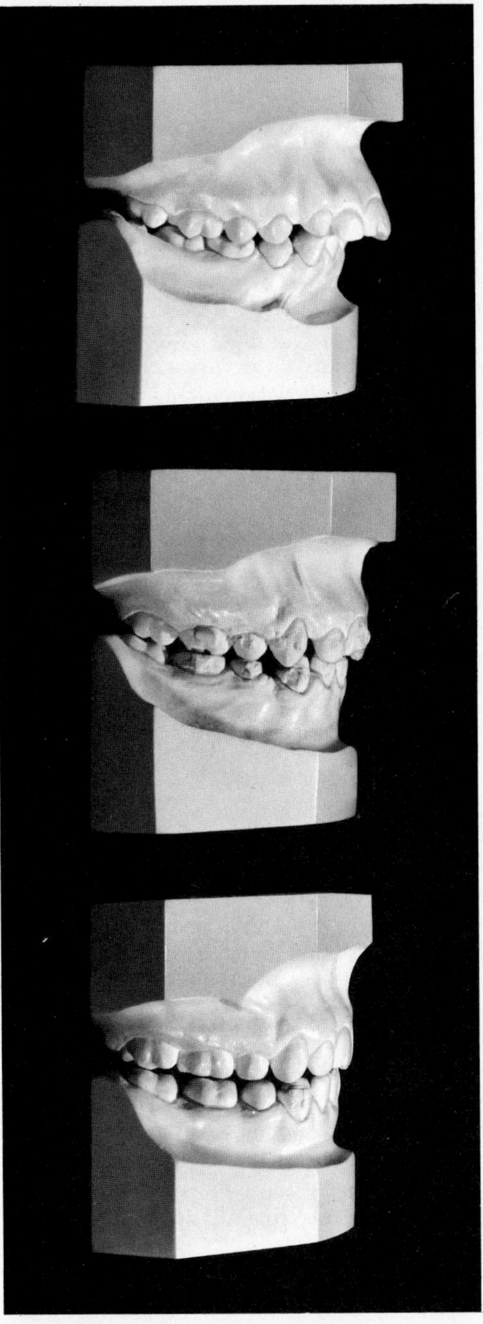

These three sets of plaster casts were made from the same boy at various times during treatment for malocclusion. The first set shows the position of the boy's teeth before braces were applied. The second casts, made about a year later, show the progress of straightening. The third casts show the position of the teeth after treatment was completed.

Breath-holding. It is not uncommon for children around the age of 1 year to hold their breath. Almost always there is a definite cause—anger, frustration, fright, or injury. A breath-holding spell usually begins with vigorous crying. The child then suddenly gasps and holds his breath until he turns blue or pale. He may even pass out briefly. If he does, the reflex mechanisms of breathing will take over, and he will come to in a few moments.

Few things frighten a parent more than seeing his child hold his breath. There is one good rule to follow when this happens: Do nothing at all. Usually the spells are not dangerous. If the child faints, place him on his side. Open his mouth so that excess saliva will flow out and not choke him. As he recovers, try not to show concern.

If your child frequently holds his breath, or if he has convulsions when he holds his breath, consult your doctor. He may be able to help you discover why the child holds his breath and how you can prevent it. M.G.

See also **Convulsions; Fainting**

Broken bones, also called fractures, are fairly common during childhood. There are several types of fractures.

- In a simple (closed) fracture, the broken bone does not cut through the skin.
- In a compound (open) fracture, a sharp end of the bone sticks through the skin. Compound fractures are more serious because of the danger of infection.
- A greenstick fracture is a type of simple fracture that occurs most commonly in children. It is a partial break in a bone. Children's bones are soft, and, like a green stick of wood, they may bend and splinter on one side.
- In an epiphyseal fracture, the growing ends of the long arm and leg bones break off or separate. This type of fracture can occur only in children. It most commonly occurs at the wrist and ankle.

Some fractures are not immediately apparent. But if the area around an injury swells and becomes very painful, call your doctor.

An obvious fracture requires immediate attention. Here are some emergency first-aid measures.

- Do not move the injured part, and do not let the child move it. Moving the sharp, broken ends of a bone may injure nerves, blood vessels, and muscles, or cut through the skin. It is especially important not to move the child if you suspect a back, neck, or head injury.
- Let the child lie where he is.
- Keep him quiet.
- To treat for shock, cover him with a blanket or with clothing.
- Then call the police or fire department for emergency help in getting the child to a hospital.

If no trained emergency help is available, put a splint on the injured part to prevent further injury when the child is moved. Do not try to straighten the injured part. Gently bind it to a board or firm object, such as a tree branch or a piece of cardboard. If possible, pad the splint by wrapping cloth around it.

- If there is a broken bone in the upper arm, and if the arm is in a bent position, use a splint that extends from the armpit to below the elbow.
- If there is a broken bone in the upper arm, and if the arm is straight, use a splint that extends from the armpit to the child's fingertips.
- If there is a broken bone in the lower arm, use a splint that extends from the armpit to the fingertips.
- For a broken wrist, use a splint that extends from the fingertips to the elbow.
- For a broken bone in the thigh, use a splint that extends from the foot to the child's armpit.
- If a bone in the lower leg is broken, use a splint that extends from the foot to the hip.
- If a bone in the ankle or foot is broken, use a splint that extends from the foot to the knee.

If a child's back is injured, and if it is essential that you move him, he should be lifted on a wide board so his back will not bend. Also, if it is essential that you move a child with a suspected neck injury, he should be carried with his head held firmly so that his neck does not move. J.J.G.

See also **Dislocation of joint; Shock**

Emergency splinting

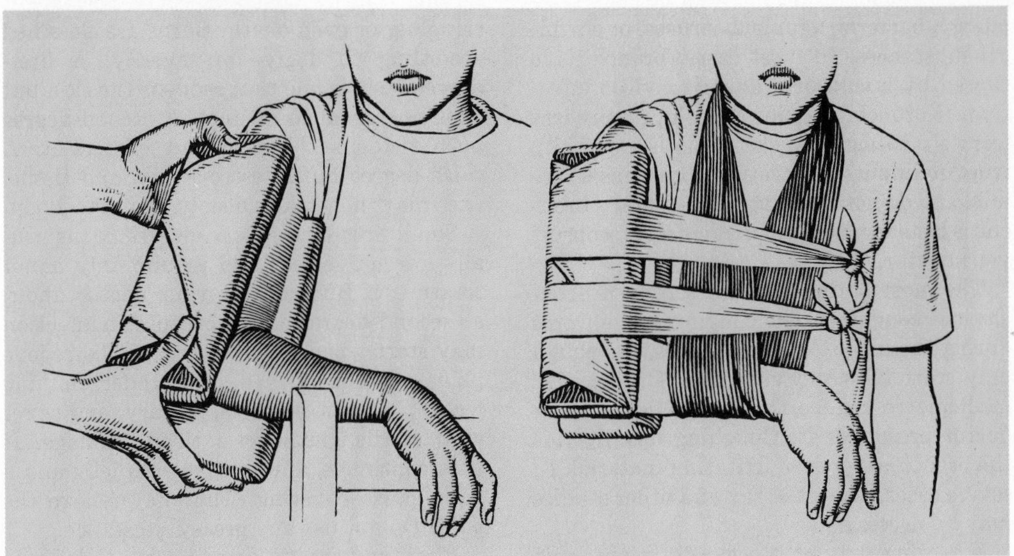

If you must apply a splint to the upper arm, and the arm is bent, use splints that reach from the armpit to below the elbow. Use a sling to support the lower arm. Then tie the splints snugly around the child's body with strips of cloth.

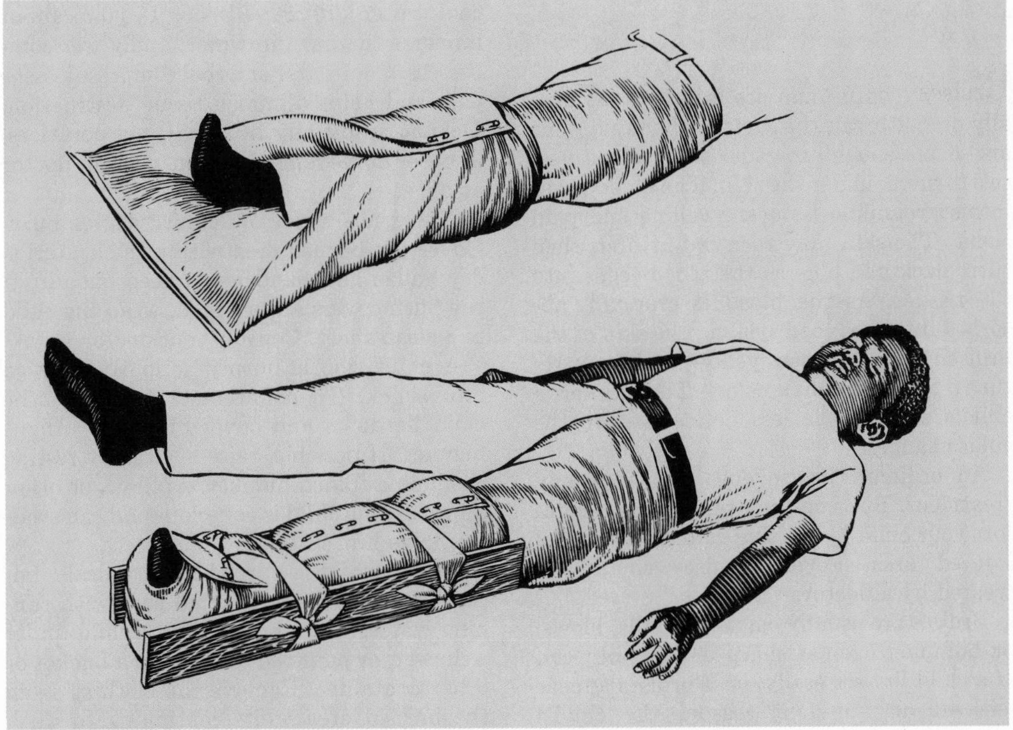

A pillow splint provides stability for a broken bone in a child's foot or ankle. Gently wrap the pillow around the foot and leg. Next, secure the pillow with safety pins. Then tie the splints snugly around the child's leg with strips of cloth.

Bronchitis is an inflammation of the lining of the bronchial tubes. It may be caused by allergy, bacteria, a fungus, viruses, or chemical substances. In most cases, bronchitis is caused by a cold or a lingering virus infection. If bronchitis follows a cold, it may last from six to eight weeks. This is especially true in infants. However, most cases are mild and do not last long. If the child's bronchitis lasts for more than a few days, consult your doctor.

The most bothersome symptom of bronchitis is coughing. The cough may be worse during the night. In severe cases, the cough may start the child vomiting. Do not give medicine to reduce the cough unless your doctor prescribes it. Coughing usually rids the bronchial tubes of irritating material. In severe cases, a chest X ray and other studies may be necessary.

Wheezing may also occur in infants and young children with bronchitis. Humidifying the child's room may help relieve the wheezing. M.G.

See also **Allergy; Colds; Coughing; Humidifying**

Bruises (contusions) are injuries that usually do not break the surface of the skin but are severe enough to cause small blood vessels to break under the skin. The blood oozes into surrounding tissues. Swelling and pain occur. The skin may turn red at first, then turn black and blue as the blood seeps into the tissues. As the blood is gradually absorbed into the blood system, the skin of the bruised area becomes yellow and then returns to its normal color. The darker a child's skin is, the less noticeable are the color changes.

An ordinary bruise does not need any treatment. But you may reassure and comfort your child by putting cold cloths on the injured area. Severe bruises should be treated by a doctor.

Bruises are usually caused by falls, blows, or bumping against sharp or hard objects. If a child bruises easily, or if bruises appear without any obvious reason, the child's blood may not be clotting normally. Inform your doctor. M.G.

See also **Blood clotting; Hemophilia**

Burns range from minor annoyances to serious injuries that can cause permanent crippling or even death. Burns are classified according to degree of severity. A first-degree burn is one that reddens the skin but does not produce blisters. A second-degree burn reddens the skin and blisters it. A third-degree burn destroys skin and tissue, and may penetrate deeply into the body.

Small first- and second-degree burns usually are not serious and require only minor treatment. But consult your doctor about all second-degree burns, because an infection may start when a blister breaks. To relieve pain, put the burned area under running water for a few minutes, pat dry, and cover with sterile gauze or a clean bandage. If pain continues, apply petroleum jelly and a light gauze covering. This may relieve the pain. Do not use any greasy substance.

First- and second-degree burns that cover a large area are more serious. Wrap the child in a clean sheet to avoid infection and take him to a hospital emergency room. If this is not possible, immerse the burned area in cool water (70° F.; 21° C). If you cannot immerse the burn in water, apply wet compresses. Cool water or a cool compress lessens pain and helps diminish tissue destruction. Do not apply oily mixtures, tea poultices, or other home remedies. Consult your doctor at once.

Never use water on a third-degree burn. Cover the burned area with a thick, sterile, dry gauze and bandage to keep out air. If the burn covers a large area, wrap the child in a clean sheet. Consult your doctor.

A child who is burned seriously may go into shock. To counteract this, have the child lie down and cover him with a light blanket. If possible, raise his legs by resting them on a folded blanket, a pillow, or other object. If the child is conscious and can swallow, give him water.

If your child is burned by chemicals, immediately wash the affected area with running water. Use a hose, put the child under a shower, or pour the water from a bucket or other container. Remove the clothing from the burned area while continuing to wash with water. Then, continue first aid, as for other burns. T.M.H.

See also **Accidents; First aid; Shock; Sunburn**

First aid for burns

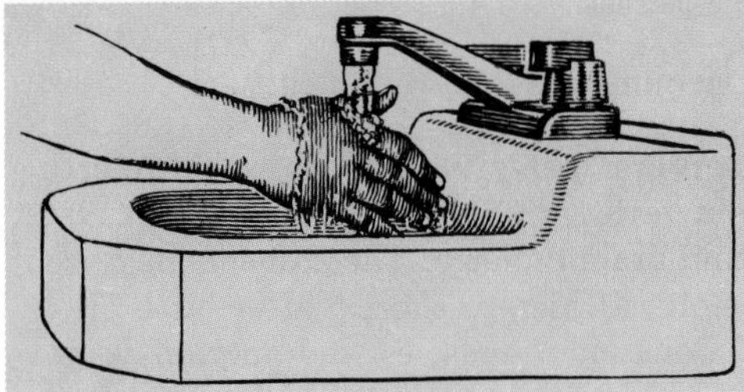

For minor burns, run cold water on the burn for several minutes. If pain continues, apply petroleum jelly and a light gauze dressing over the burn.

If the burn is a major one and you cannot get the child to a hospital immediately, immerse the child or the burned part of his body in cool water.

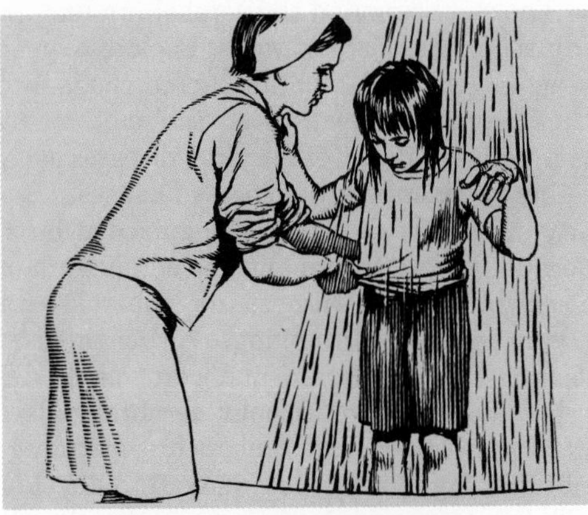

For chemical burns, immediately flood the burn with flowing water. Remove the child's clothing while rinsing the burn.

Cancer is a disease in which there is a rapid, uncontrolled growth of abnormal cells in the blood or other body tissue. The abnormal cells destroy normal ones and take their place. If cancer goes unchecked, it can spread from one part of the body to another, and may cause death. Although cancer in children is not common, it kills more children between the ages of 1 and 14 than any other disease. Scientists do not know exactly what causes cancer.

If cancer attacks the blood, an excessive number of white blood cells are produced. This condition is called leukemia. It is the most common type of cancer in children. First signs of leukemia may include anemia, tiredness, loss of appetite, enlargement of lymph glands, and prolonged and unexplained low-grade fever (up to 101° F.; 38° C). Leukemia is fatal in most cases.

If cancer attacks the body tissue, it appears as a tumor (a lump or swelling). Not all tumors are cancerous. Those that are not are called benign tumors.

Cancerous tumors may occur anywhere in the body—the bones, the eyes, the lymph glands, the muscles, the skin, the testes. Any lump or swelling which can be seen or felt and which is growing rapidly may be a sign of cancer. Other symptoms include weight loss, unexplained anemia, unexplained fever, and failure to thrive.

Tumors of the brain may cause a child to walk unsteadily. They may also cause severe headaches, repeated vomiting, convulsions, cross-eye, double vision, and unconsciousness. Tumors of the spinal cord often cause trouble with walking, stiffness of the back, or difficulties with urinating.

Doctors use blood counts, X rays, and bone marrow examinations to diagnose cancer. Generally, physicians prefer to remove all tumors—both benign and cancerous—surgically. If the tumor is cancerous, the surgeon often removes surrounding tissue to be certain that he is removing all of the cancer cells. Otherwise, the cancer may begin to grow again. Doctors also use radiation therapy and drugs to help fight cancerous tumors. The curing of a tumor depends on the type it is, where it is located, and its stage of development. M.G.

See also **Leukemia**

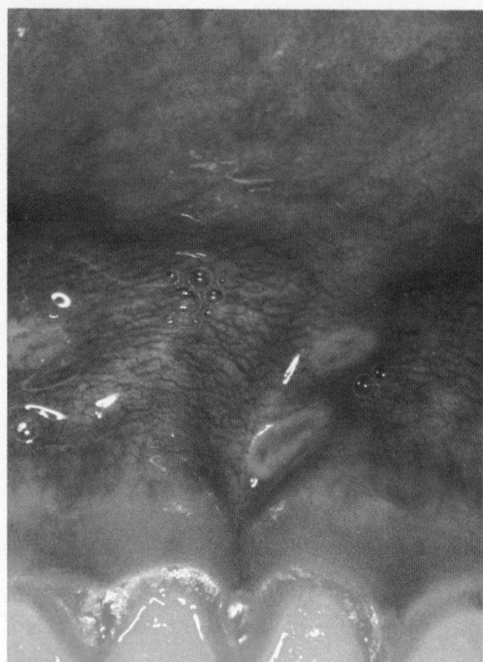

The gums are a common place for canker sores to develop.

Canker sores are tender ulcers on the inside of the mouth. One or several canker sores may develop at a time. Canker sores heal by themselves slowly over a period of 8 to 14 days. Doctors do not know what causes them.

Canker sores may first appear as tender, small blisters on the inside of the cheeks, on the tongue, or on the gums. The child may complain of a sore throat or refuse to eat or drink. After one or two days, the blister breaks and a shallow, tender ulcer appears. During the first few days, the child may have a fever (from 101° to 103° F.; 38° to 39.5° C). Give him aspirin in doses appropriate for his age. The glands below his chin may become tender, but in the early stages, he may be able to drink nonirritating beverages such as apple juice (avoid citrus juices) through a straw. After eating, he should rinse his mouth with plain water or salt water (one level teaspoonful of table salt in a glass of water). A.M.M.

Car sickness. *See* **Motion sickness**

Carbon monoxide poisoning. *See* **Poisonings and poisons**

Carbuncle. *See* **Abscess; Boil**

Cerebral palsy is a general term referring to a variety of motor disabilities that result from brain damage. The damage may occur before, during, or shortly after birth.

Control of muscles and motion is governed by the cerebrum (the largest and most complex part of the brain) and the cerebellum (a portion of the brain responsible for coordination). The cerebrum and the cerebellum send signals through the spinal cord and peripheral nerves to the muscles. When there is damage in these areas of the brain, the child's muscles receive badly organized signals from the brain. Paralysis, weakness, incoordination, lack of balance, trembling, and involuntary and unorganized movements may occur.

Brain damage sufficient to cause motor disabilities usually is so extensive that other defects in brain function occur. There may be seizures, problems with speech, and visual impairment. If damage is severe, there may be intellectual impairment.

The lack of muscle control that accompanies cerebral palsy often interferes with speech and writing. Because of this, the child cannot express himself, and it is difficult to measure his intelligence. It is also difficult to determine whether a child's performance on an intelligence test is affected by cerebral palsy or by mental retardation.

The cerebrum and the cerebellum may be injured in a variety of ways. Lack of oxygen reaching the infant's brain, hemorrhage into the brain, or infection of the mother by German measles or other virus diseases early in her pregnancy are suspected causes. Usually, cerebral palsy is not recognized at birth because the cerebrum and the cerebellum of a newborn have almost no control over crying, sucking, or moving. During the first year, as the cerebrum and cerebellum develop in the child without cerebral palsy, sitting, directed hand movements, standing, and walking appear. As these fail to develop normally in a child with cerebral palsy, a doctor can estimate the degree of injury. By that time, clues about the cause are difficult to find. Detailed information about pregnancy, delivery, and the early newborn period may provide enough information for a doctor to speculate as to the cause. But a definite diagnosis is often impossible.

Although children with cerebral palsy continue to develop and grow, their achievements in walking, self-feeding, talking, and other skills come later than for normal children. In some instances these skills never develop.

Cerebral palsy cannot be cured, but medical treatment, physical therapy, speech therapy, special education, training, and counseling can help to increase the skills of afflicted children. The type of help a child with cerebral palsy should receive depends on the type and degree of disability he has. Medical treatment may include drugs or surgery. Physical therapy may include braces or exercises. The learning ability of children with cerebral palsy varies. One may only be able to learn to feed and dress himself. Another may be able to learn skills that enable him to hold a job. A.G.S.

Chafing and chapping are two kinds of skin irritations. Chafed skin is red and often moist. Chafing results when clothing rubs against the body—at the belt line, for example—or when two skin surfaces rub together—as in the armpit or groin. Sand, perspiration, or other irritating substances may make the chafing worse.

To clear up chafing, try to eliminate the cause. If tight clothing is the cause, dress your child in loose-fitting clothes. If a child is fat, he may have to lose weight before the chafing disappears.

Careful cleansing of the skin and application of a soothing cream or lotion are helpful in treating chafing. If the chafed area is moist, apply cornstarch powder or a cornstarch paste two or three times daily to promote drying. When the child's skin is drier, discontinue the cornstarch and use talcum powder. If the chafed area is dry, apply cold cream three or four times a day. If itching occurs, cut the child's fingernails short so he will not hurt himself if he scratches. Apply cool tap water compresses for 20 to 30 minutes, four times a day. Or, give him tub baths for the same amount of time. If home treatment does not clear up the chafing, consult your doctor.

Chapping is a reddening, scaling, or cracking of the skin caused by a loss of oil in the skin. Exposure to cold, wet, windy weather may cause a child's cheeks, lips, and hands to chap. Staying indoors when the weather is bad prevents chapping. But exposure cannot always be avoided. Mittens and mufflers will help, as will an effort on the child's part not to lick his lips. If your child's skin chaps easily, apply cold cream or a good hand and face lotion to the chapped areas several times daily. This not only soothes chapped areas, but also helps prevent chapping.

Harsh soap, failure to rinse thoroughly, and careless drying can also cause chapping. Have your child use a mild soap or a cleansing lotion or cream. Encourage him to rinse and dry thoroughly after washing.

Chapped skin rarely requires medical care. But if chapping is persistent and severe, consult your doctor. A.M.M.

Charley horse and leg cramps are terms often used interchangeably, but they are not the same thing.

A charley horse is a painful muscle bruise on the front of the thigh. A blow or a muscle strain crushes and tears the muscle fibers and causes internal bleeding. These injuries often occur while playing football or any rough sport. The child feels pain when he straightens his knee, or when someone bends his knee past a right angle. The front of his thigh may turn "black and blue," and frequently a hard lump forms in the muscle. The torn muscle fibers may bleed internally for several days. Ice packs on the bruised area help to relieve pain and reduce bleeding; warm baths help the child gradually regain use of the muscle.

Leg cramps, on the other hand, usually occur at night, after the child has gone to bed. The cramps are caused by a sudden contraction of a muscle or group of muscles in the calf or thigh. J.J.G.

See also **Bruises; Cramps; Growing pains; Rheumatic fever**

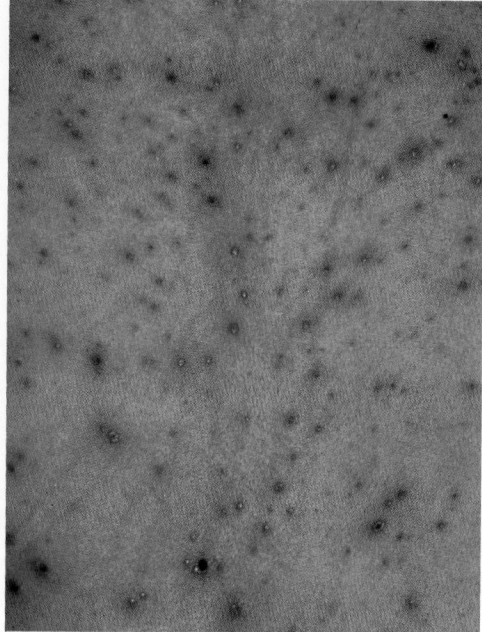

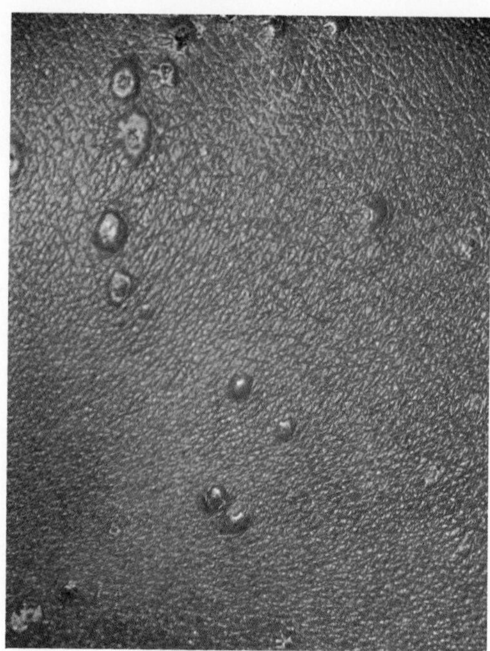

In the rash that accompanies chicken pox, new pimples form while old ones change to blisters. As the blisters dry up, scabs form and then fall off. Skin color (white, left; black, right) can affect the appearance of a chicken pox rash.

Chicken pox (varicella) is an extremely contagious disease. It is caused by a virus.

A rash usually appears first on the chest and the back, and then spreads rapidly over the rest of the body. The rash changes to pimples within a few hours and then into blisters. The blisters break in a few hours and dry into scabs. The rash occurs in successive crops—new pimples form while old ones change to blisters. This condition lasts for three or four days. The blisters dry up by the fifth to the seventh day. Most of the scabs fall off by the 10th day, but some may remain up to the 20th day.

Most children do not become very sick with chicken pox, although some may have a mild fever. Control the fever with aspirin in doses appropriate for the child's age. Some children may also vomit, and have backache and headache.

Chicken pox occurs most often in children between 2 and 8 years of age, but it can occur even in the newborn child. Call your doctor if you suspect that your child has chicken pox.

While your child has chicken pox rash, try to keep him from scratching. Scratching can open and infect the blisters, causing scars. Keep the child's fingernails short and wash his hands at least three times a day. Baking soda or cornstarch baths once or twice a day may help relieve the itching. Use one or two cups of soda or starch for each bath. If the itching is severe, your doctor may be able to prescribe medication to make the child more comfortable. Call the doctor if any of the blisters become infected.

Chicken pox appears from 14 to 21 days after exposure. Usually, a child can go back to school about a week after the disease begins. Chicken pox is contagious from about one day before the symptoms appear until the blisters have formed into scabs. A child is immune to it after one attack.

Children with serious illnesses such as leukemia, or children receiving cortisone or X-ray treatment, should be carefully protected from chicken pox. It can produce serious complications in these children. H.D.R., Jr.

See also **Communicable diseases; Virus**

First aid for choking

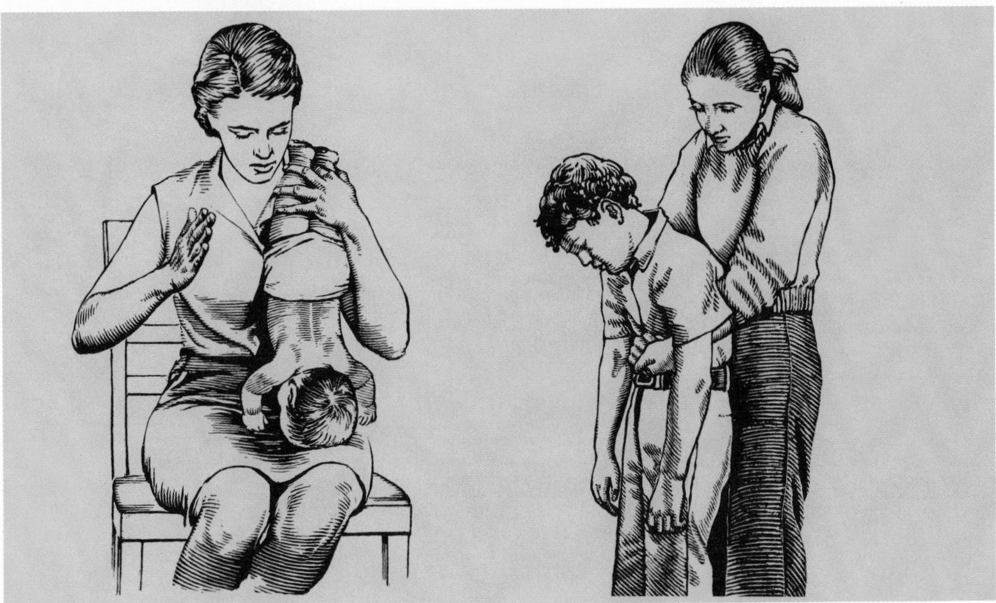

If a baby or young child is choking (*left*), hold upside down by the ankles and slap the back a few times. If an older child is choking (*right*), wrap your arms about the waist, lock your hands together, and thrust upward.

Choking. A child may choke from accidentally breathing food or other objects into the windpipe. If a child is coughing violently but still can breathe, go to the nearest hospital immediately. If possible, have someone phone your doctor to meet you and the child there. If the child is choking and cannot breathe, waste no time. Hold a baby by the ankles, head down, and slap the back a few times to force the object out of the windpipe. On a child 5 years or older, use what is known as the Heimlich maneuver. Circle your arms around the standing child's waist. Place the thumb side of your fist against the child's belly, above the navel and below the ribs. Grasp your fist with your other hand and press into the abdomen with a quick upward thrust. Repeat if necessary. *Caution:* Too much force can damage the child's internal organs.

If the child does not start breathing, give mouth-to-mouth artificial respiration (see ARTIFICIAL RESPIRATION, page 176). Then repeat back slaps or quick upward thrust. Do not reach into the child's throat with your finger or with any instrument unless you see the object clearly and can easily grasp it. If choking continues, rush the child to the nearest hospital.

Babies and toddlers can choke on small objects they place in their mouths. Encourage your child to give you any such objects found, then thank the child and substitute a safer object. Make sure that stuffed toys and dolls do not have eyes made of buttons, beads, or glass.

Children can also choke on food particles. Train your child to chew food thoroughly and not to talk while eating. Do not give a child under 4 years of age small, hard foods, such as peanuts or popcorn, which can easily cause choking. M.G.

See also **Accidents; Artificial respiration; Coughing; Gagging; Swallowed objects**

Chorea. *See* **Saint Vitus's dance**

Chromosomes. *See* **Heredity**

Cleft lip. *See* **Harelip**

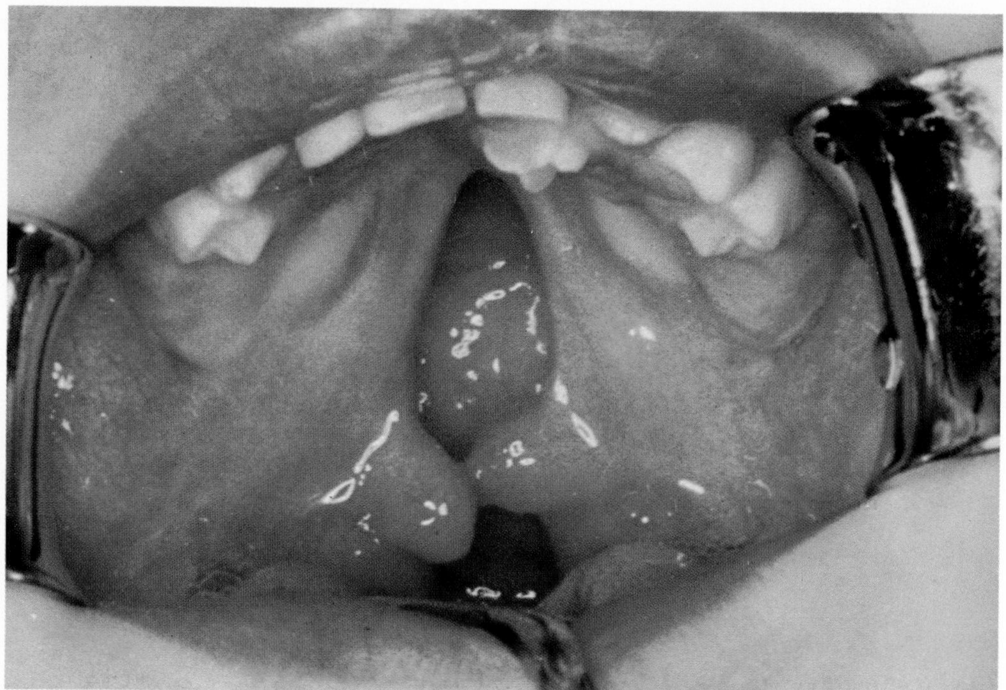

A cleft palate is a split in the palate (roof of the mouth). It is present at birth.

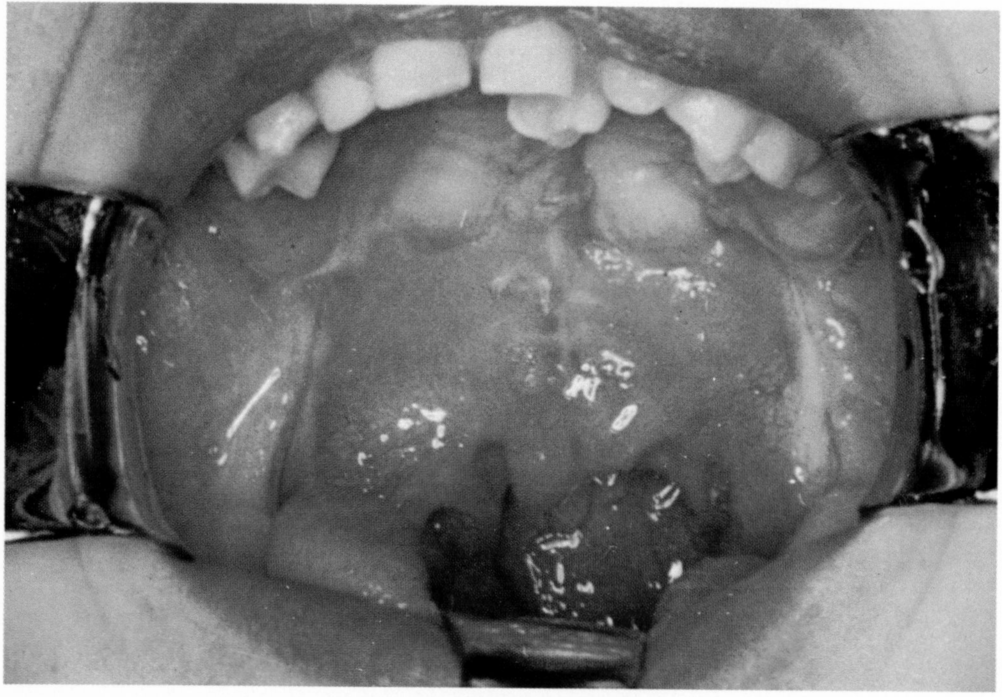

Doctors sometimes use surgery to join the two parts of a cleft palate.

Cleft palate is an opening in the roof of the mouth that keeps the nose and mouth from being adequately separated. The opening may be very small, or so large that the mouth and nose are practically one cavity. Often the cleft extends through the upper lip as well as the palate. Sometimes cleft palate is hereditary, but often something has interfered with normal development of the mouth before the baby was born.

An infant with cleft palate may have difficulty in nursing and may need special feeding. Also, a child with cleft palate tends to have middle-ear infections, so he should be watched carefully for this complication.

Your physician may recommend surgery to correct the cleft palate, although he may delay the surgery until the child is 2 years old. Or he may suggest the use of a dental appliance instead of surgery. The aim is to give the child a good appearance, to enable him to eat and speak normally, and to allow him to enjoy normal physical, emotional, and social growth. T.M.H.

See also **Harelip**

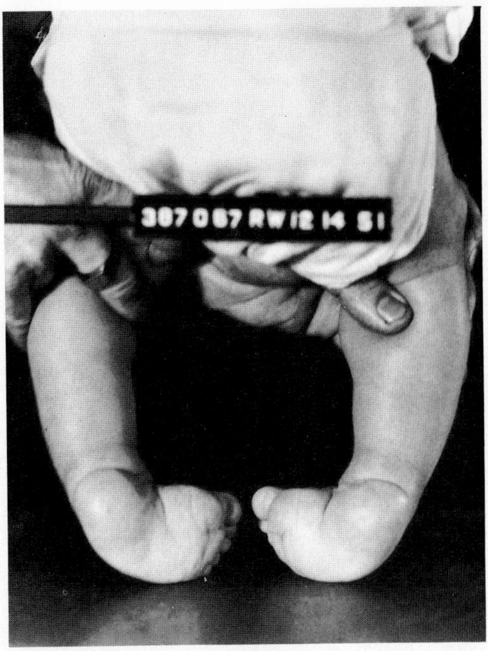

This infant was born with clubfeet, Corrective treatment was begun before the child was a year old.

Clubfoot is the most common foot deformity a baby may be born with. Usually, a clubfoot is twisted inward and downward, making the entire leg resemble a club. Clubfoot tends to run in families, and occurs about once in every 1,000 births. It is more common in boys than in girls.

Clubfoot may occur in one or both feet, and it varies in severity from a very mild deformity requiring little treatment to a severe case requiring extensive care. An orthopedic surgeon (bone specialist) usually directs the care of a child with a clubfoot. Treatment may include massage; the use of special shoes, splints, and plaster casts; and in some cases, surgery. Best results are obtained when care is started early, preferably before the child is a year old. When treatment is delayed, it takes longer to correct the deformity, and the results may not be so successful. J.J.G.

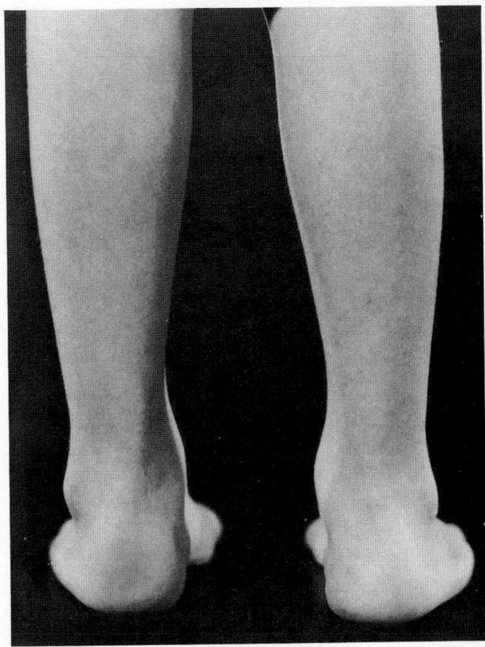

By the time the child was 6 years old, the clubfoot condition was corrected to an almost normal position.

Cold sore. *See* **Fever blisters**

Coagulation of blood. *See* **Blood clotting**

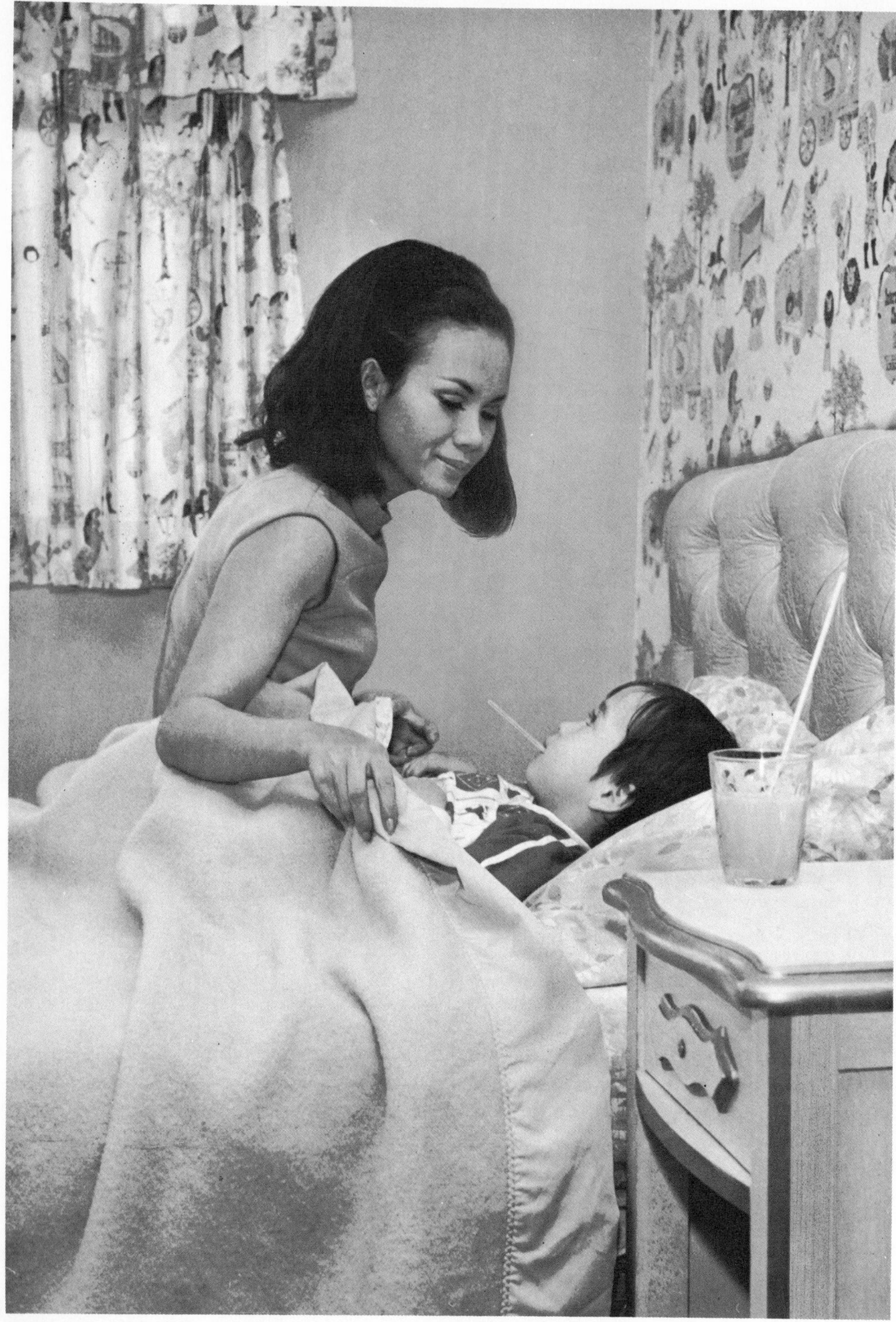

If your child has a fever of 102° F. (39° C) or higher, or a fever and a sore throat, call your doctor. Try to make the child as comfortable as possible.

Colds. Sneezing, a stopped-up or runny nose, sore throat, and a cough usually are signs of the "common cold," a malady with which parents are all too familiar. Colds may be caused by many different viruses. These viruses are spread through the air in droplets from sneezes and coughs. If a child with a cold covers his mouth and nose whenever he sneezes or coughs, he will decrease the number of cold germs that he sprays into the air.

For mild colds with no fever or only a slight fever, you do not have to call your doctor. However, you should call your doctor if your child has a fever of 102° F. (39° C) or higher, if he has a fever and a sore throat, if his cold seems severe, or if the cold lasts more than a few days.

Because cold viruses lower a child's resistance to bacteria that can cause ear infections, sinusitis, or other illnesses, your doctor may prescribe antibiotics to prevent or treat such complications. But the antibiotics have no effect on the cold virus. In fact, there is no way to cure a cold. All you can do is make the child as comfortable as possible, follow the doctor's instructions, and remember the following points.

- If a child with a cold does not feel very sick and has only a slight fever, he does not have to stay in bed. If a child feels ill, he may wish to be in bed.
- Relieve a child's fever with aspirin in doses appropriate for the child's age or with other fever medicine recommended by your doctor.
- Generally, coughing should not be suppressed. It helps rid the bronchial tubes and windpipe of mucus and other irritating material. However, if your child coughs so frequently that he tires himself, irritates his throat, or cannot sleep, your doctor may want to prescribe a cough medicine.
- Increasing the humidity in the child's room, especially if he is an infant, may soothe his inflamed nose and throat.
- Gently wipe the child's runny nose to prevent his skin from becoming chafed. Use nose drops or nasal sprays only when your doctor advises them. If a baby's nose is stuffed-up, your doctor may recommend using a syringe to suck the mucus out of the baby's nose.
- Let the child decide if and how much he wants to eat or drink. Do not force foods or liquids on him.

Infants usually suffer only mild colds—a runny nose and a slight cough. However, a baby may be very uncomfortable because eating is difficult for him when he cannot breathe through his nose. A baby also is more likely to develop bronchitis, middle-ear infections, pneumonia, and other complications. So anyone with a cold, including members of the immediate family, should stay away from a baby. If you have a cold and you must care for a baby, do not breathe directly into the baby's face. Also, wash your hands before you handle anything—teething ring, foods, the bowl of a spoon, toys, nipples—that goes into the baby's mouth. M.G.

See also **Allergy; Bronchitis; Communicable diseases; Coughing; Croup; Drugs; Earaches; Fever; Hay fever; Humidifying; Laryngitis; Measles; Nose drops; Pneumonia; Sinusitis; Sneezing; Sore throat; Strep throat; Virus; Whooping cough**

Colic is a common, uncomfortable condition that some babies experience during the first three months of life. The baby cries hard and seems to be in great pain, as if he has a severe stomach-ache. His legs may stiffen, or he may pull them up against his abdomen. Often, his abdomen is hard and tense, and he may pass gas. Colic occurs more often in the evening, and, with a few babies, it may occur almost every night. If you think your baby has colic, consult your doctor.

No one is certain what causes most colic. It occurs both in breast-fed babies and in bottle-fed babies. Some doctors believe that colic is due to an immaturity of the baby's intestinal tract, because colic almost always disappears by the time a baby is 3 months old. Colic usually is not caused by allergy.

Emotional factors may affect colic. High-strung babies are more prone to develop the condition than placid ones. Anxiety or tension in the family may increase the frequency of colic. Whatever the causes, colic does not interfere with the baby's health or development. Here are some of the things

(**Colic,** *continued*) you can do to prevent or lessen your baby's colic.

- If your baby is formula-fed, have your doctor review the formula. He may want to change it.
- Check rubber nipples to make sure the holes are the proper size.
- Do not feed the baby too rapidly or for too long.
- Burp the baby frequently during his feedings so he can release swallowed air.
- During an attack of colic, quiet rocking or holding may soothe the baby.
- Sometimes a colicky baby is more comfortable lying on his stomach.
- A pacifier often relieves colic.

In addition to the above, your doctor may prescribe sedatives for the baby.

If your baby has colic, have some part-time help, if at all possible, so that you can take an afternoon nap. An afternoon away from home once a week may also help you cope with this fatiguing experience. And, remember: Worrying about colic only makes it harder to cope with. M.G.

Colitis is an inflammation of the colon (the large bowel). Colitis may be either transient (of short duration) or chronic (lasting for a long time). Consult your doctor if you suspect that your child has colitis.

Simple colitis (a transient form) is a sudden irritation or infection of the colon, accompanied by diarrhea. Some cases are caused by bacteria and viruses. A child with simple colitis should eat bland foods, drink plenty of liquids, and rest.

Children with chronic colitis have symptoms either continuously or recurrently over several weeks or months. There are two types of chronic colitis—ulcerative and spastic.

Ulcerative colitis can endanger a child's life. While doctors do not know what causes it, they do know how to manage it. The inflamed lining of the colon bleeds easily and becomes ulcerated. The most common symptom is diarrhea that may contain mucus and blood. The child may also have a poor appetite, recurrent abdominal pain, arthritis, fever, and anemia.

A child with ulcerative colitis may have to be hospitalized. Doctors prescribe drugs to fight the inflammation and infection. If the child is anemic, the doctor may prescribe vitamins, iron, or a blood transfusion. Surgery may be necessary in extreme cases.

Spastic colitis tends to occur in emotionally sensitive children. It may be caused by anxiety or other emotional factors. Symptoms are recurrent abdominal pain and either diarrhea or small, hard stools.

Regional enteritis is a long-lasting disease similar to colitis. Regional enteritis is usually an inflammation of the small bowel, but the inflammation sometimes extends to the colon. Symptoms include fever; recurrent abdominal pain, particularly after eating; diarrhea; constipation; and a feeling of rapid fullness of the stomach at meals. Ulceration of the small bowel may cause fistulas (abnormal channels within the body).

Doctors do not know what causes regional enteritis. Drugs may relieve the symptoms, but sometimes the inflamed section of the bowel must be removed surgically. M.G.

Color blindness is an inability to tell certain colors apart. A child who is color blind may see certain colors as gray. To most color-blind children, red and green appear as gray. Only a very few children see all colors as gray. Some color-blind children fail to recognize pastel shades.

In most cases, color blindness is inherited. Women are less likely to be color blind than men are. More than 4 of every 100 men are color blind, while about 1 of every 200 women is color blind. No cure has yet been found for color blindness.

Color-blind people often do not realize that their eyesight is defective because they learn to use the color names that everyone else uses. They do not realize that they are not seeing the colors as others see them.

If you notice that your 5- or 6-year-old child has difficulty identifying colors; if he wears mismatched socks; or if he cannot take the correct crayon from a box when asked to select one by color, you should have his vision checked. R.O.S.

See also **Heredity**

Coma is a state of unconsciousness caused by injury, poison, or disease. A coma may occur suddenly, or it may be preceded by confusion, disorientation, or stupor. A coma is always an emergency situation that demands immediate first aid and immediate medical attention.

Here are the steps to take if your child goes into a coma.

- Be sure that nothing obstructs the child's breathing.
- Place him on his side with his mouth open and slightly downward so that saliva and any vomit may roll out of his mouth.
- If the child's tongue falls toward the back of his mouth, pull it forward. You may have to use a handkerchief or a towel to get a grip on the tongue.
- If the child has a convulsion, place a folded handkerchief between his teeth so he will not bite his tongue.
- Call your doctor. If you cannot reach a doctor, take the child to the nearest hospital emergency room.

Severe head injury is a common cause of coma. A child may lose consciousness immediately after the injury. Or he may go into a coma hours later. Rarely, he may go into a coma days, or even weeks, later. Always consult your doctor when your child receives a severe head injury. The doctor will decide if the child should be hospitalized immediately or if he can be cared for safely at home.

If your child is in a coma and you suspect he has swallowed a poisonous substance, take him to a hospital immediately. Also, take along the container the substance was in to help the doctor identify the poison and perhaps determine how much the child has taken.

Coma in children may also be caused by a brain hemorrhage, a stroke, or a brain tumor. Diseases such as diabetes, meningitis, and encephalitis may also cause coma.

A child who is in a coma requires hospital care. Coma is treated according to its cause. For example, if the coma is caused by diabetes, the doctor will give the child insulin and fluids. M.G.

See also **Convulsions; Diabetes mellitus; Fainting; Head injuries; Meningitis; Poisonings and poisons; Sleeping sickness**

Communicable diseases. Most communicable diseases of childhood begin in much the same way. A child may wake up in the morning with a miserable case of sniffles, or he may come dragging home from school, aching and irritable. At this stage, there is a big question about what the symptoms mean. It could be that the child just has a cold. But, there is no question about what you should do.

- Put the child to bed in a room by himself and keep everybody else out.
- Take his temperature.
- Look for a rash on his arms, face, neck, or chest.
- Call your doctor.

Do not think you are being overcautious by following this procedure. The child may indeed have only a cold. But, if the illness does turn out to be contagious, the earlier and more complete the isolation, the better for other members of the family, especially for babies and elderly relatives. The sooner you get medical advice, the better the chance to determine the nature of the illness and to treat it.

The table on pages 202 and 203 provides information about the incubation period, common symptoms, isolation period, and preventive measures for nine communicable diseases. The listing is alphabetical, with medical names of the disease in parentheses. Each disease is discussed more completely in a separate article in the Medical Guide.

"Incubation period" means the length of time between exposure to a disease and the appearance of the first signs or symptoms. This is the time usually required by the viruses or bacteria, once they are in the body of a susceptible person, to grow and reproduce themselves in sufficient quantity to cause illness.

"Common symptoms" are the signs that alert parents to call a doctor. Only a doctor should make a diagnosis and prescribe any treatment.

Isolation of the child who has the disease is recommended for each communicable disease. Quarantine of the child who has been exposed to the disease is recommended for some of the diseases. H.D.R., JR.

See also **Fever; Immunization; Rash; Shots; Virus**

Communicable diseases

Disease	Incubation period	Common symptoms
Chicken pox (Varicella)	14 to 21 days.	Mild fever, upset stomach, headache, blisterlike rash that appears suddenly. Blisters become crusted in 1 to 3 days.
Diphtheria	1 to 10 days (average, 2 to 6 days).	Severe sore throat, fever, yellowish-gray patches on tonsils, throat, or palate. Breathing may become tight and difficult.
German measles (Rubella)	about 14 to 21 days (average, 17 days).	Sore throat and headache. Rash on face and head, spreading to neck and trunk. Slight fever during rash. Rash lasts 2 or 3 days. Glands at back of head and neck and behind ears become enlarged.
Measles (Rubeola)	Fever, 10 days after exposure. Rash, 14 days after exposure.	Resembles cold. Fever, runny nose, watery eyes, cough. White spots on inside of cheeks. Rash begins on forehead, spreads downward.
Mumps (Infectious parotitis)	About 14 to 21 days (average, 18 days).	Swelling and pain in one or more salivary glands. Difficulty in chewing and swallowing.
Poliomyelitis (Infantile paralysis)	7 to 21 days (usually, 10 to 12 days).	Fever, sore throat, dull pain on bending neck, headache, muscle spasms, stiff back. Symptoms may begin suddenly or gradually.
Scarlet fever	2 to 5 days.	Begins very suddenly with headache, chills, fever, sore throat, vomiting. Neck glands enlarged and tender. Tongue coated and pitted looking at first, then becomes red and rough. Rash appears about 3 days after first symptom.
Smallpox (Variola)	10 to 14 days (usually, 12 days).	Begins suddenly with chills, fever, vomiting, severe headache, and backache. Red spots that change to blisters filled with pus. Scabs in 10 to 12 days.
Whooping cough (Pertussis)	5 to 21 days (average, 10 days).	Increased nose and throat secretions. Spells of coughing, which are worse at night. Slight fever. Whooping develops in 2 weeks. Coughing spasm may end in vomiting.

Isolation period of infected child	Isolation period of exposed child	Preventive measures
Isolate for 6 days after rash appears.	None.	None. One attack usually gives immunity.
Isolate until doctor has taken 3 consecutive bacteria-free cultures, one every 24 hours.	Quarantine 7 days and until 2 consecutive bacteria-free cultures have been taken, with a 24-hour time span between them.	Shots of diphtheria toxoid (usually begun as part of 3-in-1, DTP shots in infancy). One attack usually gives immunity.
Isolate from first symptoms to 5 days after rash.	None.	Vaccination. One attack usually gives immunity.
Isolate from first symptom to 5 days after rash.	Quarantine 7 to 14 days under some conditions, but quarantine of no value during epidemic.	Vaccination of all susceptible children. Gamma globulin in special cases for temporary immunity. One attack usually gives immunity.
Isolate until swelling subsides, 7 to 10 days.	None.	Mumps vaccine. One attack involving one or both sides usually gives immunity.
Isolate for 7 days from onset, or for duration of fever.	None usually, except to avoid exertion.	Oral polio vaccine should be given beginning in infancy.
Isolate about 7 days, or longer if doctor advises.	None. But should have throat culture.	None. One attack usually gives immunity.
Isolate confirmed cases until all scabs are gone. Isolate suspected cases until doctor has made diagnosis.	Observe for 16 days from date of exposure.	Vaccination when traveling in countries where smallpox occurs regularly.
Isolate for 4 weeks from onset, or 3 weeks after coughing begins.	Quarantine for 14 days after exposure.	Shots (usually begun as part of 3-in-1, DTP shots). Early immunization important. One attack usually provides immunity.

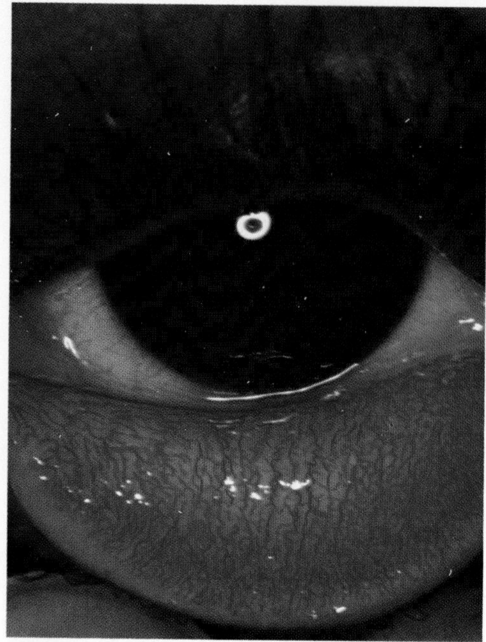

When a child has conjunctivitis, the lining of the eyelid and the membrane covering the eyeball become inflamed.

Conjunctivitis is an inflammation of the membrane covering the outer, front layer of the eyeball and the lining of the eyelid. It is caused by bacteria, viruses, or such chemical irritants as smoke or soap. Conjunctivitis usually occurs by itself, but it may appear in connection with colds, measles, chicken pox, and other diseases.

If your child complains of "something in my eye," he may have conjunctivitis. This feeling is often a first symptom, followed by a discharge of water or pus, or swelling accompanied by itching, burning, and discomfort from light. Symptoms are usually more intense in the evening after the eyes have been used and will vary with the amount of inflammation. In the morning, a child's eyelids frequently will be stuck together from the discharge that has dried during the night. Wash the eyes open, but apply no other home treatment. If the inflammation does not clear in a very short time, consult your doctor. Some forms of conjunctivitis are contagious. R.O.S.

See also **Allergy; Eye health**

Constipation is a bowel disorder in which the stools are small, hard, and dry; and they are difficult for the child to expel. You cannot tell if your child is constipated just by watching him have a bowel movement, because some completely healthy children grunt, strain, and get red in the face just before and after they have a bowel movement.

Some mothers worry unnecessarily about constipation and become overly concerned about the "regularity" of their child's bowel movements. Babies, like adults, vary a great deal in the frequency of bowel movements. Most young babies have one to three movements a day, but some have four or five regularly every day. Occasionally, a breast-fed baby has one bowel movement every two or three days, but breast-fed babies usually have four to eight movements each day.

Most babies have an occasional, mild episode of constipation with some discomfort for a day or so. This is common in illnesses with fever. Usually, no special treatment is necessary except to offer the baby an extra amount of water.

If your baby's stools are especially dry, try a few changes in diet. Extra water is the first step. If the baby is entirely formula fed, try substituting one tablespoon of dark corn syrup for one of the tablespoons of regular sugar in the formula. Do not increase the total amount of sugar given.

Cereal may be mildly constipating. If the baby eats other solids, give him more fruit (except bananas). Occasionally, one-half ounce (15 milliliters) of prune juice mixed with an ounce (30 milliliters) of sterile water will help. Never give your baby laxatives, suppositories, or enemas without consulting your doctor.

Occasionally, an extremely hard stool may cause a small tear in the anus. This may, in turn, cause some pain in the passage of stools and some bright red blood on the outside of the stools. Consult your doctor if this occurs. He will probably prescribe medication to soften the baby's stools.

Quite frequently, older children will be constipated for short periods of time. Occasionally, this condition represents some resistance to toilet training, but most often

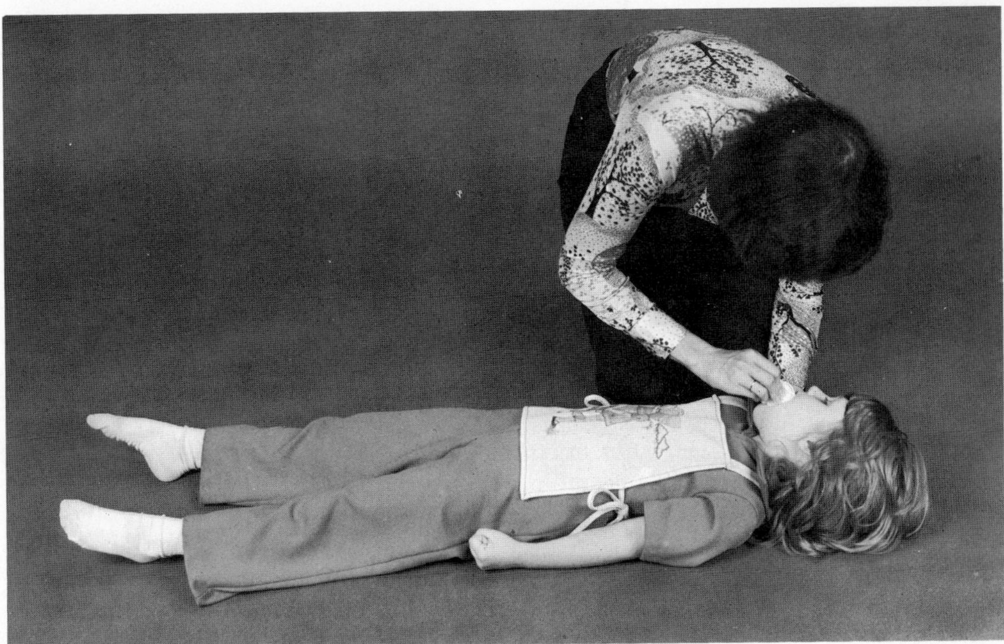

There is always a chance of self-injury during a convulsion. Turn the victim's head to one side to prevent choking on vomit. To keep the victim from biting the tongue, roll a handkerchief into a small wad and place it between the teeth on the high side of the mouth. Call a doctor as soon as possible.

it starts around the age of 2, when the child is learning to exercise his own will and to say "no." He even says "no" to his own body needs, ignoring them while he continues to play. Or he says "no" because he is upset over the arrival of a new baby in the house. Never battle over this withholding of stools, because a child who feels he must defend his right to exercise his own control can become very stubborn. Do not focus undue attention on his bowel habits.

To avoid constipation, your child should have a balanced diet, regular exercise, and plenty of liquids. Consult your doctor if your child is persistently constipated, especially if the child resists going to the toilet and soils his underpants repeatedly during the day. M.G.

See also **Appetite; Enema; Laxatives; Nutrition; Suppositories**

Contagious diseases. *See* **Communicable diseases; Immunization**

Contusions. *See* **Bruises**

Convulsions are involuntary contractions of muscles. During a convulsion, a child's muscles may jerk or twitch. He may lose consciousness. His eyes may roll, stay open, or almost close. He may clench his teeth. He may become rigid, with his neck arched, his arms and legs stiff, and his toes pointing. Sometimes during a convulsion, the child involuntarily urinates or moves his bowels. Although convulsions are frightening to witness, they usually are not dangerous.

If your child has a convulsion, try to remain calm and reassuring. Unless he is in a dangerous place, let the child stay in the position in which he falls—on his back, on his side, or on his stomach. Keep the child from hurting himself. Turn his head to one side to keep him from choking in case he should vomit. Place a folded handkerchief between his jaws so that he will not bite his tongue. The convulsion usually stops within a few minutes. After the convulsion, the child generally sleeps deeply for a while.

Call your doctor if your child has a convulsion. The doctor will want to examine the

(**Convulsions,** *continued*) child to determine the cause.

Convulsions are brought on by brain disturbances. The most common cause of convulsions in children between the ages of 1 and 3 is a high fever. If high fever tends to bring on convulsions in your child, the doctor may place him on daily doses of an anticonvulsant medicine for a couple of years. You should also take precautions whenever your child has a high fever (102° F.; 39° C) by giving him

- appropriate doses of aspirin
- a sponge bath in lukewarm water

Convulsions may also occur in connection with diseases causing unusually low blood sugar or unusually low levels of calcium in the blood. In diseases such as tetanus (lockjaw) or infections of the brain, such as meningitis, convulsions are often frequent and severe. Convulsions may occur after birth injuries or after brain injuries resulting from accidents. Epilepsy, too, is characterized by convulsions. M.G.

See also **Epilepsy; Fever; Head injuries**

Cot death. *See* **Crib Death**

Coughing usually indicates that something is irritating the breathing passages and that the body should be rid of it. Some of the most common causes of coughing are the following.

- Respiratory infections such as bronchitis, the common cold, croup, pneumonia, sinusitis, and whooping cough
- Allergies such as asthma and hay fever
- Accidentally breathing small objects such as coins, tiny toys, safety pins, beads, or small food particles into the windpipe or lungs
- Accidentally breathing chemical substances into the windpipe or lungs

Chronic coughing may be caused by tuberculosis or cystic fibrosis. Occasionally, a child coughs just to gain attention.

The way you treat a cough depends largely on its cause. Consult your doctor to determine the cause. He may advise chest X rays and allergy tests.

Usually, a child's coughing should not be suppressed. It is the normal way to get rid of irritating material in the respiratory system. But if coughing tires your child or interferes with his sleep, the doctor may prescribe a cough medicine for the child or tell you to give the child cough drops. Never give cough medicine to a child unless your doctor prescribes it.

Here are some other steps your doctor may take to relieve your child's coughing.

- In cases of respiratory infection, he may prescribe antibiotics. He may also advise you to increase the humidity in the child's room. The moistened air makes breathing easier for the child.
- In cases of nasal allergies, he may prescribe antihistamine drugs to prevent or lessen allergic reactions.
- If a foreign object has been breathed into the windpipe or lungs, he may have to remove the object surgically. M.G.

See also **Asthma; Bronchitis; Colds; Croup; Cystic fibrosis; Hay fever; Humidifying; Measles; Pneumonia; Sinusitis; Swallowed objects; Tuberculosis; Whooping cough**

Cradle cap is a scalp condition that may occur during the first few months of a baby's life. Whitish scales form on the baby's scalp, and then flake off. If the condition is not treated, the scales form a heavier crust that is yellowish and greasy. When cradle cap reaches this stage, the scalp may look a little red and irritated, and a rash may develop on the baby's face and chest.

The best way to prevent cradle cap is to shampoo the baby's scalp thoroughly (including the soft spots) at the beginning of his bath. Use soap and water and a washcloth. Do not use ointments.

If your baby has already developed cradle cap, repeat the following steps once or twice a day.

- Comb the scalp with a fine-tooth comb.
- Wash the scalp with a mild soap.
- Dry the scalp thoroughly.
- Apply several drops of baby oil to the scalp and rub it in thoroughly.

If the condition does not improve in a few days, consult the baby's doctor. A.M.M.

Cramp is the sudden, painful contraction of a muscle or group of muscles. Cramps may occur in any part of the body. Leg and stomach cramps are the most common.

Leg cramps usually occur at night, after the child has gone to bed. Cramps in the calf and thigh muscles may awaken him. You can usually relieve the pain by massaging the cramped muscles.

The most common cause of muscular leg cramps in a child is flat feet. The abnormal arch of the foot strains the leg muscles, and they develop cramps during rest periods. Consult your doctor if your child has leg cramps frequently. Arch supports in shoes may relieve the condition.

Abdominal and intestinal cramps may occur in girls during the menstrual period. Applying heat may relieve the pain. Abdominal and intestinal cramps may also be caused by an ulcer, food poisoning, or emotional upset. If the cramps are not relieved after 36 hours, call your doctor. J.J.G.

See also **Charley horse; Colic; Colitis; Flat feet; Food poisoning; Growing pains; Menstruation**

Crib death (Sudden Infant Death Syndrome or SIDS) is the sudden and unexpected death of an infant, usually while asleep. Ongoing research has not yet established the cause or causes of death. It is estimated that up to 10,000 babies die in the United States each year because of crib death.

Some stricken infants are reported to have had a mild respiratory infection a week or two earlier. But many seemed in excellent health just before death. Some even had a satisfactory physical examination on the day they died.

Crib death is the most frequent cause of death in infants between 1 week and 7 months of age, with most deaths occurring between 2 and 4 months of age. Boys are affected more often than girls, and infants of low birth weight are more likely to be affected than those of average or high birth weight. While crib deaths may occur at any time during the year, they are most frequent from late autumn through spring.

Parents who have had a baby die from crib death often feel responsible for the death. Their guilt feelings, while natural, are not supported by facts. There is no way in which crib deaths can be predicted or prevented. These infants do not suffocate in their bedclothing. And they do not die because of poor care. Crib deaths can occur to infants of the most capable parents.

Parents who have had one child die from crib death usually worry about the possibility of a second baby dying in the same manner. No evidence exists that there is a family tendency toward crib deaths. It is highly unlikely that a later baby will also die suddenly. However, the parents may tend to overprotect the next baby and to watch very closely for rapid breathing or other signs of illness. These parents should discuss their concerns with their doctor. They need more reassurance than parents who have not experienced crib death.

Contact the National Sudden Infant Death Syndrome Foundation, 310 South Michigan Avenue, Chicago, Illinois 60604, for information on crib deaths. M.G.

Cross-eye (strabismus). Many babies' eyes "drift" during the first few months of life. One eye or the other will turn in occasionally, making the child look cross-eyed. Let your doctor decide if the condition of your child's eyes requires attention. If the eyes are still not straight by the time the child is 6 months old—if they turn in, float up or down, or swing out—your doctor will probably suggest that your child be referred for a special eye examination.

If treatment for cross-eye is started early, chances of correcting the weak muscles that cause the disorder are excellent. The doctor may recommend eyeglasses or eye exercises designed to strengthen the eye muscles. He may recommend that the child wear an eye patch over the good eye to make the crossed eye work harder to develop good vision. If these corrective measures fail to straighten the child's eyes, a surgical operation may be necessary.

If crossed eyes are not corrected, the child may lose the sight of the crossed eye. R.O.S.

See also **Eye health**

Croup is an inflammation of the air passage leading to the lungs. Young children often develop croup as a result of laryngitis. The child becomes hoarse, has a brassy cough, and stridor (harsh, high-pitched, wheezing noise heard when the child takes a breath). He may also have a fever.

Croup makes it difficult to breathe, and this may frighten a child. Call your doctor immediately if you think your child has croup. He can diagnose and prescribe proper treatment. In a severe case of croup, a child may find it so difficult to breathe that the doctor may have to perform a tracheotomy (incision into the windpipe) to get air into the lungs.

Spasmodic croup—in which the child does not have a fever—is the most common and mildest type of croup. Some children develop spasmodic croup repeatedly. Until a doctor can be reached, humidify the child's room with a cold-mist humidifier. Hot-steam humidifiers are potentially dangerous because of the possibility of the child's burning himself if he knocks the humidifier over.

You can make the humidifier more effective if you make a "croup tent."

- Tie the handle of an opened umbrella to the back of a straight-backed chair.
- Place the chair against the child's bed.
- Put the humidifier on a chair near the bed.
- Drape the largest bed sheet you have over the bed, the umbrella, and the humidifier.

The humidified air then goes directly to the child. (See HUMIDIFYING, page 246, for an illustration of a croup tent.)

While the cold-mist humidifier or the croup tent is being set up, take the child into the bathroom, close the door, and run hot water in the bathtub or run a hot shower. Stay with the child to be certain he cannot get into the hot water and scald himself. The heat will steam up the room. When the child breathes the moist air, he should improve rapidly.

If the croup is severe, steaming may relieve the cough and tight breathing only partially. Put your child under the supervision of a doctor as soon as possible. If you cannot reach your doctor, take the child to a hospital. M.G.

See also **Coughing; Humidifying; Laryngitis**

Cuts and scratches. The best way to treat small cuts and scratches is with soap and water. First, wash your own hands. Then, wash the cuts with plenty of soap and water, using cotton or a clean cloth. After this, rinse away the soap and cover the cut with a small sterile gauze square or a bandage to keep it clean. You do not have to apply any antiseptic to a wound that is thoroughly washed. If areas around the cuts or scratches become inflamed, consult your doctor. Inflammation is caused by infection.

If a cut is large and deep, take the child to a hospital emergency room. Stitches may be necessary to close the wound. But in many cases a doctor can use strips of adhesive tape to bring the edges of the wound together.

A deep cut may bleed profusely. Such bleeding is good for a short time, because it helps to cleanse the cut. You can usually control bleeding by applying a sterilized dressing or clean cloth over the cut and pressing down until the bleeding stops. If the bleeding continues, do not remove the first dressing. Place another dressing on top of it and continue pressing.

Cuts in the scalp and face may bleed profusely for a few minutes. In most cases, the wound is not as serious as it appears. Wash away the blood, and then decide whether a doctor should examine the cut.

A cut on the inside of a finger, palm, or wrist may injure a nerve or a tendon. Have the child flex his fingers and make a fist. He will not be able to do this if nerves or tendons have been cut. If you think that your child has a cut nerve or tendon, take him to a hospital emergency room.

Always consult your doctor about puncture wounds; wounds that do not bleed readily; or wounds that may have been contaminated with soil from pastures, barnyards, lawns, gardens, or other areas fertilized with animal manure. These three types of wounds may contain bacteria that cause tetanus (lockjaw), a disease that affects the brain and nerves. The doctor may want to give the child a shot of tetanus toxoid or antitoxin to safeguard against tetanus infection. M.G.

See also **Bites and stings; Bleeding; First aid; Medicine cabinets; Tetanus**

Treatment for cuts

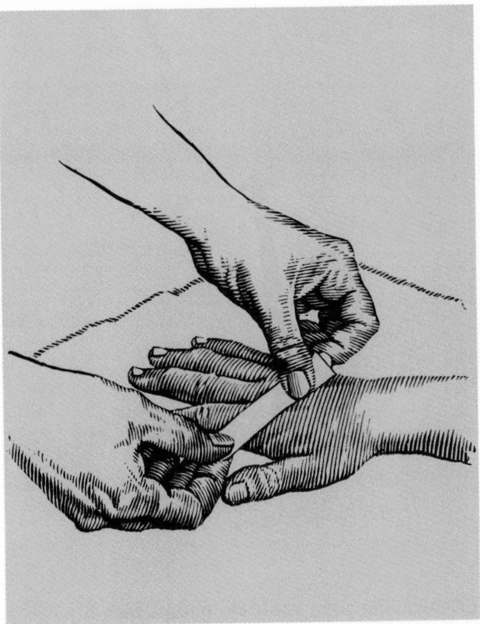

Wash a small cut with plenty of soap and warm water. Then rinse the cut thoroughly and cover it with an adhesive bandage strip.

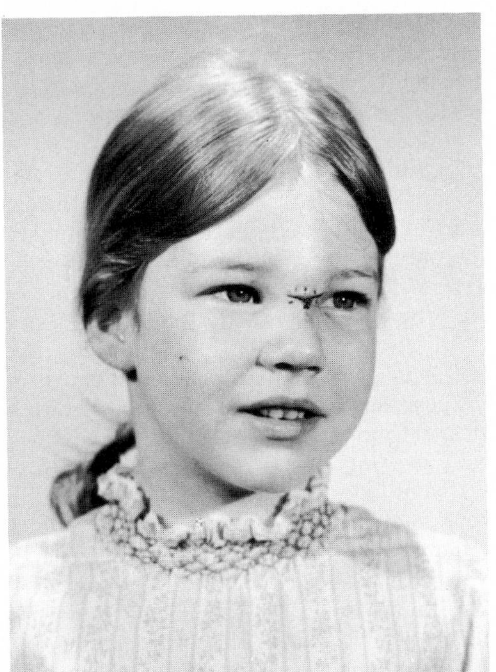

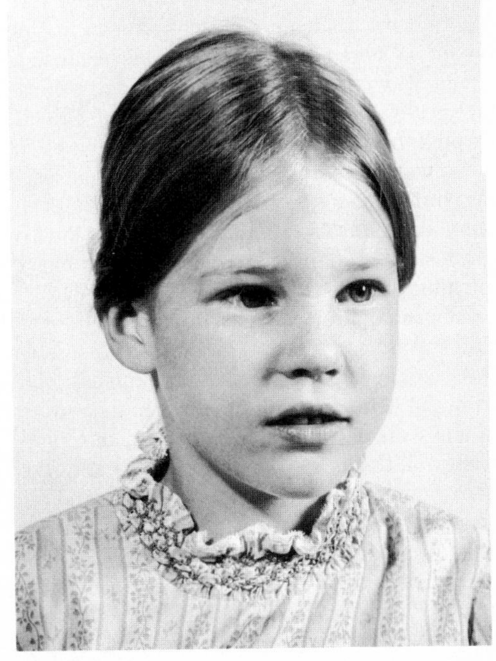

Some cuts require stitches to bring the edges of the cut together. This helps the wound to heal and usually avoids unsightly scars.

A normal heart and an abnormal heart

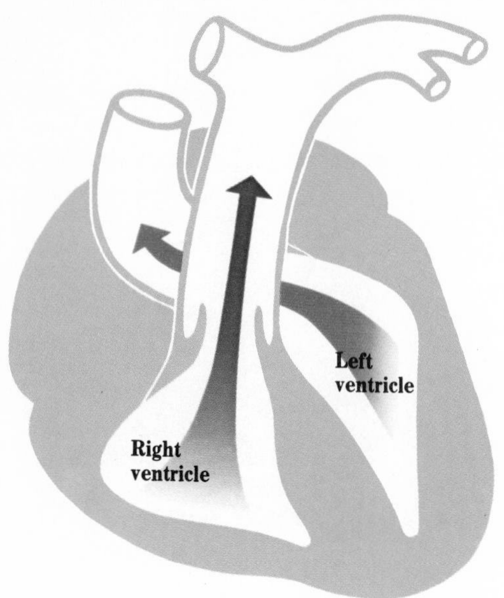

Normally, the right ventricle pumps blood to the lungs, where oxygen is added. The blood then flows back into the heart, and the left ventricle pumps it to the body.

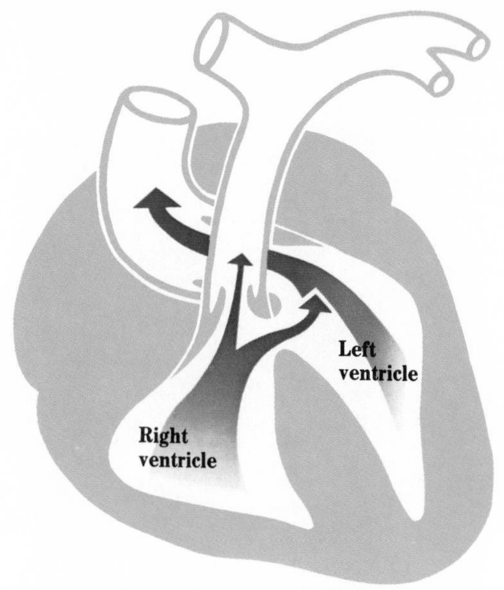

In this heart, much of the blood flows through a hole in the wall between the ventricles and by-passes the lungs. The left ventricle then pumps it to the body.

Cyanosis is a bluish coloring of the skin and lips that results from a lack of oxygen in the blood. A "blue baby" has cyanosis because a congenital (present at birth) heart defect interferes with the circulation of blood through his heart. Cyanosis in a blue baby is not always apparent when the baby is resting, but it may become noticeable when the baby cries or is very active. In addition to cyanosis, the baby may also have a heart murmur and respiratory problems.

Congenital heart defects. Cyanosis due to congenital heart defects is usually caused by the passage of unoxygenated, bluish blood from the veins through an abnormal opening in the wall between the right and left ventricles of the heart. In a normal heart, the unoxygenated blood from the veins is pumped from the right ventricle through the pulmonary artery to the lungs, where oxygen is added. Then, the bright red, oxygenated blood is pumped into the left ventricle and into the aorta and other arteries. In a child with cyanosis caused by a congenital heart defect, part or all of the blood by-passes the lungs. Because of an abnormal opening between the ventricles, the unoxygenated blood is pumped from the right ventricle directly into the left ventricle, and then into the aorta.

In addition to an abnormal opening between the left and right side of the heart, there may be an obstruction or narrowing of the pulmonary artery. This obstruction or narrowing also prevents the blood from being properly oxygenated.

Another congenital heart defect that causes cyanosis is transposition (change in the position) of the aorta and the pulmonary artery. Cyanosis may also indicate that the baby has only one ventricle in his heart.

If your baby has a congenital heart defect, your doctor will probably refer you to a pediatric cardiologist (a children's doctor who specializes in the treatment of the heart and its diseases). The cardiologist will take a chest X ray and an electrocardiogram (EKG), which records the size and shape of the electrical impulses of the heart. He may examine the heart by cardiac catheterization. A long tube is inserted in the heart through a vein in the arm, and the path of the tube is viewed on an X-ray screen. The cardiologist may also introduce a dye into the baby's circulation to help temporarily outline the defect.

Some heart defects can be corrected by surgery, but the timing of the operation depends on the baby. As long as he is gaining weight and does not have severe breathing difficulty, the operation will probably be delayed until after he is 2 years old. Corrective operations include by-passing the narrow passage which impedes the flow of blood to the lungs and closing off the abnormal opening between the right and left sides of the heart. Many congenital defects can be completely corrected so that the child has no disability.

Other causes. Cyanosis can also be caused by a collapsed lung, pneumonia, suffocation, shock, or other conditions. Treatment consists of relieving the condition that is producing the lack of oxygenated blood, and, if necessary, giving the child oxygen. M.G.

Cystic fibrosis is an inherited disease in which glands produce abnormally thick mucus that clogs up body organs and hinders their normal operation. Breathing and digestion are most often affected. Doctors do not know exactly what causes it or how to cure it completely. Although cystic fibrosis is eventually fatal, early diagnosis and treatment have made it possible for many afflicted children to lead fairly normal lives until they are adolescents or young adults. Children with cystic fibrosis should be under a doctor's care.

The most common and serious symptoms of cystic fibrosis are a persistent, hacking cough and repeated attacks of bronchitis or pneumonia. These are caused by blocked air passages. Some newborn babies who have cystic fibrosis may have difficulty with bowel movements because of an obstruction in the intestines. The infant may have frequent bowel movements that are bulky, loose, pale, and unusually foul-smelling. He may fail to gain weight even though he has a good appetite.

A child with cystic fibrosis loses an excessive amount of salt when he sweats. For this reason, he should have extra salt in his diet during the hot summer months.

If the disease has settled in the respiratory tract, your doctor may suggest that you have the child sleep in a mist tent. Special sprayers (nebulizers) produce a foglike atmosphere in the tent that thins out the secretions in the child's breathing passages so that mucus can be brought up to his throat, and he can spit it out. At specified times, the child may also wear a special face mask through which you can spray decongestants or antibiotics in solution.

The doctor may also prescribe physical therapy, breathing exercises, and positions for the child to lie in so that the secretions can drain from his bronchial tubes.

The doctor generally prescribes a diet high in protein and calories, and moderately low in fat content. Because pancreatic juices necessary for digestion become blocked in the pancreas, pancreatic enzyme preparations may have to be given by mouth. M.G.

Cysts are abnormal, fluid-filled sacs within the body. A cyst has no opening. Usually the lining of the cyst produces the material that fills the cyst.

Cysts are of all sizes and may occur almost anywhere in the body. They may be congenital (something the child is born with), or they may result when a gland opening becomes plugged. Sometimes, doctors cannot determine their cause. Only rarely are cysts malignant.

Some cysts are simple and harmless. They eventually disappear by themselves. Often, however, cysts have to be removed. Some, such as a thyroglossal cyst (in the neck), tend to become infected. Other cysts have to be removed because they interfere with proper functioning of a body organ. For example, cysts on the lungs may interfere with breathing.

Cysts that are close to the surface of the skin can be removed by simple surgery in the doctor's office. Cysts that are deep in the abdomen or chest require a major operation and hospitalization. T.M.H.

A child who is hard of hearing usually needs special speech lessons.

Deafness is the partial or complete inability to hear.

In a child with normal hearing, sound waves pass through the ear canal. They strike the eardrum, a thin membrane which separates the ear canal from a tiny chamber. The eardrum and three small bones in the chamber are called the middle ear. When the eardrum moves, the movement is transmitted along a chain of the bones—the hammer, the anvil, and the stirrup—to the inner ear. There, the cochlea (an organ shaped like a snail's shell) changes the vibrations into nerve impulses which are sent along the auditory nerve to the brain. Deafness may result if anything interferes with the healthy operation of any of these parts.

There are three main types of hearing loss. If sound waves are not conducted adequately to the child's inner ear, the hearing loss is called conductive. If sound waves reach the child's inner ear, but they are not properly changed into nerve impulses, the hearing loss is called nerve deafness or perceptive deafness. If the child's hearing loss is the result of both conductive and perceptive impairments, the hearing loss is called mixed deafness.

Causes of deafness. Deafness can develop before birth. It can be inherited. It also can develop in an unborn child if the mother has German measles or other diseases during her pregnancy, or if she takes certain drugs.

Or, deafness can be caused after birth by a number of illnesses or injuries, especially head injuries such as skull fractures or concussions. German measles, measles, meningitis, mumps, scarlet fever, and whooping cough are some of the diseases that may cause perceptive deafness. Infected adenoids, tonsillitis, and the common cold can cause temporary deafness if the infection spreads to the middle ear. An obstruction in the ear canal—an accumulation of wax, a boil, a small object like a marble—may cause deafness. Deafness can also result if the eardrum is ruptured by a sharp instrument, a violent noise, or sneezing.

Detecting hearing losses. These signs can warn parents that their child may be deaf.

- From birth to 6 months—The child is not startled by noises. He is not responsive to pleasant or cross voices. He does not turn his head toward the source of familiar sounds.
- From 6 months to 18 months—The child does not understand words. He babbles a few sounds. He does not turn his head in response to sounds.
- From 18 months onward—The child does not speak words. He makes his wishes known by pointing and gesturing. He does not identify objects when they are named. He depends on sight more than on hearing.

If you have any doubt about your child's ability to hear, consult your doctor. He may recommend that you take the child to an otologist (a doctor specializing in ear conditions) for examination.

Various tests can be made to determine the state of your child's hearing. These tests include the use of the voice, a watch, tuning forks, and an audiometer (an electronic device that measures the range of a child's hearing, from the lowest sound to the highest). An audiometric examination helps a doctor determine whether a child is deaf, how much hearing he has, the character of the hearing loss, and whether a hearing aid will be helpful. Audiometric graphs or records also provide a means of measuring hearing loss for a particular child over a long period of time. A record of hearing loss can be kept and compared with new records, enabling the doctor to tell whether the child's hearing is unchanged, improving, or becoming worse.

Deafness and speech. Detecting a hearing loss is important at any age, but it is especially important in babies because speech normally develops from hearing. A child who is born totally deaf cannot learn to talk without special training. He usually enters a school when he is about 4 or 5 years old. Some schools have parent education programs to help you guide your child even before he enters school. Excellent parent education programs are also available by mail. (See AGENCIES AND ORGANIZATIONS INTERESTED IN THE WELFARE OF CHILDREN, page 150.) With special schooling and guidance, a totally deaf child can grow into a mature, self-supporting person.

A child with only a partial loss of hearing usually needs special speech lessons, too. He does not hear all the sounds in every word.

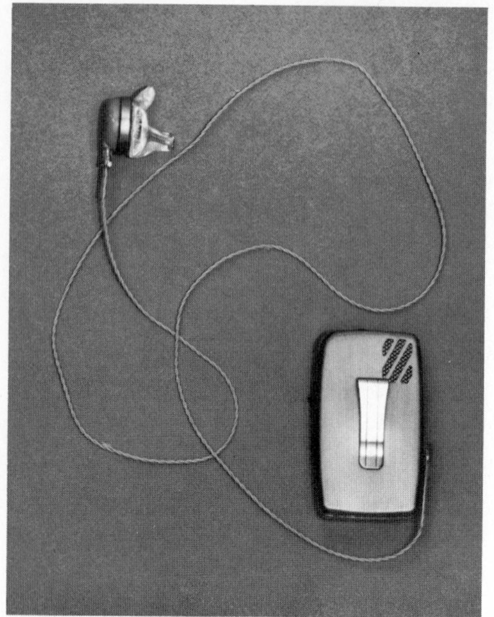

A hearing aid can warn a hard-of-hearing child that a car is approaching. A microphone in the case of the hearing aid (*shown above left*) picks up sound waves and amplifies them. The sound is then transmitted to a receiver in the child's ear.

(**Deafness,** *continued*) Because he says the words in the same way that he hears them, he will have a speech defect unless he has special training. He may also need a hearing aid or some medical treatment to improve his hearing.

Hearing aids. A hearing aid consists essentially of a microphone, an amplifier (also called a transmitter), and a receiver. The microphone picks up sound, and the amplifier makes it louder and transmits it to the receiver by means of a wire. The receiver is small and usually made to fit in the child's ear. Most amplifiers are made to be worn on a jacket lapel or some other place where they can receive sound freely.

There are two types of hearing aids—the air conduction aid and the bone conduction aid. An air conduction aid amplifies sound, transmitting it directly to the ear itself. Bone conduction aids transmit sound waves to the bony part of the head, usually in the mastoid region behind the ear. The air conduction aid is by far the more popular and usually the more effective. But the molded ear insert used in the air conduction aid is too uncomfortable for some children, so the bone conduction aid may be best for them.

A hearing aid will not restore or bring hearing to normal, but it will amplify sound so that it can be heard. Many of the sounds will seem new or strange at first. Voices may sound different because they lack some of the qualities and timbre of normal speech. This is especially true if the child had normal hearing at one time and then lost it, either through disease or injury.

A child with partial deafness can frequently hear some tones better than others, and his hearing aid can be adjusted to amplify tones he has difficulty hearing so that they sound more normal to his ear. Hearing aids also help a child to hear warning sounds, such as approaching cars.

An ear specialist will tell you whether a hearing aid will help your child. He can also tell you whether the child will benefit most by using a hearing aid at all times or only when it will help him most—during school, for example. C.F.F.

Dehydration is a condition that results when the water content of the body drops excessively. It is sometimes accompanied by a loss of certain body minerals, such as sodium and potassium.

Dehydration is caused by one of two things. The first is an increase in the loss of water from a child's body, as may occur with persistent vomiting, persistent diarrhea, excessive sweating, high fever, severe burns, or increased urination. The second cause of dehydration is a decrease in the intake of water, as may occur when a child does not or cannot drink sufficient fluids for his body's normal functions. Sometimes, both factors may cause dehydration. For example, a child who is vomiting is losing water from his body. At the same time, he may not be able to drink any liquids.

The severity of dehydration depends upon the amount of water and the amount of minerals lost. Generally, the child's skin is dry, and his tongue and the lining of his mouth are parched. His skin may become less elastic. Babies and young children lose weight. Occasionally, the child may run a fever of 102° F. (39° C) or higher. In more severe cases of dehydration, the child may be listless and his eyes may be sunken. The soft spots (fontanels) in an infant's head may become depressed.

If your child shows signs of dehydration, call your doctor. If you cannot reach him, take the child to a hospital. If the diarrhea, vomiting, or other cause of the dehydration has stopped, give the child water or cracked ice. If he can keep this down, then give him small amounts of weak tea, a mixture of half water and half orange juice, or a carbonated soft drink.

The doctor will judge the severity of the dehydration on the basis of what has caused it and on any signs of dehydration the child has. He may also examine samples of the child's blood and urine to determine if there has been a mineral loss. If the dehydration is not severe, he may advise oral medication. If it is severe, and especially if there is persistent loss of fluids, the doctor will probably advise hospitalization and the giving of fluids intravenously. M.G.

See also **Diarrhea; Fever; Soft spots; Urinary disturbances; Vomiting**

Diabetes mellitus is a disease in which the body fails to utilize sugar properly. The failure occurs when the pancreas does not produce enough of the hormone that enables the body to store and burn sugar in its normal manner. This hormone is called insulin. Although diabetes is more common in adults, it can occur at any age.

A child with untreated diabetes usually eats a great deal more than is normal, drinks large quantities of water, and urinates frequently or in large amounts. A doctor can diagnose the child's condition by analyzing the child's urine and blood. A child who has diabetes will show an excess of sugar in both blood and urine. If the diagnosis is not made promptly and treatment begun, the child loses weight rapidly, breathes deeply and rapidly, is nauseated, vomits, gradually becomes weaker, and may become drowsy or go into a diabetic coma.

All diabetics should be under a doctor's care. Although diabetes cannot be cured, it can be controlled through the use of insulin injections. Oral substitutes for the insulin injections are not recommended for most children. Some insulin preparations act for many hours, so the child may need only one or two injections a day. Care must be taken to regulate the amount of insulin given, for too much may lower the blood sugar to a point where the child may feel unusually hungry or nauseated. The child may perspire and grow pale, or faint and lose consciousness—sometimes with a convulsion. This condition is called insulin shock. If a child appears to be developing insulin shock, offer orange juice or some other sugar-containing food, and promptly call your doctor.

In addition to giving insulin, many doctors prescribe specific diets consisting of foods that are low in sugar content.

Although the diabetes will be lifelong, it should not interfere with the child's psychological and social development. Encourage him to participate in the usual childhood activities and to take care of his own dietary and insulin needs. Diabetic children can grow to adult life able to carry on normal activities. M.G.

See also **Convulsions; Diets; Drugs; Endocrine glands; Heredity**

Diaper rash is so frequent in its mild form that almost every baby has it sometime. The skin in the diaper area looks red and chafed, and sometimes there are a few pimples and rough red patches on it. The rash may spread and the baby may be uncomfortable. Boys who have the sores of severe diaper rash on the penis may have pain when they are urinating.

Severe diaper rash usually results from an interaction of the bacteria on the skin and the urine on the wet diaper. This interaction produces ammonia, which irritates the skin and causes the rash.

To treat diaper rash, change wet or soiled diapers frequently. Avoid using waterproof pants over the diapers, especially on very young babies or on those with sensitive skin. Rinse the diapers thoroughly after washing them. The "rinse" cycle of an automatic washing machine usually rinses the diapers adequately.

When your baby's skin is chafed, let him lie without diapers for about an hour after each diaper change. The air will help dry and heal the skin. Apply a protective preparation, such as zinc oxide paste or a baby lotion, after the skin has been cleaned and dried. Your doctor may want to recommend a preparation.

For severe diaper rash, rinse the diapers in a vinegar solution—use ½ cup of household vinegar in the tub of rinse water. Rinse the diapers in this solution after they have been completely washed and rinsed. After rinsing them in the vinegar solution, wring the diapers out, or let them go through the "spin" cycle of an automatic machine, and dry them in the usual way.

Occasionally, diaper rash occurs because enzyme- and bleach-containing detergents are used in washing the diapers. You can lessen the chances of this if you use a mild soap and rinse the diapers thoroughly. Boiling the diapers for half an hour or more after washing may be helpful if the measures listed above are ineffective.

If the diaper rash looks like a chemical burn, develops blisters, or becomes infected, consult the baby's doctor. Impetigo (a blister-forming skin disease) is a fairly common complication of severe diaper rash. A.M.M.

See also **Impetigo**

Diarrhea is an intestinal disorder marked by frequent loose, watery bowel movements. Diarrhea can be serious, especially when it is accompanied by mucus or blood in the stools, listlessness, failure to eat, vomiting or fever. If your child's diarrhea persists or appears to be serious, call your doctor.

Diarrhea in babies is often caused by problems in feeding. Sometimes the baby's formula is not sterilized adequately or is made in incorrect proportions (too much sugar or too little water). Check with your doctor about your formula preparation and the amounts you are feeding the baby. Sometimes a baby has one or two loose stools when he starts eating new solid foods, particularly when chopped or bite-size foods are replacing strained ones. To help your baby adjust more easily to new solid foods, cut down on the amount of the foods and start him on them slowly. Occasionally, diarrhea may be caused by a food allergy.

Mild diarrhea may accompany a general infection. Your doctor may prescribe medicine for the general infection. He may also suggest that you give your child extra fluids (water, diluted formula, apple juice, or very weak tea) to help replace the fluid lost in the diarrhea bowel movements. And he will probably tell you to feed the child a bland diet consisting of such foods as applesauce, cereal, and gelatin.

Sometimes a specific bowel infection causes diarrhea. Be careful to prevent spreading the infection to other members of your family. Wash your hands after handling the baby or his diapers. Place the diapers in a covered container and wash them separately from other clothing. Boil the diapers or iron them to kill germs.

In older children, diarrhea is usually milder but it occurs for similar reasons—bowel infection, as part of a general illness, or food that the child has trouble digesting. Diarrhea may also be a symptom of tension or anxiety that occurs at times of stress or excitement, such as a school examination or a special party. If these situations frequently cause diarrhea, consider ways to relieve your child of his stress or to help him avoid too much excitement. M.G.

See also **Allergy; Dehydration; Food poisoning; Influenza; Sterilizing**

Diets. A balanced diet contains all the food elements that a child needs to grow and stay healthy. A child requires proteins to build body tissues, fats and carbohydrates for energy, and minerals and vitamins for growth, maintaining body tissues, and regulating body functions.

Your doctor may prescribe a special diet for your child if the child has an illness, a food allergy, or a weight problem. Be certain you know why the diet is being prescribed and how you can best carry it out.

Here are some questions you may want to ask your doctor when he advises a diet.

- Is the quantity of food eaten important? If so, how can you keep a record of what the child eats?
- If your physician advises a gelatin dessert, does he mean one made from plain, unsweetened gelatin or from prepared, sweetened products?
- How urgent is it to follow the diet closely? In some metabolic diseases, where the child's body cannot digest certain component materials in foods, it is vitally important to follow the dietary prescription to the letter.

Encourage your child to stay on the diet. If there are choices among foods, use those the child prefers, especially if he must remain on the diet for a long time. Let the child who can understand assume some responsibility for eating needed foods and avoiding others. Most children are happy to have this trust placed in them. An older child often can help plan what he will eat. Helping to make such decisions may give him the incentive to carry them out.

Make diet food as appealing as you can. For instance, a white cream soup, beautifully smooth and served in a colorful bowl or cup with a bright garnish, usually perks up the appetite of a child on a bland diet.

A child on a diet has to learn to go without eating certain foods, but try not to put an extra strain on his willpower. For example, a child who is allergic to eggs has to accept the fact that he cannot eat eggs for breakfast even though the rest of the family has eggs. But, serve eggless desserts so he can eat the family dessert. M.G.

See also **Allergy; Anorexia nervosa; Appetite; Nutrition; Overweight; Underweight; Vitamins**

Diphtheria is a severe, contagious disease in which a membrane forms in the throat or nose. This membrane may hinder breathing and eventually cause choking, or even death. Diphtheria is caused by bacteria. Once common, diphtheria is no longer widespread because almost all children are vaccinated against it.

Diphtheria usually begins about two to six days after exposure. A child with diphtheria may have a sore throat, fever, headache, backache, drowsiness, and vomiting. Yellowish-gray patches may appear on the throat, the tonsils, or the roof of the mouth. Sometimes, the membrane so completely obstructs the throat that the child cannot breathe. A doctor may have to perform a tracheotomy (incision into the windpipe) to get air into the lungs. Call your doctor immediately if you suspect that your child has diphtheria.

Inoculations of diphtheria toxoid are routinely given in a single shot along with tetanus (lockjaw) toxoid and pertussis (whooping cough) vaccine. These inoculations, called DTP shots, are usually given at 2, 4, 6, and 18 months of age. As further protection, a DTP booster is given at 4 to 6 years of age, or when entering kindergarten or first grade.

For nonimmunized children over 6 years of age, two Td shots (combined tetanus and diphtheria toxoids) are given eight weeks apart. A third shot a year later completes the immunization.

For continued protection, all immunized children should have a Td booster shot every ten years.

After your baby receives a DTP shot, he may run a fever, lose his appetite, and be cranky. The area around the injection may be sore and red. This reaction occurs because of the whooping cough vaccine. Give aspirin in doses appropriate for the baby's age to relieve fever. Your baby should feel better the next day. Be sure to tell your doctor if your baby does have a reaction. He may want to change the amount of the injection. H.D.R., JR.

See also **Communicable diseases; Fever; Immunization; Shots; Tetanus; Whooping cough**

Disinfecting. *See* **Sterilizing**

Dislocation of shoulder joint

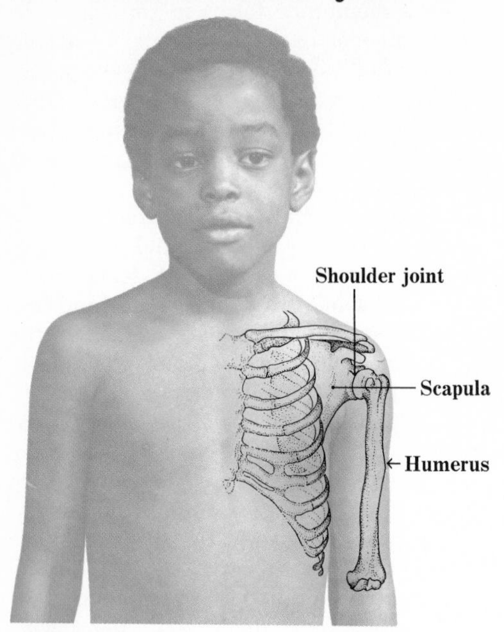

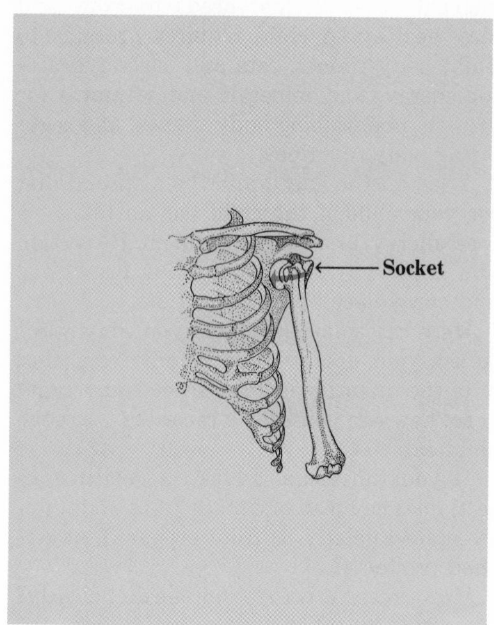

The shoulder joint consists of two bones—the humerus and the scapula. When the humerus slips out of the socket of the scapula (*right*), the shoulder is dislocated and the child experiences immediate pain.

Dislocation of joint. A joint is dislocated when the two bone ends that make up the joint become separated and no longer work together. Most dislocations occur in the shoulder, elbow, ankle, or finger joints.

Dislocation causes a child immediate pain and rapid swelling, and he cannot use the joint normally. The bone may be broken, so call a doctor at once and do not move the child. If you cannot reach a doctor, protect the joint by putting splints on the injured part in the most comfortable position. Do not pull on the bones. After applying the splint, immediately take the child to a hospital for X-ray examination and proper care. The child will probably be given an anesthetic, and the doctor will gently manipulate the bones of the joint back into their proper position. Then the doctor will usually apply a splint or cast to protect the healing joint.

Sometimes, a joint—usually the shoulder or kneecap—continues to dislocate periodically. Surgery is required to correct it. J.J.G.

Drowning. *See* **Artificial respiration**

Drugs are used to provide comfort and to prevent and cure disease. Drugs are obtained from plants, animals, and minerals. Or, they can be produced synthetically.

- Insulin is a hormone extracted from animal tissues. Doctors use insulin to control diabetes mellitus, a disease in which the body does not produce enough insulin.
- Most antibiotics are produced from molds that live in the soil. Doctors use antibiotics to treat blood poisoning, boils, osteomyelitis (bone infections), pneumonia, scarlet fever, and tuberculosis.
- Sulfa drugs are synthetic drugs, produced from chemicals. Doctors may use sulfa drugs against blood poisoning, meningitis, pneumonia, and urinary tract infections.
- Vaccines are made from the growth of bacteria or viruses. Vaccines have been developed to prevent diphtheria, poliomyelitis, measles, German measles, whooping cough, tetanus, and other diseases.
- Silver nitrate is a drug derived from a mineral. Doctors drop silver nitrate into the eyes of a newborn baby to prevent infection.

The same drug often may be dispensed in different forms. For the child who cannot swallow capsules or tablets, a doctor may prescribe a syrup, drops, or chewable tablets. If a child is vomiting, the drug may be given as a suppository. A doctor injects a drug if he wants a rapid effect, or if the drug is ineffective when taken by mouth. Time-release capsules allow the action of the drug to be spread over a period of hours.

Many drugs can be bought without prescriptions, but there are dangers in giving them to children. Many illnesses have similar symptoms but are treated differently. Your doctor will diagnose the illness and prescribe the proper drug and dosage. An overdose of any drug may be harmful. Do not even give vitamins to your child without first checking with your doctor.

After your child recovers from an illness, discard the unused drug prescribed for him. Medicines often deteriorate with time. Also, they may be hazardous to a child exploring the medicine cabinet. (See also THE DRUG PROBLEM, page 121.) M.G.

Ear, objects in the. If your child says that something is in his ear, do not try to remove the object yourself. Just the attempt to remove a foreign object may injure the ear canal or eardrum. Or the object may be pushed farther down the ear canal, making it harder to get out. Call your doctor. If you cannot reach him, take your child to a hospital emergency room.

Children are prone to put such things as peas, beans, or corn kernels into their ears. These vegetables absorb moisture and swell, causing intense pain and blocking the ear. Paper also swells and causes pain and blockage. Beads, buttons, and stones that fit into a child's ears can cause painful irritation. Sometimes an insect lodges itself in a child's ear canal, causes discomfort because of its movement, and frightens the child with its buzzing. Matches or hairpins may break the skin and cause a painful infection.

Caution your child never to put anything into his ears. Try to keep small objects out of his reach. C.F.F.

See also **Earaches**

Dyslexia is a reading disability that doctors believe is inherited. It occurs much more often in boys than in girls.

Dyslexic children read slowly and with considerable effort. They may also have difficulty telling right from left. Children with dyslexia tend to reverse letters and words at an age when this is no longer normal. Frequently, they guess at words when they are asked to read.

Most children with dyslexia are not intellectually retarded and do not have eye problems or brain damage. But they may become emotionally disturbed because they are unable to read as well as their classmates.

Doctors know of no specific cure or treatment for dyslexia, but qualified reading tutors may help the child.

Many children with dyslexia are subjected to considerable pressure under the mistaken notion that they are not trying to learn. If parents and teachers recognize that the child is truly handicapped, and if they exert less pressure, the child will suffer less emotional stress. M.G.

Earaches are usually caused by infections. The infection may occur in the outer, middle, or inner ear.

Ear infections. The common cold is the most frequent cause of an ear infection. Cold germs travel from the nose to the middle ear through a short tube called the Eustachian tube.

Frequent swimming, especially in fresh water, can cause ear infections. The outer ear canal—the part you can see when you look directly into the ear—is especially susceptible to infection during hot, humid weather.

A child may also start an infection of his ear canal by scratching and poking his ear with his fingernails, bobby pins, matches, or other objects. With these objects, he may break the skin surface and germs can cause a boil or an abscess to form.

Call your doctor whenever your child has an earache, especially if he also has a fever, or if there is draining from the ear. Your doctor may prescribe antibiotics or sulfa drugs to treat the infection. Occasionally,

(**Earaches,** *continued*) however, these drugs are not used soon enough, or they encounter germs that resist them. Then, your doctor may make a small opening in the eardrum to allow the infection to drain.

Infection of the ear canal is often painful. To ease the pain of earache, apply an electric heating pad, a hot-water bottle, or hot compresses to the ear. Or, put 3 or 4 warm drops of mineral oil in the ear. Aspirin may also help.

Other causes. Sometimes earaches occur even when the ear itself is healthy. If your child complains of an earache and no ear infection is present, he should have his teeth, nose, and throat examined. An unerupted wisdom tooth, a sinus infection, or tonsillitis may be the cause of the pain.

Wax in the ear seldom causes earache. The wax is not an accumulation of dirt, but a natural body secretion. If a plug of ear wax is moistened while the child is swimming or bathing, it may expand and cause temporary deafness. Prompt removal of the wax by a doctor will cure this. C.F.F.

Eczema is a rash that is usually caused by an allergy to a food, drug, or some other irritating substance. Patches of skin become red and itch persistently. Often the itching is so intense that the child scratches himself until he bleeds. Scratching opens the skin. This lets a colorless fluid ooze from the rash. The skin becomes thick, coarse, dry, and scaly. In an infant, the rash appears mainly on the cheeks, and in the folds of the neck, arms, and sides of the legs. In an older child, it appears mainly as chronic, thickened areas behind the knees, in front of the elbows, or in the creases of the neck. In severe cases, it may spread over the entire body. If you think that your child has eczema, consult your doctor.

The cause of eczema is often difficult to determine. Your doctor may suggest eliminating a certain food from the infant's diet to find out if that particular food is causing the allergic reaction. In more severe cases, he may perform skin tests on the child to see which substances he is allergic to. If he can discover what is causing the eczema, you can sometimes prevent the condition by removing the offending food from the child's diet or by removing the irritating material from his surroundings.

Eczema usually begins in infancy. It occurs more often in children with a family history of allergies. It usually clears completely by the time the child is 18 to 24 months old. Sometimes, however, it persists through puberty and into adult life. The skin of a child who has had severe eczema usually heals without any scars. However, some children may retain uneven pigmentation of the skin, which is exaggerated by sunburn. Many children with eczema develop hay fever or asthma as they get older. A child may also have both eczema and a respiratory allergy at the same time. If your child has eczema, certain precautions may reduce the discomfort produced by the rash.

- Do not let the child's skin come into contact with wool or clothing made of synthetic fibers. Cotton material is preferable.
- Avoid clothing that causes an excessive amount of perspiration.

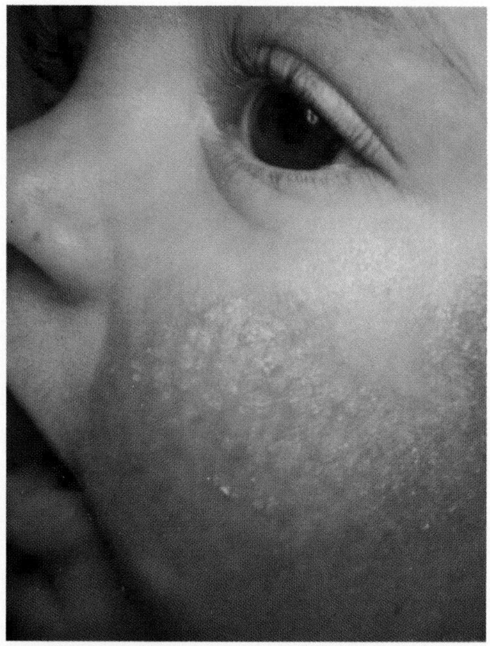

In infants, eczema usually starts on the cheeks and then spreads to the folds of the neck and other parts of the baby's body.

- Avoid irritating soaps and detergents, and excessive bathing.
- Keep the fingernails short to lessen damage from scratching.
- Antihistamines and other drugs may reduce itching, but they should be used only when prescribed by a doctor.
- When the skin is red and oozing, wet compresses help relieve itching and inflammation. Your doctor may also prescribe lotions and ointments to lessen itching.
- Keep a baby with eczema clothed because scratching becomes more violent when his clothes are off.
- Keep the child occupied to help take his mind off the itching.

The skin changes caused by eczema make the child's skin more susceptible to infection. A child with eczema must not be vaccinated against smallpox because the virus may spread and make him seriously ill. He must not even come in contact with anyone who has been recently vaccinated. Other immunizations are usually safe. J.S.H.

See also **Allergy; Itching**

Freeing a child from a live wire

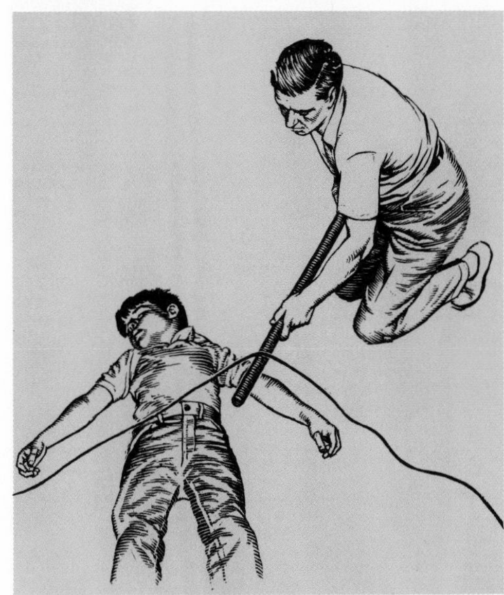

To get a live wire off your child, stand or kneel in a dry place and move the wire with a broomstick, or with any other object that does not conduct electricity.

Electric shock is usually much easier to prevent than to treat. It is very dangerous and can kill or seriously injure anyone.

If your child suffers electric shock, remember that while seconds count, do not be careless of your own safety. If you find the child unable to let go of an electric wire, keep calm. Do not touch either the wire or the child with your bare hands while electricity is still flowing. Pull the main switch if it is near, or jerk the plug from the socket. If you cannot turn the electricity off, you will have to move the wire off the child or the child off the wire. Use anything dry that does not conduct electricity—boards, branches, wooden poles, folds of cloth or newspaper, or rubber or heavy cloth gloves. And be sure that you are standing on a dry surface.

As soon as the child is free, start giving him artificial respiration if he has stopped breathing. (See ARTIFICIAL RESPIRATION, page 176). Have another person call the doctor and the fire department inhalator squad. If you are alone, restore breathing before calling the doctor. If an electric spark has caused a burn, treat it later.

A child suffers electric shock usually because an adult has forgotten how curious and investigative a child can be, or because the adult does not realize how little a child knows of danger or caution. To a child, an electric outlet is a fascinating hole in the wall, just right for poking with a stray bobby pin. To a child, an appliance cord is for pulling—he doesn't know that it may be faulty. To a child, it is quite possible that he can find his favorite television character by poking into the rear of the television set.

Make your home safe, keep your eye on your child, and let him understand that in dealing with dangers your "No" means "Positively no!" Even the crawler learns to stay away from outlets if you repeatedly pick the child up, say a firm "No," move him to another spot, and hand him a distracting toy. For added safety, you can buy special plastic plugs that cover the electric outlets. M.G.

See also **Accidents; Artificial respiration; Burns**

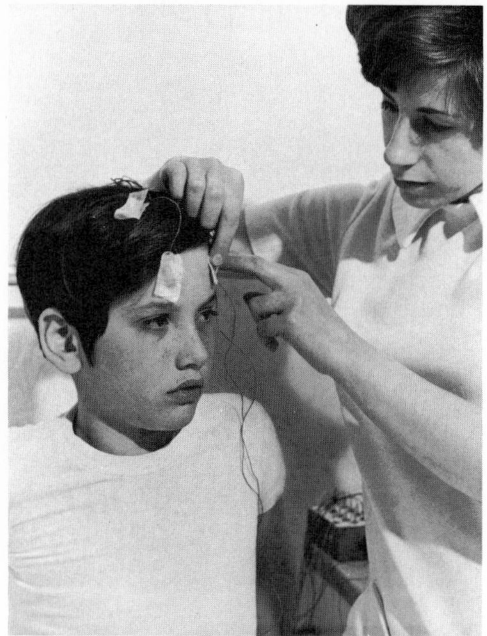

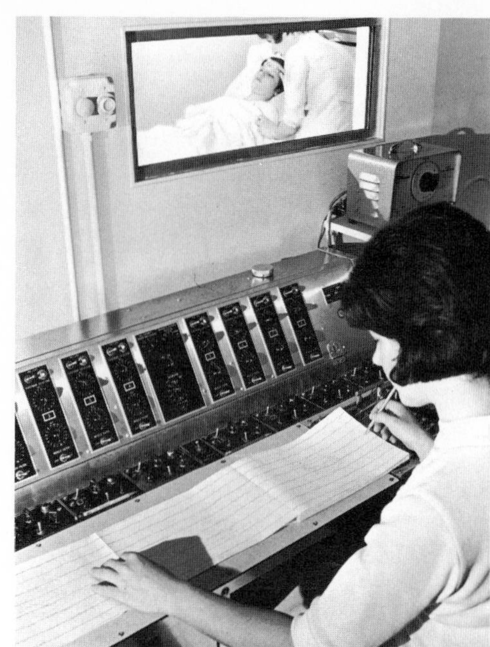

An electroencephalograph records brain waves. Wires attached to the child's head pick up electrical impulses from the brain. The impulses are then recorded on a strip of paper.

Electroencephalography is the recording and study of brain waves. An instrument called the electroencephalograph records electrical impulses sent out by the cortex (the thin layer of nerve cells that covers most of the brain). The electrical impulses are picked up by wires attached to the scalp, either with glue or with needles, and recorded on a strip of paper. The record (the electroencephalogram, or EEG) looks like a series of parallel, wavy lines. The child's hair does not have to be shaved off, and he feels no pain from the electroencephalograph.

Abnormal patterns may be recorded if the child has epilepsy, a brain tumor, encephalitis, drug intoxication, or a degenerative disease of the brain. In some cases, especially in epilepsy, doctors can determine the cause of the abnormal electrical pattern from the electroencephalogram. In other cases, the abnormal pattern indicates only that brain destruction or deterioration has occurred, and the electroencephalogram cannot be used to establish a definite cause of the destruction or deterioration. A.G.S.

Emetics are medicines that cause vomiting. Inducing vomiting is a recommended treatment for certain types of poisoning. But, remember: Never induce vomiting if the child is asleep, unconscious, semiconscious, or has convulsions; or if the child has swallowed a corrosive substance or a petroleum product.

Vomiting is more effective if the child first drinks some liquid. The best emetic is syrup (*not fluid extract*) of ipecac. If you do not have syrup of ipecac, put one teaspoon of mustard in half a glass of water, or three teaspoons of salt in a glass of warm water, and have the child drink the mixture. If none of these remedies is available, make the child vomit by finger-tickling the back of his throat.

Any time you induce vomiting, be sure to keep the child's head lower than his hips so that all the vomit flows out of his mouth and not back into his throat. Also, be sure to catch and save the vomit for the doctor to analyze. M.G.

See also **Poisonings and poisons**

Location of endocrine glands

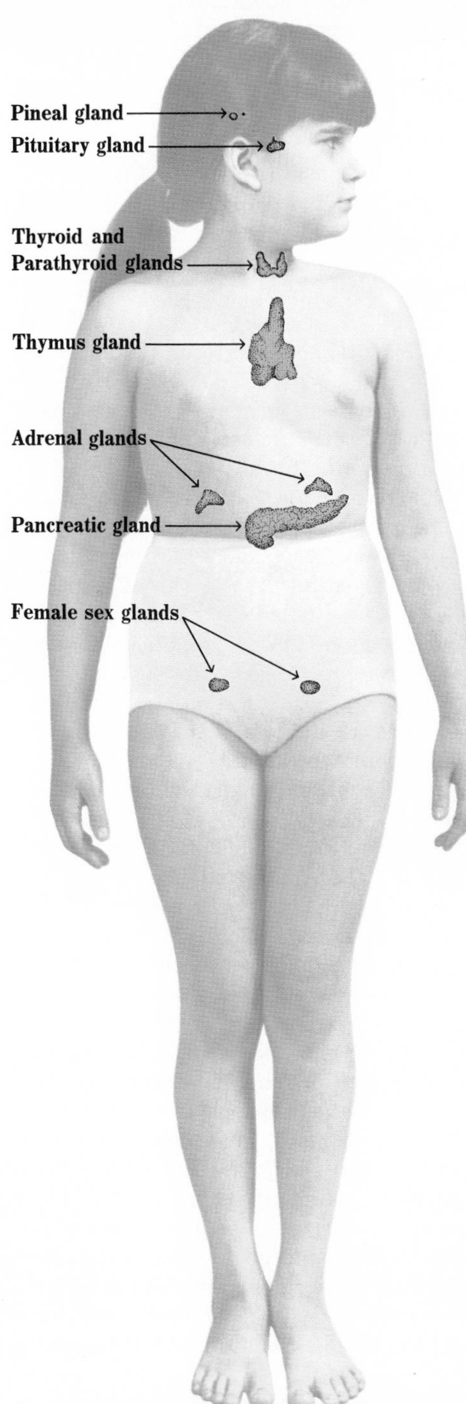

Each type of endocrine gland produces one or more hormones. These hormones regulate growth, sexual development, metabolism, and other body functions.

Endocrine glands produce vital chemical substances called hormones. Hormones regulate body growth and shape and various functions of the body. Endocrine glands are also called the ductless glands because their hormones enter the blood stream directly instead of through ducts.

The "master" endocrine gland is the pituitary. This gland, approximately the size of the end of your thumb, produces many hormones. One hormone regulates a child's growth. Other hormones regulate other endocrine glands—thyroid, adrenal, and sex glands.

The thyroid gland produces thyroid hormone, which regulates metabolism (chemical process of utilizing foods). The adrenal glands produce hormones that regulate growth, sexual development, sugar metabolism, and the use of salt. Part of the pancreatic gland produces insulin, which regulates the use of sugar within the body. The sex glands produce hormones that affect growth and the development of masculine or feminine characteristics. M.G.

Enema is the introduction of fluid into the intestine through the rectum to flush the bowels. The fluid remains in the intestine for a short time and, when eliminated, it washes out feces from the bowels. Enemas are usually given to empty the bowels before certain types of surgery.

Do not use enemas for constipation unless a doctor prescribes them. He may do so in the rare case of an impaction (a severe piling up of feces in the bowels). But constipation is best treated by a prescribed diet and increased exercise. Regular use of enemas for constipation may have harmful effects.

- They may make a mild case of constipation more severe, because they tend to destroy the healthy muscle tone of the bowels.
- They may frighten a young child.
- They may make a child focus too much attention on his anus and bowels.
- They are uncomfortable physically. M.G.

See also **Constipation**

Enuresis. *See* **Wetting**

Epilepsy is a chronic (long-lasting) disorder of the nervous system. Some forms cause convulsions and loss of consciousness. The exact cause of epilepsy is unknown, but it may be the result of any condition or disease that affects the brain. Epilepsy is not inherited, although there may be a family tendency toward the disease, as there may be toward heart disease.

Types of epilepsy. The two most common types of epilepsy are known as *grand mal* (pronounced "gran mahl") and *petit mal* (pronounced "petty mahl"). Some doctors prefer to use the terms "convulsive seizures" for grand mal and "absence attacks" for petit mal. When a child suffers a grand mal seizure, he loses consciousness, falls, and his muscles may stiffen or become rigid. He then begins to twitch and jerk, first rapidly, then more slowly but more violently. Saliva may flow more freely during convulsions and not be swallowed, and the child may lose control of his bowels and bladder. The convulsions usually last only a few minutes, but afterward the child may be drowsy and sleep for a time.

A seizure is dramatic and frightening, but children rarely suffer serious injury during them. You cannot do much for a child suffering an epileptic seizure except place a coat, pillow, or folded blanket under his head; loosen his clothing; and remove objects from the path of moving arms and legs. You may place a folded handkerchief between his teeth to keep him from biting his tongue or cheek. After the attack, turn the child on his side.

In a petit mal seizure, the child loses consciousness for a few seconds, but he usually can maintain his balance and does not fall. He may appear dazed momentarily after the seizure, but he soon resumes conversation or normal activity. Petit mal seizures occur frequently, perhaps dozens in a single day. They may interfere more with a child's learning than will the infrequent grand mal seizures, because they interrupt a child's concentration.

Not all convulsions are caused by epilepsy. An infant with a high fever may have convulsions. If the child is younger than 4, and if the convulsions occur only with a fever—and not very often—the convulsions will probably cease to be a problem by the time the child is about 6 years old. If the convulsions occur without fever and continue after the child is older, the doctor will suspect epilepsy.

Any child suffering from convulsions should have immediate medical attention. Parents should be completely frank in describing the child's convulsions, in reporting head injuries or illnesses involving high fevers, and in recalling any history of convulsions in the family. The doctor, who seldom is able to observe the seizure, will need this information and the results of diagnostic tests to make a proper diagnosis. He probably will request that an electroencephalographic study be made. This is a painless recording of the brain's activity picked up by sensitive wires that are pasted to the child's scalp. (See ELECTROENCEPHALOGRAPHY, page 222.) The recording appears on paper as an ink tracing of wavy lines.

Drugs can eliminate or reduce seizures in about 85 per cent of all epileptics, but some time may be required before the doctor can determine the proper combinations and dosages of drugs. Success of the treatment for epilepsy will depend largely upon how carefully and continually the doctor's instructions are followed.

Day-to-day living. Epileptic children need the same affectionate guidance, patient understanding, and satisfactions from life that all children need. Epilepsy itself is usually not a serious handicap, but the attitudes of adults and the child's playmates may create difficulties. Parents of an epileptic child should tell friends and neighbors about their child's condition, and give them accurate information about epilepsy.

However, epilepsy may impose some restrictions on a child's life. Swimming, bicycle riding, climbing, driving, and other activities may have to be limited. Most epileptic children can go to school. However, the parents of an epileptic child should inform the principal, teacher, and school nurse about the child's condition. An explanatory note from the child's doctor may also be helpful in case the child has a seizure at school and needs help. A.G.S.

See also **Convulsions; Electroencephalography; Fever**

Eye, objects in the. Your child will tell you immediately if he has something in his eye because it hurts. If he is still an infant, he will probably tell you by crying and rubbing his eyes.

Do not try to remove an object from your child's eye. Most foreign objects are washed out in a few moments by the extra tears the irritated eye produces. If the object does not wash out, call a doctor or take the child to a hospital. Many amateur attempts to remove objects from an eye result in loss of sight, usually from infection.

If a harmful fluid gets into your child's eye, wash the eye immediately with plenty of water. After you apply first aid, call your doctor. If you cannot reach him, take the child to a hospital emergency room.

If an eye is injured by a sharp object such as a dart, an arrow, or a knife, do not try to open the eyelids. Cover the injured eye with a clean cloth and take the child to a doctor or to the emergency room of the nearest hospital. R.O.S.

See also **Eyelids**

Eyeglasses. Eyeglasses cannot cure poor eyesight, but in many cases they can help a child to see better. Even when a child has no obvious eye defect, parents should be alert to signs of eye trouble. This is especially true of 2-year olds. By this age a child's eyes should be functioning effectively. But if he overreaches or underreaches in his attempts to grasp objects, seems overly sensitive to bright light, or squints or rubs his eyes excessively, he may have some visual deficiency.

Children should have a complete eye examination by the time they reach 3 years of age. They should have frequent reexaminations as they grow and their eyes change. If a serious visual deficiency is neglected in a preschooler, by the time the child is ready for school even glasses may not be of much help.

Parents should remember that often a young schoolchild with blurry vision may not complain about it because he thinks everyone sees as he does. The schoolchild who is mentally, emotionally, and physically healthy, but fails to keep up with his classmates, may have a visual problem. He may misbehave in class because he is frustrated by his inability to see clearly. Often, parents and teachers find that when such a child begins to wear glasses, his learning and behavioral problems tend to lessen and disappear. It is easier for a child to learn when he does not have to strain to see words on a page or on the blackboard.

The child who wears glasses need not wear them all the time unless his doctor tells him that he should. Some children need to wear glasses only when reading or doing close work. If this is the case with your child, let his teacher know it so that she can help your child use his glasses to the greatest advantage. Teach your child to take care of his glasses. Show him how to put them on and take them off without stretching the earpieces, how to keep his glasses clean, and how to handle them without scratching the lenses. Remind him that his glasses are a necessary tool to help him learn about the world through his eyes.

Eye health. A good rule for the care of normal eyes is to let them alone except for periodic medical examinations. When eyes seem abnormal in any respect, a complete eye examination is in order. Self-diagnosis and self-treatment of eye disorders can be disastrous.

Contrary to popular opinion, no known exercises will correct near-sightedness, farsightedness, or defective color vision. Also, extra vitamins or special foods rarely help in treating eye disorders or in developing normal eyes. The varied diet of food available to most people in the United States and Canada contains all the vitamins needed for eye health.

Infants. A child sheds no tears when he cries until he is several weeks old. Infants produce only enough tears to keep their eyes moist. Tears drain through two small openings in the inner corner of each eyelid into a tiny sac and then enter the nose, causing it to "run." Occasionally, this tear system becomes blocked and tears constantly run over the edges of the lid. Or the tear sac

(**Eye health,** *continued*) near the nose may swell. If this happens, call your doctor.

In the first few weeks of life a baby's eyes look crossed at times. Do not be alarmed at this lack of eye coordination. Let your doctor decide if the condition warrants attention. But if the baby's eyes are constantly out of line at 6 months of age, your doctor will probably refer your child for a special eye examination. If treatment is started early enough, it can often eliminate the need for surgery.

Older children. All children should have a complete eye examination before they enter the first grade. About one out of five children examined will need help with some visual problem. In most states, children receive visual screening tests when they enter school. Many children with poorly functioning eyes have received correction as a result of these tests. However, rather than count on the tests at school to discover if your child has a visual problem, it is wiser to have your child's eyes examined beforehand. Then have your child's eyes examined every two years.

Also, be alert to the following danger signs which can indicate eye difficulty.

- The child frequently stumbles or bumps into furniture.
- He squints, frowns, or blinks excessively while reading.
- He holds reading material close to his eyes.
- He has sore or unusually red eyes or eyelids.

Good lighting and correct posture ensure more efficient use of the eyes and often prevent eye discomfort. Do not restrict reading to save your child's eyesight. Restriction can actually prevent him from fully developing his visual ability. Like muscular ability, visual ability improves with practice and use.

Distinct contrasts in lighting may contribute to eye fatigue, as when a child watches television in a darkened room or studies at a desk where a single lamp leaves the rest of the room in darkness. Some other light should be on in the room.

To read well, a child must be able to see well. But if tests show his eyes to be normal, if his I.Q. is normal, and if he still is having difficulty in reading, perhaps he has an emotional problem. Because of emotional difficulties, some children who see words clearly find it almost impossible to understand their meanings. If this appears to be true of your child, consult your doctor.

Accidents. In the United States alone, children suffer about 95,000 serious eye accidents each year. About a thousand of these cases are so severe that the child loses the sight in one or both eyes. Most of these accidents could have been prevented.

Do not allow your child to handle sharp-pointed scissors. Allow him to use a BB gun, a bow and arrow, or sharp tools only if he is mature enough to understand the dangers involved.

If your child suffers an eye injury, get professional help immediately. Do not put liquid into the eye (except to wash out irritants such as acid or gasoline). Gently cover the eye, and take the child to a doctor. R.O.S.

See also **Astigmatism; Color blindness; Conjunctivitis; Cross-eye; Dyslexia; Eyelids; Farsightedness; Nearsightedness**

Eyelids protect the eyes and help keep them clean. Any disease of the eyelids should be checked by a doctor.

A sty, a common disease of the eyelid, is an infection in one of the glands in an eyelid. It is a small boil that forms at the lid edge. Usually it comes to a head, breaks, drains, and cures itself. Hot compresses held against the sty may hasten the process and relieve minor irritations.

One sty often leads to another because as a sty breaks and drains, it can infect other areas of the eyelid. To avoid this, your doctor may recommend antibiotic eye ointments or drops. If your child has one sty after another, a doctor should examine him.

Other diseases of the eyelids may produce redness, burning, itching, crusting, or swelling of the lids. There may also be tumors or notches in the eyelids, or the lid margin may be red. R.O.S.

See also **Conjunctivitis; Eye health**

Eyestrain. *See* **Eye health; Far-sightedness; Near-sightedness**

Fainting is a brief period of unconsciousness. It usually occurs suddenly, when the blood pressure falls to a point at which the brain does not get enough blood to maintain consciousness.

A child may feel weak and numb just before fainting. He may become nauseated and lightheaded, have blurred vision, and appear pale. He may salivate excessively and sweat, yawn, or sigh. Sometimes these symptoms end in a fainting spell, but other times they do not.

If your child faints, he will probably remain unconscious for only a few seconds. Place him flat on his back. Do not put anything under his head. Loosen his clothing and elevate his feet slightly. Blood will flow back into his brain, and he will regain consciousness. Call a doctor if your child has fainted and does not regain consciousness promptly.

A sudden fright or threat often causes a fainting spell. For example, fainting may occur as a reaction to pain, or to an unpleasant sight. Fatigue; fasting; standing motionless for long periods; hot, crowded quarters; and many other conditions may also cause fainting. The fainting spell usually occurs when a child is standing. It rarely happens when he is lying down.

Some children faint more easily than others. If your child faints easily, teach him to lie down or to sit and place his head between his knees as soon as the symptoms start. If he is in a very hot room, he should walk to a cooler area if possible. He should avoid situations which he knows may cause him to faint.

Usually, fainting is not a sign of any serious condition. However, if your child faints repeatedly, tell your doctor. He will want to determine the cause.

Fainting is only one cause of unconsciousness. Diabetic coma, head injury, and poisoning are others. M.G.

See also **Breath-holding; Coma; Convulsions; Diabetes mellitus; Head injuries; Poisonings and poisons**

Fallopian tubes. *See* **Menstruation**

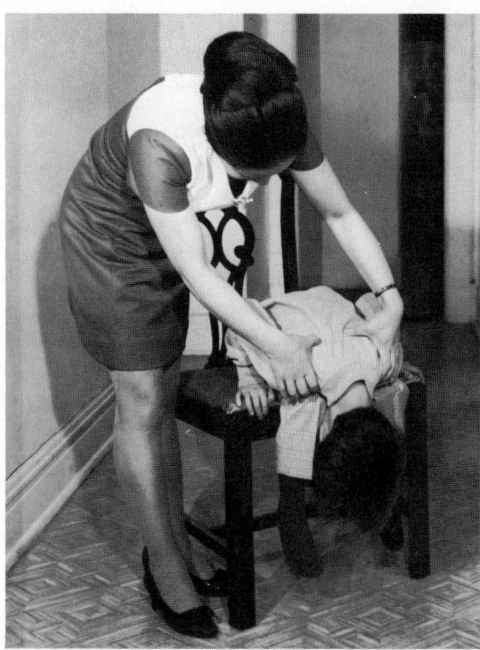

A child who faints easily should be taught to place his or her head between the knees as soon as fainting symptoms start.

Far-sightedness (hyperopia). A child who is far-sighted sees distant objects fairly well, but near objects are blurred. The reason for this is that a far-sighted eye is shorter from front to back than a normal eye. Light rays from an object strike the retina of the eye before they can be brought into focus.

Most far-sighted children see well at the beginning of a task involving reading or other close work. But if the task is prolonged, they may complain of blurred vision, eye discomfort, and headaches. A far-sighted child may become inattentive and cranky after studying or watching television or movies for too long a time.

Some children are poor readers because they are far-sighted. It is work for a far-sighted child to see because the child must focus the lenses of the eye more than a person with normal vision in order to see clearly. Because it is difficult to read, the child may daydream instead.

If you suspect your child is far-sighted, consult your doctor. A complete eye examination may be in order. R.O.S.

Fever. The normal oral temperature of the human body is about 98.6° F. (37° C). A higher temperature usually is called a fever. However, a child may be healthy and still have a temperature above normal.

A child's temperature goes up and down a little during each day, depending on the time of the day and what the child is doing. Usually, a child's temperature is slightly lower in the morning and slightly higher in the afternoon. Exercise, a hot bath, drinking warm liquids, or merely being out in the sun may raise a child's temperature by several tenths of a degree, or even an entire degree. If you want to know if your child has a fever after he has engaged in any of these activities, wait about half an hour before taking his temperature.

A below-normal temperature (around 97° F.; 36° C) may occur at the end of an illness. As long as the child feels well, do not be concerned.

A fever usually means that some infection is present in the child's body. If the fever is low grade (under 101° F.; 38° C), your child may lack energy and be drowsy, especially in the afternoon. Or, he may be irritable and restless. If the fever is above 101° F. (38° C), he will probably lack energy, complain of being ill, and want to remain quiet or go to bed. Headache and muscular aching often occur.

Reducing a fever. If your child has a fever, give him aspirin in doses appropriate for his age. (Use the table accompanying this article as a guide.) Or, your doctor may recommend using an aspirin substitute because in certain instances aspirin substitutes are easier to give, they are less likely to cause the child to vomit, and they are less dangerous. Call your doctor if the aspirin or aspirin substitute does not control the fever; if the fever is 102° F. (39° C) or higher; or if the child has a rash, a sore throat, or an earache.

Some children have convulsions if a fever develops rapidly. If your child tends to have fever convulsions and he is running a high fever, try to lower his temperature. Give him aspirin or aspirin substitute in doses

Proper dosage of aspirin and aspirin substitutes.

Avoid overdosage. Check with your doctor before giving more than two doses.

Age of Child	Amount	Frequency
6 months old	½ tablet of baby aspirin, or 0.3 milliliter aspirin substitute	Every 3 to 4 hours
1 year old	1 tablet of baby aspirin, or 0.6 milliliter aspirin substitute	Every 3 to 4 hours
2 years old	1½ tablets of baby aspirin, or ½ to 1 teaspoon aspirin substitute	Every 3 to 4 hours
3 years old	2 tablets of baby aspirin, or 1 teaspoon aspirin substitute	Every 3 to 4 hours
4 years old	3 tablets of baby aspirin, or 1 to 1½ teaspoons aspirin substitute	Every 4 hours
5 years old	4 tablets of baby aspirin, or 1 to 1½ teaspoons aspirin substitute	Every 4 hours

(Four baby aspirins equal one 5-grain (320-milligram) adult aspirin)

How to take a child's temperature

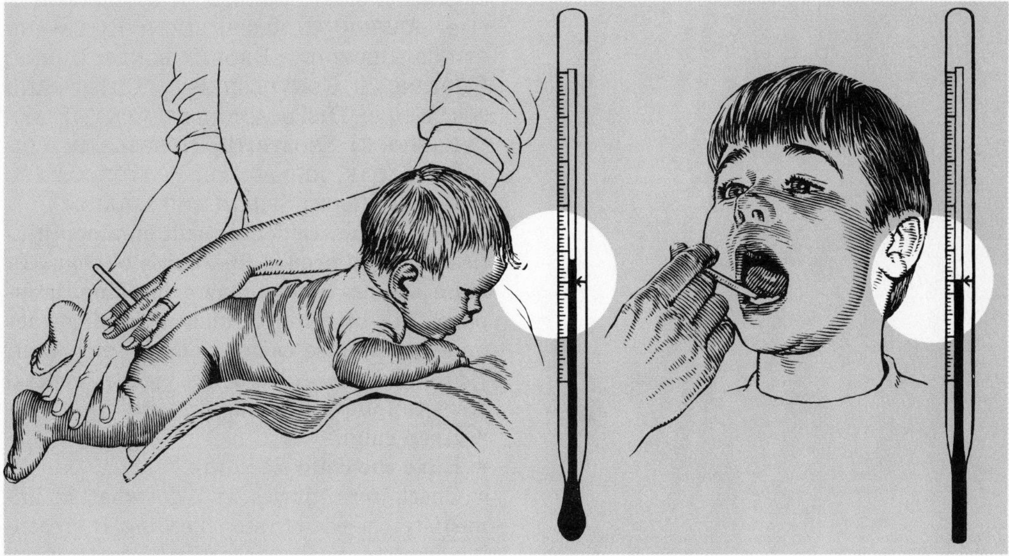

To use a rectal thermometer, lay the child face down. Insert the bulb of the thermometer about an inch (2.5 centimeters) into the rectum and hold it in place gently. Normal rectal temperature is about 99.6° F. (37.5° C). Use an oral thermometer for older children. Place the bulb under the tongue. Then the mouth should be kept closed. Normal oral temperature is about 98.6° F. (37° C).

appropriate for his age. Also, sponge his skin with cool or lukewarm water. If he does have a convulsion, call your doctor.

Taking a child's temperature. The three most common ways of taking a child's temperature are by rectum, by mouth, or by armpit. Rectal temperature registers about a degree higher than oral temperature. The temperature by armpit registers about a degree lower than oral temperature. When you report the temperature, tell your doctor how you took it.

Take the temperature of an infant or young child rectally, using a rectal thermometer. Check the mercury-filled bulb of the thermometer to be certain it is not cracked. Then lubricate the tip with petroleum jelly or cold cream. Lay the child on his stomach across your knees. Gently insert the thermometer about an inch (2.5 centimeters) into the child's rectum. Let the thermometer find its own direction. Then, place your hand on the child's buttocks and hold the thermometer like a cigarette so that the child will not injure himself if he moves. Leave the thermometer in place for two or three minutes.

When the child is a year old, you may want to start taking his temperature in his armpit. Undress the child so that he has no clothes on between his arm and his chest. Use either an oral or a rectal thermometer. Place the bulb in his armpit and hold his arm against his side for five minutes.

Temperatures can be taken orally with school-age children. Place the thermometer under the child's tongue for three to five minutes. Be sure he keeps his mouth closed.

To read a thermometer, hold it at the end opposite the mercury bulb. Do not hold it by the bulb because the heat of your fingers may raise the temperature. Rotate the thermometer until the mercury column appears. After you have read the temperature, wash the thermometer with alcohol or cool, soapy water. Hold the thermometer tightly by the end opposite the bulb. Shake it down by snapping your wrist. Keep shaking it until the mercury falls. M.G.

See also **Convulsions; Dehydration**

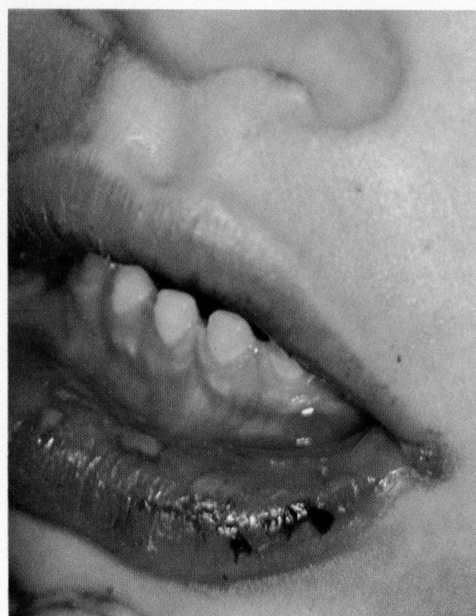

A fever blister starts as a patch of red, burning skin. Then yellowish blisters develop. When these blisters break, they ooze and form a crust.

Fever blisters (herpes simplex) usually form on the lips or around the mouth, but they sometimes form inside the mouth. They also may occur on the mucous membrane of a girl's genitals and the surrounding skin. Fever blisters are also called cold sores. They are caused by a virus.

Fever blisters often occur along with certain illnesses that cause fever, such as the common cold or the flu. The blisters also tend to recur, particularly when the child is subjected to physical or emotional stress.

The blisters are infectious, so the infected child should have his own washcloth and towel and should avoid spreading the fluid in the blisters. The blisters usually dry in three or four days and develop a crust. The crust drops off in another three to five days.

Call your doctor whenever your child is badly troubled by fever blisters. The doctor may prescribe the application of camphorated oil or a salve to make the child more comfortable. M.G.

Fingernails. *See* **Nail care**

First aid. (NOTE: First aid for particular emergencies is described in separate articles—ARTIFICIAL RESPIRATION; BITES AND STINGS; BLEEDING; BROKEN BONES; BURNS; CHOKING; CONVULSIONS; CUTS AND SCRATCHES; DISLOCATION OF JOINT; ELECTRIC SHOCK; FROSTBITE; NOSEBLEED; POISON IVY, OAK, AND SUMAC; POISONINGS AND POISONS; SHOCK; SPRAIN AND STRAIN.)

Most home accidents result in minor injuries, and the needed first aid is obvious. In more serious cases—severe bleeding, stoppage of breathing, and poisoning—act quickly, because each second is important.

First-aid rules. Here are some general steps to follow in giving first aid.

- Keep calm.
- Have the child lie down.
- Check for injuries and do what is immediately needed to stop bleeding. If breathing has stopped, give artificial respiration. If the child has been poisoned, give the proper antidote.
- Call the doctor. If possible, have someone else call him while you give first aid.
- Keep the child quiet and continue first-aid treatment until the doctor arrives.

First-aid kits. To do its job properly in the home, in the family car, or on a hike through the woods, a first-aid kit should contain sufficient materials for its probable use. It should be arranged so that you can quickly remove any item without scrambling the contents of the entire kit. Individual items should be wrapped separately so that unused materials do not become soiled or contaminated.

Surgical supply manufacturers package first-aid kits according to Red Cross specifications. First-aid kits available in most drugstores and department stores are not standardized. Examine the contents and packaging of a kit before buying one.

To meet most emergencies, you should have the following items:

An assortment of adhesive bandage strips
Several gauze pads
A roll of adhesive tape
A roll of sterile gauze bandage
A tube of burn ointment
A package of folded, sterile gauze totaling one-half square yard (0.5 square meter) or more. M.G.

Fistulas are abnormal tunnels or openings in the body. Generally, they connect one organ with another organ, or an organ with an abnormal opening in the skin.

Fistulas occur in three ways.

- They may be congenital.
- They may result from infection when an abscess ruptures into two organs, or into an organ and the skin.
- Or, they may result from an injury that penetrates the body.

Symptoms of fistulas include pain and a discharge of pus or other matter.

Congenital fistulas. In rare cases, a child is born with a fistula leading from the navel to either the bowel or bladder. If the bowel is involved, contents from the intestines ooze from the navel. If the bladder is involved, urine oozes from the navel. Another fistula that may be present at birth connects the trachea (windpipe) and the esophagus (tube that carries food to the stomach). When the baby is first fed, milk gets into the trachea and he has difficulty breathing.

Infections. Anal fistulas are commonly caused by infections and abscesses near the rectum. This fistula (called fistula in ano) leads from the rectum to the anus. Pus, and occasionally excrement, oozes through the abnormal opening. Regional enteritis (an inflammation of the intestine) sometimes causes fistulas to develop between loops of the intestine, from the intestine to the abdominal wall, or from the intestine to the bladder.

Injuries. An injury, such as a gunshot wound or a fall onto a sharp object, can harm an artery and a vein and result in an arteriovenous fistula. Blood runs directly from the artery into the vein, putting an increased workload on the heart.

If your child has a draining sore on his skin, consult your doctor. Most fistulas are corrected by surgery. The complexity of the operation depends on the organs affected. Some, such as the fistula in ano, may close spontaneously and heal. Sometimes, fistulas are cured by a minor operation requiring only about a day in the hospital. Those that involve blood vessels or the trachea are more complicated and require major operations for correction. T.M.H.

See also **Colitis**

Normal foot and flat foot

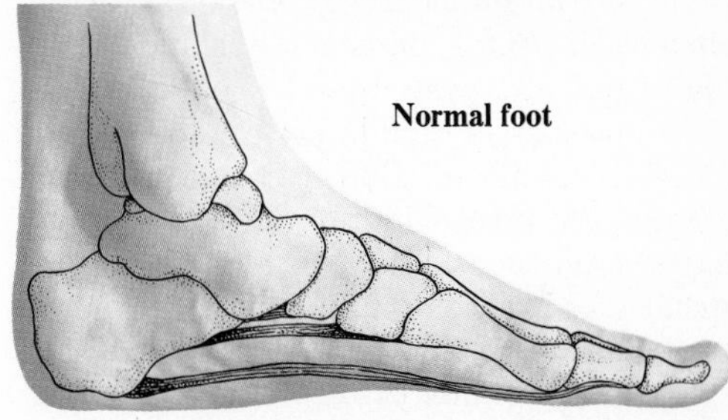

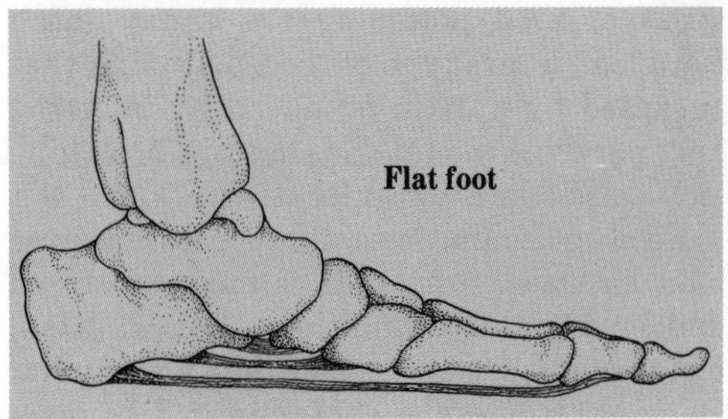

The bones in the arch of a normal foot are supported by muscles and ligaments. When these muscles and ligaments are weak, the arch flattens.

Flat feet. The arch of the foot consists of several bones, all fitting next to one another in a curve that is supported by muscles and ligaments that attach to the bones. When these muscles are weak, the arch relaxes and flattens out, and the child develops flat feet. Soreness, pain, and fatigue may develop.

Most babies look as though they have flat feet. Their feet are usually quite plump, and fat partially hides the foot arch. As a child uses his feet and learns to walk, the muscles strengthen and hold the bones of the foot in a firm arch. If your child still appears to have flat feet when he is about 2 years old, if he is having pain in his feet or legs, or if he tires easily, consult your doctor. The doctor may suggest applying wedges to the inner heel of each shoe.

Until your child is about 2 years old, he should wear soft shoes with flexible high tops and flexible leather soles. These soles allow the muscles of his feet and ankles to move and become stronger. J.J.G.

Flu. *See* **Influenza**

Food poisoning can result from eating food that is contaminated by bacteria or by chemicals. Some mushrooms and other plants can also cause food poisoning.

Symptoms of food poisoning include nausea, vomiting, diarrhea, and stomach cramps. Younger children and infants may have convulsions. Call your doctor if you suspect food poisoning. In most cases he will prescribe drugs and a diet to control the symptoms. Serious cases of food poisoning may require hospitalization. However, most types of food poisoning are rarely fatal. Botulism, a rare type of food poisoning that is caused by a toxin produced by bacteria, may paralyze the muscles used in breathing and cause death by suffocation.

Food poisoning usually occurs because food has been prepared, canned, or stored under unsanitary conditions. Potato salad, meat salads, custards, chicken, and similar foods easily become contaminated by bacteria. Keep these foods refrigerated until they are served. M.G.

See also **Poisonings and poisons**

Foot care. Probably the most common questions parents ask about their child's feet are, "When should he start wearing shoes?" and "What type of shoes should he wear?" For the first year, a baby does not need shoes. He does not need even booties or socks on his feet unless the house or floor is unusually cold. Even when he starts standing and walking, he does not have to wear shoes unless he is outdoors in cold weather, or walking where he might injure his feet. There is real value in letting him go barefoot under suitable conditions until he is 2 or 3 years old. Going barefoot helps strengthen foot and leg muscles, and helps build up foot arches.

Buy your child his first pair of shoes when he begins walking. The proper first shoe should have a flat, flexible sole and a high top. When he is about 2 years old, he can begin wearing the regular low-cut oxford.

Does the shoe fit your child properly? When your child stands, his longest toe should be from ¼ to ½ inch (6 to 13 millimeters) from the end of the shoe. To check the width of a shoe, lightly pinch the material over the child's toes. It should form a little fold if the shoe is wide enough. Later, when your child wears sturdier shoes, you can check the width by pressing in the sides of the shoe while he is standing. If the shoe is wide enough, a slight bulge should form.

Proper fitting socks are important, too. Your child's socks, like his shoes, should have from ¼ to ½ inch (6 to 13 millimeters) extra room at the toe end. Cotton and wool are the best materials for socks because they cushion the foot and absorb moisture. Change your child's socks every day. When your child is old enough to put on his own socks, check to be sure that he puts them on correctly, with the heel of the sock covering the heel of his foot.

Until your child is about 5 or 6 years old, check his shoes every few weeks to be certain they are still long enough and wide enough. The average toddler needs a new pair of shoes about every 3 or 4 months. Children usually outgrow their shoes before they wear them out, but never let a child wear a pair of shoes that are run-down at the heels or on the soles. Run-down shoes put extra pressure on parts of the child's feet and may cause aching feet, calluses, and other foot disorders.

An older child may not tell you that his shoes do not fit or that they hurt his feet. Look for certain signs. If a child appears to walk with discomfort, or if he takes off his shoes as soon as he gets into the house, his shoes are probably too small. An indication of short shoes is redness at the base of the big toenails. Red spots or blisters indicate that the shoes may be rubbing against the child's feet.

Do not pass shoes down from an older child to a younger child. Feet have different shapes, and the older child has impressed the shoes with the shape of his feet. Even though hand-me-down shoes may be the right size, they can force the younger child's feet out of their own, individual shape and into the shape of the shoes. J.J.G.

See also **Bowlegs; Flat feet; Hip, congenital dislocation; Knock-knee; Nail care; Ringworm; Warts**

Fracture. *See* **Broken bones**

If your child's hands or feet become frostbitten, warm them gradually by soaking them in lukewarm water.

Frostbite results when the body is exposed to extreme cold. It usually occurs in the ears, fingers, nose, and toes. The immediate effect of frostbite is that the frostbitten area becomes whitish and numb. This occurs because the blood and moisture in the tissues freeze and circulation is cut off. Further damage varies. The tissue of a frostbitten finger may be completely destroyed. Or the child may experience no more than a mildly painful burning sensation every time the finger is exposed to cold, even months after the original injury.

If you think your child has frostbite, follow these procedures.

- Consult a doctor as soon as possible.
- Do not massage the frostbitten area, because you may damage the tissues.
- Do not rub the frostbitten area with snow or ice, because you may remove the skin and injure the tissues.
- Take the child indoors and let the frostbitten area warm gradually.
- Do not apply hot pads, heating pads, or hot-water bottles.
- Do not put the child close to a hot stove or under a heat lamp.
- Soak frostbitten fingers or toes in lukewarm water (90° to 100° F.; 32° to 38° C). Apply warm (not hot), wet towels to frostbitten nose or ears.
- If blisters occur, cover them with a bandage to protect them from infection.

Frostbite can be prevented by following certain precautions.

- Dampness increases the chance of frostbite, so teach your child to come indoors to change wet or damp clothing, particularly his mittens, shoes, and socks.
- Be certain that his ears, hands, and feet are adequately protected in cold weather.
- When he is ice-skating, skiing, or otherwise going to be exposed to the cold for a long time, he should wear a protective face mask. M.G.

See also **Blister**

Fungus diseases. *See* **Ringworm; Thrush**

Furuncle. *See* **Boil**

Gagging is a reflex action at the back of the throat. Sometimes it produces vomiting. If your baby gags, it is a sign that he is not able to cope with whatever is in his mouth and may need your help. Older children sometimes gag just to get attention.

Many young babies gag easily and this may cause "spitting up." Occasionally, a baby may gag because a bit of dust or lint gets into his mouth, or because a nipple is pushed too far into his mouth. Sometimes babies gag during feeding simply to show that they have had enough to eat. A child also gags if he is nauseated and about to vomit.

Babies often gag when first offered solid food, such as cereal. This is quite natural, because the solid food is strange in consistency and is difficult for them to swallow. To avoid the gagging, make the food more fluid and offer it in smaller amounts.

Gagging is an important protection against the entry of solids into the larynx and breathing passages where they could cause choking and suffocation. M.G.

Gamma globulin is one part of plasma, the liquid part of blood. Gamma globulin contains antibodies that help the body fight infection. When an infection begins, the body manufactures gamma globulin that includes antibodies to fight that infection. In some cases, after the infection has cleared up, enough of the gamma globulin remains in the body to prevent the child from getting that disease a second time. That is why it is unusual for a child to have a disease like measles twice.

Pooled gamma globulin serum—that is, gamma globulin taken from a number of people—may be injected into a susceptible child who has been exposed to a disease. For example, a doctor may inject gamma globulin into a child who has been exposed to measles or hepatitis. The injection may prevent the disease or make it milder.

Some children lack gamma globulin completely. These children must receive regular injections of the substance. J.S.H.

See also **Allergy; Communicable diseases; Immunization; Shots; Virus**

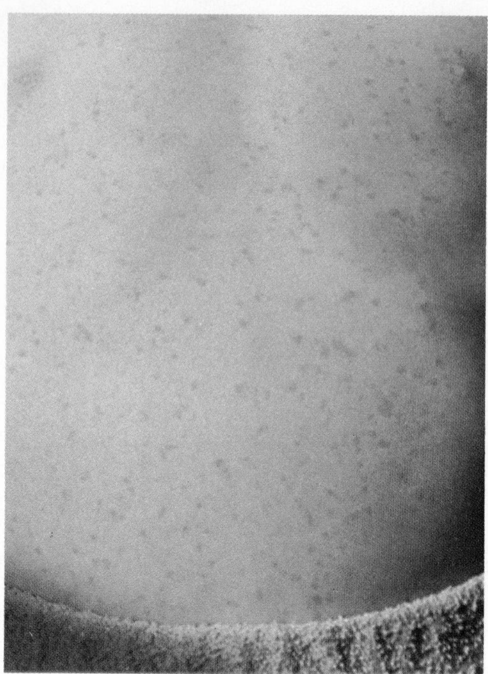

One of the symptoms that may accompany German measles is a rose-colored rash.

Genes. *See* **Heredity**

German measles, also called rubella or three-day measles, is a contagious disease caused by a virus. It is preventable. A child is usually immunized against German measles at 15 months of age.

German measles occurs most frequently in children between the ages of 5 and 15. Outbreaks of German measles usually occur during late winter and the spring.

First symptoms of German measles are low fever, sore throat, headache, and a swelling and hardening of the glands in the neck and behind the ears. These symptoms appear from 14 to 21 days after exposure. A rose-colored rash may appear next, although some cases are so mild that they produce no rash. The rash begins on the face, spreads over the rest of the body, and lasts two or three days. The spots are separate at first, but then run together, causing a flushed appearance. In young children, the rash may be the first symptom. On darker skins, the rash may not be apparent.

If you suspect that your child has German measles, call your doctor. Most cases of German measles are so mild that the child usually does not have to stay in bed. German measles is contagious from about seven days before the rash appears until about five days after. A child who has had German measles can usually go back to school one week after the rash appears. An attack of German measles usually gives a child permanent immunity to the disease.

German measles can harm an unborn child. If a woman gets the disease during the first three months of pregnancy, the child may be born with cataracts, deafness, mental retardation, and other defects. If a pregnant woman is exposed to German measles, she should see her doctor as soon as possible. H.D.R., Jr.

See also **Communicable diseases; Immunization; Shots; Virus**

Glands. *See* **Endocrine glands; Swollen glands**

Glandular fever. *See* **Mononucleosis**

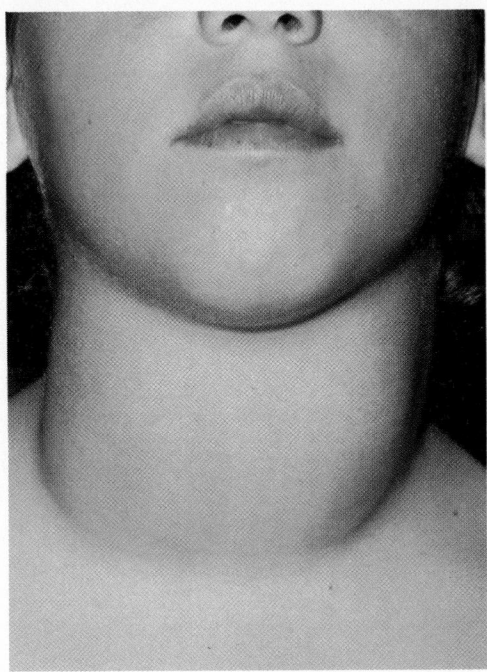

The swelling in this child's neck is caused by a goiter.

Goiter is an enlargement of the thyroid gland. This gland is located in the front of the neck between the top of the breastbone and the Adam's apple. The goiter is usually visible as a prominent bulge. In children, goiters most frequently develop just before the beginning of puberty, and they are more common in girls than in boys. If you suspect that your child has a goiter, consult your doctor.

One type of goiter is called a simple goiter. Several conditions can cause simple goiters.

- The thyroid does not produce enough thyroid hormones. Goiters caused by this can usually be treated with medication.
- Certain medications or foods may contain goiter-producing agents. Treatment requires discontinuing the use of those medications or foods.
- The thyroid may be chronically inflamed. Doctors do not know what causes the inflammation. The goiter generally disappears without treatment, but thyroid medication is usually prescribed.
- The diet may lack a sufficient amount of iodine. This condition is rare in the United States and Canada because of the widespread use of iodized salt.

Another type of goiter is called a toxic goiter. This type of goiter causes an excessive production of thyroid hormone (hyperthyroidism). Doctors do not know exactly what causes toxic goiters.

Toxic goiters may produce emotional instability, increased nervousness, an increase in appetite, and weight loss. The child may lose weight even though he eats large amounts of food. He may sweat excessively, his hands may tremble, and his eyes may protrude. The goiter may cause a feeling of pressure in the neck or even some difficulty in swallowing.

Thyroid-suppressant drugs are generally used to treat toxic goiter. The drugs must be taken regularly for a number of years. However, they may not effectively control and eliminate the goiter. In some cases, an operation is needed to remove part of the thyroid gland. M.G.

Growing pains. Doctors do not believe that growth causes pain in the feet or legs of children. If your child complains of pain in his feet and legs, try to find the cause.

Poor alignment of the bones, ligaments, and muscles of the feet and legs causes the body's weight to be carried unevenly by the feet and legs. This is the most common cause of foot and leg pains in young children. A doctor should examine a child who limps because of pain or a child who complains that one or both of his hips or knees hurt.

Occasionally, a child may have fleeting pain and swelling—sometimes with redness—in one or more joints. If your child has these symptoms, call your doctor. This condition may indicate arthritis, osteomyelitis, rheumatic fever, or other diseases.

Also, when a child exercises a great deal, he may become fatigued and complain of pain in his feet or legs, or he may have cramps in them during the night. Sprains, bruises, and bumps are also possible causes of pain in the feet and legs. M.G.

Washing your child's hair

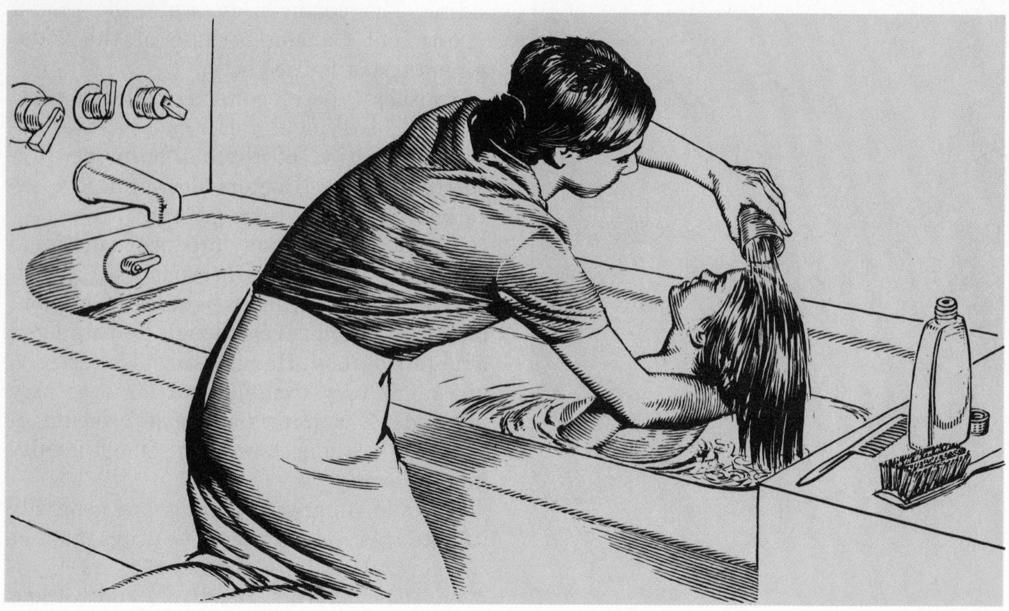

One of the easiest ways to wash a child's hair is to do it when he or she is in the bathtub. Then the child can tilt his head backward. This avoids having shampoo or water run into his eyes and stinging.

Hair care. The color of your child's hair, its texture, and its abundance are physical characteristics for which you and his ancestors are responsible. But its luster, vitality, and attractiveness depend mostly on the child's general health and on the kind of hair and scalp care he receives.

Your child's hair needs a daily brushing of at least 100 strokes to give it gloss, to remove loose scales, and to stimulate the scalp. Boys with short hair require less brushing. Begin brushing a child's hair regularly as soon as he has hair to brush. Be sure to use a brush with soft bristles that will not scratch or irritate his tender scalp. Separate the hair into sections and brush up and away from the scalp, one section at a time. Move your wrist with each stroke so that the brush goes through a rolling motion.

If you use a comb, pick one with blunt teeth because sharp edges may injure the scalp and hair. Take a small section of tangled hair, and start combing it about two inches from the free end of the hair. When the comb passes freely to the end, place it a little higher in the section and comb through to the end again. Repeat the procedure until the comb passes freely from the scalp to the end of the hair.

Combs and brushes are as individual as toothbrushes. Each child should have his own. Wash combs and brushes frequently in warm soapy water to keep them clean and fresh.

If your child's hair is brushed and combed each day, a shampoo once a week or every ten days is probably enough. Use only gentle shampoos. Until puberty, most children do not have much oil in their hair, and strong shampoos may irritate the scalp and make the hair unmanageable. And if some lather runs into a child's eyes, a strong shampoo will burn or sting much more than a specially prepared gentle one.

Brisk towel drying may break and split a child's hair, so blot the hair dry. A cream rinse may help your daughter if her hair snarls and tangles after shampooing. If she has long hair, avoid styles such as tight pony tails that pull excessively on the hair.

Haircuts can also be a part of proper hair care. They help keep hair from getting so thick that it is hard to keep clean.

As adolescence approaches, your child may develop dandruff—small, whitish scales that form on the scalp and then flake off. Simple dandruff, with or without mild itching, is not regarded as a scalp disease. A shampoo once a week usually controls dandruff. Also, encourage your child to brush his hair and scalp, or to massage his scalp gently with his fingertips for about 10 minutes each day. If dandruff is excessive, uncontrollable, and accompanied by itching and inflammation of the scalp, your child may have a scalp disease. Consult a doctor.

Encourage your child to take care of his own hair at the first sign of willingness on his part. Girls, especially, benefit from learning to care for and arrange their own hair. And do not forget to compliment your child on his hair care. It will be added encouragement for him. M.G.

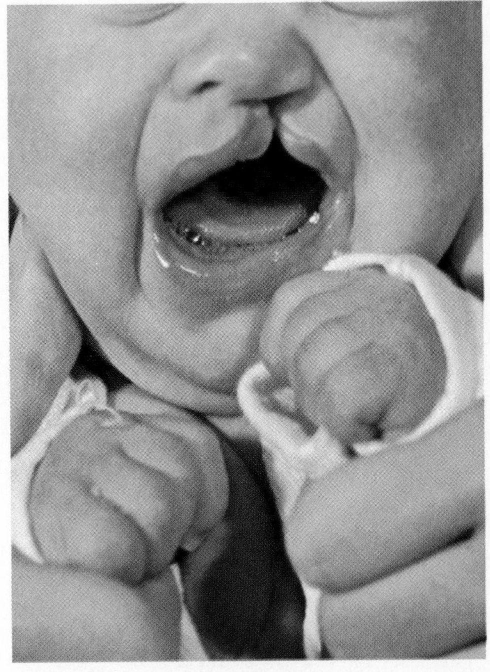

A harelip is a split in the child's upper lip. It is present at birth.

Hard of hearing. *See* Deafness

Harelip

Harelip (cleft lip) is a cleft (split) in the upper lip. It is congenital (present at birth). The cleft may be just a small notch on the lip or it may extend to one or both sides of the nose. Harelip may occur by itself or along with cleft palate or other body defects such as deformed, additional, or missing teeth.

Doctors cannot always determine the cause of harelip. Sometimes harelip is inherited, but often something has happened during the course of the mother's pregnancy to affect the normal development of the child's lip.

If the child has no other abnormalities, harelip can be treated by plastic surgery, usually when the baby is a few weeks old. Treatment is more difficult if the cleft occurs on both sides of the nose, but the defect can be corrected. Sometimes more than one operation is needed to correct the abnormalities. If the child also has a cleft palate or other defects, care of all the problems must be planned together. T.M.H.

See also **Cleft palate; Heredity**

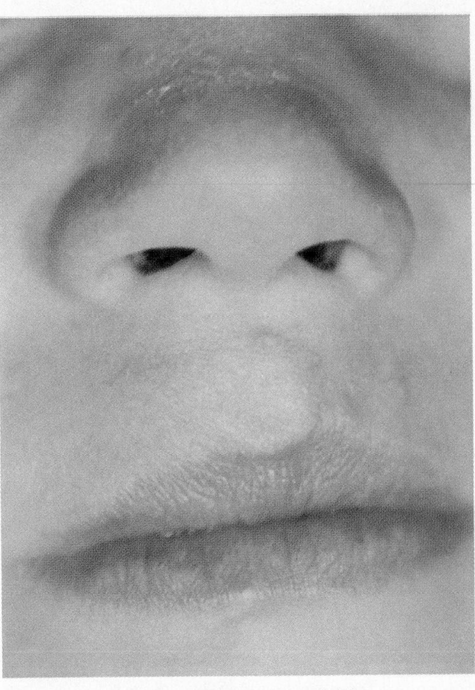

Plastic surgery is highly successful in the correction of a harelip.

The pollen from ragweed causes hay fever in many children. One ragweed plant can produce a billion pollen grains.

Hay fever (seasonal allergic rhinitis) is an allergic reaction of the nose and eyes that is caused by pollen, molds, dust, and other substances floating in the air. Common symptoms include sneezing; stuffiness; difficult nasal breathing; runny nose and eyes; and itching of the eyes, nose, ears, and the roof of the mouth. A fever is not one of the symptoms. Some children who have hay fever also develop asthma.

Hay fever occurs at certain times of the year and is usually caused by pollens from grass, trees, ragweed and related weeds, or by airborne molds.

If typical hay fever symptoms last all year, your child may have perennial allergic rhinitis. Substances in the air other than pollen, such as dust and animal dander (particles from skin, hair, and feathers) are some of the substances that cause perennial allergic rhinitis. If your child seems to have a constant cold, he is probably allergic to something.

If you think your child has either seasonal or perennial allergic rhinitis, consult your doctor. He may recommend sending the child to an allergist (a doctor specializing in the treatment of allergies). The allergist will probably perform tests to determine what substances (called allergens) are causing the reaction. Once the allergens are identified, you may be able to eliminate them from the child's surroundings, or at least reduce them. Sometimes, the allergist can immunize the child against the allergens. The allergist may also prescribe drugs to relieve symptoms.

If your child has year-round symptoms, the allergist may suggest that you do several things.

- Eliminate stuffed toys, woolen blankets, and feather pillows from the child's room—possibly from the entire home.
- Keep no pets that have either fur or feathers.
- Encase the child's mattress and box spring in a zippered, plastic or latex-muslin cover to reduce dust.
- Keep windows closed to minimize the entry of pollen.
- Use an air conditioner with a good filter, or other devices to clean the air. J.S.H.

See also **Allergy; Asthma**

Head injuries are fairly common among children, but relatively few are serious. However, if your child loses consciousness—either at the time of a head injury or later—he should be examined by a doctor immediately. Any blow that knocks the child unconscious could cause brain injury from bleeding inside the skull.

If your child receives a severe bump on the head, keep him quiet for a while and watch him closely for these danger signs.

▪ Severe headache. Aspirin or aspirin substitutes in doses appropriate for your child's age should relieve any headache that follows a head injury. If aspirin does not relieve the headache, or if the headache gets worse, call your doctor.

▪ Persistent vomiting. If your child vomits more than once or twice after a head injury, call your doctor.

▪ Difficulty in speaking. If your child's speech is slurred or if he is not able to talk as well as he usually does, call your doctor.

▪ Unequal pupils. If the pupils of your child's eyes are not the same size, call your doctor.

▪ Double vision. If your child complains of double vision, or if you notice that he squints one eye to prevent seeing double images, call your doctor.

▪ Weakness of one side. If your child is unsteady in walking, or if he limps, call your doctor. If he cannot use one arm or leg as well as the other, call your doctor.

▪ Excessive sleepiness. Your child may go to sleep after a head injury. If you cannot awaken him easily, call your doctor.

▪ Convulsions. If convulsions start, turn your child's head to one side to keep him from choking if he vomits. Put a folded handkerchief between his teeth to keep his mouth open. Call your doctor as soon as possible.

If your child shows none of these symptoms for 12 hours after a head injury, he is probably all right. In rare cases, persistent headache, drowsiness, and a change in the child's normal behavior may develop days or weeks after a head injury because of a slowly accumulating blood clot. If any of these symptoms does appear, call your doctor immediately. A.G.S.

See also **Coma; Convulsions; Fever**

Headaches can usually be relieved by aspirin in doses appropriate for the child's age. If your child has a headache that does not respond to aspirin, consult your doctor. Headaches have many causes.

▪ A child with a sudden infection and fever may develop a headache. The headache usually subsides as the infection clears up.

▪ Fatigue and overexposure to sun can cause headaches.

▪ Emotional tension can cause persistent or recurrent headaches in children.

▪ Eyestrain can also cause recurring headaches. If headaches occur frequently, have your child's vision checked.

A few children have quite severe headaches called migraines. If a child has a migraine, he may see spots before his eyes, become nauseated, and even vomit. Unusual excitement, nervous strain, emotional upset, or excessive fatigue may cause migraines. The child may feel better if he lies down in a quiet, darkened room. A doctor can prescribe specific medicine to relieve migraine headaches. M.G.

Hearing aid. *See* **Deafness**

Heart murmur is an unusual sound produced by the heartbeat. A normal heart makes "lub-dub," "lub-dub" sounds every time it beats. The "lub" sound occurs when two valves inside the heart close. The "dub" sound is made when the valves in the aorta and the pulmonary artery close. A heart murmur is a purring, rumbling, or scratchy noise.

A very common group of heart murmurs are called functional or innocent murmurs. These murmurs are completely harmless and tend to disappear when the child reaches adolescence.

Other murmurs are caused by abnormal blood currents flowing through channels narrowed by disease, through defective channels present at birth, or through holes in walls within the heart.

Usually, heart murmurs are discovered during a doctor's examination. Most heart murmurs are harmless and do not interfere with the child's normal life. M.G.

If your child is suffering from heat exhaustion, first move the youngster to a cooler place and offer some water. Call your doctor as soon as possible.

Heatstroke (sunstroke) is a condition that can result when the body's heat-regulating system stops functioning normally. Heatstroke is caused by excessive heat, not by the sun itself.

One way the body normally cools itself is by sweating. A child with heatstroke stops sweating. His skin may become flushed, hot, and dry; and he may lose consciousness. When the child stops sweating, his body temperature rises. The temperature may go as high as 112° F. (44° C) and may cause brain damage, so it is necessary to lower the temperature immediately.

Place the child in a bathtub of cold water until his temperature goes down to 102° F. (39° C) or lower. If this is not practical, take off the child's clothing and put wet cloths and ice bags directly against his skin. Call a doctor at once.

Be sure you know the difference between heatstroke and heat exhaustion. A child with heat exhaustion continues to sweat; a child with heatstroke stops sweating. M.G.

See also **Heat exhaustion**

Heat exhaustion is one of the body's reactions to overheating. It usually occurs when a child sweats more than usual and his body loses too much water and salt. Heat exhaustion is not the same as heatstroke. A child with heat exhaustion continues to sweat; a child with heatstroke does not.

A child with heat exhaustion may be pale and weak. He may become nauseated and vomit, and he may lose consciousness. His skin feels moist and clammy, and his pulse may be weak and irregular. Move the child to a cooler place but do not let him become chilled. Call your doctor.

To prevent heat exhaustion, dress your child in lightweight, loose-fitting clothing that is light in color. Keep strenuous play to a minimum during extreme heat, and see that the child drinks a lot of water and gets an adequate amount of salt. The amount of salt ordinarily used in food is usually sufficient, but during extreme and prolonged heat, your doctor may suggest salt tablets for older children. Occasional tepid baths also help. M.G.

First aid for heatstroke

If you cannot put the child into a tub of cold water, put wet cloths directly against the child's skin. If possible, put ice packs against the back of the child's neck.

Hemoglobin. *See* **Anemia; Blood count**

Hemophilia is a hereditary disease in which the blood does not clot properly and bleeding is difficult to stop. Hemophilia occurs almost entirely in males. Women rarely show signs of the disease, but they carry it and transmit it to their sons.

Hemophilia varies from severe forms in which bleeding occurs after almost any activity, to milder forms in which only major injuries or surgery produce excessive bleeding. The bleeding may occur internally as well as from a cut on the skin. Internal bleeding usually occurs in body tissues, muscles, or in joints such as the knee, ankle, elbow, or hip.

No cure has yet been found for hemophilia, but bleeding can be controlled with normal blood plasma or with concentrates of clotting factors (medicines that help clot the blood). Prompt medical treatment can prevent large hemorrhages that might permanently damage joints, tissues, or organs. Surgery and dental extractions can be performed without danger of hemorrhage if the child with hemophilia is first treated with plasma or the concentrates of the clotting factors.

Hemophilia is sometimes apparent in newborn infants. They bleed excessively from the umbilical cord or following circumcision. More commonly, the disease becomes evident when the child begins to crawl or walk. Small bumps cause large bruises and swelling which are signs of large areas of hemorrhage. If this happens, have the child examined immediately by your doctor. If you know there is a history of hemophilia in your family, report this to the doctor who will deliver the baby and to the baby's pediatrician. The baby's doctor will probably want to examine the child when he is about 3 months old.

Once hemophilia is diagnosed, doctors usually recommend protecting the child from activities that might produce injury. For example, discourage tree climbing or physical contact sports such as football or hockey. F.O.

See also **Blood clotting; Bruises; Heredity**

Hemorrhage. *See* **Bleeding; Hemophilia**

Hepatitis is an inflammation of the liver caused by a virus. The two most common types of the disease are infectious hepatitis and serum hepatitis.

Symptoms of infectious and serum hepatitis include headache, loss of appetite, and loss of energy. The child may also be nauseated, vomit, and have abdominal pain. His urine may look greenish-yellow, and his stools may be pale. Older children often run a temperature ranging from 100° to 104° F. (38° to 40° C) for two to five days. As the fever subsides, jaundice (a yellowing of the skin and whites of the eyes) usually appears. Normally, jaundice lasts from 8 to 11 days. As it fades, the child regains his appetite and feels better. If you suspect that your child has hepatitis, call a doctor.

Usually, a child gets infectious hepatitis when he eats food or drinks water that has been contaminated by a person infected with the disease. But infectious hepatitis may also be spread by direct contact. The incubation period (time from infection to the appearance of the first symptom) ranges from 14 to 50 days. It averages 25 days. A child with infectious hepatitis should be isolated for at least one week after the onset of the disease. Hepatitis is communicable for at least two or three weeks before and one week after the onset of acute illness. An injection of gamma globulin, if given early to those exposed to infectious hepatitis, often provides temporary protection or lessens the effects of the disease. Take care to protect others in the family. Be certain that everyone washes his hands before meals and after bowel movements. Provide separate eating utensils for the sick child and sterilize them after use. One attack of infectious hepatitis usually gives permanent immunity.

Serum hepatitis can be transmitted through a transfusion of blood or blood product (such as plasma) taken from a person infected with the virus or by the use of contaminated syringes or needles. It is less common than infectious hepatitis and has an incubation period ranging from 50 to 160 days. Children with serum hepatitis do not have to be isolated. Gamma globulin injections offer little or no protection to those exposed. H.D.R., JR.

See also **Gamma globulin; Jaundice**

Heredity. The kind of person your child will be is determined to a great extent at the moment of his conception, when the sperm from the father unites with the egg from the mother. If scientists could translate the chemical code inside the tiny fertilized egg, they could tell whether the child is to be a boy or girl, blue- or brown-eyed, blond or dark-haired. The storehouse of this information lies in the chromosomes. Under a microscope, chromosomes appear as dark strings in the nucleus of each body cell. With the exception of the sex cells (the sperm and the egg), 46 chromosomes are in each cell of the human body. Egg and sperm cells each have 23 chromosomes. In fusing, they give the fertilized egg the total of 46 chromosomes.

Whether the fertilized egg develops into a boy or a girl is determined by two special chromosomes—the sex chromosomes. Every egg bears a chromosome known as the X chromosome and every sperm bears either an X or a Y chromosome. When the sex chromosomes meet in the fertilized egg, an XX baby will be a girl and an XY baby, a boy.

When an egg cell is fertilized by a sperm cell, it starts to grow. First, it divides into two cells; then into four cells; then into eight cells, and so on—until it produces all the cells in a baby's body. During each cell division, the 46 chromosomes in a cell duplicate themselves so that each new cell gets an identical group of 46 chromosomes. The 46 chromosomes are composed of two sets—one set of 23 chromosomes from the individual's father and one set of 23 from his mother. Each chromosome in one set of 23 can be matched to a particular chromosome in the other set. In a girl, the 23 pairs of chromosomes are alike. In a boy, one pair of chromosomes, unlike the other 22 pairs, are not alike. In a girl, the two sex chromosomes (XX) look alike. In a boy, the two sex chromosomes (XY) do not look alike.

Genes determine heredity traits. Hundreds of tiny particles called genes are arranged in a line along the length of each chromosome. Genes control a child's inherited traits, such as blood group, blood-clotting ability, sensitivity to certain tastes, and hair color.

DNA (deoxyribonucleic acid) is the key chemical compound of a gene. DNA is a molecule that consists of two threadlike strands that are connected by crosspieces. The two strands are wound around each other. The structure (called a double helix) looks like a rope ladder twisted into a spiral. A DNA molecule makes an exact duplicate during cell division.

Except in certain instances of sex-linked traits, there are two genes for every trait—one gene on a chromosome in the set of 23 from the individual's mother, and one gene on the matching chromosome in the set of 23 from his father. In many traits, the action of one gene overpowers the action of the other. The more powerful gene is called dominant, and the other gene is called recessive. The gene for brown eyes is dominant over that for blue eyes. If a child gets a gene for brown eyes from his father and a gene for blue eyes from his mother, he will have brown eyes. Except in certain instances of sex-linked traits, it takes two recessive genes to make a recessive trait show up. Both chromosomes must carry the gene for blue eyes for a child to have blue eyes. The indi-

Identical twins look almost exactly alike because they develop from a single egg cell and, therefore, inherit the same genes.

vidual with one gene for blue eyes and one for brown may transmit either gene to the next generation, because only one chromosome from the pair (and therefore only one gene), goes into the sperm or egg cells.

Genes are not always either dominant or recessive. This situation is called incomplete dominance. Three genes—which may be designated *A*, *B*, and *a*—control the inheritance of blood-group types. (Even though there are three genes, the most any person can have is two.) *A* and *B* are dominant to *a*, but they are incompletely dominant to each other. If a child inherits a dominant *A* gene from each parent or if he inherits a dominant *A* gene from one parent and a recessive *a* gene from the other, he has blood type A. If he inherits a dominant *B* gene from each parent or if he inherits a dominant *B* gene from one parent and a recessive *a* gene from the other, he has blood type B. However, if he inherits an *A* gene from one parent and a *B* gene from the other, his blood type is neither A nor B. It is type AB because of incomplete dominance between genes *A* and *B*. If he inherits a recessive *a* gene from each parent, his blood type is O.

Sex-linked traits. The genes on the X and Y chromosomes determine traits that are called "sex-linked" because these genes are carried on the sex chromosomes. Color blindness is one sex-linked trait.

Color vision is controlled by a gene located on the X chromosome. The Y chromosome has no gene for color vision. A boy (XY) has only one X chromosome, and, therefore, only one gene for color vision. A girl (XX) has two X chromosomes, and, therefore, two genes for color vision. If a boy inherits a gene for color blindness, he is color-blind. But, since the gene for normal vision is dominant and the gene for color blindness is recessive, a girl is color-blind only when she inherits two genes for color blindness—one from her mother and one from her father. If she inherits only one gene for color blindness, she has normal vision, but she is a carrier of color blindness. Since a father does not pass on his X chromosomes to his sons, the sons of a color-blind father never have the disorder unless their mother is a carrier. However, the daughters of a color-blind father are carriers and transmit the defective X chromosome to about half their sons and half their daughters.

Another example of a sex-linked trait is hemophilia, a disease in which blood does not clot normally. Queen Victoria passed hemophilia on to many of her descendants, but she was just a carrier and did not have the disease. Because she was XX, the gene on her "good" X chromosome overcame the recessive hemophilia gene on the other X chromosome. Those of Queen Victoria's male descendants who received her defective X chromosome had the disease, and those who received the good X chromosome did not. Those of Queen Victoria's female descendants who received her defective X chromosome became carriers of the disease.

Not all hereditary diseases are caused by sex-linked genes. Some hereditary diseases, such as sickle cell anemia, always require two recessive genes.

Hereditary diseases. Scientists are studying hereditary diseases, trying to discover how body chemistry sometimes goes wrong. If the mistake can be corrected—by a drug or a change in diet—the person with an inborn defect of metabolism, for example, can lead a normal life. Diabetes mellitus is a condition in which the body does not utilize carbohydrates normally. It can be controlled by giving insulin, a hormone that the diabetic does not produce in sufficient quantity.

Phenylketonuria (PKU) is a hereditary disease in which the newborn child cannot properly use part of the protein in milk. If this abnormality goes unchecked, it eventually causes mental retardation. A blood test or a test of a diaper wet by urine shows the doctor whether the disease is present. If it is, he immediately prescribes a special diet to help the child develop normally.

Another important area of genetic research is the detection of carriers of hereditary diseases. The carrier of a recessive gene that causes a hereditary disease is apparently different from the normal person. In the case of the phenylketonuria gene, a blood test indicates that individuals with one gene for the disease can be identified, even though they are not sick in any way. Scientists are searching for tests to detect carriers of bad genes, because if one carrier

(**Heredity,** *continued*) marries another, the chances are one out of four that any child of theirs will have the disease in question. Marriage between cousins is more likely to produce a child with a hereditary disease. If one partner carries a recessive gene, a member of his family is more likely than usual to carry it, too.

Mutations and abnormalities. Occasionally, changes take place spontaneously in genes. This change is called mutation. A mutant gene is transmitted in the same way that normal genes are. All the bad genes mentioned (those that cause such diseases as hemophilia and diabetes mellitus) arose from mutations. Radiation from X rays, ultraviolet light, and fallout may also cause mutations. Some mutations are the cause of early miscarriages.

Besides mutations, there are chromosomal abnormalities consisting of too many, too few, or altered chromosomes. Down's syndrome (Mongolism), a form of mental retardation, is characterized by an extra chromosome or an altered chromosome. M.G.

Location of inguinal hernia

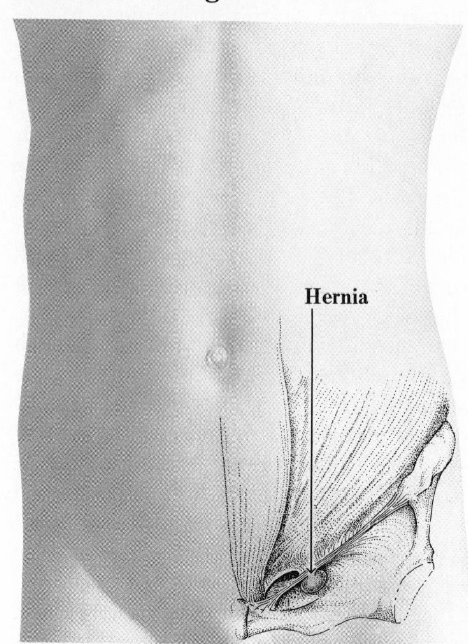

An inguinal hernia allows a loop of intestine to slip through the abdominal wall and into the groin or scrotum.

Hernia, or rupture, is a weakness or break in a muscle wall that lets tissue or a body organ push out of its normal place and into another part of the body. This causes a bulge that may become larger when the baby cries, then may become smaller or disappear when he stops crying. There are two common types of hernias in children—inguinal and umbilical.

An inguinal hernia occurs when a loop of intestine slides through an opening in the abdominal wall and into the groin or the scrotum (the pouch containing the testicles). Inguinal hernias may occur on one or both sides of the body. They are more common in boys than in girls.

If you suspect that your child has an inguinal hernia, contact your doctor. An inguinal hernia can be corrected only by surgery. The operation can be performed on children only a few weeks old, if necessary. A young child will be in the hospital from 24 to 36 hours after the surgery, an older child from three to four days. Convalescence takes only a few days.

If your child has an inguinal hernia for which no immediate operation is planned, watch him carefully. If the child feels pain in the area of the hernia, or if you cannot gently push the intestine back into the abdomen, call your doctor immediately.

An umbilical hernia occurs at the navel of some newborn infants. It develops because the muscle tissues surrounding the navel are still weak and allow part of the intestine to push through. Umbilical hernias usually disappear without surgery or special treatment by the time the child is from 2 to 4 years old.

Other hernias are quite uncommon in children, but you should notify your doctor promptly if you notice a bulge in your child's body tissue.

Sometimes, a hernia is confused with a hydrocele (a collection of fluid in the sac surrounding the testicle). Frequently, a boy may have both a hernia and a hydrocele. If he does, the doctor will probably want to repair both in the same operation. T.M.H.

See also **Hydrocele**

Herpes simplex. *See* **Fever blisters**

Hiccups occur when short, jerky contractions of the diaphragm interrupt the breathing cycle. The diaphragm, a large muscle that divides the chest from the abdomen, normally contracts and relaxes rhythmically to aid breathing. But sometimes the diaphragm contracts suddenly and air is pulled through the larynx (voice box). The air hits the vocal cords and the epiglottis (the cap on top of the larynx) and produces the "hic" sound.

Babies have hiccups frequently—sometimes several times a day. Burping or a drink of warm water may help a baby stop hiccuping. You may help an older child by giving him a drink of water, or you may try some other common remedy such as having him hold his breath, or having him breathe into a paper bag. Usually, however, hiccuping stops by itself after a few minutes. In rare instances, hiccups continue for several hours. If this happens to your child, call your doctor. M.G.

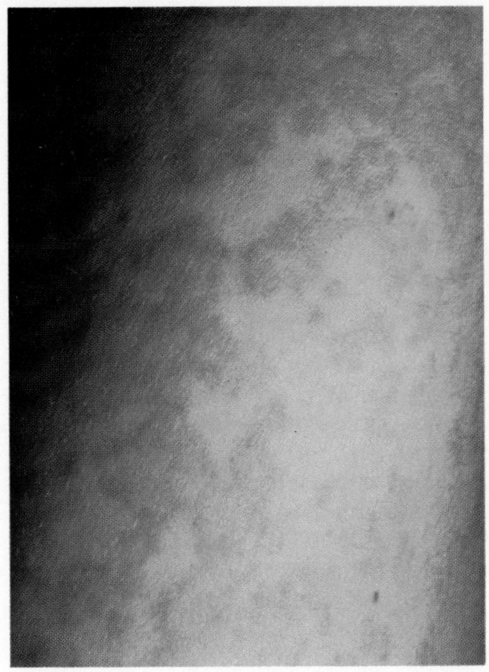

The raised welts on this child's leg are typical of hives. They often itch.

Hip, congenital dislocation. In congenital dislocation of the hip, the ball of the thighbone is not in the socket formed by the pelvic bones. Although the exact cause is unknown, heredity is believed to be a significant factor. The condition is more common in girls than in boys. Congenital hip dislocation is a common cause of pigeon-toe.

Congenital dislocation usually affects only one hip. The affected leg is shorter. The skin folds in the upper thigh and buttock are different from the other side. A dislocated hip prevents the thigh from bending out as far as normal. Putting diapers on the baby may be difficult. If the condition is not discovered before the child walks, he will have a pronounced limp.

If you think your child has a congenitally dislocated hip, consult your doctor. The condition should be treated as early as possible to prevent serious hip trouble. Early treatment consists of using splints to keep the hips in a frog position. In more severe cases, casts, and sometimes surgery, may be necessary. J.J.G.

Hives are an allergic reaction of the skin. They look like mosquito bites—raised, whitish welts on reddened skin—and they often itch. Hives may last for a short time and suddenly disappear, or they may continue for months. They may occur anywhere on the body. Sometimes, swelling occurs around the eyes or lips. In rare cases, swelling occurs inside the throat or larynx and interferes with breathing. Prompt medical or surgical treatment may be required. Consult your doctor if you suspect that your child has hives. He may recommend that you take the child to an allergist (a doctor specializing in the treatment of allergies).

A child may be allergic to such foods as milk, eggs, fish, nuts, berries, shellfish, or pork. Eating them or inhaling their odors may cause hives. Keeping a record of what your child eats and systematically eliminating certain foods from his diet may help you to determine which foods cause the allergic reaction.

Certain drugs such as aspirin, antibiotics, and vitamins can also cause hives. A child

(**Hives,** *continued*) who is highly sensitive to penicillin may even break out in hives after drinking milk from cows that have received the antibiotic.

The stings of bees, wasps, hornets, or yellow jackets may cause hives and swelling in a susceptible child. The child can be desensitized to the stings over a period of years. His doctor will give the child repeated injections of gradually strengthened extracts from the insects.

Hives may occur after the child has had an infection of his ears, sinuses, teeth, tonsils, or other body parts. Hives can develop when the child comes into contact with cosmetics, wool, or other substances. Hives can result from sensitivity to cold, heat, or light. Food preservatives and other substances may cause hives. Psychological factors may be the cause of hives.

Doctors treat hives by trying to discover and eliminate the cause. They may prescribe antihistamines, tranquilizers, or adrenalin to relieve some of the symptoms. J.S.H.

See also **Allergy**

Humidifying a child's room is often recommended by a doctor when the child has bronchitis, a cold, croup, laryngitis, whooping cough, or other diseases that make breathing difficult. Humidifying provides moisture that can loosen secretions in the child's bronchial tubes and nasal passages, and make breathing easier.

The safest way to add moisture to the air is with a cold-mist humidifier. A hot-steam humidifier is dangerous because a child may get burned by touching it or knocking it over. Usually, placing the humidifier close to the child's bed supplies enough moisture. However, if the doctor has told you to have the moist air go directly to the child's bed, make a "croup tent."

- Tie the handle of an opened umbrella to the back of a straight-back chair.
- Place the chair against the bed.
- Put the humidifier on a chair near the bed.
- Then drape the largest bed sheet you have over the bed, umbrella, humidifier, and chair. M.G.

See also **Croup**

How to set up a croup tent

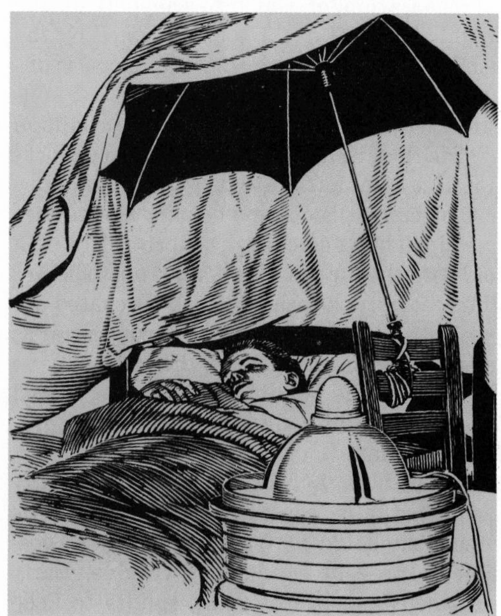

Tie an umbrella to the back of a chair. Move the chair next to the child's bed, and place the humidifier near the bed. Then cover the bed, the umbrella, the humidifier, and the chair with the largest sheet you have.

Hydrocele is a collection of fluid in the sac surrounding the testicle. You may first notice it as a swelling of the scrotum (the pouch that contains the testicles). A hydrocele is often confused with a hernia, and it frequently occurs with a hernia. The swelling from a hydrocele alone, however, remains about the same size all the time, and the swelling from a hernia tends to come and go. If your son has a scrotal swelling, have a doctor examine him.

An acute hydrocele, one that appears abruptly, may be caused by an infection around the testicle or by a twisting of the testicle inside its sac that cuts off the blood supply to the testicle. This type of hydrocele causes severe pain and should be examined by the doctor at once.

A hydrocele in a boy less than a year old may disappear without any treatment unless it is acute. If a boy is older, or if he has an acute hydrocele, an operation and a day or two of recuperation in the hospital may be necessary. T.M.H.

See also **Hernia**

Hydrocephalus. The brain is suspended within the skull in clear and watery cerebrospinal fluid. This fluid also occupies four interconnected cavities (ventricles) within the brain. Cerebrospinal fluid, continually secreted by organs within the brain, flows through the ventricles and into the space around the brain, where it is absorbed into the blood. Normally, the amount of fluid stays the same because it is absorbed at the same rate it is secreted. Sometimes, however, the amount of cerebrospinal fluid increases abnormally. This condition is called hydrocephalus.

The most common cause of hydrocephalus is an obstruction in the pathway of the cerebrospinal fluid. The obstruction keeps the fluid from being absorbed as fast as it is secreted. As a result, the volume of fluid increases, enlarges the ventricles, and compresses the brain. Brain damage can occur.

Hydrocephalus most frequently occurs in young infants with underdeveloped pathways for the cerebrospinal fluid. The earliest sign is an abnormally rapid rate of growth of the baby's head. His brow enlarges, and his scalp is shiny. The fontanels (soft spots) may bulge. Because the compressed brain does not function normally, the infant may also fail to develop on schedule such skills as sitting, crawling, and standing.

Hydrocephalus is often treated by providing an artificial drainage route for the cerebrospinal fluid from the ventricles into the blood. In one method, a small plastic tube is placed in one of the ventricles. It leads down through the body and drains into the right atrium (upper chamber) of the heart. Removing the organs that secrete cerebrospinal fluid has also been tried with some success. In some cases, hydrocephalus may stop by itself.

Early detection of hydrocephalus requires attention to head circumference during the first two years of life. Routine examinations by a doctor during these years usually include measuring the head size of the child. A.G.S.

See also **Soft spots**

Hysteria is a mental illness that may occur suddenly in adolescents or preadolescents. The child may develop a severe anxiety that leads to an irrational, persistent fear. Or, he may develop what appears to be a physical disability, even though a medical examination shows that there is no physical cause for it. A seeming paralysis of an arm, a leg, or another part of the body is a common symptom of hysteria. Pricking, tingling, or creeping sensations are also common. Other symptoms include blindness or decreased vision, deafness, inability to speak or to speak above a whisper, fainting spells, convulsions, and inability to urinate.

Usually, children with hysteria are unconcerned about their symptoms, and the symptoms may worsen if the child receives extra attention. A child with hysteria generally requires psychiatric help.

The word "hysterical" is not always connected with the illness hysteria. "Hysterical" usually means a lack of control over laughing, crying, rage, or other emotions. These outbursts can occur in any child. M.G.

Immunization schedule

Age	Disease	Date given
2 months	Diphtheria, whooping cough, and tetanus; polio	
4 months	Diphtheria, whooping cough, and tetanus; polio	
6 months	Diphtheria, whooping cough, and tetanus; polio *	
15 months	Measles, mumps, and German measles	
18 months	Diphtheria, whooping cough, and tetanus; polio **	
4 to 6 years	Diphtheria, whooping cough, and tetanus booster; polio booster	
14 to 16 years	Diphtheria and tetanus booster	
Every 10 years thereafter	Diphtheria and tetanus booster	
Special immunizations (When your doctor advises)	Cholera	
	Infectious hepatitis	
	Influenza	
	Plague	
	Rabies	
	Smallpox	
	Tuberculosis	
	Typhoid Fever	
	Typhus	
	Yellow Fever	

* The American Academy of Pediatrics considers this third immunization for polio to be optional and generally desirable only in areas where polio is present.
** The American Academy of Pediatrics recommends that this fourth immunization for polio be given at 12 months of age in areas where polio is present.

Immunization. The purpose of immunization is to protect a child from disease. Children are immunized with vaccines which contain substances called antigens. Antigens are prepared from the bacteria, viruses, or toxins (substances produced by the bacteria or viruses) that are the cause of a particular disease.

Immunization generally starts when a child is 2 months of age, but some doctors may begin a month sooner. A child's first vaccine combines immunization against diphtheria, tetanus (lockjaw), and pertussis (whooping cough). The combined shot is called a DTP vaccine. Oral polio vaccine is given separately, usually at the same time as the DTP shots. MMR, a combined vaccine against measles, mumps, and rubella (German measles), may be given when the child is 15 months of age.

Combined doses. Early in a child's life, combined doses of DTP and MMR set up immunity against common childhood diseases. The combined doses save the doctor's time, as well as time and money for parents —and the child undergoes less pain and anxiety.

A combined dose is no harder on a child medically than single ones. Reactions are rarely severe. If your child does react—with swelling or reddening at the site of the injection, or with a fever, unusual sleepiness, or a convulsion—after a dose of triple antigens, tell the doctor before the next dose is given. The doctor may give a smaller dose or omit the whooping cough vaccine at that time.

Early immunization. Immunization is begun at a young age so that a child will become immune as soon as possible. Inherited immunity from an immune mother cannot be depended upon to protect a child from whooping cough, polio, tetanus, and diphtheria. Immunity to these diseases is not achieved until more than a month after the last of the primary doses, and the doses are given about two months apart. Even with an early start, the child is several months old before becoming immune.

But, perhaps the most important reason for early immunization is to prevent whooping cough, which is a most serious and sometimes fatal disease during the first year of life. Measles is also a dangerous disease, and during an outbreak, 6-month-old babies may be inoculated, with another shot given at 15 months of age.

In the past, smallpox vaccinations were mandatory. They were given routinely to all children between 1 and 2 years of age except those who had eczema or some other chronic skin disease. Because of these mandatory inoculations, smallpox has virtually disappeared in the United States. There has not been a case of smallpox reported in the United States since 1949.

Public health officials no longer recommend routine smallpox vaccinations for all children. They believe that the risk of complications that might result from the vaccination is greater than the risk of catching the disease. However, travelers to or from countries where smallpox epidemics occur, must be vaccinated against the disease.

Booster doses. A periodic booster dose is routine procedure for maintaining immunization against diphtheria, whooping cough, tetanus, and polio. An emergency booster dose may be given when an immunized child is exposed to a disease. Also, a dose of tetanus toxoid may be given to an immunized child when he is bitten by an animal, when he steps on a nail, or when he has a burn contaminated by soil.

Special vaccinations. Special immunization is needed if you and your child are going to travel to places where he may be exposed to diseases other than those for which he has had vaccinations, or where food and water may be contaminated. His immunizations against diphtheria, whooping cough, tetanus, and polio should also be brought up-to-date. A smallpox certificate, signed by the doctor and countersigned by the local or state department of health, is required before entry into some foreign countries and sometimes at the point of re-entry into the United States. If you talk with your doctor well ahead of your departure, he can provide the kinds of immunization required. M.G.

See also **Allergy; Bites and stings; Communicable diseases; Diphtheria; Eczema; Gamma globulin; German measles; Hepatitis; Impetigo; Influenza; Measles; Poliomyelitis; Shots; Smallpox; Tetanus; Tuberculosis; Virus; Whooping cough**

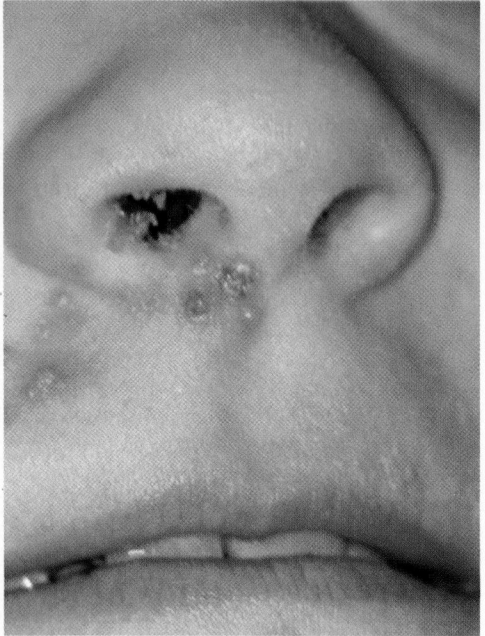

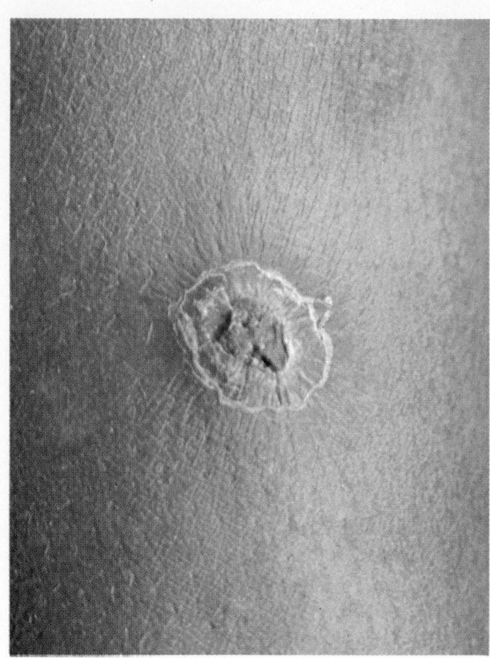

Small blisters are the first sign of impetigo. These blisters break, releasing pus which forms a crust. The coloring of the crust may vary, depending on the skin coloring. A darker skin produces a darker crust.

Impetigo is a highly contagious skin infection that most often affects children. It is caused by bacteria that grow on the skin.

Small, blisterlike sores containing pus develop on the skin. These sores usually open and a thick, honey-colored crust develops over them. The crust drops off in from four to six days.

To lessen chances of spreading infection, a child with impetigo should keep fingers away from infected parts and avoid scratching. Separate washcloth, towels, and tableware should be used. Bed linen should be changed daily. The child should not be allowed to return to school until the condition has completely cleared up.

If your baby shows symptoms of impetigo, consult your doctor. Babies with impetigo should be watched carefully. The bacteria may get into the blood and cause blood poisoning. A.M.M.

Infantile paralysis. *See* **Poliomyelitis**

Infectious mononucleosis. *See* **Mononucleosis**

Influenza (flu or grippe) is an infectious disease caused by a virus. There are several types of influenza, caused by different viruses that are present in secretions and other discharges from the nose and mouth of an infected person. Doctors believe that influenza is spread mainly by coughing and sneezing.

Usually, influenza lasts a relatively short time. Symptoms may include: a chill, aching muscles (especially in the back), vomiting, diarrhea, and a fever as high as 105° to 106° F. (40.6° to 41° C). The child usually has a hacking cough and may complain of a sore throat. The symptoms last several days and gradually fade if no complications develop. Afterwards, the child may lack his usual energy for a time.

If you suspect that your child has influenza, call your doctor. Keep the child's diet light—mainly liquids. To relieve aching muscles and fever, give the child aspirin in doses appropriate for his age.

The most serious problem with influenza is the complications that may develop.

The disease leaves the child feeling weak. He is also susceptible to middle-ear infections, pneumonia, and inflammation of the brain.

There is no drug that cures influenza, but doctors sometimes prescribe antibiotics to guard against secondary infections. Vaccines for preventing influenza are also available, but their protection lasts only a short time, possibly only six months to a year. Also, no one vaccine can immunize against all types of influenza. And, in rare cases, children react to the vaccine (for example, fever and other symptoms of influenza). Consequently, doctors do not generally recommend the vaccines unless an epidemic of influenza appears to be developing. Children with diseases such as tuberculosis, diabetes, muscular dystrophy, heart disease, and lung disease, should receive the vaccine if an epidemic is likely. H.D.R., Jr.

Inguinal hernia. *See* **Hernia**

Inoculations. *See* **Immunization; Shots**

Itching is a symptom of many diseases and conditions. Cool, moist compresses may help relieve itching, but you must find the cause before you determine the treatment. Here are some causes of itching.

- Allergies including hives and eczema cause severe and, at times, uncontrollable itching. Sometimes, a child who has completely recovered from eczema may continue to scratch when he goes to bed, when he is undressed, or when he is emotionally upset.
- Hay fever may cause itching of the eyes, ears, nose, throat, or the roof of the mouth.
- Pinworms cause intense itching around the anus, usually during the night.
- Athlete's foot (ringworm of the feet) causes itching between the child's toes.
- Mosquito, flea, and bedbug bites can cause itching.
- Chicken pox causes itching when it is forming blisters.
- Poison ivy, oak, or sumac causes a burning itch, blistering, and crusting. J.S.H.

See also **Allergy; Chicken pox; Pinworms; Poison ivy, oak, and sumac; Ringworm**

Jaundice is a yellow discoloring of the skin and eyeballs that results from an excess amount of bile pigment in the blood stream. It is a symptom of disease rather than a disease itself. If your child appears to have jaundice, call your doctor. He will determine the cause of the jaundice and prescribe proper treatment.

Ordinarily, bile pigment enters the blood as a result of the normal breakdown of red blood cells. The liver converts the bile pigment from a complex to a simple chemical form, so that it can pass through the bile ducts and into the intestinal tract where it is excreted in the stools.

A number of different conditions may cause jaundice.

- An increased destruction of red blood cells (as may occur in rapidly developing anemia)
- An inability of the liver to excrete bile pigment (as when the liver is damaged)
- An immaturity of the liver that limits its capacity to handle the pigment
- An obstruction of the bile ducts
- An infection of the liver (as in hepatitis)

Jaundice in infants may be completely normal or may indicate a serious disorder. Normal jaundice occurs in the majority of newborn babies, especially premature babies. Such jaundice usually begins when the baby is only 2 or 3 days old and disappears by the 5th or 7th day. It may occur because the immature liver lacks enough enzymes to process the bile pigment. Usually, no treatment is needed for this condition.

Jaundice that appears within the first 24 hours of a baby's life usually is more serious. Incompatibility between the blood types of the mother and the infant is one of its common causes. In such cases, the mother is usually Rh-negative and the baby Rh-positive, but other blood incompatibilities may also be the cause. The baby may need one or more exchange transfusions. In an exchange transfusion, the baby's blood, which has a high content of bile pigment, is replaced by blood which has a lower level of bile pigment. High levels of bile pigment in the baby's blood may lead to brain damage or even to death. M.G.

See also **Anemia; Blood type; Hepatitis; Heredity; Rh factor**

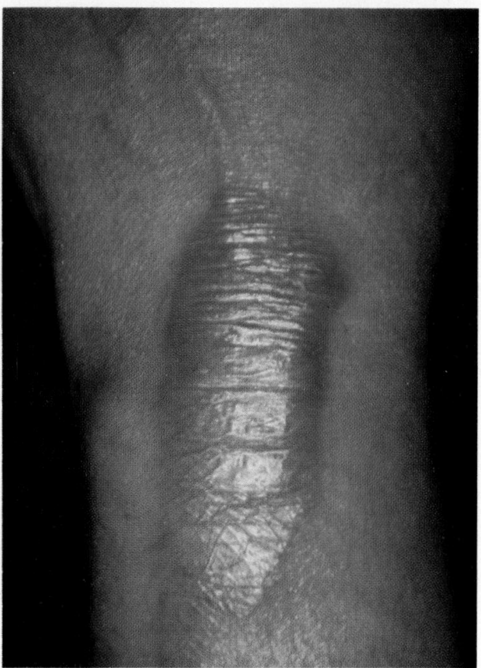

This typical keloid developed around a burn on a boy's wrist.

Knock-knee is a condition in which the legs bend inward and the knees come close together. Sometimes, a knock-kneed child also looks pigeon-toed—his toes point together and his heels point outward.

Knock-knees may result from the position in which a child holds his legs. This cause is more common in heavy children. The condition generally gets worse until the child is 5 or 6 years old. Then it improves gradually. The condition usually corrects itself by the time the child is 9 years old and no treatment is necessary. However, if the condition is quite noticeable in a young child, a doctor may recommend corrective shoes and a reduction in the child's weight.

Knock-knees may also result from injury or disease affecting the knees. If injury is the cause, usually only one knee is affected. Knock-knees caused by injury or disease do not always correct themselves. Braces and surgery may be necessary to correct the knock-knee condition. J.J.G.

See also **Bowlegs; Flat feet; Foot care; Overweight; Rickets**

Keloid is a harmless overgrowth of scar tissue that may develop around cuts, punctures, surgical incisions, or burns. Keloids occur more often in Negroes than in Caucasians. Doctors do not know exactly what causes a keloid.

For the first few months, keloids are usually red or pink. Later they lose this color. They frequently itch and are tender, especially when clothing rubs against them. You can lessen the itching and discomfort.

- Dress the child in loose-fitting clothing of nylon or silk. Avoid wool and cotton.
- Try to keep the child from getting overheated.
- Gently massage the keloid with lanolin every day.
- Your doctor may also recommend X-ray treatment or the injection of a special cortisone preparation. This may reduce the size and discomfort of the keloid.

In rare cases, a doctor may remove surgically an uncomfortable or disfiguring keloid. Unfortunately, keloids tend to recur even after they are removed. T.M.H.

Laryngitis is an inflammation of the larynx (the organ in the throat that contains the vocal cords). A baby with laryngitis may be hoarse. An older child with this condition will have definite hoarseness.

There are many causes of laryngitis. A common cause at all ages is a brief and severe infection of the respiratory tract. Many of these cases are caused by viruses. Watch babies and young children carefully during such attacks. If the larynx swells, the breathing passages may close. In very severe cases, the doctor may have to make an opening into the windpipe below the larynx so that the child can breathe.

Too much talking or shouting may also cause laryngitis. This type of laryngitis responds quickly to rest.

If you suspect that your baby or young child has laryngitis, call your doctor immediately. Treatment depends upon the cause. If the child is constantly hoarse, your doctor may suggest that you consult an ear, nose, and throat specialist. M.G.

See also **Croup; Humidifying; Virus**

Laxative is a medicine that induces bowel movements. Mineral oil, castor oil, and Epsom salts are common laxatives. Do not give laxatives to your baby except on the advice of a doctor. Never give a laxative to a child who has abdominal pain.

Ordinarily, parents worry unnecessarily about their child "keeping regular." Do not worry if your child misses a day. Some children have bowel movements only every second or third day, but if the stool is soft and normal there is nothing to worry about. Hard, dry stools indicate constipation. They will usually become softer after a minor change in diet, such as using a different form of sugar in the baby's formula, increasing the amount of fruit and vegetables, or decreasing the milk intake.

If laxatives are used repeatedly, they may make the problem worse by interfering with the normal muscle tone of the bowel. For this reason, a laxative should not be used unless the child has a special bowel problem. In that case, your doctor will probably recommend a specific mild laxative. M.G.

Lead poisoning. *See* **Poisonings and poisons**

Leukemia is a form of cancer in which the white blood cells multiply and grow wildly. The first signs include easy bruising, weakness, loss of appetite, anemia, enlargement of the lymph glands, and fever. The disease is diagnosed by examining samples of bone marrow and blood. As yet, the cause of leukemia is unknown.

The several kinds of leukemia are classified according to the type of white blood cell affected. All kinds may be either acute (rapidly developing), or chronic (slowly developing). The acute form is seen most often in children. The chronic form usually occurs in adults.

The kind of leukemia most common in children is acute lymphocytic leukemia. As the name implies, those white blood cells called lymphocytes multiply rapidly in the body's lymph system. Most children with this kind of leukemia respond to drug treatment and irradiation.

About half the children treated will stay disease-free for at least five years—and may never have a recurrence. The others will have one or more periods of improvement, called remissions, during which they act and appear normal. But the symptoms may gradually return. As drugs become less effective, the white blood cells multiply rapidly and interfere with the production of red blood cells. The abnormal white cells may also invade vital organs, reducing the body's ability to fight infection and control bleeding.

During periods of remission, the child should be allowed to live as normally as possible, and treated as before the onset of the disease. Any sudden, excessive pampering may be confusing and make the child difficult to handle.

Researchers in the United States and other countries are striving to find the cause of leukemia, to develop new methods of treatment, to extend remissions, and, hopefully, effect a cure. F.O.

Leukorrhea. *See* **Vaginal discharge**

Lip blister. *See* **Blister; Fever blisters**

Lockjaw. *See* **Tetanus**

Lymph glands. *See* **Swollen glands**

Malocclusion is the failure of the teeth of the upper and lower jaw to meet properly in biting, or when the mouth is closed. It is caused by irregular placement of the teeth. Malocclusion is also called poor bite.

Malocclusion may occur in both primary (baby) teeth and permanent teeth. It may be inherited; it may be acquired; or a combination of these factors may cause it.

Some children lose their primary teeth too early because of decay or injury. Then, when the permanent teeth come in, they may shift out of position because the guiding channels left by the primary teeth may have changed. Some primary teeth stay in too long and push the permanent teeth out of position. Children who suck their thumbs or fingers excessively after the age of 5 or 6, when the permanent teeth are coming in,

(**Malocclusion,** *continued*) may also develop poor bite.

Loss of permanent teeth can leave gaps in the child's jaws and cause the remaining teeth to drift (lean out of position) into the gap.

A child with malocclusion may encounter several problems. He may not be able to chew his food properly or he may have trouble cleaning his teeth. Protruding front teeth or teeth crowded into small jaws may make him feel self-conscious because he does not look like other children. Too much space between the teeth may impair his speech.

All children should start going to a dentist when they are about 3 years old, and they should visit the dentist periodically. If the dentist checks your child's teeth regularly, he will be able to recognize signs of malocclusion when they occur. He can advise you if he thinks the child should see an orthodontist (a dentist who specializes in correcting irregularities of teeth and jaws). Malocclusion can be corrected by braces. M.G.

See also **Braces, dental; Teeth and teething**

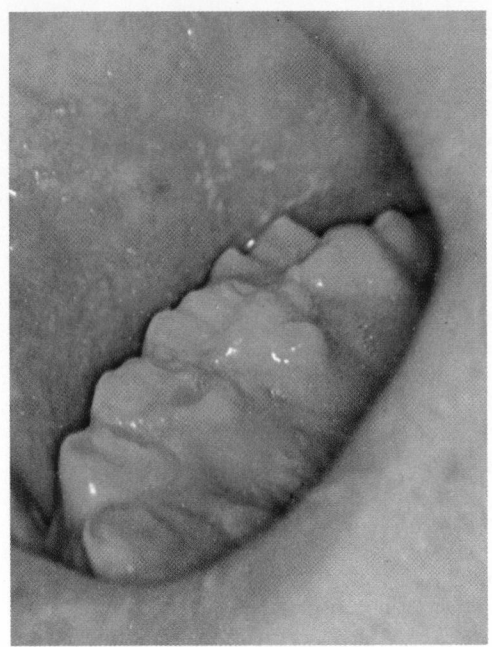

An early symptom of measles is the appearance of tiny white spots on the insides of the cheeks, next to the molars.

Measles (rubeola) is a highly contagious disease caused by a virus. Measles can be prevented by vaccination, and doctors usually recommend vaccination because of the complications that can follow measles.

The first symptoms of measles are similar to those of a cold. The child has a hard, dry cough; red and watery eyes; and a fever that may go quite high. The fever appears about 10 days after exposure. Then, usually within a day or two, tiny white spots called Koplik spots appear on the insides of the cheeks, next to the lower molars. About two days later, a blotchy red skin rash begins at the hairline, spreads down the trunk, and reaches the feet after three days.

Call your doctor if you suspect that your child has measles. The doctor will probably advise bed care, in a partially darkened room if light bothers the child's eyes. He may also prescribe a drug to control the cough. While the child is feverish, he loses his appetite almost completely, so the doctor will probably suggest that the child's diet be composed mainly of liquids.

A child who has measles can usually get out of bed two days after his fever is gone. About a week after the rash begins, if all the cold symptoms are gone, he can go outdoors and play with other children. The disease is contagious from about four to five days before the rash appears until five days after. An attack of measles gives a child permanent immunity.

Some of the complications that may follow measles are pneumonia, middle-ear disease, bronchitis, and encephalitis. Every child who has not had measles should get live measles vaccine at 15 months of age. In the event of exposure, babies as young as 6 months can be vaccinated, but the child should be revaccinated at 15 months. A child not vaccinated during infancy may be immunized at any time. If an unvaccinated child is exposed to measles, gamma globulin may give temporary protection, or make the disease milder.

H.D.R., JR.

See also **Communicable diseases; Gamma globulin; Immunization; Virus**

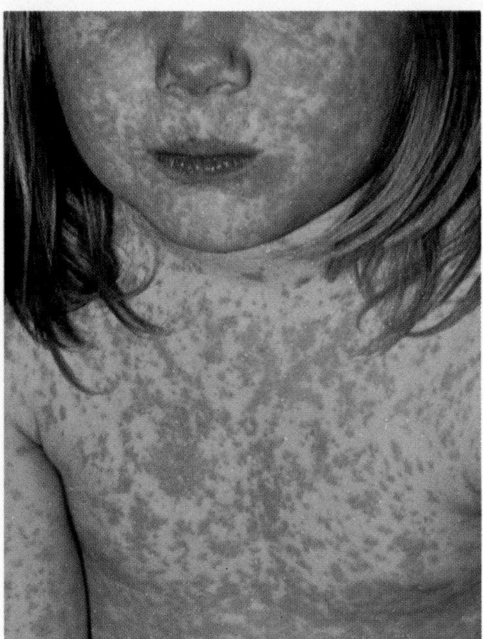

A blotchy red skin rash is the most obvious symptom of measles. It begins at the child's hairline and then spreads.

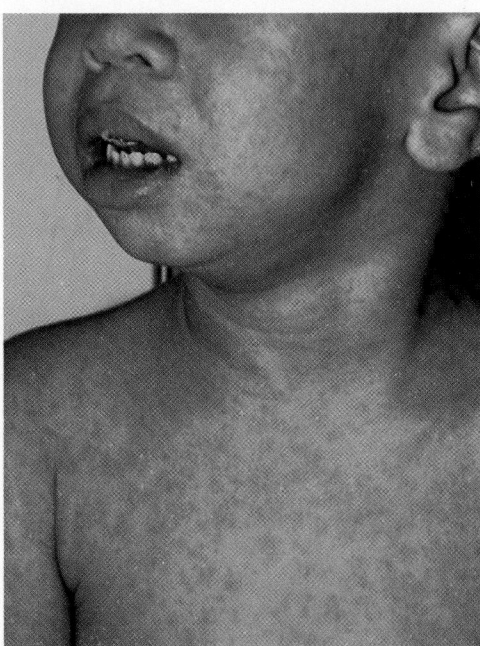

A rash on a darker skin is sometimes quite difficult to see. The measles rash on this child's body is an exception.

Medicine cabinets have a dangerous fascination for young children. To child-proof your medicine cabinet, follow these safety precautions.

- Keep all sedatives, pills, or other medicines—including aspirin and all solutions containing wood alcohol—locked up or out of a child's reach.
- Keep razors, nail files, and nail scissors on the more inaccessible top shelves of the medicine cabinet. Leave the lower shelves for cotton, bandages, gauze, adhesive tape, and other harmless supplies.
- Always throw away prescriptions when the illness for which they were ordered is over. Empty leftover medicines into the toilet bowl. Rinse out the medicine bottles before throwing them away in the trash containers.
- Every jar, box, or bottle should be labeled to show what it contains, what the contents are for, and how they are used.
- Identify anything "for external use only" with a symbol marked in nail polish.
- Clean out the medicine cabinet at least every three months, discarding anything that is useless or spoiled.

A well-stocked medicine cabinet will enable you to take care of most cuts, aches, and pains. It should contain:

Sterile gauze bandages, 3 inches (7.5 centimeters) square
Sterile bandages, 2 inches (5 centimeters) wide
Sterile bandages, 1 inch (2.5 centimeters) wide
Adhesive tape, 1 inch (2.5 centimeters) wide
Sterile absorbent cotton
Box of small prepared bandages
Petroleum jelly
Aspirin
Calamine lotion
Rubbing alcohol (70 per cent)
Syrup (not fluid extract) of ipecac
Rectal thermometer

Other supplies that could be part of a household's medical equipment are an oral thermometer, a medicine dropper, a heating pad, an ice bag, a hot-water bottle, tweezers, and a cold-mist humidifier. M.G.

See also **Accidents; Drugs; First aid; Poisonings and poisons; Prescriptions**

Meningitis is an infection of the membranes covering the brain and spinal cord. Most cases of meningitis are caused by bacteria that are carried by the blood to the brain from a nose, throat, or lung infection.

In older children, meningitis often begins with a fever, irritability, headache, nausea, and vomiting. A rash of bright red spots may also appear. Gradually, the child's back stiffens, and he cannot bend his neck forward. The child may have convulsions and may lose consciousness.

In infants and young children, the signs of meningitis are somewhat different. Frequently the child has no fever, and infants rarely have a stiff neck. However, the membrane covering the fontanels (soft spots in the skull) may stretch and become tight.

If you suspect that your child has meningitis, call your doctor. A child with meningitis must be hospitalized in order to receive proper examination and proper treatment. Early treatment with antibiotic drugs is necessary to avoid serious complications or even death. H.D.R., JR.

Menstruation. All parents who have a daughter want her to grow up enjoying her femininity. It follows that all girls should learn to accept menstruation as a normal and necessary part of feminine life, essential to the process of reproduction.

Unfortunately, too many young girls fear menstrual periods and become emotionally upset when they begin the process. They may have heard their mothers or their friends refer to menstruation as "having the curse" or "being sick." Or they may have been told that menstruation is painful; that they will feel weak; or that they cannot exercise, dance, swim, take baths, or wash their hair.

When a girl becomes about 8 years old—or earlier if she asks questions—her mother should start to tell her about menstruation. Present it to her as the wonderful phenomenon it is—preparation for a special day when she is to be a mother. The explanation is not difficult.

Begin by telling your daughter about the two ovaries, one on either side of her uterus (womb), and about the vagina. The ovaries produce eggs capable of developing into babies if they are fertilized by sperm. The uterus is the special place in the mother's body where the baby will grow until it is ready to be born. It is a pear-shaped organ in the middle of a woman's body. The vagina is the birth canal, through which the baby is born. It is below the uterus.

Menstrual cycle. Once a girl enters puberty, generally by the time she is 12 or 13, the ovaries start to produce one egg a month. This egg is smaller than the head of a pin. About two weeks after menstruation, the egg passes from the ovary through a tube, called the Fallopian tube, to the uterus. The uterus prepares itself in case the egg is fertilized. If a baby is going to grow from this tiny egg, it must receive food. This food is brought to the uterus in the mother's blood. The lining of the uterus becomes thick and spongy to receive the egg and help feed it. If the egg is not going to develop into a baby, this lining is not needed. The lining breaks down, and most of the lining and a little blood pass out of the body through the vagina. This discharge occurs about once a month unless a woman is pregnant. Menstrual periods do not occur during pregnancy and for a month or so afterwards.

Some girls associate bleeding with injury and are frightened by the thought of menstrual bleeding. The amount of blood discharged during menstruation varies with the individual. It is usually about 1½ ounces (44.5 milliliters), not enough to make a girl anemic or weaken her. The body quickly replaces this small amount of blood.

Reassure your daughter that an irregular menstrual cycle is not uncommon for the first couple of years. There may even be lapses of two or three months between periods. After that, the cycle should recur every 26 to 30 days, each period usually lasting about 5 days.

The cycle, once established, is fairly regular for each girl, but it may occasionally vary. Excitement or nervousness may cause irregularity. Many girls skip menstrual periods when a great change in their normal routine occurs—for example, when they are away at summer camp or during their first year at college.

The menstrual cycle

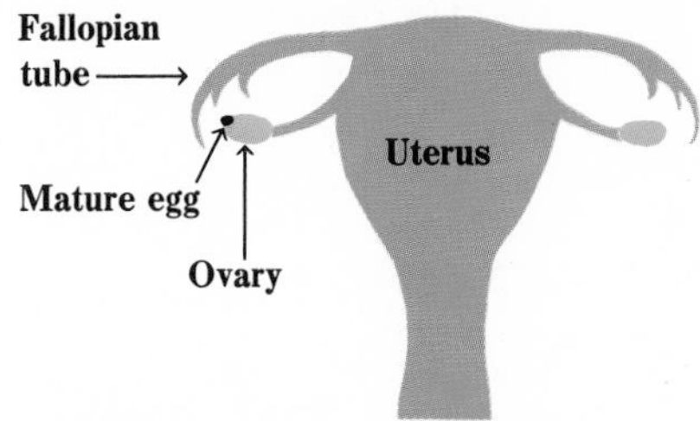

1. Although each ovary may contain thousands of potential eggs, usually only one egg matures during each cycle.

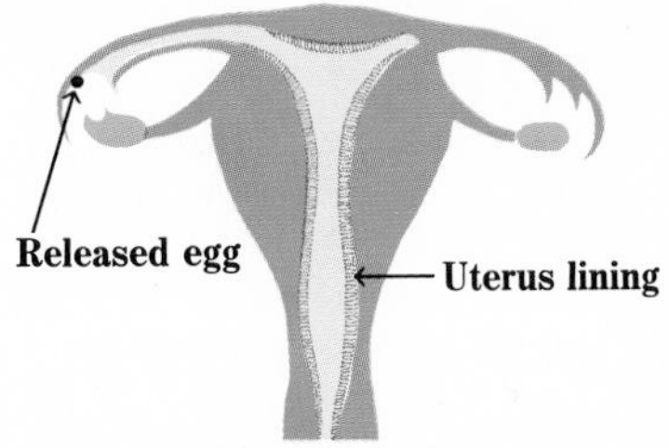

2. The ovary releases the mature egg. The lining of the uterus starts growing to receive and feed the egg if it is fertilized.

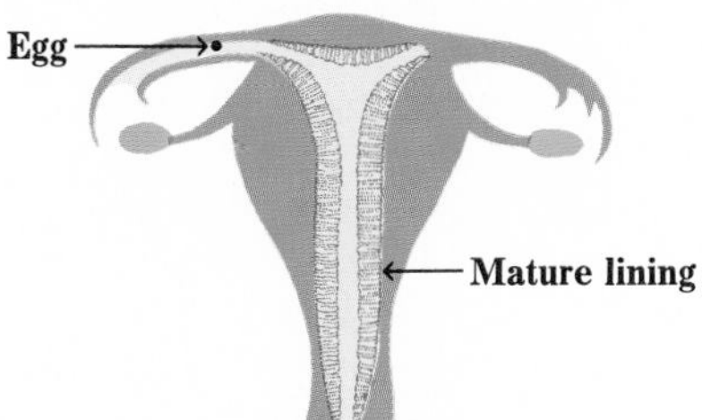

3. The egg slowly moves down the Fallopian tube to the uterus. Fertilization, if it occurs, takes place in the Fallopian tube.

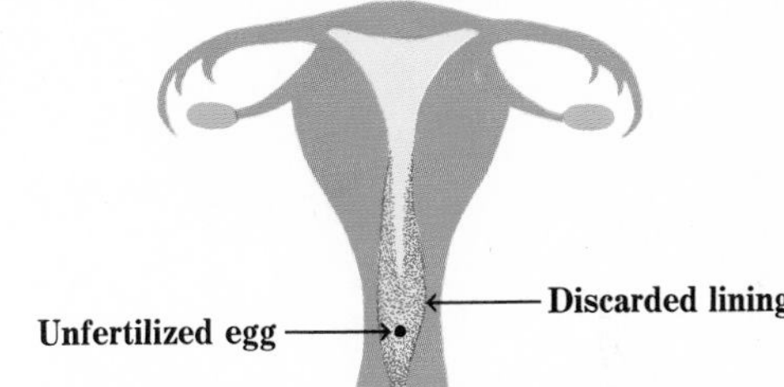

4. If the egg is not fertilized, the lining of the uterus is not needed. The lining breaks down and passes out of the body.

Care during the period. During the menstrual period, some girls use soft, absorbent, gauze pads called sanitary napkins to absorb the menstrual flow. The pads are held in place by a narrow elastic belt, called a sanitary belt. Other girls use tampons—small rolls of compressed, absorbent material that are inserted into the vagina.

Some girls worry about offensive odors that may occur during menstruation. These odors result not from the freshly discharged blood but from changes in the blood as it dries. Frequent changing of sanitary pads or tampons provides greater comfort and less concern about personal hygiene.

Many girls ask if menstruation will hurt. Pain or discomfort does not necessarily accompany menstruation. Some girls get cramps, but the cramps usually last only the first day. Some girls have cramps because of their negative attitude toward menstruation. Other cramps have physical causes. Most cramps can be relieved by medication, a hot-water bottle, a heating pad, and warm drinks. But if the pain is too severe, consult a doctor. Tenderness of the breasts, backache, a feeling of heaviness, and a slight gain in weight may also accompany the menstrual period.

A girl usually can continue her normal activities during her menstrual periods. She may dance, skate, and ski; and she may wash her hair and take showers. If tampons are used, a girl may swim at any time during her period.

What to tell boys. Boys, too, ask questions about menstruation. "Do boys menstruate?" "Does it hurt?" These questions should be answered truthfully. Explain to them that menstruation is simply a process of getting rid of material that was ready inside the body with food for a baby. Since men cannot have babies inside of them, men do not menstruate. Tell them also that menstruation does not usually hurt. Some girls are uncomfortable, and may be a little cross, but they go right ahead with school or work or whatever they have to do. Reassure them that menstruation is not like bleeding from an injury. M.G.

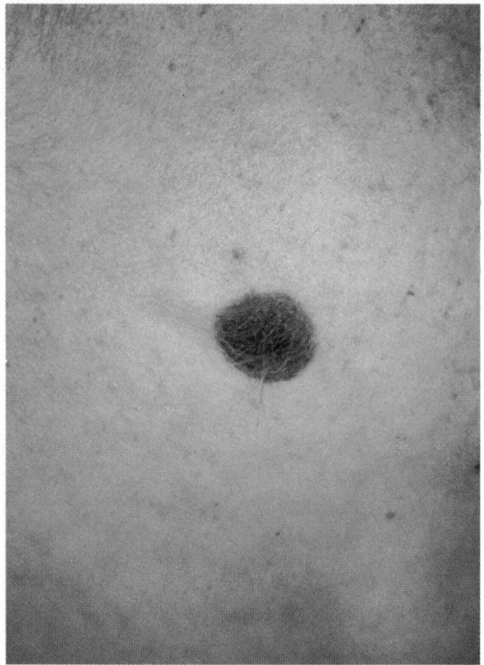

The common soft, hairy, brown mole, such as the one on this child's cheek, is harmless.

Mononucleosis is a contagious disease that most commonly strikes older children, adolescents, and young adults. It occurs both sporadically and in epidemics. Doctors believe that it may be caused by a virus. Mononucleosis is also called infectious mononucleosis and glandular fever.

A typical case of mononucleosis begins with chills, fever, headache, dizziness, and sore throat. Lymph glands in the neck or in other parts of the body may swell. The child may feel exhausted, he may feel depressed, and he may lose his appetite. In some cases, a reddish rash may spread over the trunk and other parts of his body. Call your doctor if you suspect that your child has mononucleosis.

A child with mononucleosis should be kept in bed, but he does not have to be isolated. Symptoms of the disease may last from two to six weeks, but it may take several months for the child to regain his usual energy. H.D.R., Jr.

See also **Communicable diseases; Hepatitis; Jaundice; Virus**

Moles are commonly found in the older child and adolescent. Large amounts of dark pigment in the cells give moles their color. Moles may be black, brown, grey, purple, or bluish black. Some may also have hair in them, especially the larger moles. Sometimes moles are just small spots or marks, but other times they cover large areas of skin.

Usually, moles are not harmful and do not change in appearance over the years. In rare instances, however, they can begin to grow and become cancerous. If a mole enlarges, changes color, bleeds easily, or becomes painful, consult your doctor. Tell your child not to pick or otherwise irritate a mole, for the irritation may cause it to start growing. If a mole is in a place where irritation cannot be avoided, such as at the belt line, on the palms, on the soles, or on the genitalia, the doctor may remove it. Moles may be removed very easily. Usually, the doctor uses a local anesthesia and simply cuts out the mole and a small portion of the surrounding skin. A.M.M.

See also **Birthmark**

Motion sickness. Some children become nauseated and vomit when they ride in a car, bus, train, ship, or plane. No one knows why one child shows more sensitivity to motion than another, but children who have more anxiety about traveling seem more prone to motion sickness.

Some children become sick when riding in almost any type of conveyance, and others are bothered by only one or two. If the motion is very bumpy, as in a small airplane, almost any child will become sick.

Here are a few steps you can take to reduce chances of your child's suffering motion sickness while traveling.

- Place the child where he can easily see out of the vehicle.
- Avoid seats where motion may be especially bumpy, such as the back of a bus or the tail of an airplane.
- Do not let the child eat rich or heavy foods before traveling.
- Ask your doctor to prescribe a drug that will help prevent motion sickness. M.G.

See also **Vomiting**

Multiple sclerosis (MS) is a disease that affects the brain and spinal cord. The myelin (material coating the nerves) breaks down and becomes spotted with hard scar tissue. The scar tissue hinders the normal functions of the nerves which carry messages from the brain to all parts of the body. Multiple sclerosis may strike children, but it usually affects people between 20 and 40 years old. Doctors do not know what causes it, and they have not yet found a cure.

First symptoms may be blurred vision in one or both eyes; double vision; an unsteady walk; or numbness of an arm, a leg, or a part of the trunk. These symptoms may last only a few days and be followed by a period of complete recovery. Then other attacks may occur—weeks, months, or even years later. Symptoms often differ from one attack to another.

Some persons never completely recover from the first attack of multiple sclerosis and become more disabled with each new attack. Others recover almost completely from a series of widely spaced attacks. A.G.S.

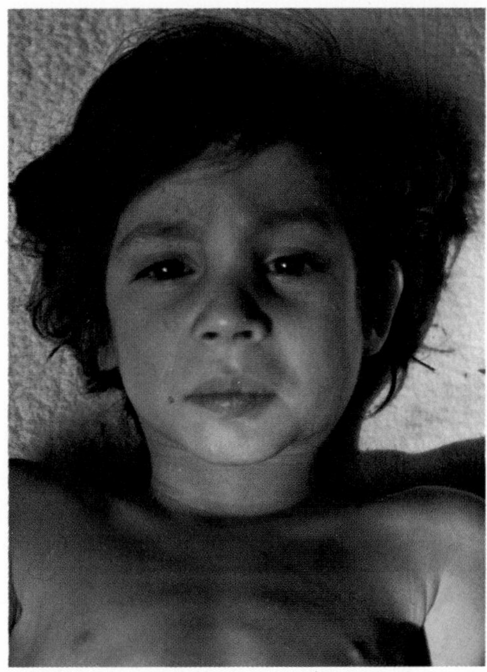

Mumps may cause swelling of the salivary glands on one or both sides of the neck.

Mumps (infectious parotitis) is a contagious disease caused by a virus. It occurs most often in children.

Mumps begins with a pain below and in front of the ear. Next, the child has difficulty chewing and swallowing. Then, the salivary (parotid) glands just below and in front of the ears swell and become tender. In most cases, one gland swells first and the gland on the other side of the neck swells a few days later. Sometimes only one side swells. Other salivary glands may also be affected, but only the doctor can determine this. In about 30 to 40 per cent of all cases, swelling of the glands cannot be seen.

A child with mumps may find it painful to swallow sour or highly seasoned food. Fever and chills may also appear. If you suspect that your child has mumps, consult your doctor.

When mumps attacks male adults and adolescent boys, the sex glands may be affected. But this complication rarely causes sterility. Another complication of mumps affects the meninges (membranes that surround the brain and the spinal cord). The child may have a high fever and headache; he may vomit and become delirious. But this complication (called mumps meningitis) rarely produces serious aftereffects.

In some mild cases of mumps, the doctor may not insist on bed rest. If the case is severe, or if the child is an adolescent boy, the doctor will probably suggest that you keep him warm and quiet in bed.

Symptoms of mumps usually appear from 14 to 21 days after exposure. Mumps is contagious from about 7 days before symptoms appear until from 7 to 10 days after, or until the swelling disappears. The child may return to school when all swelling has disappeared. A child who has had mumps in either or both parotid glands almost never has the disease again.

The MMR shot (measles, mumps, rubella), given at 15 months of age, protects against mumps. Mumps vaccine alone may be given to children, particularly boys, who have not had the shot or mumps. H.D.R., Jr.

See also **Communicable diseases**

Muscular dystrophy is an inherited disease that causes muscles to grow weak and waste away. It usually attacks the muscles that control arm, leg, and face movements. Scientists have not yet found the cause or the cure for the disease.

Muscular dystrophy may occur in newborn babies, but it is more common in older children and teen-agers. There are several forms of muscular dystrophy. Some forms spread rapidly and cause severe disability; others spread slowly and cause less disability. Some result in early death. Others do not affect the life span.

A child with muscular dystrophy has difficulty in going up stairs, has a tendency to fall, and walks with a waddling gait. He may be able to attend school for some time after the onset of the disease. But as the disease progresses, he may have to wear braces in order to stand and walk. Finally, he may need a wheel chair.

Physical therapy cannot cure muscular dystrophy, but it can help to slow down the crippling effects of the disease. J.J.G.

Nail care. A child's nails require regular care to keep them clean. Wash them in warm water and scrub them with a moderately stiff brush. Use either manicure scissors or an emery board to keep them short. Trim and shape fingernails to a rounded point. Toenails should be cut straight across so that they will be less likely to curve into the flesh and become ingrown. Ingrown nails can become painful and infected.

If a toenail becomes ingrown, cut the nail straight across and do not trim the corners. Soak the child's foot in warm water and dry it. Then, use a toothpick to tuck a small piece of cotton under the corner of the ingrown toenail. Each night, for four or six weeks, remove the cotton, soak the foot, then insert a fresh piece of cotton. If this does not relieve the pain and make the nail grow out, or if there is still an infection, consult your doctor.

To prevent hangnails (pieces of skin hanging by one end at the side or base of a nail), show your child how to push back the cuticle with a towel when he dries his hands. M.G.

Care of ingrown toenails

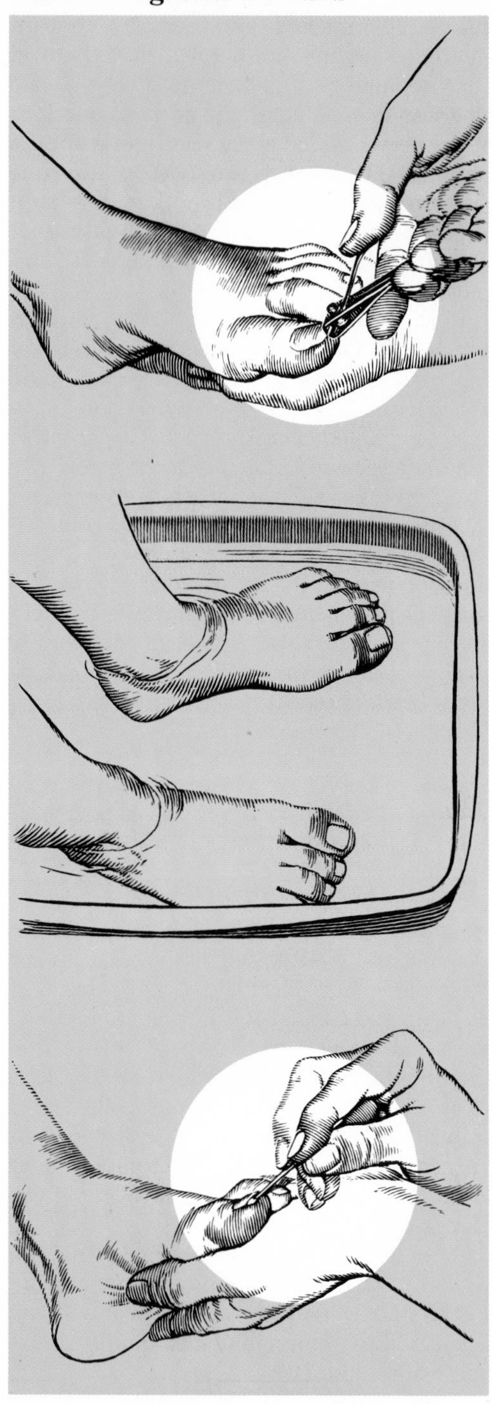

Cut your child's toenail straight across with toenail clippers or scissors. Do not trim the corners. Soak the foot in warm water and dry it. Then tuck a small piece of cotton under the ingrown corner of the nail.

Navel. The umbilical cord attaches an unborn baby to the placenta (the organ attached to the inside of the uterus) of its mother. Food and oxygen flow from the mother to the unborn baby through blood vessels in the cord. Waste material from the baby flows through the cord to the placenta, where it is picked up by the mother's blood. At birth, the cord is clamped and cut close to the baby's abdomen. The resulting scar is called the navel.

The small piece of cord that remains gradually dries up and turns dark. It falls off in about a week. Afterwards, the navel may look a little red for a few days. Report any redness, swelling, or bleeding around the navel to your doctor. Keep the navel clean and dry until it is healed. Your doctor may recommend cleaning the navel each day with alcohol and giving sponge baths rather than tub baths until the navel heals. He will probably tell you not to cover it with a dressing because the navel heals better if it is exposed to air. M.G.

See also **Hernia**

If a child is near-sighted, the world may look like this photograph—near objects are in focus but distant objects are blurred.

Near-sightedness (myopia) is a defect in sight. A near-sighted child sees close objects fairly well, but distant objects are blurred. The reason for this is that the eyes are longer from front to back than the normal eye, and light rays from an object are brought into focus too far in front of the retina.

Near-sightedness usually develops in childhood and adolescence. It is rarely present at birth. A near-sighted child may hold things close to see them; but so will a far-sighted child on occasion. Near-sighted children may also keep their eyelids partially closed, making a tiny slit that helps them to see more clearly.

If you think your child is near-sighted, consult your doctor. An eye examination may be in order and glasses may be prescribed. Near-sighted children should have their eyes checked biannually for the first few years, then annually. A child with near-sighted parents should have an eye examination before entering school because there is a family tendency toward near-sightedness. R.O.S.

When a near-sighted child wears corrective glasses, distant objects are brought into focus.

Nephritis is a disease that affects the kidneys. It most often follows a streptococcus infection, usually a sore throat. Generally, it does not affect children under the age of 3. Nephritis may be chronic—slow to develop, long lasting, and incurable—or it may be acute—quick to develop, of short duration, and easily cured. Acute nephritis is the more common type found in children.

Acute nephritis varies in severity. Some children become seriously ill. But the outlook is almost always excellent. Generally, acute nephritis begins from one to three weeks after an untreated streptococcal infection. The child's urine often contains blood, giving the urine a smoky color similar to that of a cola drink. The child may also be tired and have a fever, severe headache, and swelling around the eyes. Call your doctor if you suspect that your child has nephritis. Bed rest and antibiotics for the streptococcal infection will probably be prescribed. Recovery usually begins in a week or two. M.G.

See also **Urinary disturbances**

Nightmares. A young child—especially between the ages of 2 and 5—may frequently wake from his sleep because of a dream—usually a frightening one. Frightening dreams may serve as safety devices for getting rid of unpleasant feelings. Fears and frustrations of the day spill over into the night, resulting in dreams that may make a child wake up crying or screaming. Alone and terrified in the dark, your child needs all the comfort you can give him. Speak to him soothingly and encourage him to tell you about his dream. Listen carefully, even if he gives a garbled account. There may be a clue to the cause of the dream, or to problems that have been troubling him.

You cannot eliminate all worry and anxiety in your child, so there is no way to prevent bad dreams. But perhaps a little more attention to his emotional security—shielding him from family problems, spending extra time with him—will help him sleep more peacefully. If your child has frequent nightmares, consult your doctor. M.G.

See also **Sleep**

Nose, objects in the. Sometimes by accident, and sometimes just to find out what will happen, a child puts objects into his nose. If the child's nose bleeds, or if you cannot see the foreign object, call your doctor immediately.

Occasionally, the child may get the object out of his nose quite easily by himself. He may sneeze it out. Or he may force it out by blowing his nose. Ask a child to blow his nose only if you know he will not sniff in instead of blow out.

You may be able to remove a soft object from your child's nose by using a pair of tweezers. Do this only if you can see the object. And be careful not to injure the child's nostril. Warn him not to move his head while you are trying to remove the foreign object.

Never try to remove a smooth, hard object from a child's nose. The object may be pushed farther into the nose quite easily and might get into the throat and choke the child. Call your doctor immediately, and let him remove the object. C.F.F.

Nose drops help clear up a stuffy nose. Some also kill germs. Doctors occasionally prescribe nose drops in the final stages of a cold, but not ordinarily in the early stages when the nose is runny.

Use nose drops for your child only when your doctor advises, and only in the amounts he specifies. Young children can suffer from an overdose of the drugs in these solutions. Never continue nose drops indefinitely.

If your baby struggles when you try to put drops in his nose, wrap him in a blanket. Put him in your lap or lay him on a bed, whichever is more convenient and comfortable for you. Put one arm around him or over him to keep him still, and hold his chin with your hand. Leave your other hand free to put in the drops.

Another common method of giving nose drops is to take the baby on your lap and lay him back with his head between your knees. In this way, you can confine his head with your knees, hold his hands with one of your hands, and still have one hand free for inserting the drops. C.F.F.

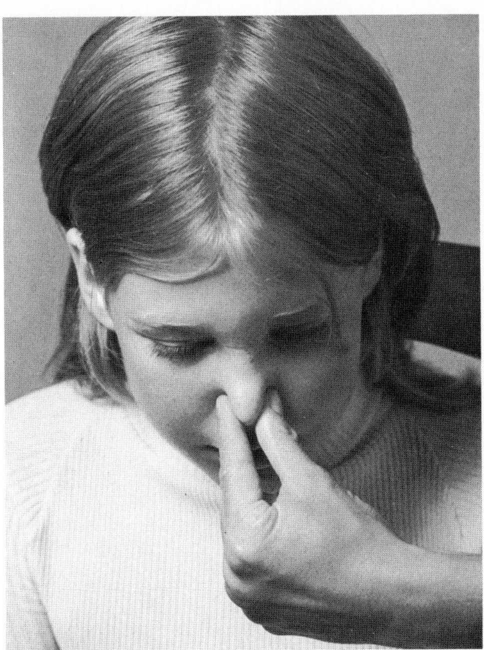

One effective way to stop a nosebleed is to pinch the nostrils shut while the child is sitting up and leaning forward.

Nosebleed may be caused by a punch in the nose or a fall. A child's nose may also bleed if he picks it, pokes something into it, or blows it too hard. Colds, other infections, and extremely dry air may also rupture tiny blood vessels. Fortunately, most nosebleeds in children occur in the front, central part of the nose, where you can easily apply pressure to stop the bleeding.

If your child has a nosebleed, have him sit up and lean forward, if possible. Or, place him in a reclining position with his head and shoulders raised. Pinch his nostrils shut for at least 10 minutes as he breathes through his mouth. If bleeding continues, put a small pad of cotton or gauze in the bleeding nostril and apply pressure.

When the bleeding stops, do not let your child blow his nose for a while. If he does, he may disturb the blood clots and start another nosebleed. If bleeding does not stop in 10 to 15 minutes, call a doctor. He may pack the nose with gauze, or he may cauterize the small bleeding points. C.F.F.

Pressing a wad of cotton under a child's upper lip is another common method of stopping a nosebleed.

Nutrition. The nutrients in food can be divided into certain groups—proteins, carbohydrates, fats, vitamins, and minerals. Water is sometimes considered a nutrient.

Proteins are necessary for the growth and repair of cells. Proteins help build blood and form antibodies to fight infection. They also supply energy. The proteins in food are broken down by the body's digestive system into amino acids. Then body cells use the amino acids like building blocks to put together new and different proteins.

There are 10 essential amino acids. The body can make other amino acids if it gets these 10, but it cannot manufacture these 10. Some foods contain all 10 of the amino acids. These foods, called complete proteins, include meats, poultry, fish, milk, cheese, and eggs. Other foods contain some of the essential 10 amino acids. These foods, called incomplete proteins, include cereals, dried beans, dried peas, and nuts.

Carbohydrates. Starches and sugars, two carbohydrates, supply quick energy. Starches are found in cereals, bread and

(**Nutrition,** *continued*) other baked goods, rice, noodles, macaroni, spaghetti, potatoes, lima beans, and corn. Sources of sugars include candy, fruit, honey, jams, jellies, syrup, and milk.

Other important carbohydrates are celluloses. Celluloses cannot be digested, but they supply roughage. Roughage stimulates muscle contractions in the intestine walls. This helps the body eliminate wastes. The leaves of vegetables and the skin and pulp of fruits are good sources of roughage.

If a child does not eat enough digestible carbohydrates, his body burns protein for energy. A child needs carbohydrates so that the proteins are spared for body-building. Nutritionists recommend meeting the carbohydrate needs of a child mainly through bread, cereals, fruits, green vegetables, milk, and potatoes. If a child takes too much of his carbohydrate requirement in the form of sweets, his supply of vitamins, minerals, and proteins from vegetables and fruits may be lowered. Also, a diet high in refined sugar, such as candy, can cause tooth decay.

Excess carbohydrates are converted into fat and stored in the body as fatty tissues. If a child eats more starches and sweets than are needed for his daily energy requirements, he may become overweight.

Fats are highly concentrated sources of energy. They supply more than twice the energy of an equal amount of carbohydrates or proteins. However, fats are digested slower and cannot be used for quick energy. Fats also supply vitamins A and D. Foods containing fats include cream, butter, margarine, cheese, egg yolk, fat in meats, salad oils, peanut butter, nuts, and chocolate.

Fat that is not burned up is stored as body fat. Body fat supports and protects vital organs and areas such as the eyeballs, the kidneys, the liver, and the joints. A layer of fat under the skin protects the body from losing an excessive amount of heat. If a child eats too many fats, excess body fat is formed and he becomes overweight.

Fats can be divided into two types—saturated and unsaturated. Saturated fats

Basic food groups

The basic seven	
Group 1	Meats, poultry, fish, eggs, dried beans and peas, and nuts
Group 2	Leafy, green, and yellow vegetables
Group 3	Citrus fruits, raw cabbage, salad greens, and tomatoes
Group 4	Potatoes and other vegetables, and noncitrus fruits
Group 5	Breads, cereals, and flour
Group 6	Butter and fortified margarine
Group 7	Milk and milk products

The basic four	
Meat Group	Meats, fish, poultry, eggs, dried beans and peas, nuts
Vegetable-Fruit Group	Vegetables and fruits that provide vitamin C; dark green, leafy vegetables and deep yellow vegetables and fruits; other fruits and vegetables
Bread-Cereals Group	Bread, muffins, macaroni, spaghetti, rice
Milk Group	Fresh whole milk, skim milk, dried milk, evaporated milk, cheese, ice cream

Nutritionists recommend that a child have 3 or more glasses of milk each day. A teen-ager needs 4 or more glasses. Milk products may also fulfill this need. With the Basic Seven system, nutritionists suggest one daily serving from each of the remaining six groups. With the Basic Four system, they recommend four or more servings from both the vegetable-fruit and bread-cereal groups, and two or more servings from the meat group.

are usually solid at room temperature, and unsaturated fats are usually liquid at room temperature. Some doctors recommend reducing the amount of saturated fats in the diet and replacing them with unsaturated fats, because they believe that saturated fats may raise the level of cholesterol, a fatty chemical found in the blood stream. A high level of cholesterol in the blood may lead to heart disease.

Foods high in saturated fats include chocolate, fatty beef, fatty dairy products, luncheon meats, and pork. Liver, most margarines, poultry, and veal are lower in saturated fats. Foods high in unsaturated fats include corn oil, fish, mayonnaise, and special margarines. Fried foods are full of the kind of fat they are cooked in.

Minerals. Several minerals are also required by the body. These minerals include calcium, iron, and iodine.

Calcium helps build bones and teeth, helps blood clot, helps muscles and nerves work, and helps the body regulate the use of other minerals. Milk, cheese, ice cream, shellfish, canned sardines, egg yolk, soy beans, and green vegetables supply calcium.

Iron combines with protein to make hemoglobin, the red substance in blood that carries oxygen to cells. Good sources of iron include lean meats, egg yolk, dried beans and peas, green leafy vegetables, prunes, raisins, dried apricots, liver, heart, kidney, liver sausage, shellfish, and enriched or whole grain bread, cereal, and cereal products.

Iodine helps control the rate at which the body uses energy. Seafoods and iodized salt supply iodine.

Vitamins are essential for the utilization of foods for normal growth and for prevention of certain diseases. Some vitamins, such as vitamins A and D, may be stored in the body. Other vitamins must be supplied constantly because the excess is eliminated.

Vitamins can be divided into two general classes. Vitamins A and D, and others are called fat-soluble because they dissolve in fat. Vitamin C, B-complex vitamins, and others are called water-soluble because they dissolve in water. For more information on vitamins, see VITAMINS, page 302.

Water helps carry nutrients to cells and waste products away from cells. It also helps build tissues and regulate body temperature. Water is obtained from liquids and from foods with a high percentage of water.

Nutrients and diet. A well-balanced diet usually provides all the essential nutrients in sufficient quantity. If your child does not eat exactly the recommended amounts every day, do not be concerned. If, however, during a week he eats much more or much less than the suggested amounts, try to determine the cause. Through regular physical examinations, a doctor can determine if your child is well nourished.

Conserving nutrients. Store and prepare foods in ways that preserve nutrients.

- Keep meat, fish, and poultry in a refrigerator or freezer, wrapped in wax paper or foil.
- Keep frozen food frozen until it is used, and cook it as soon as it is defrosted. Frozen food loses vitamins after thawing and refreezing. Never refreeze frozen foods.
- Wash leafy vegetables and store them in plastic in a refrigerator.
- Cook vegetables for the shortest possible time in as little liquid as possible. M.G.

Osteomyelitis

Osteomyelitis is a bone infection. It is usually caused by bacteria that are carried to the bone by the blood stream from a source of infection in another part of the body. The infection may be a boil on the skin or an infected ear.

Osteomyelitis takes two forms—acute and chronic. The acute (brief and severe) form is more common in the growing child than in the adult. The child has a fever, is irritable, and has pain and tenderness in the bone. The chronic (long-lasting) form is more common in the adult and is characterized by bone pain and draining skin sinuses (a type of abscess).

Osteomyelitis is a serious disease. Avoid home remedies. If you suspect that your child has osteomyelitis, call your doctor promptly. He may give the child intravenous fluids to keep up the child's strength and antibiotics to cure the infection. Early medical attention cures most cases of osteomyelitis. J.J.G.

Otitis media

Otitis media. *See* **Earaches**

Overweight. Many children who appear to be overweight are not. For example, a child with a stocky build and a large body frame is not necessarily overweight. Nor is the preadolescent girl or boy who gains weight rapidly just before a rapid increase in height. If you think your child is overweight, consult your doctor. By examining the child, your doctor can determine what his weight should be for his age and his body frame. If your child is overweight, the doctor can determine the cause and prescribe whatever treatment may be necessary.

In rare instances, a child may be overweight because of a disorder of the pituitary, thyroid, or adrenal gland. Usually, however, excessive eating or decreased physical activity (or both) is the cause. The child is consuming more calories than he is burning through body activity. Sometimes there are underlying emotional problems. Overweight may start after a family crisis or after the child recovers from an illness or operation. The child may eat because he feels anxious and wants to achieve a sense of satisfaction and comfort.

In some families, there is a tendency to overweight. When both parents are overweight, there is a 75 per cent chance that their children will also be overweight.

A little extra weight probably is not harmful. But if a child is quite heavy, he may significantly increase the workload of his heart, he may have trouble performing normal physical actions, or he may be ridiculed and rejected by his classmates.

If your child is overweight, he needs your help to lose the extra weight. Do not keep tempting foods such as cookies, candy, cakes, soft drinks, ice cream, and potato chips around the house. Discourage between-meal eating. When the child does snack, offer him fruit, carrot sticks, and other raw vegetables. Encourage him to develop an interest in athletics and other activities that will provide physical exercise. If you want to treat him, do not take him out for a soda. Take him to the bowling alley, swimming pool, or skating rink. Praise him for even the slightest weight loss. When he loses weight, some new clothes in his new size may be an added incentive. M.G.

See also **Anorexia nervosa; Diets**

Pacifiers commonly are made of a small plastic or rubber nipple attached to a flat disk that keeps the infant from swallowing the nipple. A pacifier offers no nourishment, yet it often soothes a hungry, irritable, or colicky baby. It also gives the infant a chance to satisfy his basic need to suck—a very strong need in infants.

Many parents who object strongly to having a child suck his thumb are not distressed if he sucks a pacifier. They feel that they can offer the pacifier as they wish, whereas the thumb is always at the baby's disposal. One disadvantage of the pacifier is that a baby may be agitated if he has trouble keeping the pacifier in or near his mouth. Never put a pacifier on a ribbon or string around the baby's neck or wrist in order to keep it handy. The danger of the baby's choking himself is too great. M.G.

See also **Thumb-sucking**

Pimple. *See* **Acne**

Pinkeye. *See* **Conjunctivitis**

Pinworms are thin white parasites that live in the intestines. They are about ¼ inch (6 milliliters) long. They may be seen in the child's stool, or even protruding from the anus or vagina. Children with pinworms itch about the anus and scratch the area severely. The itching is worse at night after the child goes to bed. Pinworms may cause a vaginal discharge in young girls.

If one child has pinworms, the entire family should be examined by a doctor. The adult pinworm crawls out of the anus or vagina to lay its eggs. The eggs may fall from the infected child onto his bedding or clothing. The child may pick the eggs up under his fingernails, or they may float in the air because they are so light. Other persons may pick up the eggs by inhaling them or by touching the child's bedding, clothing, or hands. If the eggs are swallowed, they reach the intestine and become adult pinworms.

Pinworms are harmless unless they occur in large numbers. Doctors usually prescribe drugs to eliminate them. M.G.

Pneumonia is an inflammation of the lungs. It is usually caused by bacteria and viruses. Most children get pneumonia as a complication of a cold, or of such other diseases as influenza, measles, and tuberculosis. Certain fungi may be inhaled and cause pneumonia. Pneumonia can also develop if a child swallows a chemical substance such as kerosene or furniture polish. Other cases of pneumonia may occur if a child breathes foods, talcum powder, or other foreign materials into his windpipe.

A child with pneumonia usually breathes rapidly, sometimes with a grunting sound, and he may develop a cough and a high fever. (Infants usually run a lower fever than older children.) The child usually is listless and, in severe cases, appears desperately ill. An older child may complain of pain in his chest or abdomen.

If you suspect that your child has pneumonia, call your doctor. He may hospitalize the child, because the child may need oxygen and intravenous fluids. M.G.

See also **Colds; Virus**

Poison ivy leaves grow in clusters of three, all from the same stem. The edges of the leaves may be lobed or notched.

Poison ivy, oak, and sumac are three common and closely related plants that cause skin rashes. If your child spends a great deal of time in woods and fields, show him what these plants look like so he can avoid them.

Poison ivy grows as a vine or shrub. Some forms of poison ivy are called poison oak. Poison ivy always has three smooth leaves on one stem. The leaves are shiny green in summer and turn red or orange in the fall. Bunches of small, green flowers grow on the main stem close to the leaves. In autumn and winter, the plant bears clusters of white, waxy berries.

Poison sumac grows as a shrub or small tree in swampy areas. It has narrow, fern-like leaves and drooping clusters of white berries.

Poison ivy or poison sumac rash is caused by an irritating oil in the leaves, flowers, fruit, stem, bark, and roots. Clothing that has come in contact with poison ivy may irritate the skin just as much as the plants themselves. Wash or clean the clothing before the child wears it again. Dogs and cats that have come in contact with the poison ivy may also cause the rash. Decontaminate your pets by bathing them.

If you think your child has touched poison ivy, immediately wash his hands and exposed portions of his skin thoroughly in a generous lather of mild soap. Rinse with plenty of cold water, lather again, and rinse again. Do not rub too hard and do not use brushes, sponges, or other rough or harsh materials. Washing with soap removes or lessens the irritation of the oil.

Poison ivy rash may appear a few hours or a few days after the child touches the plant. At first the child's skin itches or burns. Then the skin becomes inflamed, and it usually develops blisters. Scratching may cause an infection. Cut the child's fingernails short. To reduce itching, soak the rash-covered skin in plain or salt water for 20 to 30 minutes, four or five times daily. Use one level teaspoon of table salt in one pint (0.5 liter) of water. Apply calamine lotion every two or three hours. Your doctor may prescribe medicine to reduce itching. A.M.M.

Poisonings and poisons. Each year in the United States, some 500,000 children under 5 years of age are accidentally poisoned. About 500 of them either die or become so ill they must be hospitalized.

Treatment of poisonings. Here are the steps to take if your child is poisoned and you know what the poison is.

- Give the appropriate antidote. Often antidotes are printed on the containers of poisonous substances. Or, use the chart in this article. However, do not give any liquids to an unconscious child even if liquids are part of the antidote.
- Induce vomiting only when it is part of the antidote. However, do not induce vomiting if the child is having convulsions or is unconscious.
- Call your doctor or take your child to the nearest hospital emergency room. Take the container with its label so that the doctor can identify the poison and possibly determine how much the child has taken.

If your child is poisoned, and you do not know what the antidote is, follow these instructions.

- Call your doctor.
- Or, call your poison control center. (Ask your doctor for the number of the nearest poison control center, and keep the number posted near the telephone.) The center will tell you what emergency first-aid procedures to take.
- Or, take the child to the nearest hospital emergency room.

If you discover that your child is eating or drinking some product, but you do not know if the product is poisonous, remember this caution: Any nonfood substance that is eaten or drunk is a potential poison. Call your doctor or poison control center to find out whether the substance is poisonous and, if so, the antidote.

Symptoms of internal poisoning are not always immediately apparent, but they include cramps, diarrhea, pallor, stupor, nausea, and vomiting. If the child has taken a corrosive poison, he may be burned around the mouth and tongue. Aspirin and tranquilizers may make him sleepy, or even unconscious.

How children are poisoned. The kitchen, bathroom, garage, basement, and bedroom are all likely places for poisonings to occur. Household cleaning agents and solvents, and even insecticides, are often stored in kitchen and bathroom cupboards easily accessible to children. Insecticides and gasoline are kept in the garage. Bathroom medicine cabinets contain pills and cosmetics. Bedroom night tables may hold tranquilizers, sleeping pills, and aspirin. All of these, if taken in sufficient quantity, can kill a child.

The smell or taste of a substance will seldom prevent a child from eating or drinking it. The child who annoys you by refusing to drink his milk or his orange juice may gulp ink, kerosene, or lighter fluid with gusto. Children will also eat or drink glue, crayons, paint, solvents, tobacco, matches, reducing tablets, turpentine, flashlight batteries, cosmetics, and countless other common

---

How to induce vomiting

- Give the child syrup of ipecac, one tablespoon (one-half ounce, or 15 milliliters) in half a glass of water, or
- Tickle the back of the child's throat with your finger until he gags, or
- Give him one teaspoon of mustard in half a glass of water, or
- Give him three teaspoons of salt in a glass of warm water.

When you are inducing vomiting, have the child lie on his stomach on a bed with his head hanging down over the edge. Or, turn him over your knees. This position prevents him from breathing vomit into his lungs. Put a large pan on the floor under his head to catch the vomit. Save the vomit. The doctor may want to analyze it to determine what type of poison the child has taken.

Antidotes for external poisons

- If a child comes in contact with strong acids, alkalies, or other corrosive substances, remove his contaminated clothing immediately. Quickly wash the affected skin area with lots of water. If the poison is oily or does not wash off with water, cleanse the skin thoroughly with soap and warm water, and rinse. Then call your doctor or take the child to a hospital emergency room.
- If the poison spatters into the child's eye, hold the eye open and rinse it with a stream of water for several minutes. Then call your doctor or take the child to a hospital emergency room.

Antidotes for internal poisonings

Acids. Do not induce vomiting. Give one ounce (30 milliliters) of milk of magnesia in a large glass of water.

Alcohol. Give a glass of milk. Induce vomiting. Then mix a tablespoon of baking soda in a quart (1 liter) of warm water, and have the child drink as much as he will take.

Alkalies. Do not induce vomiting. Give two tablespoons of vinegar in two glasses of water. Then give the whites of two raw eggs or four tablespoons of olive oil.

Ammonia. See Alkalies.

Antifreeze. See Alcohol.

Aspirin and headache tablets. Give a glass of milk. Induce vomiting. Then mix one tablespoon of baking soda in a quart (1 liter) of warm water. Have the child drink as much as he will accept.

Barbiturates. If the child is conscious, induce vomiting. Give two tablespoons of Epsom salts in two glasses of water. Then give strong coffee or a cola drink and try to make the child walk. If the child is unconscious, keep him warm until a doctor comes or until you have taken him to a hospital. Give artificial respiration if breathing stops.

Carbon monoxide. Carry the child into fresh air. Give artificial respiration if necessary.

Cleaning fluids. See Petroleum products.

Codeine. If the child is conscious, give him a glass of milk. Then give him two tablespoons of Epsom salts in two glasses of water. Keep the child moving. Give him strong, black coffee. If the child is unconscious, keep him warm until a doctor arrives. If the child stops breathing, start artificial respiration.

Cold tablets. Give a glass of milk. Induce vomiting. Mix one tablespoon of baking soda in a quart (1 liter) of warm water. Have him drink as much as he can.

Cologne. See Alcohol.

Cough syrups. See Codeine.

Drain cleaners. See Alkalies.

Food poisoning. Induce vomiting. Then give two tablespoons of Epsom salts in two glasses of water.

Furniture polish. See Petroleum products.

Gasoline. See Petroleum products.

Insect and rat poisons

with arsenic. Give a glass of milk. Then induce vomiting.

with DDT. Induce vomiting. Then give two tablespoons of Epsom salts in two glasses of water.

with phosphorus. Induce vomiting. Then give eight tablespoons of mineral oil. Do not give vegetable or animal oil. Then give eight tablespoons of hydrogen peroxide. Finally, mix one tablespoon of baking soda in a quart (1 liter) of warm water. Have the child drink as much as he can.

with sodium fluoride. Give two tablespoons of milk of magnesia. Then give a glass of milk. Then induce vomiting.

with strychnine. Give a glass of milk. Induce vomiting. Give artificial respiration if necessary. Keep the child quiet.

Iodine. Mix cornstarch or flour with water into a thick paste and give to the child. Mix four tablespoons of salt in a quart (1 liter) of warm water. Have him drink this until he vomits a clear fluid. Finally, give him a glass of milk.

Kerosene. See Petroleum products.

Laundry bleach. Give the child one or two glasses of milk.

Lighter fluid. See Petroleum products.

Lye. See Alkalies.

Nail polish remover. See Alcohol.

Oil of wintergreen. A very small amount can cause death. Give a glass of milk. Then induce vomiting. Mix a tablespoon of baking soda in a quart (1 liter) of warm water. Have the child drink as much as he can. Call your doctor.

Paregoric. Give a glass of milk. Then give two tablespoons of Epsom salts in two glasses of water. Keep the child awake.

Pep pills (amphetamines). Give a glass of milk. Then induce vomiting.

Petroleum products. Do not induce vomiting. Give a glass of water or milk. Then give four tablespoons of vegetable oil.

Rat poisons. See Insect and rat poisons.

Shaving lotion. See Alcohol.

Sleeping pills. See Barbiturates.

Toilet cleaners. See Alkalies.

Tranquilizers. See Barbiturates.

Turpentine. See Petroleum products.

Antidotes for plants that are poisonous when eaten

(Notify doctor if any of these plants is eaten.)

Buttercup. All parts are poisonous, especially the juice. Give the child one or two glasses of milk and four tablespoons of vegetable or mineral oil.

Castor bean. All parts, and mainly the seed, are poisonous. Induce vomiting.

Cherry tree. The twigs and leaves are poisonous. Induce vomiting.

Daffodil. The bulb is poisonous. Induce vomiting.

Hyacinth. The bulb is poisonous. Induce vomiting.

Iris. The leaves and the rootstocks are poisonous. Induce vomiting.

Jimson weed. The berries are poisonous. Induce vomiting.

Lily of the valley. The leaves, flowers, and roots are poisonous. Induce vomiting.

Mistletoe. The berry is poisonous. Induce vomiting.

Mushrooms, poisonous. All parts may be poisonous. Induce vomiting. Then give two tablespoons Epsom salts in two glasses of water.

Narcissus. The bulb is poisonous. Induce vomiting.

Poinsettia. The juice of the leaves, stems, flowers, or fruit is poisonous. Give milk and/or four tablespoons of mineral or vegetable oil.

Potato. The green "sunburned" spots and sprouts of potato tubers, green stems, and leaves are poisonous. Induce vomiting.

Rhubarb. The leaf blade is poisonous. Give milk and induce vomiting.

Wisteria. The seeds and pods are poisonous. Induce vomiting.

(**Poisonings and poisons,** *continued*) household items that can be harmful even though they seem harmless.

More children are poisoned by drugs than by any other product. And of all medications, aspirin causes the greatest number of child poisonings. If a youngster swallows several adult-sized aspirin tablets, or if he swallows a large number of child-sized tablets, he is in grave danger.

Household chemicals are the second leading cause of child poisonings. Metal polishes, drain and toilet bowl cleaners, waxes and polishes for floors and furniture, bleach, ammonia—all are in daily use and too often in reach of children. Many parents are unaware of, or disregard, the warnings on the containers of these products. Soaps and detergents are often stored in low cabinets where youngsters can easily reach them, as are dangerous furniture polishes, floor polishes, and waxes. Many parents do not realize that the kerosenelike solvent found in these waxes and polishes is an extremely dangerous ingredient.

Insecticides, weed killers, and rat poisons are also a leading cause of child poisonings. And swallowing these substances is not the only way a child can be poisoned by them. Some of these products can be absorbed through the skin. Prolonged inhalation of their vapors may also be harmful. Read all warnings on these containers and follow the manufacturers' directions for using and storing the products.

Preventing poisonings. Protect a young child by keeping all poisonous substances out of his sight and his reach. As he grows older, teach him that it is dangerous to eat, drink, or smell strange liquids or powders he may see about the home or yard. Teach him to ask you about each new thing. Always remember that curiosity is part of the normal development of a young child. Even while you are teaching him, you must keep a watchful eye on him.

To "poison-proof" your home, follow these precautions.

- Flush unused pills and liquid medicines down the toilet. Do not discard them in

Plants that are poisonous when eaten

Lily of the valley

German iris

Field buttercup

Mistletoe

Poinsettia

(**Poisonings and poisons,** *continued*) trash containers where they may be found and taken by children.

- Store medicines after each use. Do not leave them any place where a child might reach them.
- Do not refer to medicines as "candy."
- Do not put household cleaning products in teacups, drinking glasses, soft-drink bottles, or food containers.
- Do not leave cleaning cloths or sponges saturated with furniture polish or other cleaning fluids lying about.
- Do not let yourself be interrupted when using a poisonous substance. Let the phone or doorbell ring until the substance is returned to a safe place.
- Check regularly to be sure no poisonous products are within reach of children.
- Never store foods and poisons in the same cabinet. M.G.

See also **Accidents; Artificial respiration; Bites and stings; Coma; Convulsions; Emetics; Food poisoning; Medicine cabinets; Poison ivy, oak, and sumac; Prescriptions; Vomiting**

Poliomyelitis (infantile paralysis or polio) is a serious contagious disease that is characterized by inflammation of the brain and spinal cord. It is caused by a virus.

Symptoms of polio may at first resemble those of a common cold. The child may have fever, chills, sore throat, headache, severe intestinal upset, stiff back, muscle spasms in the neck or thighs, or pains and stiffness in the legs, back, and neck. Some children become paralyzed, but most do not remain paralyzed permanently. All children with polio should be under a doctor's care.

Vaccine has almost eliminated polio in the United States and Canada. The first vaccine perfected was the inactivated Salk vaccine, in which the virus is dead but still able to cause production of antibodies. Later, a live oral vaccine was developed by Albert Sabin. This vaccine contains the living poliovirus, but the virus has been weakened so that the child does not catch the disease. Live vaccine provides longer-lasting immunity, so children who have been immunized with the Salk vaccine should also receive oral vaccine.

Giving the oral vaccine is simple. Two drops of the vaccine are dropped directly into the child's mouth or onto a small lump of sugar which is then fed to the child.

Three types of viruses cause polio, so a child must be protected against all three. Type I is the most frequent cause of polio. Type III is the next most frequent cause, and Type II is the least frequent cause.

There is an oral vaccine for each of these three types. The doses can be given separately. These vaccines, called MOPV (monovalent oral poliovirus vaccine), are most helpful to doctors during an epidemic caused by a single type of polio.

For routine immunization, most doctors prefer TOPV (trivalent oral poliovirus vaccine). This vaccine protects against all three types of polio. It is usually given at 2, 4, and 6 months of age, with a fourth dose a year later at 18 months of age. Many doctors also recommend a fifth dose of TOPV at 4 to 6 years, or when children enter kindergarten or first grade. H.D.R., Jr.

Posture is the way a child holds his body as he stands, sits, and moves. Good posture is important for good appearance and good health.

When a child with good posture stands, he holds his head up. His head is balanced over his shoulders. His chest is held high, his shoulders are back, and his abdomen is drawn in. His weight rests equally on both of his feet. When a child with good posture walks, his feet point nearly straight ahead and he leads with his thighs and knees.

If a child has poor standing posture, his head falls forward, his shoulders are rounded, his back curves, his chest slopes, and his abdomen sags.

When a child with good posture sits, his hips are against the back of the chair and his feet are flat on the floor. The weight of his body rests on both of his thighs to evenly distribute his weight. If he leans forward to write, he bends from his hips, instead of curving his back.

When a child with good posture lifts heavy objects, he uses his leg muscles, not

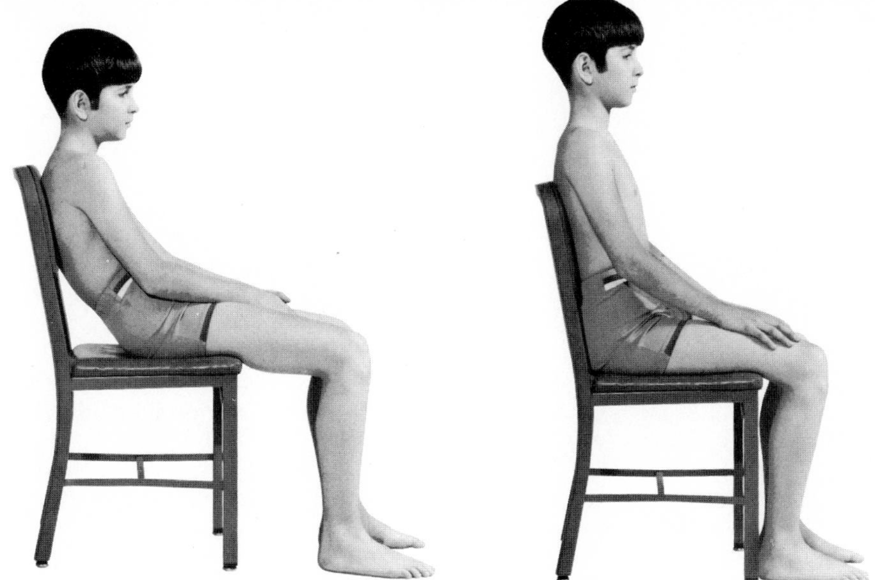

Poor sitting posture (*above left*) can cause swayback, backache, round shoulders, spinal curvature, muscle strain, and can hinder normal functioning of body organs. In a good sitting position (*above right*), a child should sit well back on the chair, with both feet squarely on the floor. The head should be over the shoulders, and the back should be straight.

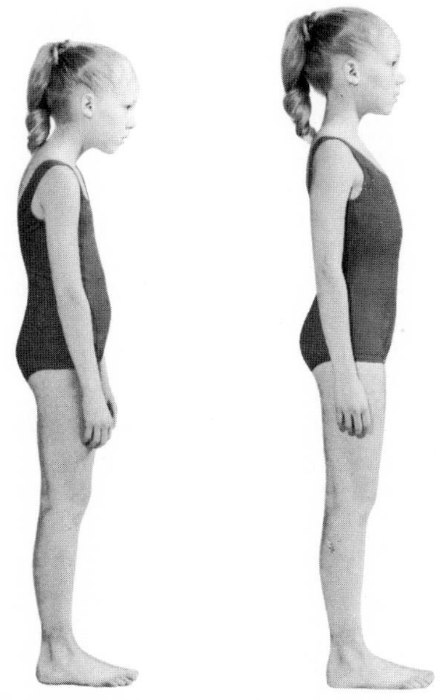

Poor standing posture is shown above left. In a good standing position (*above right*), the head should be balanced over the shoulders, the chest held high, the shoulders back, and the abdomen drawn in.

his back muscles. He stands close to the object, bends his knees, keeps his back straight, and lifts the object.

Poor posture can cause swayback, spinal curvature, round shoulders, and backaches. Organs in the chest may be crowded together and hinder efficient functioning of the lungs. The diaphragm, liver, stomach, and other organs in the abdomen may sag. Body weight is abnormally distributed and can strain leg muscles. Lifting heavy objects with the body in poor posture can strain back muscles.

Nagging a child to "Stand up straight!" and "Square your shoulders!" does not help him acquire good posture. A child with the double problem of bad posture and nagging parents is likely to sag and slump all the more. A child often listens to a doctor and takes part in good-posture campaigns at school more readily than he responds to parental insistence. Bicycling, walking, basketball, and other sports may also help improve your child's posture. M.G.

See also **Scoliosis**

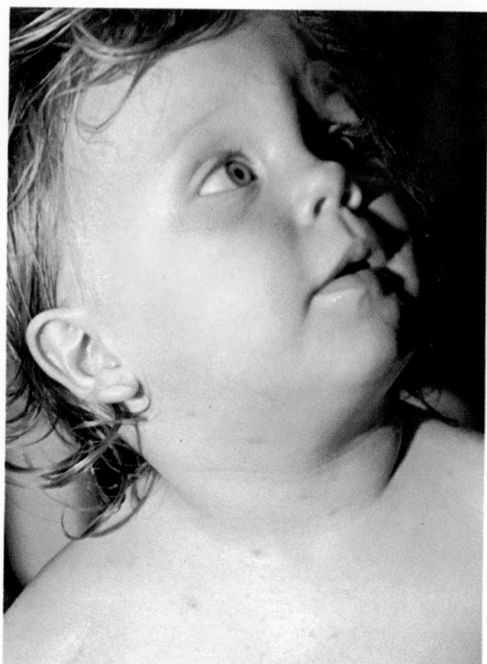

Prickly heat rash consists of raised, red, pinpoint spots.

Prickly heat is a skin rash caused by excessive heat or humidity. The rash is made up of raised, red, pinpoint spots. The surrounding skin also becomes red. Prickly heat occurs especially in areas of the body where perspiration accumulates. In fat babies and young children, it may be found in the groin folds, neck folds, and over the shoulders.

Prickly heat may cause itching and scratching. The skin may become raw, irritated, and infected. Try to clear the condition promptly. Sponge the child's skin frequently with cool tap water, or give him a cool bath. Avoid clothing that may irritate the affected areas. Leaving the skin exposed to the air can help keep it dry. The child's room should be well ventilated and the room temperature should be cool (about 70° F.). Medicines usually are not necessary if the child can be kept cool and clean. A dusting powder made of cornstarch or talcum may be helpful. Apply the powder three or four times daily after a cool bath. If prickly heat does not clear up, call your doctor. A.M.M.

Prescriptions are usually written directions provided by a doctor to prevent or treat an illness. Most prescriptions are for medicines, but prescriptions may also be given for diet, physical therapy, eyeglasses, and exercises. At the top of the prescription form you may notice an ℞ which stands for the Latin word *recipe*, meaning "take." Doctors used tc write their prescriptions entirely in Latin, but today most of them use English except for a few signs and symbols.

Have all prescriptions filled by a qualified pharmacist. Follow exactly the doctor's instructions for giving the medicine. Remember that almost all medicines are harmful if taken in larger amounts than prescribed by the doctor.

And a last word of caution: never give medicine prescribed for one member of the family to another whose symptoms seem to be similar. The cause and treatment of the second illness may be entirely different from the illness for which the medicine had been prescribed. M.G.

See also **Drugs; Medicine cabinets**

Rash. Since it is difficult to tell a mild, relatively harmless rash from a serious one, consult a doctor if your child develops a rash. Skin color can affect the appearance of a rash. A severe rash on a dark skin may appear milder than it really is. The following are some common causes of rashes.

- Measles—blotchy red rash
- German measles—rose-colored rash, low fever, swollen glands in neck and behind ears
- Roseola infantum—flat pink rash on the chest, abdomen, and neck
- Scarlet fever—a rash that looks like a sunburn with goose pimples
- Chicken pox—separate, raised pimples, some of which blister, then break and crust
- Eczema—patches of itchy, rough red skin
- Hives—itchy white welts on red skin
- Ringworm—circular, rough patches
- Impetigo—blisterlike sores that crust
- Prickly heat—raised, red, pinpoint spots, usually in the groin and neck folds
- Diaper rash—red, chafed-looking skin
- Poison ivy—blisters and inflammation accompanied by much itching. A.M.M.

Reye's Syndrome is an uncommon disease that occurs in children from a few years of age to adolescence. It involves the liver and brain and often follows an attack of chicken pox or influenza.

A child may be recovering from a mild respiratory infection when suddenly there is persistent vomiting. This is followed by behavioral changes consisting of lethargy alternating with irritability, hyperactivity, and hallucinations. Should your child show such symptoms, call your doctor immediately. If the diagnosis is Reye's Syndrome, the patient needs emergency treatment and should be taken to a hospital equipped to give all the help necessary.

This disease is named for Dr. R. D. K. Reye, who, with Australian colleagues, first described cases of it in 1963. Its cause is still uncertain and proper treatment is unclear. The general aim is to reduce the brain swelling and restore normal liver metabolism. Most patients also have a high blood ammonia level which must be lowered. S.L.K

Rh factor is a chemical substance that most people have in their blood. It gets its name from rhesus monkeys, in whose red blood cells it was first discovered. The Rh factor is inherited. If the factor is present in a child's blood, his blood is Rh-positive. If the factor is absent, his blood is Rh-negative. Both types of blood are normal and healthy, but they do not always mix safely.

For example, if a child with Rh-negative blood receives a transfusion of Rh-positive blood, the Rh-positive blood may cause production of antibodies that attack the child's normal red blood cells. The child may become seriously ill or even die. Hospital technicians test a child's blood to determine the Rh factor before transfusions are given.

It is also important to know the Rh factor when a woman is pregnant, or when a husband and wife are planning to have a baby. The child of an Rh-negative mother and an Rh-positive father may be Rh-positive or Rh-negative. If the child is Rh-negative, there is no problem. But if he is Rh-positive, his blood may cause the mother's Rh-negative blood to produce antibodies against the Rh factor. These antibodies may then return to the baby's blood and destroy his red blood cells. The infant—commonly called an "Rh baby"—may die before birth or may be born with mild to severe jaundice and anemia. The opposite condition, that is, an Rh-positive mother and an Rh-negative baby, does not cause trouble.

Once the blood of an Rh-negative woman starts to produce antibodies, the level of antibodies becomes progressively stronger with each Rh-positive pregnancy. Generally, an Rh-negative woman with an Rh-positive husband can have two or three healthy Rh-positive babies because her antibody production may be slow enough that these first babies escape its effects. But if an Rh-negative woman has ever had a transfusion of Rh-positive blood, her blood may already contain antibodies that can react dangerously with her baby's Rh-positive blood.

With correct and immediate treatment, a seriously affected Rh baby can usually make a good recovery and be normal. Doctors can detect Rh incompatibilities by simple blood tests that measure the level of antibodies. If the level rises threateningly, the doctor may induce early labor so that he can deliver the baby before the level of antibodies becomes dangerously high. Sometimes, exchange transfusions must be given to the baby immediately after birth to replace the baby's blood with fresh blood. In rare cases, transfusions of blood have been given to unborn infants. Transfused blood must be Rh-negative because Rh-positive blood would be destroyed by the antibodies in the baby's system.

For protection in future pregnancies, a vaccine is available to prevent the production of antibodies in the mother's blood. It may be given to a mother with Rh-negative blood within 72 hours after delivery or miscarriage of an Rh-positive baby.

The best protection against the heartbreak of an Rh baby is competent prenatal care. A doctor can take proper measures to have on hand the equipment, typed blood, and other materials for treating the Rh condition. F.O.

See also **Anemia; Blood type; Jaundice**

Rheumatic fever is a disease that follows an untreated infection by group A beta hemolytic streptococcal bacteria. The infection is usually a strep throat. About one strep throat in a hundred results in an attack of rheumatic fever. Rheumatic fever usually first strikes between the ages of 5 and 15.

Symptoms of rheumatic fever generally appear within two to five weeks after the strep infection has cleared up. St. Vitus's dance (chorea), uncontrollable twitching of muscles, may be one of the first symptoms. Or, the child may have vague pains in his muscles. (However, the great majority of children with muscle pains in their legs at night do not have rheumatic fever.) These pains may become intense. The joints in the child's legs and arms may become painful and swollen. The child may also have a fever and a skin rash. At the same time, the heart and the heart valves usually become inflamed. This inflammation causes a heart murmur.

Rheumatic fever can cause permanent damage to the child's heart, but not always. When permanent damage does occur, it usually results from inflammation of either or both of the valves on the left side of the heart. As the inflammation lessens, a scar forms on the valve. This scar prevents the valve from opening and closing properly. The damaged valve may allow blood to leak back when the heart contracts. Or, the valve may become so puckered and shrunken that the child's heart can scarcely force blood through it.

If you suspect that your child has rheumatic fever, consult your doctor. He will likely advise hospitalization of the child. Bed rest during the severe phase of the disease is essential for a child with rheumatic fever. Convalescence at home may be necessary for a time. The doctor will probably prescribe a gradual increase of physical activity. He may also prescribe aspirin, and, in special cases, cortisone to relieve the symptoms.

A child who has had rheumatic fever is not immune to it. He is susceptible to recurring attacks. Each additional attack may damage the heart valves. Eventually, the valves may become so scarred that an operation is necessary. Strep infections are a greater threat to a child who has already had rheumatic fever. To protect the child, the doctor will prescribe a long-term program to prevent a strep infection. The child may receive a daily oral dose of a sulfa drug or an antibiotic such as penicillin. Or, he may have an injection in the buttocks of a long-acting antibiotic once a month. This protective treatment may be continued until he is about 21 or even older.

The best way to fight rheumatic fever is to prevent it. Call your doctor if your child has a sore throat with a fever, if he has a persistent sore throat, or if he has an extremely sore throat. The doctor may want to take a throat culture, because this is the only way to identify the beta hemolytic streptococcus. If the doctor finds this streptococcus, he will prescribe antibiotics immediately. This treatment will continue until another throat culture shows that the infection has cleared up. Fortunately, most sore throats are not strep throats. M.G.

See also **Arthritis; Cramps; Growing pains; Heart murmur; St. Vitus's dance; Strep throat**

Rickets is a bone disease caused by a metabolic disturbance in the body. Some children with rickets do not get enough vitamin D in their diets. Others have an inherited disability that prevents absorption of vitamin D from food. Rickets is extremely rare in the United States and Canada.

In most cases rickets occurs before the child is 3 years old. The bones of the child do not calcify (harden) adequately. They are so soft that they can bend out of shape. Bumps can also develop on the bones. Severe rickets causes bowed legs and deformed skull, rib, spinal column, and pelvic bones. Bone damage can be corrected if it is not too severe. If rickets is not corrected, the bones may eventually harden and leave the child misshapen.

Although vitamin D enriched milk and food are available, and although enough exposure to the ultraviolet rays of the sun can prevent most cases of rickets, your doctor may not want to rely completely on these sources. He may prescribe extra daily vitamin D for your baby. M.G.

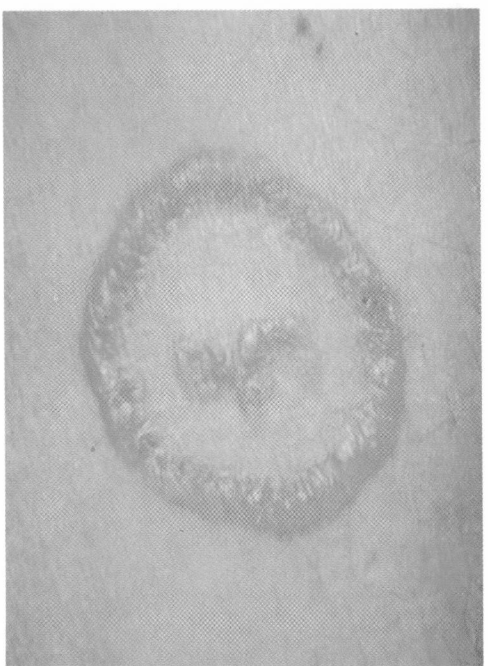

Small, circular patches of pink skin are characteristic of ringworm of the body.

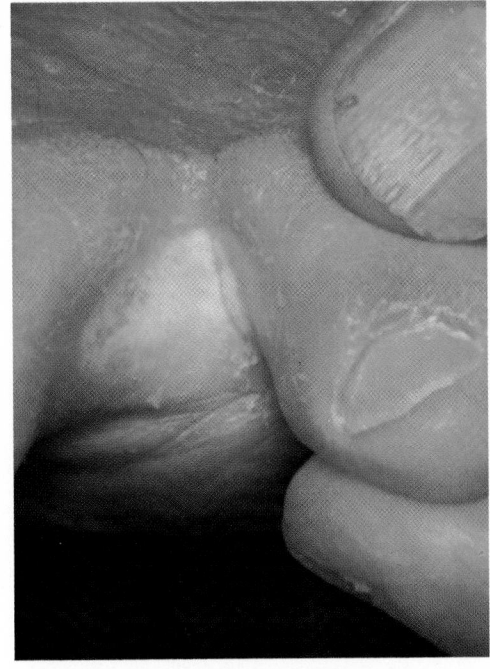

Athlete's foot usually produces cracked, itchy, tender skin between the toes.

Ringworm is a contagious skin disease caused by fungus. It is sometimes itchy. Ringworm of the body usually appears as small, circular, pinkish patches. As a patch grows larger, the center clears and the eruption looks like a ring. Ringworm of the scalp is characterized by round, red, scaly patches in which hairs break off close to the scalp. Ringworm infection of the feet, commonly called athlete's foot, usually appears in the webs of skin between the toes. It usually produces cracked, itchy, tender skin. Blisters and scaly skin may appear on the soles and sides of the feet. If you think your child has ringworm, call your doctor. Antifungal drugs can clear up the disease.

Ringworm may be spread by contact with infected persons, infected dogs or cats, or infected brushes, combs, and furniture. If your child has ringworm, make sure that he uses his own comb, brush, washcloth, towel, and other personal articles. Caution him against scratching the infected area. If he scratches it, he may spread ringworm to other parts of his body. A.M.M.

Roseola infantum is a disease characterized by a rash and a fever. Doctors believe that it is probably caused by a virus. Roseola infantum usually affects children between 6 months and 3 years of age. It is the most common illness that causes a fever and a rash in children under 2 years of age.

Roseola infantum usually begins with a fever of 103° to 105° F. (39.4° C to 40.6° C). After three to five days, the child's temperature suddenly drops to normal or below. Then, a rash of small, pink, flat spots appears on his chest, abdomen, and neck. Only rarely does it spread to his face, arms, and legs. The rash may last a few hours or one or two days. One attack usually provides permanent immunity.

Call your doctor if you suspect that your child has roseola infantum. He will probably tell you to give the child aspirin to bring down the fever and liquids to prevent dehydration. You do not have to isolate a child with roseola infantum. H.D.R., JR.

Rubella. *See* **German measles**

Saint Vitus's dance (chorea) is a disease of the nervous system which causes uncontrollable twitching of muscles in the face, arms, legs, or of the entire body. An attack of chorea usually lasts about six weeks, and it gradually subsides without damaging the child's nervous system. The disease most commonly affects children from 7 to about 15 years of age. Doctors do not know what causes chorea.

The twitching may be mild and infrequent, or it may be severe and almost continual. The child may have difficulty in writing or in feeding himself. He may walk awkwardly and be clumsy when carrying things. In severe cases, the muscular jerking may cause the child to fall out of bed. A child with chorea may become nervous, irritable, and emotionally upset.

Call your doctor if you suspect your child has chorea. He may prescribe sedatives and bed rest. A.G.S.

See also **Ataxia; Rheumatic fever; Tic**

Scald. *See* **Burns**

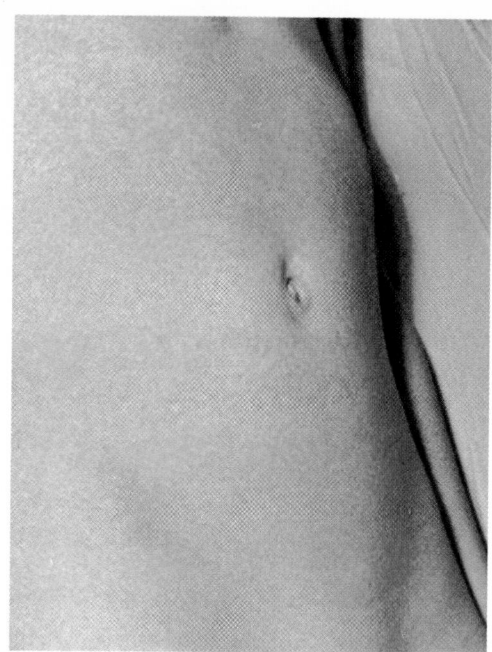

The deep red rash that a child develops with a case of scarlet fever looks like a sunburn with goose pimples.

Scarlet fever is a contagious disease that is caused by the same streptococcus bacteria that produces sore throats, swollen glands, tonsillitis, ear abscesses, and other infections. A person with a streptococcic infection can spread scarlet fever even though he does not have scarlet fever. For example, a child may develop scarlet fever after picking up the bacteria from someone in whom the streptococcus produced only a sore throat.

First symptoms of the disease come on suddenly—high fever, sore throat, chills, vomiting, and headache. Early treatment prevents spreading of the disease to others, so call your doctor whenever your child has a sore throat and a fever.

About three days after the first symptoms appear, the child breaks out in a deep red rash. The rash resembles a sunburn with goose pimples. It consists of pinhead-sized, raised spots that are close together. The rash begins on the child's neck and in his groin and armpits. Then it gradually spreads over the rest of his body and the sides of his face. The area around his mouth is pale, his

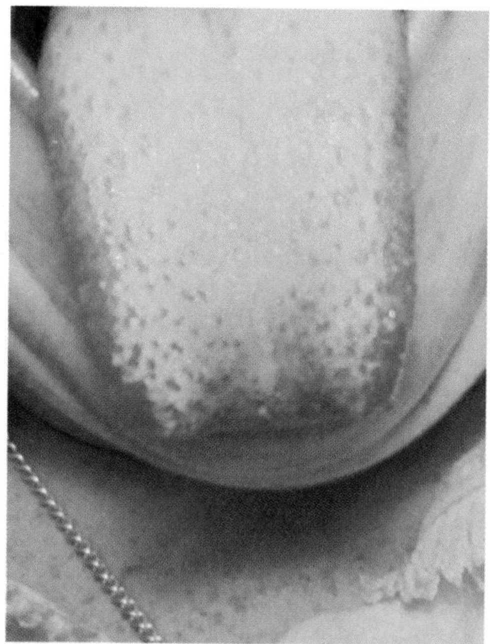

In the early stages of scarlet fever, the tongue is coated. Then it becomes red and pitted looking (strawberry tongue).

throat is inflamed, and his tongue becomes red and pitted looking. After the rash fades, the child's skin usually peels or flakes off for from three to eight weeks. If the rash is widespread, peeling will be extensive. Scarlet fever usually affects children between 3 and 12 years old.

Doctors usually prescribe penicillin or other antibiotics to treat scarlet fever. Isolate the child for about seven days—or longer if the doctor so advises. Remind the child to cover his mouth and nose when he sneezes or coughs. Have him use paper tissues for this. When he is done, burn the tissues in a safe place. Scarlet fever is contagious for from two to five days before symptoms appear and for about 24 to 48 hours after treatment with antibiotics starts. One attack of the disease usually gives a child permanent immunity.

Scarlet fever was once considered a very serious disease, but prompt use of antibiotics in treating streptococcic throat infections has greatly reduced its threat. H.D.R., Jr.

See also **Sore throat; Strep throat**

Structural scoliosis

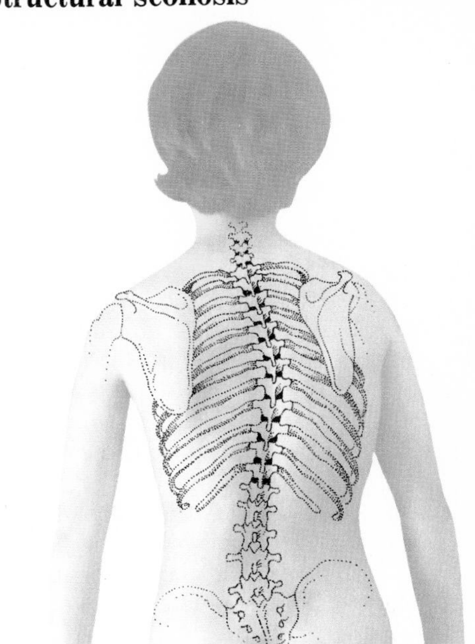

The curve in this girl's spine makes her right shoulder and right hip higher than her left shoulder and left hip.

Scoliosis (curvature of the spine) is a condition in which the spine curves from one side to the other. Scoliosis occurs in about 2 per cent of the population. It is more common in girls than in boys. Consult your doctor if you suspect that your child has scoliosis. He may suggest that you take the child to an orthopedist (a surgeon specializing in deformities and diseases of bones and joints).

There are two types of scoliosis—functional and structural. Functional scoliosis may be caused by poor posture, a short leg, or muscle spasms. It does not result in any bone changes. Functional curves are flexible and disappear when the child lies down. Functional scoliosis can be treated by correcting posture, by fitting the child with special correction devices such as a built-up shoe, or by drugs to relax muscles.

Structural scoliosis is a spinal deformity that begins in childhood and usually results in permanent bone changes. Some cases may be caused by a spinal deformity that was present at birth, or by a disease that deforms the bones of the spine during growth. For example, it can follow paralysis of the spine muscles caused by poliomyelitis. However, doctors do not know what causes about 80 per cent of all cases of structural scoliosis.

Although structural scoliosis is rarely painful, it causes deformity. A structural curve, unlike a functional curve, does not disappear when the child lies down. Frequently, one hip or one shoulder appears higher than the other. The chest appears off-center in relation to the pelvis. The back of the ribs bend out, pushing out the shoulder blade. When the child bends forward, a hump appears on one side of the upper back. The deformity caused by structural scoliosis frequently worsens as the child grows. Early diagnosis and treatment are important.

Treatment of structural scoliosis depends on the severity of the curve. An orthopedist may prescribe spinal muscle exercises, a heel lift to straighten the pelvis, casts or braces, or surgery. Structural scoliosis can rarely be completely cured, but early treatment can lessen its crippling effects. J.J.G.

Shock is one of the body's reactions to physical or infectious stress. The normal flow of blood is upset and normal functions of the body are weakened. A child suffering from shock may be weak or faint; may become pale; may have cold, clammy skin; and may have weak, irregular, or "fluttering" pulse. Nausea and vomiting are also common in shock.

Bleeding, major burns, severe pain, infection, and severe injury such as a broken bone may cause shock. Fear or other strong emotions may cause a different kind of shock.

A child in shock should be placed on a flat surface. If blood has been lost, elevate the feet a little. To prevent loss of normal body heat, wrap the child in a blanket. Do not use a hot-water bottle or other artificial heat. Too much heat draws blood to the skin and away from more vital organs where it is needed.

Call your doctor promptly or take the child to a hospital. Most forms of shock need immediate, specific treatment. M.G.

Hypospray is a painless way of giving shots. Air pressure forces the liquid drug or vaccine through pores of the child's skin and into the child's body.

First aid for shock

A child in shock should be placed on a flat surface. Wrap the child in a blanket. This will help keep the body temperature normal.

Shots that children usually receive may be divided into three categories: (1) preventive, to avoid a disease; (2) curative, to rid one of a disease; and (3) desensitizing, to decrease allergic reactions.

Children are injected with their first preventive shots early in life. Doctors usually give a diphtheria-whooping cough-tetanus shot (DTP) when a child is from 1 to 3 months old. Polio vaccine is given orally at the same time. Later, shots are given to prevent measles and German measles and may be given to prevent mumps.

Curative shots, such as antibiotic drugs, not only cure a disease, but also often prevent serious complications from a disease. Although curative drugs may be given orally, doctors may decide to give them by injection for several reasons. The drug more quickly enters the blood stream to fight the disease; the drug is not tasted (regardless of how well the taste of oral drugs is disguised, some children refuse to take a second dose, or they vomit it); and the doctor is certain that the drug has been taken.

Location of the sinuses

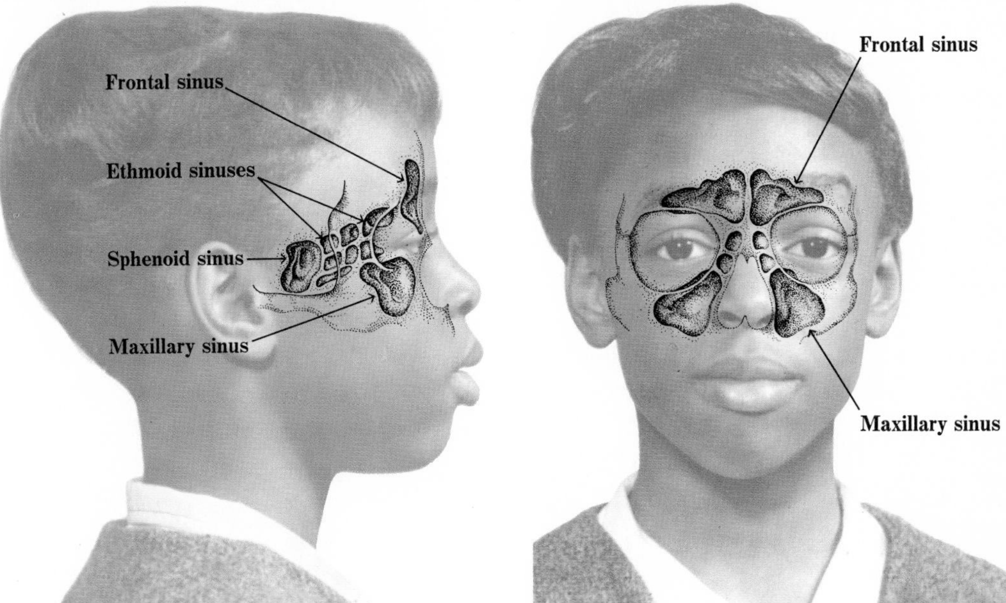

The frontal sinuses are above the eyes. The maxillary sinuses are in the cheek bones, below the eyes. The ethmoid sinuses are above the nasal cavity. The sphenoid sinuses are behind the ethmoid sinuses.

Doctors give desensitizing shots to many children who are allergic to substances from which they cannot constantly be protected. These shots are injected into the child in small, but increasing doses. As a result of the repeated shots, the child's body manufactures antibodies and effects cellular changes that lessen the allergic reaction.

If your child is allergic and your doctor does not already know about the condition, tell him. Penicillin and other drugs may cause undesirable reactions, especially when a child has eczema, hay fever, or asthma.

Your attitude and that of the doctor and nurse can influence the child who is fearful of the shot he is to get. Be truthful when a child asks, "Will it hurt?" You might tell a toddler that it will hurt a tiny bit, but not much; that all his friends have had shots; and that the doctor is his friend and wants to keep him well. You can minimize your infant's crying or even prevent it if you lean over his face so that he can see you when the doctor gives him the shot. M.G.

See also **Allergy; Immunization**

Sinusitis is an inflammation of one or more sinuses. The sinuses are cavities in the skull. They are lined with mucous membranes that are the same as, and join with, the mucous membranes of the nose. When a child has a cold or other infection in the nose, the infection often spreads to these membranes.

Normally, mucus drains from the sinuses into the nose through tiny openings. When the membranes of the sinuses become infected, they swell and block drainage. Pressure then builds up, and a child may have severe, throbbing pain over one or both cheeks. Or, he may have a severe headache without being able to say where the pain is. Also, his face may swell. If the sinusitis is chronic (constant), the symptoms may not be so severe, but the child may have a nasal discharge (sometimes with a foul odor).

If you think your child has sinusitis, consult your doctor. He may recommend nose drops, an oral decongestant, or antibiotics. Home treatment also should include humidifying the child's room and applying hot compresses to the child's nose. C.F.F.

Most children find it enjoyable to have stories read to them at bedtime.

Sleep. To avoid needless concern about your child's sleeping habits, remember: (1) the length of time a child sleeps decreases as he grows older and (2) two children of the same age do not necessarily need the same amount of sleep. Each child develops his own sleep pattern. This sleep pattern may be affected by several factors.

For example, a preschooler may be so busy learning new things that he is stimulated to a point where both the amount and the quality of his sleep suffer. When he becomes overtired, he may resist going to bed. He may have difficulty going to sleep. And when the preschooler finally does go to sleep, he may not sleep peacefully.

Another factor that affects a child's sleep pattern is illness. A sick child may need more sleep than usual until he completely recovers from his illness.

Children may use sleep, often unconsciously, to escape from situations that disturb them. Dread of school, fear of failure, and fear of neighborhood bullies can cause a child to resist getting up in the morning. However, these same fears may make another child sleepless.

Amount of sleep. Your newborn needs more sleep and spends more time sleeping than he ever will again. In the first few days after birth, he may sleep as much as 23 hours a day. But many newborns sleep much less. The new baby's sleep is often restless, and broken up into short and long periods. He is aroused mainly by hunger or other discomfort. After the first few days, he spends more time awake or half awake—being fed, being bathed, or being diapered.

As a baby grows older, he stays awake during the day for longer periods of time. When he is about 3 months old, he may start sleeping 12 hours through the night and taking several naps during the day. Gradually, as he requires less sleep, he takes fewer naps during the day. When he is a year old, he may sleep 14 to 15 hours a day, including two naps. When he is 2 years old, he may sleep 13 to 14 hours a day, including one nap. When he is 4 years old, he may sleep 11 to 12 hours a day, including a nap.

After your child enters school, bedtime is affected by homework and the family pattern of living. Some children feel tired enough to go to bed as early as 8:30 P.M. A child between the ages of 6 and 10 years may need only 10 or 11 hours of sleep. When he reaches junior high school, homework and extracurricular activities may keep him up later. At the same time, his sleep requirements may be reduced to about nine hours.

Sleeping arrangements. Proper sleeping arrangements can help a child fall asleep and sleep peacefully. An infant should sleep in a crib with high sides to keep him from rolling over and falling onto the floor. Until he is about 3 years old, use a smooth, flat, moderately hard mattress. Pillows and heavy bedcovers are hazardous because a baby may get so tangled up in them that he has trouble breathing easily.

Do not expect a young baby or toddler to lie under bedcovers all night long, or even throughout a nap. Keep him warm and snug in sleepers or a sleeping bag that suits the season. Even preschoolers continue to appreciate one-piece pajamas with feet in them for winter wear. Too much clothing and cover is almost as bad as too little, because your child will surely be restless if he is too warm. In warm weather, your baby requires nothing more than a diaper and a lightweight shirt.

Your baby can easily fall asleep in the midst of normal activity, but keep him away from harsh and unnecessary sounds. If he is sleeping outdoors, protect him from insects with mosquito netting. And keep him out of range of dust and smoke.

Do not make a child who is afraid of the dark sleep without some kind of night light. Some children have trouble falling asleep after daylight-saving time goes into effect because it is still light outside at bedtime. They usually adjust in a week or two.

Sleeping in parents' bedroom. No child should share his parents' bedroom if it can be avoided. If for some reason you have to keep your baby in your room at night, find another place for his bed before he becomes too dependent on your presence.

Except for unusual circumstances, do not take a child into your bed to give him a sense of security when he is frightened. Such togetherness brings mutual comfort for a short time, but few children are willing to return to their own beds when the fear passes. Even

(**Sleep,** *continued*) during illness or periods of fearfulness, encourage and comfort your child in his own bed, in his own room.

Movement and positions. Babies and older children move frequently in their sleep. Healthy young babies make trembling and sucking movements with their lips, their eyelids flutter, and their hands and feet twitch. They whimper as if talking in their dreams. Their breathing is normally fast and irregular. Older babies and toddlers sleep restlessly at night, moving from one part of the crib to another. They also assume positions that seem most uncomfortable—neck turned sharply to one side, arms and legs bent acutely on the chest and abdomen, legs extended beyond cribside; or on the stomach with head turned to one side, knees brought up close to the chest. These positions are common, normal, and healthy for most infants and young children. Lying on the stomach is safe if there are no pillows or loose bedclothes to interfere with breathing. This position helps to drain secretions from the nose and throat of a child with a cold.

Sleep resistance. Many babies resist going to sleep when they are between the ages of 6 and 9 months. The child, even though he is tired, cries when he is put into his bed. His mother picks him up and holds and rocks him. Then, when she puts him down, he starts crying again and she picks him up again. This routine is repeated over and over, night after night.

To interrupt this cycle, parents have to be firm and be prepared to withstand about ten to twenty minutes of crying for a few nights. At bedtime, put the baby in his bed and leave his room. Try not to look in on the baby while he is crying. At least, do not let him see you looking. Usually, the length of the baby's crying period decreases each night, and the crying may disappear by the end of three nights.

Sleep resistance usually crops up again toward the end of the second year, when the child has learned to climb over the side of his crib. If this occurs, put the toddler back in his own bed promptly and firmly and leave the room.

If a child fears the dark, keep a night light on in the room.

Dreaming. If your child is restless while sleeping, if he talks in his sleep, or if he cries out, you can be fairly sure that he is dreaming. Sometimes the dreams are pleasant. Sometimes they are nightmares.

Changes in routine—for example, toilet training or starting nursery school—may cause nightmares. The child will look to you for comfort. He may want you to come to his bedside and cuddle or rock him. He may settle for a few reassuring words and a drink of water, or he may demand that a light be left on close to his bedroom for the rest of the night. The contents of his dreams often seem irrational. For example, he may find animals friendly and acceptable during the day, but they become fierce and frightening in the night.

Many times, dreams are carry-overs from things a child saw or did the day before—television and radio programs, events at school, or other activities. Let him talk about his dreams, particularly those that are upsetting. This unburdening may help prevent recurring nightmares. Usually, the preschool child cannot remember his dreams. A school-age child may not only remember them, but he may also spontaneously tell you about them.

Rituals and routines. Everybody goes through some kind of ritual in preparing to go to sleep. For an adult or older child, it may simply involve undressing, taking a bath, brushing teeth, and getting into a comfortable sleeping garment at a certain time each night. A young child may want you to read a story out loud, or he may get a favorite stuffed animal ready for bed, kiss everybody good night, recite his prayers, or wait for you to tuck him in. The child who is accustomed to a certain routine continues to demand it. Routine gives him a sense of security and makes him happier than a series of irregular and unpredictable performances. Routine should not be rigid or punishing or threatening, and certainly there should be no implication that going to bed is unpleasant. Going to bed can become a game in which your child enjoys an opportunity to learn new skills—to undress himself, arrange his clothes, and take a bath. But any bedtime routine should not be too long, too exciting, or too complex.

If your child is uncooperative at times, he may have had too long a nap in the afternoon. In this case, postpone bedtime or prolong the routine. Some children regularly fight going to bed. They want a drink of water. They have to go to the toilet. They want to hear another story. They want still another drink of water. Anger is useless. If you can be firm and limit the ritual, yet keep it flexible, your child will probably respond to the limitations set. He may argue less and be more willing to part from you and go to sleep.

Many toddlers go to bed with a toy, a favorite blanket, or some object that represents security to them. To other children, thumb-sucking offers bedtime security. Sometimes parents, feeling that their child is now a "big boy" or a "big girl," attempt to stop these bedtime habits. There really is no need to worry, because a child assumes increasing responsibility for putting himself to bed after about the age of 4. He relies less and less on rituals and routines. M.G.

See also **Nightmares; Thumb-sucking**

Sleeping sickness is a commonly used term for encephalitis. Encephalitis occurs when an inflammation of the brain alters normal functioning of various parts of the brain. The child may become excessively drowsy and go to sleep. Other symptoms include headache, fever, paralysis, convulsions, and tremors. Call your doctor if you suspect that your child has encephalitis.

Encephalitis is caused by several kinds of viruses. These viruses can be transmitted by mosquitoes and other insects. Or, encephalitis may accompany infections such as mumps, measles, or influenza. Preventive measures include insect control and vaccinations, if available, against the specific viruses that cause encephalitis.

Care of a child with encephalitis is extremely difficult, especially when he is in a period of sleep. He must then be fed artificially, usually through a tube passed through the nose or mouth into the stomach. Chances of recovery from encephalitis vary with the degree of brain damage and the area of the brain involved. H.D.R., JR.

Smallpox is a contagious disease. It is spread by a virus through direct contact with the coughing or sneezing of a smallpox patient, or the pus from his sores, or by articles he has used—tissues, linens, and clothing.

The disease starts with chills, fever, vomiting, headaches, and backaches. A child's temperature may rise to 104° F. (40° C) or higher. Ulcers develop in the mouth and throat. Red spots appear about three or four days later—first on the face and the arms, then on the trunk (especially on the back), and on the legs. Later, these spots change to blisters filled with pus. As the child recovers, the fever drops and the blisters dry up and form scabs.

When smallpox was widespread, the federal and local governments in the United States, in an effort to control the disease, instituted regulations making smallpox vaccinations routine for all persons. Usually, these vaccinations were given to children between the ages of 1 and 2. They were not given when a child or a member of the household in which he lived had eczema, some other chronic skin disease, or any other contraindication. Revaccination was recommended every five years.

Mandatory smallpox vaccinations have virtually eradicated the disease in the United States, where there has not been a recorded case of smallpox since 1949. The U.S. Public Health Service now recommends that, except in certain cases, the practice of giving routine vaccinations be discontinued. It is generally felt that the risk of complications resulting from vaccination is greater than the risk of getting the disease.

Throughout the rest of the world, the World Health Organization is helping to eradicate the disease with increasing success. Although importation of smallpox into the United States is unlikely, a constant watch is maintained. All suspected cases are investigated and, if necessary, measures are taken to prevent the spread of the disease.

Vaccinations are still required for anyone traveling to and from countries where smallpox occurs regularly, and for health service workers who are exposed to smallpox patients. H.D.R., Jr.

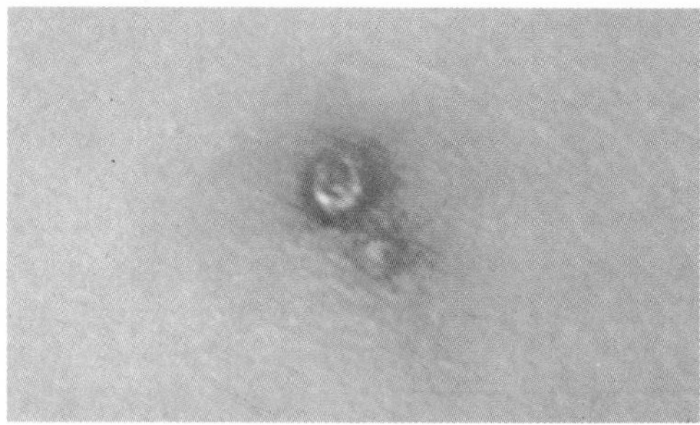

About three days after a smallpox vaccination, a small, red, itchy pimple appears.

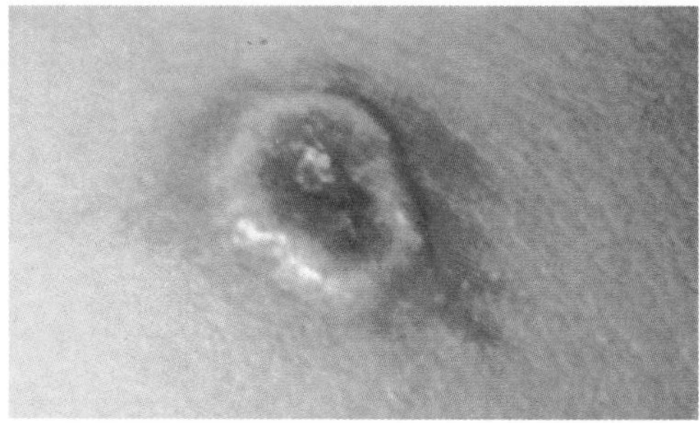

About nine days after vaccination, the pimple develops a white-colored blister.

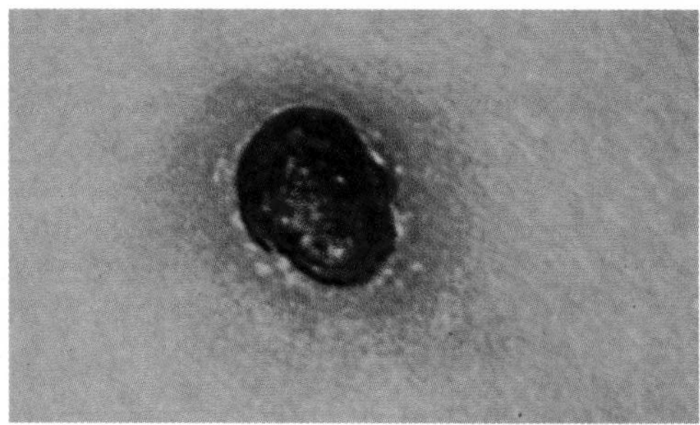

About 14 days after vaccination, the blister dries up and forms a scab.

About 21 days after vaccination, the scab falls off and leaves a scar.

Smothering. *See* **Suffocation**

Sneezing. Most babies sneeze occasionally, even when they do not have a cold. Sneezing is how a baby cleans dirt, lint, or mucus from his nose. Tiny hairs that line the nose move the mucus and other material down the nose. This material usually collects in a ball on the large hairs near the opening at the front of the nose. This collection tickles the baby and makes him sneeze the material out of his nose.

Usually, you can tell when your baby is getting a cold because there will be more than the normal drop or two of mucus in his sneeze. Also, a baby with a cold is more apt to be irritable; he may have trouble eating because of nasal congestion, he may lose his normal appetite, and he may show other signs of illness.

Lint frequently irritates a baby's nose and makes him sneeze. You can eliminate some of the lint in new blankets and baby clothes if you wash them before using. M.G.

See also **Colds**

Soft spots (fontanels) are areas of a baby's skull where the bones have not yet joined and hardened. In place of bone, a very tough membrane covers the area.

A baby may have as many as six soft spots at birth. Generally, you can feel only two of them. Gradually, through the months, the soft spots disappear as the skull bones grow and harden. By the time a baby is a year old, it is usually hard to find the soft spots.

The largest soft spot is shaped like a diamond and is about 1 to 1½ inches (2.5 to 4 centimeters) on a side. It is just in front of the top of the child's skull. The fontanels vary in size in different babies.

Although the brain may seem unprotected in these softer areas, the tough membrane is actually very strong. Mild shampoos and ordinary handling of the head and scalp will do no harm. In fact, shampooing the baby's scalp, including the soft spots, is necessary to prevent cradle cap, a scalp condition that causes whitish scales. M.G.

See also **Cradle cap**

Sore throat usually results from an infection. It may range from a mild soreness to a painful condition in which the child has difficulty in swallowing.

Children often have sore throats. The infection can accompany colds, tonsillitis, and other illnesses. Call your doctor if your child has a fever along with his sore throat, if his throat is more than mildly sore, or if his sore throat persists.

Because most sore throats are caused by viruses, they cannot be cured with antibiotics. Your doctor will probably prescribe aspirin to control fever. Doctors generally do not recommend gargling for children, but throat lozenges for children may help relieve minor irritations. The doctor may examine secretions from the child's throat to check for streptococcic infection (strep throat). If your child does have strep throat, your doctor will prescribe antibiotics. M.G.

See also **Colds; Communicable diseases; Strep throat; Tonsillitis; Virus**

Spine, curvature of. *See* **Scoliosis**

Splinters usually penetrate the upper layer of the skin only and lie embedded there. But they can be very painful and annoying because they press on nerves underneath.

A splinter is usually easy to remove. First, wash the area around the splinter with warm water and soap. This cleanses and softens the skin and makes the splinter easier to remove. Sterilize a sharp needle or a pair of tweezers either with alcohol or by passing the needle or tweezers through a flame. Then, pick out the splinter. The tweezers will probably be less upsetting to the child, but sometimes they are not effective in catching hold of the splinter. You may have to ease the splinter up with a needle and then pull it out with the tweezers. A school-age child may be able to remove the splinter himself.

After the splinter is removed, swab the area with alcohol and apply a sterile dressing. If inflammation begins, if the splinter has not been completely removed, or if the splinter is deeply embedded, consult the child's doctor. T.M.H.

First aid for sprains

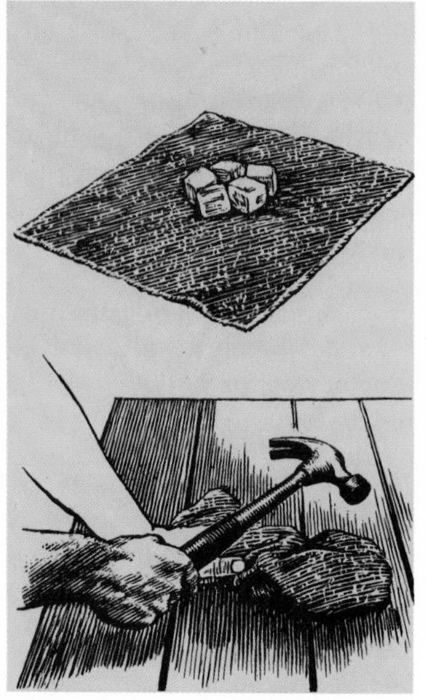
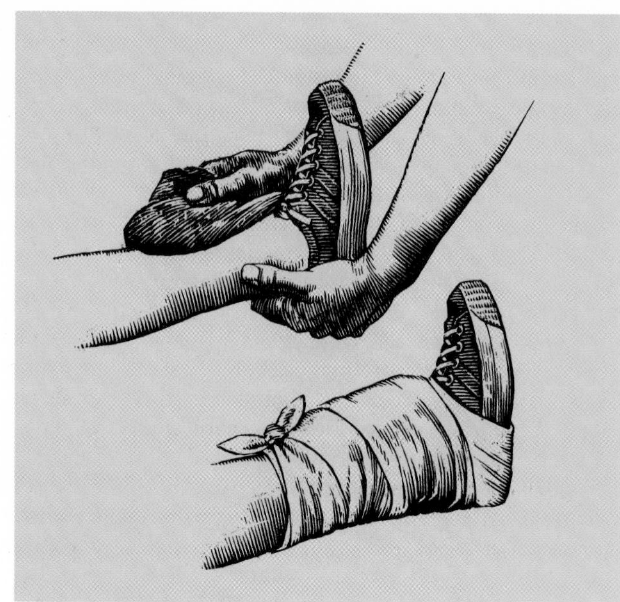

Wrap some ice in a cloth and crush the ice with a hammer. Elevate the sprained limb and apply the ice pack. Then wrap the cloth around the ankle to hold the ice pack in place. Leave the child's shoe on to prevent swelling.

Sprain and strain. A sprain is the stretching of ligaments (the tough bands of fiber that connect bones) or the stretching of the tissue around a joint (the capsule). Sprains may occur with or without fracture of the bone.

Sprains may occur in any joint but are most common in the ankle, wrist, knee, and shoulder. They may result from a strong, sudden wrench or from jumping or falling. They occur frequently in basketball, hockey, and other athletic competition.

A sprain usually causes a rather rapid swelling because fluid (and sometimes blood) accumulates in the tissues around the injured area. Bruises usually appear. There is pain, especially when the child tries to use the joint.

Immediate first-aid measures for a sprain are to leave the child's shoe on, rest and elevate the injured limb, and apply cold water or, if available, ice. This treatment reduces swelling. Call a doctor and take the child to the hospital for X rays to find out whether bones have been broken and for proper treatment of the sprain.

Your doctor may wrap the joint with an elastic bandage to provide support. Or he may even apply a plaster splint or cast. Heat, massage, and hydrotherapy (specialized treatment using water) may be necessary following some sprains.

Strain refers to a stretching injury of a tendon, or a stretching and tearing injury of a muscle. When a muscle or a tendon has undergone unusual stress, there may be soreness and tenderness to the touch, but without the damage to tissues such as may occur in sprains or fractures. As a rule, all that a mild strain requires is rest of the muscles or tendons involved and, perhaps, the application of heat or warmth for comfort. If pain is intense and persistent, consult the child's doctor. J.J.G.

See also **Broken bones; Charley horse; Dislocation of joint**

Stammering. *See* **Stuttering**

Steaming. *See* **Humidifying**

Sterilizing means destroying all germs. Disinfecting means destroying only disease germs or other harmful microorganisms.

Sterilizing baby's formula. Most mothers begin their sterilizing chores with the baby's formula or with bottles and nipples for baby's juice. Formula equipment and formula can be sterilized in two ways. In the first method, the equipment—bottles, nipples, caps, measuring utensils—and the formula ingredients are sterilized separately. Then, the formula is mixed and poured into the bottles. Mothers also use this method to sterilize the water that babies drink. They boil the water for three minutes and then pour it into bottles that have been boiled previously.

In the second method of sterilizing formula, the formula and the bottles, caps, and nipples are sterilized together. The formula is mixed and poured into the bottles, the nipples placed on, and the caps screwed on loosely. Then, the bottles are boiled, formula and all.

Other needs for destroying germs. In every home, there occasionally will be other reasons to kill germs by sterilizing or disinfecting. Different methods are used. You can use heat, chemical germicides, or soap and water.

- You can sterilize a needle that will be used to probe for a splinter by putting the point of the needle directly into a flame.
- You can sterilize some liquids, including water and milk, by boiling them for 5 to 10 minutes.
- You can disinfect diapers by hanging them out to dry in the sun or by ironing them.
- You can disinfect cloth or gauze for bandaging by ironing them.
- Hands can be disinfected by cleansing with soap for 3 to 10 minutes, or by being dipped in germicidal solutions.
- You can usually disinfect a thermometer by washing it with soap and cool water.
- Wounds can be disinfected with soap and water or with medicines made for this purpose, and can be safeguarded by having sterile dressings applied by a person with freshly washed hands. M.G.

Stings. *See* **Bites and stings**

Stomach-ache is a common complaint of children, but discovering the exact cause of the stomach-ache is often not simple. Many times, a stomach-ache is a passing complaint of little consequence. In other cases, it indicates a serious disorder.

If your child has a severe, persistent, or recurrent stomach-ache, call your doctor. Until you can reach the doctor, have the child lie down. Never give food, drink, laxatives, or cathartics to a child with a sudden attack of abdominal pain.

The following are some of the causes of stomach-ache.

- Appendicitis may cause a stomach-ache that is first felt throughout the child's abdomen. In a few hours, the pain moves to the right lower abdomen. The child may also become nauseated and vomit.
- Influenza (flu, grippe) may cause a stomach-ache that is accompanied by vomiting and diarrhea.
- Colds, sore throats, and earaches are sometimes accompanied by abdominal pain that is caused by swollen lymph glands in the abdomen.
- Colic is a common cause of stomach-ache in babies less than 3 months old. The baby usually screams and cries. He may pull his legs up close to his abdomen, or he may stretch them out and become rigid.
- Food poisoning usually causes nausea, vomiting, and stomach-ache.
- Constipation can cause cramping abdominal pain.
- Eating too much food or eating an irritating food may cause stomach-aches.
- Emotional disturbances are a common cause of recurrent abdominal pain in children more than 5 years old. This is most common in children who are 9 or 10. The child may be concerned about such problems as a parent's illness, a recent death, or school difficulties. M.G.

See also **Appendicitis; Colds; Colic; Colitis; Constipation; Earaches; Food poisoning; Influenza; Sore throat; Swollen glands**

Strabismus. *See* **Cross-eye**

Strain. *See* **Sprain and strain**

Strawberry mark. *See* **Birthmark**

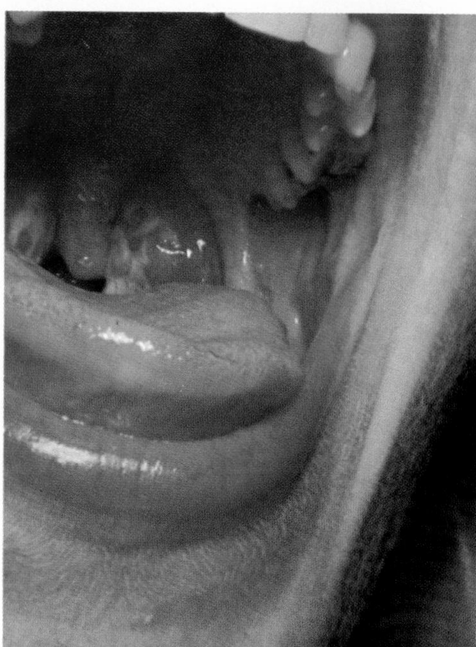

A child who has contracted strep throat may develop yellow, gray, or white patches of membranous material on the tonsils.

Strep throat is an inflammation caused by a bacterium called the streptococcus. A child with strep throat usually has a fever, lacks energy, and has a sore throat—especially when swallowing. The lymph glands in his neck are also swollen; and yellow, gray, or white patches may appear on his tonsils.

If untreated, strep throat may lead to rheumatic fever, nephritis, and other illnesses. For this reason, call your doctor if your child has a sore throat and a fever, if his throat is more than mildly sore, or if his sore throat persists.

Symptoms of strep throat are often the same as those for a sore throat that is caused by a virus. To determine whether your child's sore throat is strep throat or virus-caused, your doctor may examine samples of the secretions in the child's throat. Usually, he will treat strep throat with antibiotics.

Strep throat is contagious. Isolate your child from others outside the family. M.G.

See also **Communicable diseases; Nephritis; Rheumatic fever; Sore throat; Swollen glands; Virus**

Stuttering is an interruption in the flow of speech caused by repetition of certain sounds, prolongation of others, or hesitancy in talking. A child who stutters in normal speech may not stutter when he is singing, repeating memorized material, or acting in a play. Stuttering occurs in about 1 child in 125. It is much more common in boys than in girls, but no one knows why.

Primary stuttering. Between the ages of 2 and 5 years, most children pass through a normal period called "primary stuttering," or "transient stammering." If left alone, the problem ordinarily disappears by itself after six months or a year.

Parents who are not aware that primary stuttering is normal may make a child feel he has a serious speech problem. They may show their concern by facial expressions, by completing what the child is trying to say, or by constantly telling the child to "take his time" or "start over." The best thing to do is nothing at all. Do not ask the child to repeat what he is saying. Do not ask him to slow down. Do not scold him. Accept this temporary period of stuttering as a normal part of development.

If stuttering persists longer than usual or becomes particularly severe, you may want to discuss the problem with the child's doctor. He will probably look for emotional problems and seek ways to lessen them.

Secondary stuttering. Secondary, or true, stuttering begins when the child is aware of his nonfluency and attempts to prevent it. As he tries harder to get the words out without hesitating, the muscles involved in speech may move even less smoothly, and the child develops a stuttering block. He may attempt to break this block by stamping his foot, jerking his head, or other maneuvers. He may use similar actions in anticipating difficulty with certain words, or he may eventually avoid these words. He may be reluctant to answer questions at school or to speak on the telephone.

Children with secondary stuttering should go to a speech clinic. Your doctor can tell you where the nearest clinic is. Since little is known about the cause of stuttering, there is no standard treatment. M.G.

Sty. *See* **Eyelids**

Suffocation is a state of unconsciousness that occurs when the body does not get enough oxygen. Suffocation can cause death very quickly.

If your child is suffocating, the first thing to do is to give him air. The mouth-to-mouth method of getting air back into the lungs is the best to use with children. (See ARTIFICIAL RESPIRATION, page 176.) One person should begin this while someone else calls a doctor or the fire department inhalator squad. Continue mouth-to-mouth resuscitation until the child resumes normal breathing, or until a doctor or the inhalator squad arrives.

If a person's air supply is cut off, he will suffocate. For example, a child will drown if he stays underwater too long. Also, a child may be accidentally shut inside an airtight container such as a refrigerator, or he may be buried under a pile of dirt. A child may also suffocate if he puts a plastic bag over his head. Some children have been strangled by poorly designed harnesses intended to keep them in chairs or automobile seats. A baby may be smothered under a blanket, pillow, or thin sheet of plastic. On rare occasions a baby has been accidentally smothered by an adult with whom he is sleeping.

Suffocation may also occur when there is not enough oxygen in the air. This may occur when open-flame heating units—such as coal stoves, oil stoves, or gas stoves—are operated in close, unventilated spaces such as trailers or small cottages. These conditions produce excess carbon monoxide, which prevents the hemoglobin in the blood from carrying oxygen throughout the body. All open-flame heaters should be properly vented to the open air. If a child is suffocating because of lack of oxygen in the air, take him into the fresh air before giving him artificial respiration.

Many infant deaths once attributed to smothering have been found to be due to a type of virus pneumonia. The cause for most sudden deaths in infants is not known. Smothering is almost never to blame for sudden infant death. M.G.

See also **Accidents; Artificial respiration; Choking; Crib death; Poisonings and poisons**

Sugar diabetes. *See* **Diabetes mellitus**

Sunburn is the skin's reaction to ultraviolet rays of the sun or to artificially created rays from a sun lamp. Mild sunburn reddens the skin. More severe sunburn may blister the skin or cause a fever.

For mild sunburn, apply cold cream. For severe sunburn, give fluids and aspirin to reduce fever. Apply cold tap water compresses to relieve pain. If the condition does not improve within a few hours, call a doctor.

The safest way to avoid severe sunburn is to allow the skin's protective responses to develop by exposing the skin for a short time once daily at first (perhaps 15 minutes), and then regularly increasing the length of time. Suntan oils used before exposure may give some protection.

Children with fair skin, and especially those with red hair, are prone to sunburn. However, any skin—even if tanned—will burn if exposed too long. Do not let your child stay too long in the sunshine, especially on the beach. Reflected rays from the water intensify the effect of the sun. Burning can also occur on hazy days. A.M.M.

Suppositories are medical preparations that are usually inserted into the rectum. Most are cylinders about 1 inch (2.5 centimeters) long and $\frac{1}{4}$ inch (6 millimeters) wide.

There are two kinds of suppositories. The more common one is made of soap or glycerin and is used to induce a bowel movement. Suppositories of this kind should be used only when a doctor prescribes them. Their routine use interferes with normal bowel function.

The second kind of suppository is especially made to contain a medicine that is not easily taken by mouth. For example, a child may have a high fever, but he may be vomiting so much that he cannot keep down the medication needed to reduce the fever. In this case, a doctor may prescribe a medicated suppository to reduce the fever.

Insert a suppository gently above the muscle ring at the rectum opening. Hold the child's buttocks together for a few moments so that he will not push the suppository out. If the suppository is pushed out, wait a few minutes before trying again. M.G.

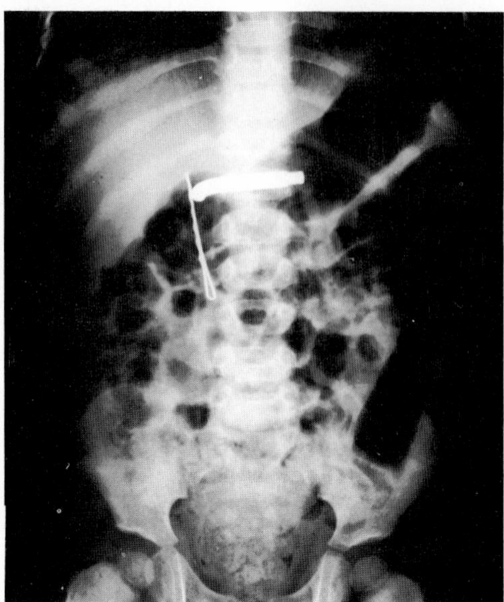

If a child swallows an iron or steel object, the doctor may have the child swallow a small magnet attached to a string. Using X rays, the doctor maneuvers the magnet until it attracts the object, and then pulls the object out.

Protect your child by keeping small objects away from him. A string of beads, for example, may be dangerous if the string breaks and the beads come loose. Keep your button box well out of reach.

When you are changing diapers, close each safety pin as you remove it. A closed safety pin will probably pass harmlessly if swallowed. An open safety pin may not.

Do not give a young child toys with detachable small parts, especially glass eyes, buttons, or bells. Do not give him a toy that might break into fragments that he could swallow or breathe into his windpipe and lungs.

As soon as your child is old enough to understand, encourage him to give you any dangerous object that he finds. You can then thank him and substitute a safe plaything. Remember, too, that children are great imitators of their parents. A child who observes his mother holding open safety pins in her mouth, or his father holding nails between his lips, will probably duplicate the deed at the first opportunity. M.G.

Swallowed objects. Children have a natural tendency to put things into their mouths. Obviously, this tendency can be dangerous because a child may swallow an object that can harm him. If your child swallows an inedible object, keep calm so that you do not alarm him. Since almost any inedible object may prove harmful if swallowed, call your doctor. If the object is a sharp one, such as a tack or an open safety pin, he may want to X-ray the child to determine whether or not surgery is needed to remove it.

Small, smooth objects such as fruit pits, coins, beads, and buttons will usually pass through a child's body without harm and come out in his stool in a few days. Do not give a laxative to the child. It will not help, and it may be harmful. Instead, feed him bread, mashed potatoes, or other starchy foods. These foods may help the object pass through the body more easily. If the child has abdominal pain, or if he vomits, call a doctor immediately. If you cannot reach a doctor, take the child to a hospital.

Swollen glands. Lymph glands (nodes) are one of the body's means of fighting infection. They are located throughout the body but are especially concentrated in the neck, armpits, elbows, groin, abdomen, and chest. When an infection invades the body, the lymph glands collect and destroy bacteria that drain from the infected area. Normally, the lymph glands range in size from as small as a pea to as large as a plum. However, when they are fighting an infection, they become enlarged and are known as "swollen glands."

- When the throat, tonsils, or gums are infected, lymph glands of the neck swell. Mumps also may cause lymph glands in the neck to swell.
- When an infection occurs on the hands or arms, lymph glands in the elbows and armpits swell.
- When an infection occurs on the leg or foot, lymph glands in the groin swell.
- When vaccinations are given, lymph glands in the area of the shot usually swell.
- When measles, scarlet fever, or some

Location of the lymph glands

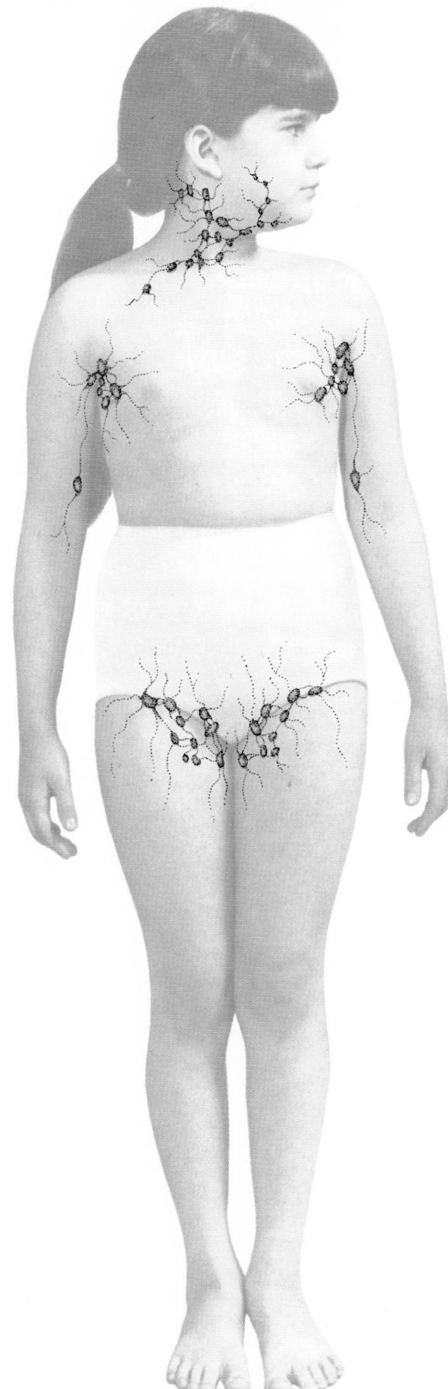

Lymph glands are located throughout the body. They swell to fight off infection. Those in the neck, armpits, and groin can be felt when they swell.

other infection affects the entire body, the lymph glands of the entire body may swell. In some infectious diseases, like German measles and mononucleosis, the lymph glands may remain quite large for some time.

Leukemia, Hodgkin's disease, and other malignant diseases of the lymphatic system may also cause swollen glands.

You can usually feel the lymph glands in the neck, armpits, and groin when they are swollen. They may be inflamed and tender to the touch. If your child has swollen glands, consult your doctor. Since the swelling is most often caused by an infection, antibiotics are usually prescribed to eliminate the infection. Sometimes, a lymph gland that is fighting an infection forms an abscess. In such a case, hot packs on the swollen gland may help to get rid of the abscess. Or, your doctor may have to lance the abscess to release the pus. M.G.

See also **Abscess; Adenoids; Communicable diseases; Fever; Immunization; Leukemia; Mononucleosis; Sore throat; Tonsillitis**

Tearing eyes. It is not unusual for a baby's eyes to water during the first few weeks of life. The doctor puts silver nitrate, or antibiotic drops or ointment, into the baby's eyes at birth to prevent infection. This often causes many tears. The watering usually disappears in a few days as the irritation subsides, and no treatment is necessary.

However, persistent watering may occur if a tear duct becomes blocked by mucus. The tear duct is a small tube leading from the tear sac (which is inside the lower eyelid next to the nose) to the inside of the nose. Normally, the duct carries away the tears that lubricate the eye. But if the duct becomes blocked, the eye waters.

Treat tearing eyes by wiping away the excess fluid with a small piece of sterile cotton that has been moistened in cool boiled water. If the condition continues after the baby is about 2 months old, if it is severe, or if it is accompanied by irritation and reddening of the eye, or by a discharge of pus, consult the baby's doctor. M.G.

See also **Conjunctivitis**

Teeth and teething. The first primary, or "baby," teeth begin to form within a baby's jaws about two months after conception. At birth, the crowns of all 20 primary teeth, and even part of the first permanent molars, are forming in the jaws. By the time a child is 3 years old, he usually has all his primary teeth. By this time, too, parts of more than 20 of his permanent teeth are developing within his jawbones.

Your baby will probably get his first tooth when he is about 6 months old. Generally, the teeth in the lower jaw appear first. By the time he is a year old, your child will probably have the four upper and four lower front teeth, which are called the incisors. The first molars appear when the child is about 15 months old. Then at about 18 months, the canines come through between the incisors and the first molars. The second molars, or "back teeth," usually appear when the child is about 2 years old.

Teething. As a tooth comes through, your baby will drool, bite, chew, and gnaw on anything he can get into his mouth. He may also thrust his lower jaw forward and move it from side to side, to rub the gums together and help the teeth push through the overlying tissue. Firm teething rings may satisfy his urge to bite. Chewing hard foods like whole carrot sticks and toasted bread may help teething and jaw development. Babies may be fussy while they are teething. This irritability may be confused with signs of illness.

Usually, a child has more difficulty getting his primary teeth than getting his permanent teeth. The primary teeth have to make their own path through the gums, whereas 20 of the permanent teeth follow the path already made by the primary teeth they replace. The 12 molars in the set of 32 permanent teeth have no channels set up for them by preceding primary teeth. Fortunately, they do not come in until the child is older. The first permanent molars usually appear when the child is about 6 years old, the second molars when he is about 12, and the third molars (wisdom teeth) after he is 17 years old.

Teething

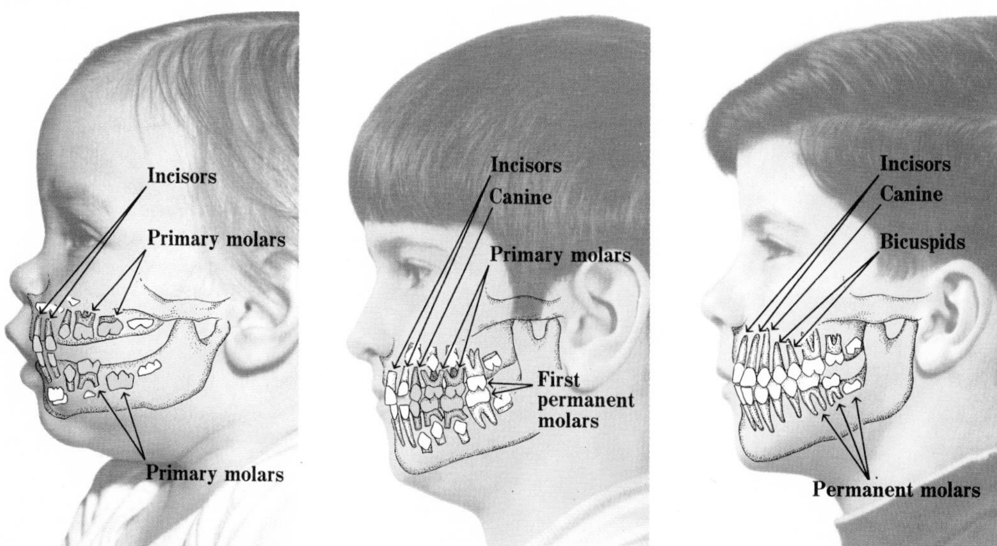

When a child is about a year old (*left*), primary incisors have pushed through the gums and primary molars are beginning to appear. By about 8 (*center*), a child has some permanent teeth—incisors and first permanent molars—and some primary teeth—canines and primary molars. At about 12 (*right*), a child has all the permanent teeth except for the third permanent molars (wisdom teeth).

How to brush teeth

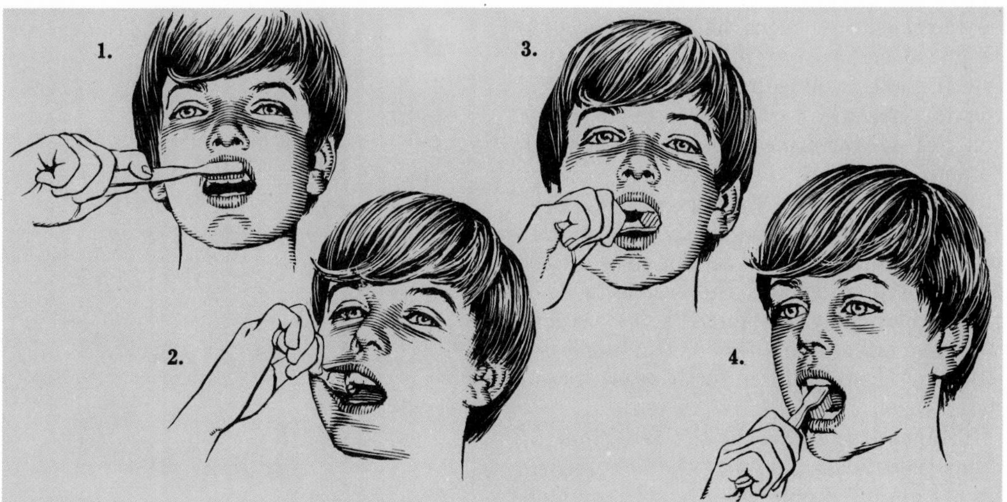

1. The hand should be twisted so that the brush moves over the gums and teeth toward the chewing surfaces. The upper teeth should be brushed downward; the lower teeth upward.
2. Be sure the surfaces next to the cheeks are brushed.
3. And be sure the surfaces next to the tongue are brushed.
4. Teach your child to use a scrubbing motion when brushing so that the chewing surfaces of the teeth are cleaned.

Dental care. Foods that are good for general health—milk, fruits, vegetables, meat, poultry, fish, eggs, and butter—are also good for teeth and gums. Fibrous vegetables and fruits that require chewing have the added value of acting as tooth-cleansing agents. Some foods can harm teeth. Sugars and starches actually encourage tooth decay.

Tooth decay usually begins in the pits and grooves on the chewing surfaces of the teeth, between the teeth, and along the gum margin on the cheek sides. Bacteria act upon food particles, producing acids and other substances that can dissolve tooth enamel and eat away the underlying dentine. Sugars are the most harmful foods because they more readily produce acids.

Many children eat far more sugar than they need for good nutrition. To reduce tooth decay, substitute fruit, nuts, popcorn, cheese, and other sugarless snacks for sweets. Try to satisfy your child's appetite for sugar by supplying sweets at one meal a day.

Teach your child to brush his own teeth when he is about 2 years old. To encourage him, let him help pick out his own toothbrush. Give him an attractive tumbler for rinsing his mouth, his own toothpaste or powder, and a sturdy stool to stand on so that he can reach the washbasin. For best results, have him brush after every meal.

Regular dental examinations are the surest way for your child to have healthy teeth and to keep his teeth for a lifetime. Your child's first visit to the dentist should be made when he is 3 years old, soon after he has all his primary teeth. Before your child's first visit, take him with you on one of your routine visits to your dentist. Arrange this beforehand with your dentist so that your child may sit in the dental chair, examine some of the instruments, and get acquainted with both the dentist and the surroundings. Then his first real visit will not be strange and alarming.

If your child has a tooth knocked out, save the tooth and call your dentist immediately. It may be possible to reinsert and retain the tooth. M.G.

See also **Braces, dental; Malocclusion**

Tetanus (lockjaw) is a disease that affects the brain and the nerves. A child with tetanus has convulsions, his muscles become stiff, and he has spasms of the jaw muscles which make it difficult for him to open his mouth. Spasms may also occur in other muscles. If you suspect that your child has tetanus, call your doctor at once.

Tetanus is caused by bacteria that produce a powerful poison as they grow. Because the tetanus bacilli cannot grow if they are exposed to oxygen, they settle in deep tissue pockets where there is no oxygen. Tetanus most often develops in puncture wounds, or in children with great tissue destruction.

Tetanus bacilli live in the intestines of domestic animals and infect the soil touched by the animal droppings. A child may step on the droppings and pick up the bacilli, but the bacilli remain harmless until they are carried deep into the tissues, usually by way of a puncture wound. For this reason, if your child has a puncture wound, or a cut that does not bleed readily, consult your doctor. In the meantime, clean the wound and cover it.

The best protection against tetanus is tetanus toxoid, a vaccine. It is usually given to babies in a DTP shot (combined diphtheria and tetanus toxoids, and pertussis vaccine). Children 6 years of age or less are given a series of three shots about two months apart, and a fourth shot a year after the third. Ideally, these shots are given at 2, 4, 6, and 18 months of age. A booster, usually as a DTP shot, is given when the child enters school. If a serious injury occurs before the DTP shots are completed, a tetanus booster is given.

A nonimmunized school-age child should get two Td shots (combined tetanus and diphtheria toxoids) two months apart, with a third shot six months to a year later, and a Td booster every 10 years thereafter.

Tetanus toxoid is almost 100 per cent effective in preventing tetanus. Tetanus immune globulin (human) should be used to treat tetanus. H.D.R., Jr.

See also **Bites and stings; Cuts and scratches; Immunization; Shots**

Thermometer. *See* **Fever**

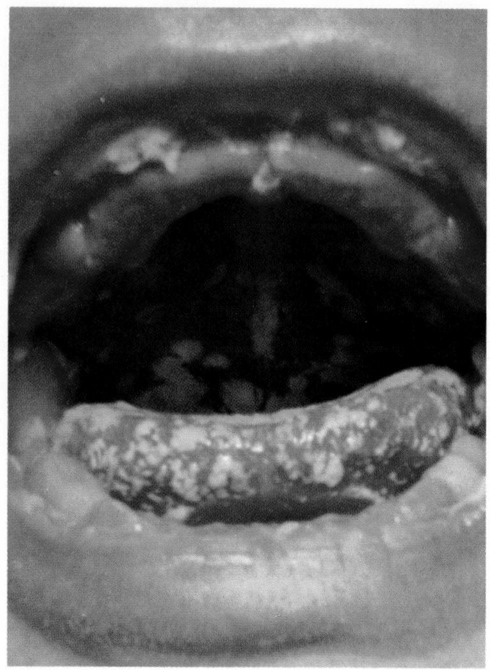

A thrush infection produces white patches on the inside of a baby's mouth.

Thrush is a mild fungus infection of the mouth. White patches that look like milk curd form on the inside of the cheeks, the roof of the mouth, and the tongue. But unlike milk curd, these patches do not wash away with a drink of water. Do not rub the patches, because the skin will bleed. The baby's mouth is usually sore, and he may be uncomfortable when he is eating. He may also have diarrhea.

Thrush is not uncommon during a baby's first few weeks of life. It is often contracted during delivery from a fungus infection in the mother's vagina.

If you suspect that your baby has thrush, consult your doctor for diagnosis and proper treatment. He will probably prescribe medication that can be swabbed on the patches in the baby's mouth after the baby has been fed. Until you can reach the doctor, give the baby cooled boiled water after he drinks milk. The water will wash the milk out of the baby's mouth, giving the thrush fungus less to live on. H.D.R., Jr.

See also **Diarrhea**

Thumb-sucking, for an infant, is almost as natural as eating. Sucking is itself a drive, a basic need. Babies can receive food only by sucking. But some babies have a greater tendency to suck their thumbs than others do. Even though satisfied at the breast or bottle, they seem determined to get further gratification by sucking fingers or thumbs. Persistent thumb-sucking is normal in babies. However, parents still often worry. If they are worried, they may ask themselves a few simple questions.

Is my baby being cuddled enough? Most babies want to be held at times, rocked and snuggled and sung to now and then.

Is he bored? Perhaps he spends too much time alone in his crib or playpen and has too few objects to handle and explore. Boredom is as real to a crawler as it is to an adult.

After a child is a year or so old, the sucking need becomes less powerful. Now, thumb-sucking may be a carry-over response to hunger or a way for the baby to lull himself to sleep. Often he stops sucking his thumb as his sleep habits change. If the thumb-sucking persists after he is 2 years old, it is evidently satisfying some further, unexplained need. Perhaps a new baby in the family has made him want to be a baby again. Perhaps he is shy when pressured too much by adults or when confronted with new playmates. Perhaps thumb-sucking is a way to feel less lonely, or perhaps only a request to be hugged.

Do not be upset if others point out that they did not let their children become thumb-suckers. Let your child alone. Do not talk about his thumb-sucking and certainly do not nag, punish, or humiliate him because of it.

Do not put distasteful substances on the thumb to discourage thumb-sucking, and do not use mechanical restraints. Unless there are problems which cause a child undue tensions, he will generally discontinue thumb-sucking on his own.

One of your biggest worries about thumb-sucking may be the effect it will have on your child's teeth and jaw formation. Most dentists feel that up until the time the second teeth appear, thumb-sucking has no permanent effect on the teeth, mouth, or jaws. M.G.

Tick bites. *See* **Bites and stings**

Tics are uncontrollable spasms of certain muscles. A child with a tic may repeatedly blink his eyes or shrug his shoulders. He may cough or sniffle. His cheek muscles may twitch; his neck may jerk to one side or the other; or, in unusual instances, his entire body may jerk. Tics usually occur more frequently and are more noticeable when the child is tense or emotionally upset.

It may be difficult for a doctor to determine why a child has tics. The cause of the tics may be psychological, even though the child may not appear troubled. Psychological tests and psychiatric consultation—perhaps in a child guidance clinic—are often helpful.

If your child has a tic, consult a doctor as soon as possible. Do not try to force the child to stop the movements. The child does not have voluntary control over the muscle spasms causing the tic, and pressure only tends to make the tics worse. M.G.

See also **Saint Vitus's dance**

Tonsillitis is an inflammation of the tonsils. The tonsils are composed of lymphatic tissue and are located in small pockets on both sides of the throat, behind the mouth. Healthy tonsils help protect the body against infection.

During early childhood, most children have an average of four infections of the upper respiratory tract each year. Each time, tonsillitis occurs. Just how severe the tonsillitis is usually depends upon the kind of virus or bacteria that causes it. Some cases of tonsillitis are so mild that the child is bothered very little.

Most often, a child with tonsillitis complains of a sore throat and has trouble swallowing. In severe attacks, the tonsils become quite swollen and red. Patches of yellowish or grayish membrane may form on them. Usually, the child has a fever and the lymph glands at the angles of his jaws swell. Other signs of severe tonsillitis are headache and vomiting.

Most attacks of tonsillitis last from five to seven days. If the tonsillitis is caused by a

Location of the tonsils

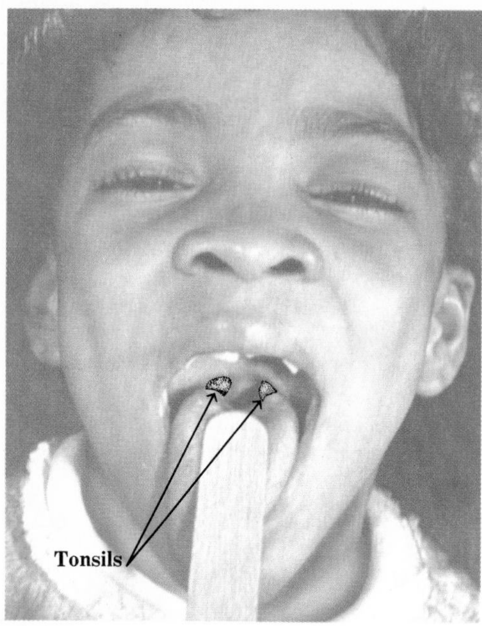

Tonsils grow on each side of the throat, in the back of the mouth. Healthy tonsils help the body to fight infection.

(**Tonsillitis,** *continued*) bacteria sensitive to antibiotics, a doctor may prescribe drugs. For example, he may prescribe penicillin for "strep tonsillitis," to shorten the attack and to reduce the possibility of complications such as nephritis or rheumatic fever.

Rarely, in severe attacks of tonsillitis, an abscess may develop in the tissue around the tonsils. Or the tonsils may remain inflamed after several attacks of tonsillitis, and the child may have a constant low fever and constant swelling of the lymph glands in the neck. In such extreme cases, the doctor may recommend a tonsillectomy (surgical removal of the tonsils). If the adenoids are also constantly infected, he may remove them in the same operation. Tonsillectomy is still a common operation, but it is performed less often than it was many years ago because the tonsils can be treated, and because surgery can produce complications. M.G.

See also **Adenoids; Nephritis; Rheumatic fever; Swollen glands**

Tourniquet. *See* **Bites and stings; Bleeding**

Tuberculosis is a serious contagious disease caused by tiny, rod-shaped bacteria called tubercle bacilli. It usually develops in the lungs, but it may appear in almost any part of the body.

The two main types of tuberculosis are commonly called primary infection tuberculosis (when a person gets the disease for the first time) and reinfection tuberculosis (when a person is infected a second, third, or fourth time).

When a child develops a primary infection, the invading tubercle bacilli are killed by white blood cells or walled up by cells and fibers that prevent their spreading through the body. Usually, the child does not feel ill or show any symptoms of the disease.

Reinfection tuberculosis may occur if the body's resistance is low because of illness, poor diet, or other causes. Then the tubercle bacilli that have been walled up break out and multiply. They may spread faster than they can be killed or walled up. A reinfected child usually has a fever, loses weight, has a cough, and is weak. Primary infection tuberculosis is more common among children who have not yet reached adolescence. An adolescent is more likely to develop reinfection tuberculosis.

If you suspect that your child has tuberculosis, or if you know that he has been exposed to it, contact your doctor immediately. With a doctor's care, a child with tuberculosis may be cured in a year or two.

A child with tuberculosis usually begins treatment in a hospital. Eventually, he may be treated at home. Doctors rely primarily on drugs to cure tuberculosis, but surgery is sometimes called for.

The tuberculin test is a simple method of learning if a child is infected with tubercle bacilli. The test may be made at 12 months, or at 15 months when the measles-mumps-rubella shot is given. A drop of harmless tuberculin (liquid prepared from dead tubercle bacilli) is injected, scratched, or rubbed into the child's skin. If after two days the spot becomes red and swollen, the test is considered positive. A positive reaction means the child has been infected by tubercle bacilli at some time. A test resulting in no reaction indicates that the child has

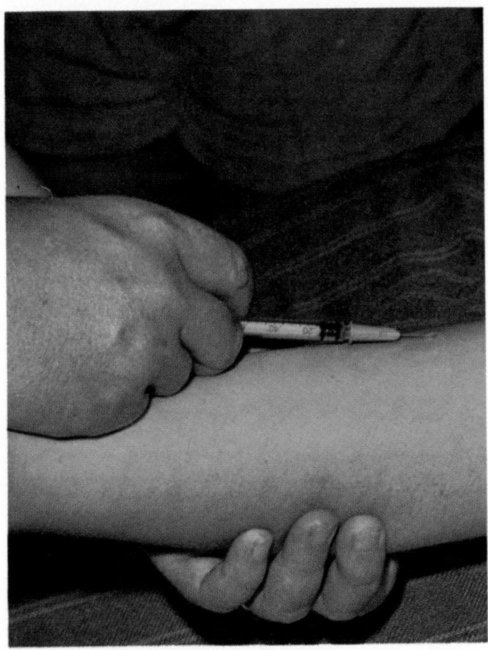

In this tuberculin test, tuberculin (a liquid prepared from dead tubercle bacilli) is injected into the skin.

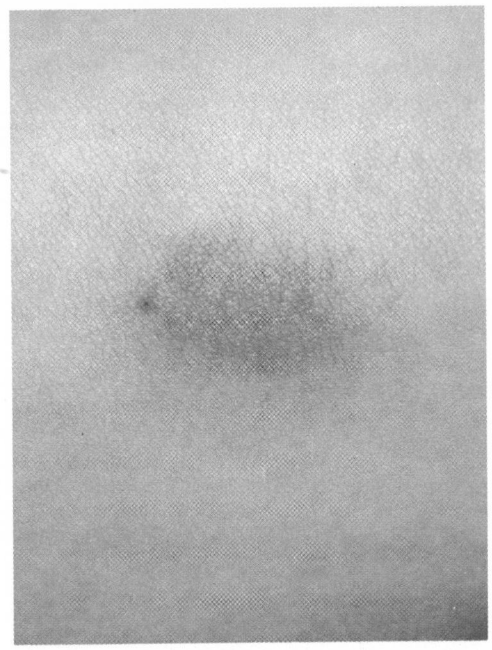

If the site of the injection becomes red and swollen after a period of two days, the test is positive.

never been infected by tubercle bacilli. If the child has a positive reaction, he should then have a chest X ray to determine if the disease is active. The doctor may also order other tests and X rays of other parts of the body. Adults who have been in contact with the child also should have chest X rays to determine who infected him. Almost all cases of tuberculosis in infants and young children are contracted from someone in the child's household. Other children in the household should have tuberculin tests to determine if they have been infected, too.

Some children who live in areas where tuberculosis is prevalent, and children in a family with an active case, may be immunized against primary infection by drugs or shots of BCG (Bacillus Calmette-Guérin) vaccine. H.D.R., Jr.

Tumor. *See* **Cancer**

Twitch. *See* **Saint Vitus's dance; Tic**

Umbilical hernia. *See* **Hernia**

Underweight. Before you worry about an underweight child, make sure that he really is underweight. Children have highly individual growth patterns, so that the "normal" weight for a given age and height varies. Let your doctor decide whether or not your child is underweight. He can also look into the cause of the child's weight problem.

Most underweight children do not eat enough. This may be caused by a chronic illness or emotional upsets.

Perhaps your youngster is eating enough food, but the food lacks nutritive value. A prescribed diet may be all that he needs to increase his weight. On the other hand, the child may be eating nutritious foods but a chronic (long lasting) disease, such as chronic diarrhea or a metabolic disorder, may prevent his body from absorbing or using food properly.

In rare cases, a young body uses food too rapidly. An overactive thyroid gland can cause such a condition.

Some children lose interest in food because their parents worry too much about

(**Underweight,** *continued*) eating habits. Too often, parents coax the child to eat.

An infant, unless he is physically sick, usually eats enough to keep gaining a reasonable amount of weight. He may briefly lose interest in food during his second year, as he begins to walk and explore his environment. Also at this time he loses the chubbiness of infancy. This loss makes many parents mistakenly believe that he is not eating as well as he should. This is not the time to coax a child to eat, because you may cause a chronic eating problem. The child usually starts eating properly again.

An illness may make a child lose his appetite for a while. Again, do not coax. The child usually recovers his appetite as he recovers his health. Jealousy of a new baby, depression, or unhappiness may also make a child stop eating his normal amount.

If your doctor tells you there is no cause for concern, stop talking about weight. Constant reminders can make a normally thin child uneasy about his body. M.G.

See also **Anorexia nervosa**

Undescended testicles. Normally, a boy's testicles descend from the abdomen into the scrotum (the pouch of skin that hangs under the boy's penis) shortly before birth. However, one or both testicles may still be in the abdomen or groin when a boy is born, particularly if he is born prematurely. In most cases, the testicles descend shortly after birth. If your son is about 2 years old and you think that one or both of his testicles have not yet descended, consult your doctor.

Many boys have highly sensitive testicles that retract into the groin or the abdomen whenever the testicles become chilled, or whenever the boy's thighs or scrotum are touched. These are not true undescended testicles. They are mobile undescended testicles. Most undescended testicles are mobile.

A doctor may have to examine a boy many times to determine whether a testicle is truly undescended. Parents can check to see if the testicle descends when the boy sits in a tub of warm water. If the testicle has been seen in the scrotum, or if the testicle can be moved into the scrotum by the doctor, the testicle is mobile. No treatment is needed. The testicle will descend normally before adolescence.

Surgery and hormone treatment are used to correct true undescended testicles. Most surgeons advise operating when the boy is from 7 to 10 years old. Some doctors recommend hormone treatment to see if the testicle will descend without surgery. If surgery is planned, the parents and the doctor should explain to the boy the reason, reassuring him that he will be completely normal after the operation.

A boy who has one undescended testicle should develop normally in terms of fertility and secondary sex characteristics such as a beard and a low voice. However, the other testicle should be brought down so that he does not consider himself different. If both testicles are undescended and no operation is performed, the testicles wither away and the boy is sterile.

Try not to show concern about undescended testicles. To do so may make the boy self-conscious. M.G.

Upset stomach. *See* **Colic; Communicable diseases; Food poisoning; Motion sickness; Stomachache; Vomiting**

Urinary disturbances. Children can develop several types of urinary disturbances, including unusual frequency of urination, decreased urination, blood in the urine, and enuresis (persistent, involuntary wetting after the child is about 4 years old). Consult your doctor if you suspect that your child has a urinary disturbance.

Unusual frequency of urination is a common disturbance. It often signals an infection of the urinary tract. Pain or a burning sensation when urinating is often part of a urinary tract infection. An infant obviously cannot use words to tell you of his discomfort, but such a child is often feverish and may be irritable and cry excessively. A doctor can determine whether infection is present by examining the urine.

Most urinary infections are cleared up with antibiotics. If an infection does not clear up, its cause may be an abnormality in the formation of the kidneys, the bladder, or the ureters (the tubes that connect each kidney to the bladder). Or, an abnormality of the urethra (the passage through which urine flows from the bladder to outside the body) may be responsible for poor urine flow and infection. When infection of the urinary passages occurs, the doctor may examine the urinary tract by indirect means, such as by a pyelogram (an X ray of the kidneys and ureters) or by direct means, such as with a cystoscope (an instrument to examine the inside of the bladder).

Unusual frequency of urination may also be a symptom of anxiety in children. Frequent urination and a large increase in the amount of urine produced may also be a symptom of diabetes.

Decreased urination may result if the child's bladder retains the urine because of an obstruction. Or, retention may be a symptom of the mental illness called hysteria. Decreased urination may also result from a decrease in the production of urine. This decrease in urine production may be caused by nephritis (a kidney disease), poisoning by certain drugs or metals, or obstructions in the urinary tract.

Blood in the urine should be reported to the doctor. Remember, however, that a child's urine may sometimes appear red after he has eaten beets. Slight bleeding may result if ammonia in the urine causes ulceration of the urinary opening of a baby boy's penis. The blood is bright red and appears in only the first few drops of urine passed. Blood in the urine may also occur because of nephritis, infection, certain types of anemia, poisoning, or some abnormality of the urinary tract.

Enuresis usually occurs during the night but may also happen during the day. Enuresis may be caused by many things—a defect in the urinary tract, a urinary infection, or emotional disturbances. Or it may just be that the child is such a sound sleeper that he is not awakened by the feeling of a full bladder. M.G.

See also **Dehydration; Diabetes mellitus; Hysteria; Nephritis; Wetting**

Vaccination. *See* **Communicable diseases; Immunization; Shots; Virus**

Vaginal discharge may result from an infection that causes the external genital area of a girl to become inflamed. It may also develop if the girl's underpants are too tight and rub against the genital region. In either of these instances, the vaginal discharge causes whitish stains in the girl's underpants. Vaginal discharge may also occur if a foreign object has been inserted into the vagina. The discharge is then usually bloody.

In all these cases, consult a doctor. He may prescribe antibiotics. He will probably also suggest bathing the external genital area by having the girl sit in a tub partly filled with comfortably warm water.

A slight discharge from the vagina is common and normal for girls who are reaching adolescence and beginning to undergo sexual growth and development. You should explain these changes to your daughter and tell her about menstruation. M.G.

See also **Menstruation; Pinworms**

Vaporizer. *See* **Humidifying**

Virus is a living organism that is so tiny that it cannot be seen under an ordinary microscope. Smaller even than bacteria, viruses enter the body in various ways—through eating or drinking, inhalation, injection, or through breaks in the skin. Once in the body, they grow inside cells and form more viruses which invade more cells.

Viruses can cause infectious diseases such as poliomyelitis, influenza, measles, chicken pox, smallpox, mumps, and the common cold. Viruses can also produce specific infections in certain cells. The liver cells are affected in hepatitis; the brain cells, in sleeping sickness; the skin cells, in fever blisters.

Doctors do not know of any cure for diseases caused by viruses, but once a person has had a virus disease, he often becomes immune to that virus. Also, vaccines can be made from certain viruses and used to immunize a child against the diseases they cause. If your child has a virus disease, your doctor will probably tell you how to make the child more comfortable and how to avoid complications of the disease. H.D.R., JR.

Important vitamins

Vitamin	Functions in the body	Food sources
A	Helps develop teeth and maintain skin, tissues lining body cavities, glands that produce digestive juices, and night vision.	Whole milk, cream, butter, egg yolks, liver, kidneys, fats, fish liver oils, green and yellow vegetables, cantaloupe, peaches, and apricots.
B_1 (Thiamin)	Gives body energy. Helps maintain appetite, a healthy mental attitude, and normal functioning of muscles.	Lean pork, organ meats, dried beans and peas, nuts, eggs, milk, whole grain cereals, and enriched cereals and breads.
B_2 (Riboflavin)	Helps carbohydrates release heat and energy in the body.	Liver, heart, kidneys, whole grain and enriched cereals, milk, cheese, eggs, and leafy green vegetables.
C (Ascorbic acid)	Increases resistance to infection. Helps form sound teeth and bones. Necessary for healthy gums and body tissues.	Citrus fruits, tomatoes, cantaloupe, strawberries, green and chili peppers, pineapple, cabbage, broccoli, asparagus, and greens of all kinds.
D	Helps body absorb calcium and phosphorus for bone growth.	Salt-water fish, vitamin D-fortified milk, and fish liver oils.
Niacin	Helps maintain healthy skin and other body tissues.	Meat, poultry, fish, and enriched and whole grain bread.

Vitamins are necessary for good health and proper growth. You can supply your child with all the vitamins he needs—with the possible exception of vitamin D—by providing an adequate daily diet of properly prepared foods.

Millions of dollars are spent each year on self-prescribed vitamin pills. Dispensing vitamin pills may make a mother feel that each child's nutritive needs are being met. But the vitamins may not be needed by the child's body.

Without your doctor's advice, you may give your child too much of vitamins A and D, and possibly some other vitamins. These vitamins are fat-soluble and may be stored in the child's body with increasingly harmful effects.

Vitamins work in subtle relationships with each other and with other nutrients. The amount of a certain vitamin needed depends on the amount of other vitamins and food elements in the body.

The contents of a vitamin pill are limited to those vitamins that have been discovered and that can be manufactured. Food may contain undiscovered but essential food substances.

It is best to rely on a good, balanced diet to supply your child with adequate vitamins, unless his doctor prescribes vitamin supplements.

One vitamin your child may not get enough of is vitamin D, which helps the body absorb the calcium and phosphorus it needs, especially during the growth of bones and teeth. Doctors and nutritionists recommend that children be given a source of vitamin D daily throughout their entire major growth period—usually until they are 20 years old. Most milk today is commercially fortified with vitamin D. One quart (1 liter) contains the required daily amount. Sunlight can also provide the body with vitamin D. The ultraviolet rays of the sun, or of a sun lamp, act on a substance in the skin and produce vitamin D.

The accompanying table shows the sources of six vitamins and how the body uses the vitamins. M.G.

Vomiting is a common symptom among infants and children. Its cause may be physical or emotional.

- Infants may vomit if they swallow too much air during feeding, or if they have an allergic reaction to a certain food, such as cow's milk.
- Any illness that is accompanied by a high fever, such as influenza, pneumonia, or scarlet fever may cause vomiting.
- Abnormalities in the formation or position of the stomach or intestines may cause vomiting.
- Disorders of organs other than the stomach, such as the kidneys or the ears, may cause vomiting.
- If a child swallows a poisonous substance, he may vomit. If you suspect poisoning, save some of the vomit for analysis. It may help a doctor decide how he will treat the child. (For ways to induce vomiting, see POISONINGS AND POISONS, page 268.)
- Appendicitis may cause vomiting that is accompanied by pain in the lower right abdomen.
- Some children vomit when they ride in cars, trains, planes, or ships.
- Vomiting may be a sign of an emotional problem. For instance, a child may vomit every morning if he is apprehensive about going to school or if he wants attention. Such children may need psychological help.

Because of its many possible causes, and since early treatment is important in many instances, never take vomiting lightly. Three instances, in particular, call for a doctor's attention: vomiting accompanied by pain in the lower right abdomen (which may indicate appendicitis), persistent vomiting (which may cause dehydration), and vomiting of green material (which may mean that some obstruction in the intestine has caused bile to back up from the intestine into the stomach). For simple vomiting, or until you can reach a doctor, keep the child quiet and give him nothing to eat. Offer him a little water, ginger ale, or weak tea. If he continues to vomit, do not give him any liquids —not even water. M.G.

See also **Appendicitis; Communicable diseases; Dehydration; Emetics; Food poisoning; Influenza; Motion sickness; Poisonings and poisons; Stomachache; Swallowed objects**

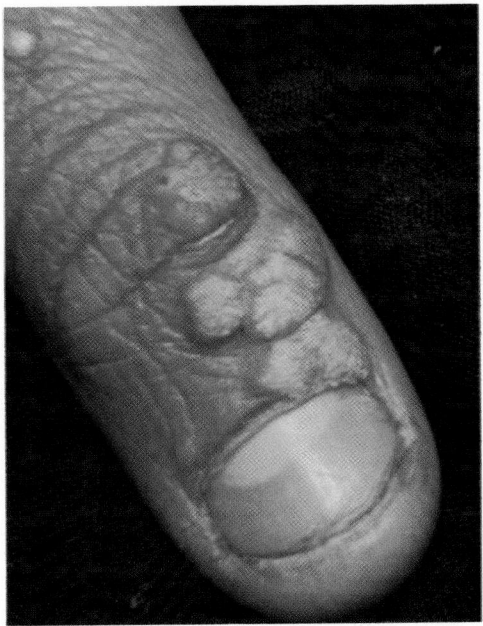

Aside from the discomfort caused if they grow at the base of a fingernail or toenail, warts do not seem to have any harmful effect on a child's general health.

Warts are small, hard growths on the skin. They tend to appear in groups of three or four, but they may appear singly or in large numbers. Most warts grow on the backs of the hands and on the soles of the feet. Warts on the soles of the feet are called plantar warts. Scientists believe that warts are caused by a virus. Caution children against "picking" at warts. This may spread the virus and increase the number of warts.

There are several effective and painless methods for removing warts, but removal should be attempted only by a doctor. These methods include blistering agents, liquid nitrogen, salicylic acid plasters, special solutions, or electrosurgery.

Some doctors prescribe suggestion therapy, a safe method that you can try at home. Suggestion therapy calls for repeated reassurance, with or without medicines or rewards, that the warts will disappear in a few months. Most warts disappear without treatment of any type within two years. Plantar warts, however, rarely disappear without treatment. A.M.M.

Wetting. Persistent wetting after a child is about 4 years old is called enuresis. Most incidents of enuresis occur at night, and are accompanied by occasional wetting in the daytime. If your child has enuresis, consult your doctor.

Some cases of enuresis are caused by a defect in the urinary tract or a chronic urinary infection. Your child may complain of painful urination, difficulty in starting or stopping urination, discolored urine, or increased frequency of urination.

Sometimes, the problem is emotional, particularly if the child's wetting occurs after he has been toilet-trained for several months or years. Usually, some difficulty in his relations with others is involved—especially with his parents, but also with teachers, brothers, sisters, or playmates. One of the most common causes for a child's bedwetting is the arrival of a new baby.

Do not threaten, punish, ridicule, or plead with a child to stop wetting. These actions may increase the child's anxiety and make wetting more persistent. He is not doing it deliberately, and he usually feels bad about it already. You can help him most by discovering what is distressing him. Is he in too high a grade level at school? Is he trying too hard to compete? He may feel that he is failing in his social as well as in his school relationships. Build up his feeling of self-confidence. Perhaps he needs only to know that you love him, to have you spend a little more time with him or show more interest in his needs. When his anxiety and tensions are reduced, wetting may stop.

Most enuretic children have no urinary tract defect and are not emotionally disturbed. Frequently, the child is a deep sleeper and may not be awakened by the feeling of bladder fullness. During the day, these children urinate often and with urgency.

Drug therapy has been used in treating enuresis, with varying success. Conditioning devices (a pad attached to an alarm which rings as soon as the child begins to wet the bed) have also been successful. But they should be used only in selected instances with children who are old enough to understand what is being attempted and who are willing to cooperate. M.G.

See also **Urinary disturbances**

Whooping cough (pertussis) is a contagious disease that is caused by bacteria. It begins like an ordinary cold. The child has a runny nose, a slight fever, and a dry cough. After a few days, he has long spells of coughing which are usually worse at night. He may begin to whoop—a long drawing in of breath that sounds like crowing—after a spell of coughing. The coughing spells may also cause vomiting.

If you suspect that your child has whooping cough, call your doctor. Also, call your doctor if your child has been exposed to whooping cough and has not been immunized against it.

Whooping cough is spread by a spray of droplets from the child's mouth or nose. When your child sneezes, have him cover his mouth and nose with a paper tissue. The paper tissues of a child with whooping cough should be burned in a safe place.

Whooping cough is communicable from about seven days after exposure to three weeks after coughing begins. If your child has been exposed to whooping cough and is not immune, your doctor will probably recommend that he be quarantined for 14 days after exposure. One attack usually provides immunity. There is also a whooping cough vaccine.

Whooping cough vaccine is usually given along with diphtheria and tetanus vaccines in a single shot, commonly called a DTP shot. The first inoculation can be given when your baby is 2 months old. However, your doctor may recommend beginning immunization when the baby is 1 month old. Other inoculations are given when he is 3 and 4 months old. If a DTP shot is not given at 3 months, it should be given at 4 and 5 months, or at 4 and 6 months. Booster shots are given at 15 to 18 months and at 4 to 6 years of age.

All infants should be immunized against whooping cough. The disease can be fatal to any child, but the death rate is far higher for infants less than a year old who have not been immunized. Immunization is so effective and widespread that the disease is less common, but it is still potentially serious for the unimmunized child. H.D.R., Jr.

See also **Communicable diseases; Diphtheria; Immunization; Shots**

Section Four

Guide and Index to *Childcraft*

Getting to know *Childcraft*

When I was a child, I spake as a child, I understood as a child;
but when I became a man, I put away childish things.

—I Corinthians 13:11

Parents of young children need to retain within themselves something of the child. But to help their children, they also need access to materials that have a direct and immediate appeal to children. *Childcraft* fulfills this need because it builds upon the known interests of children and provides information at a child's level of understanding. Because children respond to it and learn from it, it serves as an effective home resource to enrich and supplement the preschool and primary-grade curriculum, and has a direct appeal for children in the intermediate grades who need high-interest, easy-to-read material.

Philosophy and objectives

***Childcraft* is for children.** These four words represent the philosophy of these books. Implicit in the statement is a knowledge of children's interests, abilities, curiosities, and needs.

Parents will quickly recognize that *Childcraft* deals with those broad areas about which children most frequently express curiosity, that it provides the answers to many of the questions they ask, and that it supplies new and exciting information on the many subjects in which young children have a beginning interest. Thus *Childcraft* builds on the known interests of children as determined by direct observation and from contemporary educational research on their perceptions, conceptions, and interests.

Childcraft serves young children by:

1. Offering material relating to their needs, interests, and concerns, taking into account the full range of individual differences that characterizes children through the primary grades.

2. Providing a selection of the best and most interesting of traditional and contemporary children's literature, both prose and poetry. This material aims to create an awareness of cultural heritage, as well as to stimulate an interest in reading.

3. Using language that is rhythmical, pleasing to the ear, fun to listen to, fun to read, and within their range of abilities.
4. Using illustrations that are imaginative, aesthetically pleasing, and stimulating. Together, the text and illustrations provide experiences that motivate children to discuss, question, and explore.

Because *Childcraft*'s content was selected according to children's interests, because this content is presented in such a way as to capture and hold the interest of both listeners and readers, and because the organizational pattern of the informational volumes reflects the way young children naturally explore their interests—because *Childcraft* is interesting—it is a stimulus to learning. A clear indication of *Childcraft*'s universal appeal to children is the fact that it is sold around the world in an English language edition and is also published in French, Italian, Japanese, Korean, Portuguese, and Spanish.

From *About Me*, 14/270

Language

Childcraft avoids writing down to the young listener or reader. The objective is to explain clearly and interestingly—to challenge, to stimulate, and to create an appetite for more.

In the first three volumes this is accomplished by the selection of children's literature. Volume 1, *Poems and Rhymes*, and Volume 2, *Stories and Fables*, offer a selection of the finest in classic and contemporary writing for children. Volume 3, *Children Everywhere*, is an outstanding selection of modern children's stories from around the world.

The informational volumes (4 through 14) have the difficult job of providing simple explanations of complex ideas. The answers children want cannot always be expressed in simple words; but the writers, while making every effort to keep the language simple, have retained a style that appeals to children. Young children love the sounds certain words make, they love sentences that have a beat and a rhythm, and they love to discover and use new words. When it is necessary to use a specialized word, the word is used. When it is not self-explanatory within the context, it is defined and often included in a glossary.

Art and design

It is not enough to select content according to the known interests of young children. Nor is it enough to present that content in language suited both to the subject and the audience. Something else is needed. In *Childcraft*, that "something else" is the art and design. Literally thousands of illustrations—many in full color—help to identify and clarify the topics dealt with.

Good art and design arouse and develop interest. Fine illustrations have contributed to the lasting impression made by many stories for children. No one who has read *Winnie-the-Pooh* will ever be able to forget Ernest Shepard's superb and simple rendering of Pooh. There is, in fact, only one Pooh, and he can be seen on pages 46 to 51 of Volume 2, *Stories and Fables*. On the other hand, few illustrators are intimately associated with particular poems. It is important, then, that the illustrations chosen to go with poetry be selected with care. The artist must enhance visually the mood and feeling conveyed by the words of the poet.

Factual material presents another challenge for the artist, for now he must create art work that will help to make the text clear. For example, *Childcraft* uses art to show that a light switch works very much like a castle drawbridge, how a plane traveling at supersonic speed creates a sonic boom, how the pipe under the sink forms a water trap, and what makes a doorbell ring. Handled in a way that appeals to a child's imagination, while satisfying his curiosity, good art often provokes the reaction: "Hey! I never thought of it that way before!"

All told, about 4,500 pages are illustrated, of which more than half are in color. Many of the illustrations are by outstanding artists from around the world, including many of the Caldecott Medal winners. In addition, a number of internationally famous photographers have contributed their talents to the fine photographic coverage in *Childcraft.*

Organization

As indicated by the volume titles, *Childcraft* embraces a wide range of subjects (see pages 310–319 for the relationship of each volume to the school curriculum and a description of the contents of the volumes).

Volume 1, *Poems and Rhymes*, is arranged by subject; *i.e.*, "Poems for Outdoors," "Poems About Plants and Animals," and so on. Volume 2, *Stories and Fables*, is arranged by literary form; *i.e.*, "Fables," "Fairy Tales," "Myths and Legends," and so on. In Volume 3, *Children Everywhere*, the stories are arranged to achieve a variety of setting and style.

The organizing principle of volumes 4 through 14 is quite different. Insofar as possible, consistent with the material and the concepts, each page or spread (two facing pages) forms a complete unit, which in turn is part of a larger unit, usually 12 to 14 pages, on a particular topic. At no time does *Childcraft* attempt to tell a child more than he is capable of absorbing. The basic purposes are to satisfy a child's immediate curiosity, to impart fundamental understandings, and to stimulate further reading on any aspect of a subject a child finds interesting.

The people behind *Childcraft*

Since its inception in 1934, the editors of *Childcraft* have sought the advice and assistance of distinguished educators and experts in child growth and development. An Editorial Advisory Board evaluates existing content and considers new material to meet the developing interests and changing needs of children. This board is assisted by a Library Consultant Committee, a group of experienced professional librarians who are qualified authorities on children's reading needs. Both groups meet regularly with the editorial staff, and programs are implemented by a close working relationship between individual advisers and editors.

In addition, special consultants have provided technical assistance and advice in the preparation of particular volumes:

Volume 3, *Children Everywhere*

Anne Pellowski, B.A., M.S.L.S.
Director, Information Center
on Children's Cultures,
U.S. Committee for UNICEF

Volume 5, *About Animals*

Paul Bigelow Sears, Ph.D.
Professor Emeritus of Conservation,
Yale University

Loren D. Potter, Ph.D.
Professor of Biology
University of New Mexico

Volume 6, *The Green Kingdom*

Paul Bigelow Sears, Ph.D.
Professor Emeritus of Conservation,
Yale University

Volume 13, *Mathemagic*

Lola J. May, B.S., M.A., Ph.D.
Mathematics Consultant,
Winnetka (Illinois) Public Schools

Volume 14, *About Me*

Paul L. Doerring, Ph.D.
Psychological Institutes of
Michigan

Virginia Samter
Member, Association of Medical
Illustrators

Childcraft in the home

Parents have high hopes and ideals for their children. The editors and advisers of *Childcraft* share these hopes and ideals. They believe that *Childcraft* helps children get a good start toward eventual goals. *Childcraft* emphasizes inquiry and experience, process and discovery. *Childcraft* can be a valuable aid to parents and to children—but only if it is used. The section, *Childcraft*—Building Blocks for Learning (pages 320–322), contains suggestions for using *Childcraft* as a home resource—suggestions parents and children can adapt to their special needs.

What each volume is about

Childcraft is a home resource for
Literature and Language Arts

Vol. 1 Poems and Rhymes

A collection of more than 350 traditional and modern verses for young children, including Mother Goose rhymes; nursery rhymes; poems for outdoors; poems about plants and animals; rhymes of life at home; poems of play and make-believe; poems about pets and grown-ups; highway, byway, and city rhymes; verses just for fun; children's prayers; and poems and rhymes set to music. The works of more than a hundred artists, illustrators, and photographers—including such famous children's illustrators as Roger Duvoisin, Ezra Jack Keats, Robert McCloskey, Maurice Sendak, and Garth Williams—contribute to the beauty of this book. Includes author, title, first-line, and subject indexes.

Illustration for "Mice"
in *Poems and Rhymes*, 1/118

Vol. 2 Stories and Fables

A well-rounded sampling of the best-loved literature of childhood. Included are animal tales, fairy tales, folk tales, tall tales, myths and legends, and modern stories selected especially for young children. The authors include such favorites as A. A. Milne, Hans Christian Andersen, the Grimm brothers, Rudyard Kipling, Wanda Gag, Carl Sandburg, Claire Huchet Bishop, and Robert Lawson. Among the famous illustrators represented are William Pène du Bois, Marcia Brown, Ernest H. Shepard, Lynd Ward, and Brian Wildsmith. Includes author and title indexes.

Illustration for "In Which Pooh Goes Visiting and Gets Into a Tight Place"
in *Stories and Fables*, 2/46

Vol. 3 Children Everywhere

These 31 stories of the contemporary world by leading authors from 31 nations accurately reflect the universal interests, ideas, and attitudes of today's children. Each was selected for its literary quality and for the ability of the author to portray aspects of national character as well as those common traits that make the world of children one world. Six stories were written especially for this book, and 15 others are published in English for the first time. The illustrations, as international as the stories, were created especially for this volume by outstanding artists from around the world. Includes a glossary, pronunciation guide, and author and title indexes.

Illustration for "The Big Guest" in *Children Everywhere*, 3/111

Childcraft is a home resource for
Science

Vol. 4 World and Space

What is the difference between a meteor and a meteorite? Is there such a thing as a falling star? How many stars are there? Where does the wind come from? Why do geysers gush? In this book about the physical world and the far reaches of outer space, children will find the answers to these and other stimulating questions about the sky, the planets, the weather, the earth's surface, the seasons, natural resources, and map reading. Includes a subject index.

From *World and Space*, 4/152

Vol. 5 About Animals

Animals, animals, animals everywhere! More than 400 animals, from the aardvark to the zebra, from the prehistoric dinosaur to the family dog, from the giant blue whale to the microscopic paramecium, from the plodding turtle to the swift-flying eagle, fill the pages of this informative book. *About Animals* opens by explaining the difference between a pussycat and a pussy willow, and goes on to describe how various animals fit into the vast web of life, their ecological roles, and how they are being endangered on the one hand and saved on the other. More than 500 illustrations, most of them in full color, by internationally known nature photographers and artists help to introduce children to the wonders of the animal world. Includes a glossary and a subject index.

Drawing of fennec fox
for *About Animals*, 5/190

Vol. 6 The Green Kingdom

Have your children take a trip into the Green Kingdom. With the aid of 380 illustrations, they can learn about plants that swim, plants that look like rocks, and plants that "eat" insects. Why do leaves change color? What do plants do in the winter? How can you have a garden no matter where you live? The answers can be found in this volume. Children will also realize how plants give us food, paper, string, cloth, medicines, and even the oxygen we breathe. We couldn't live without plants, yet we harm them by polluting their air, water, and soil. How are people working to save plants? Explore the Green Kingdom and find out. Includes a subject index.

From *The Green Kingdom*, 6/39

Vol. 7 How Things Work

A book of mechanics and technology for young children, showing the inner workings of more than 500 simple machines and other devices—from keys and bicycle bells to electric circuits and retrorockets on space capsules. Photographs, exploded views, and informative diagrams—in color and in black and white—help explain clearly how things work. Includes a subject index.

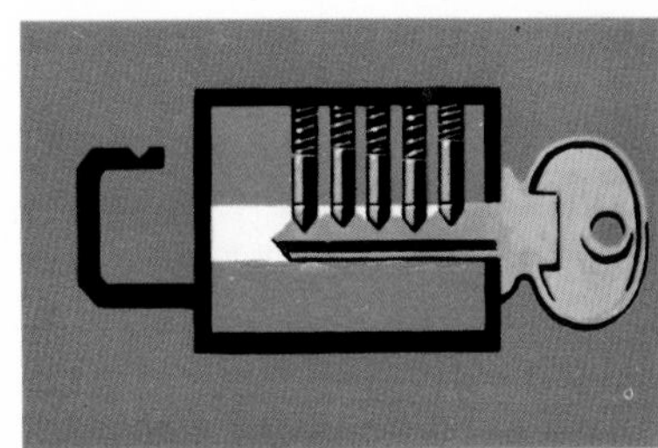

From *How Things Work*, 7/21

Childcraft is a home resource for
Social Studies

Vol. 8 How We Get Things

This *who, what, why, where, when,* and *how* book of technology, communication, transportation, and community services deals with the work people do and the products that touch our everyday lives. *Who* can give a child help when he needs it? *What* happens to recycled wastes? *Why* are there ridges on the edges of some coins? *When* is maple syrup made? *How* does a nun serve a community? Two unique sections, "What's Economics?" and "Start Your Own Town," show how people and products are affected by economics and local government and challenge children to make decisions. Includes a subject index.

Illustration for "What's Economics?" in *How We Get Things*, 8/324

Vol. 9 Holidays and Customs

Everywhere in the world a holiday is a special time to celebrate, but *how* you celebrate depends upon *where* you live or come from. In the United States, people shoot off fireworks on the Fourth of July. But in China, they shoot them off to celebrate the New Year, which usually starts in February. This volume, in effect an introduction to the cultures of the world, describes some 500 holidays and customs in more than 50 lands. It includes sections on clothing, houses, food, flags, games, toys, songs, and dances. It also features a calendar of major holidays around the world and a subject index.

From *Holidays and Customs*, 9/5

Vol. 10 Places to Know

This geography book for young children provides a glimpse of famous places around the world, as well as an introduction to the cultural heritage of man. Photographs and illustrations combine to make the strange familiar and the familiar more exciting. Here a young explorer can view the seven wonders of the ancient world, look down upon the ruins of Machu Picchu, enter the tombs of the pharaohs, stand beside Michelangelo's *David*, walk upon the Great Wall of China, gaze in awe upon the beauty of the Taj Mahal, and ponder the mystery of Stonehenge. Includes a subject index.

Wall painting in Egyptian tomb in the Valley of the Kings (Thebes), from *Places to Know*, 10/106

Childcraft is a home resource for

Creative Activities and the Arts

Vol. 11 Make and Do

Here is a resource volume of how-to-do-it projects and activities for all ages. There are step-by-step, illustrated instructions for more than 300 basic projects, costumes, games, stunts, and tricks. The craft sections have helpful hints on how to work with paper, clay, papier-mâché, wood, and string, as well as how to sew, hook, and weave. There are also pages of party and gift ideas. Everything can be made with readily available materials. Includes a subject index.

Making a stained-glass fish, in *Make and Do*, 11/55

Vol. 12 Look and Learn

In this book, more than 150 topics encourage children to learn the skills involved in really seeing. They find out that color communicates, that spaces and shapes have meaning, that gestures and facial expressions can say more than words, and how signs and symbols convey information. In addition, attention is given to the basic understandings involved in artistic concepts such as composition and perspective. Includes a subject index.

Illustration for "See What I Mean?" in *Look and Learn*, 12/103

Vol. 13 Mathemagic

Many children are often "turned off" by mathematics. But here's a book that can "turn them on" again by showing them that mathematics is really fun! For *Mathemagic* is filled with puzzles, tricks, games, stories, poems, and surprising facts that show the hidden "magic" in numbers and shapes. Children will find themselves *wanting* to do addition and multiplication in order to find the "magic number" in their name or to fool their friends with number tricks. They'll learn the basics of plane geometry as they visit, in story, a strange land where the people are triangles, squares, circles, and other shapes. And they'll delight in making their own abacus, a marvelous "counting machine" that makes working with numbers a pleasure. They'll find there's a lot more—and a lot more *fun*—to mathematics than they ever suspected!

Illustration for a poem, "A triangular tale," in Mathemagic, 12/231.

Childcraft is a home resource for
Health

Vol. 14 About Me

Through the pages of this book a child can begin to know himself. He can see himself as a physical, emotional, rational, and social being, like all other human creatures in the larger definition, yet a wonderfully unique individual as singular as his footprint. He can begin to gain both a sense of himself as a person, worthwhile in his individual strengths and weaknesses, and an understanding that his problems differ only in kind from those of other children. Some 400 photographs, drawings, and diagrams help to clarify the text. For example, the diagrams in the section "Inside and Outside of Me" show the different systems and major organs of a child's body. Includes a glossary and a subject index.

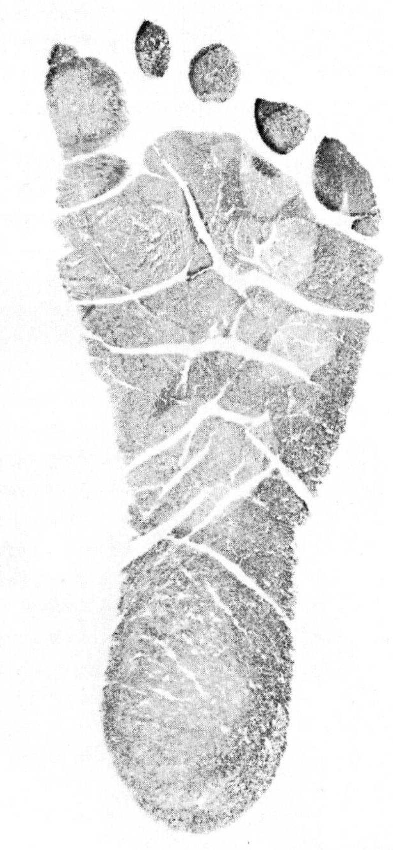

From *About Me*, 14/274

Childcraft is a home resource for

Parents

Vol. 15 Guide for Parents

This volume describes an average child's growth and development from birth to young adulthood. In so doing, the volume provides a framework against which parents can measure their children's progress. A special group of articles gives parents advice on such diverse topics as choosing a baby sitter, the drug problem, and raising a mentally retarded child. An illustrated Medical Guide contains more than 200 articles dealing with the health, safety, and well-being of children. Includes a Guide to *Childcraft* and a General Index to the complete set.

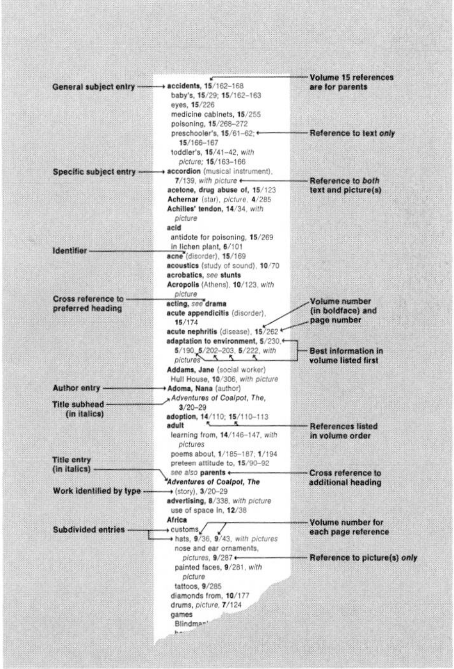

From *Guide for Parents*, 15/333

Childcraft—building blocks for learning

The education of a child is principally derived from its own observation of the actions, words, voice, and looks of those with whom it lives.

—John Jebb

Children and parents love and appreciate *Childcraft* and find it to be a valuable home resource. It reflects children's interests, recognizes the importance of the special relationship between parent and child, and provides stimulating learning experiences.

Childcraft's effectiveness in the home depends largely on how it is presented and used. It is important that you get to know *Childcraft* before introducing it to your child. Browse through each volume, noting the general content and format. Use the General Index in this volume to find specific subject matter in the set. Your familiarity and ease with *Childcraft* will enhance your ability to share it with your child.

Childcraft offers enjoyable, educational stimulation for children on several different age levels. Recognizing the cumulative nature of the learning process, each volume of *Childcraft* is a building block for further learning.

Childcraft and the toddler
(18 months to 3 years)

This is the time to introduce children to *Childcraft*. Set aside 15 or 20 minutes each day to share selections from *Childcraft* with your child. This time period may vary, but remember that a toddler has a short attention span. Sharing *Childcraft* will help to reinforce the toddler's newly acquired ability to talk and to learn more about his rapidly expanding world.

Volume 1, *Poems and Rhymes*, is specially geared for toddlers, most of whom are action-oriented. The familiar nursery rhymes and other selections relate directly to a young child's experiences. A parent's enthusiastic, animated presentation of these poems and rhymes will encourage the toddler to imitate sounds and actions. With your assurance and guidance, the toddler can sharpen his skills. "One, Two, Buckle My Shoe," for example, helps a child learn basic counting skills. Encourage the child to join in while you recite and act out the words. Use fingers, objects in the pictures, or objects in the room to show him the meaning of each number as you say it. Ask your toddler to do the same, and greet his efforts with enthusiasm and applause. The more the toddler knows that his attempts have pleased you, the more he will want to repeat the activity. Talk about what he sees in the pictures, giving him verbal clues whenever necessary. Try to relate what he sees in the pictures to real things.

Childcraft and the preschooler
(3 to 5 years)

The transition to the preschool years is marked by an expanded vocabulary, a longer attention span, and an almost total preoccupation with role-playing and fantasy. A four- or five-year-old's complete openness to learning makes sharing *Childcraft* during this period a rewarding experience for parent and child.

The preschooler still enjoys the poems and rhymes memorized from Volume 1. But he is also ready for longer literature, such as the stories in Volumes 2 and 3—stories that will take him further into the realm of ideas and indirect experiences. Look for the simpler stories and fables in Volume 2, *Stories and Fables*, and in Volume 3, *Children Everywhere*. Skim the stories yourself to see which ones are best for your child at this age. For example, "The Five Chinese Brothers" is a good story for preschoolers because it is short, simple, and has imaginative appeal.

Although most four- and five-year-olds cannot read words, they can "read" pictures to create or re-create their own stories. They love to talk about stories that are read to them. The flair and enthusiasm that went into the presentation of the poems and rhymes from Volume 1 should be just as evident when reading stories aloud. Don't rush the reading. Allow time for the child to respond and question. There is no urgency to hurry to the completion of the story unless the child suggests it. Frequent pauses to discuss pictures or particular passages will enhance the child's learning and enable him to re-create the story in his own way—a favorite pastime of the preschooler.

Preschoolers enjoy browsing through *Childcraft* on their own. Now is the time to teach your child how to care for books. Since the preschooler tries to imitate almost everything you do, the care and respect with which you handle a book will carry over to him. Talk to him about treating books kindly and gently because they provide pleasure and knowledge. He will quickly learn to follow your lead and treat books as treasured belongings.

The bright pictures and illustrations in *Childcraft* will stimulate much conversation and thought. Most often, the preschooler will want feedback to the wonders he finds in *Childcraft*. The clear, simple text will enable you to respond to your child's questions and comments in terms he will understand.

Childcraft in the primary grades
(Kindergarten through Grade 3)

The acquisition of reading skills in the primary grades broadens a child's involvement with *Childcraft.* He will begin to explore more and more of the material on his own. If he has had positive experiences with *Childcraft* in his early years, he will easily develop the habit of "checking with *Childcraft*" for the kinds of information he now needs.

The books should be placed where the child can see them and reach them easily. Remind him frequently that these books are for his use at any time, but that he has a responsibility to care for the books. This, too, is a learning process.

Through the first grade, most children will continue to seek out some adult help in exploring *Childcraft.* In the second or third grade, however, they will begin to make much more use of the books without parental help. This is also an age when children become intensely curious about themselves. Volume 14, *About Me,* will help children and parents during this period. The inevitable question, "Where did I come from?" is answered clearly and simply in the section "Becoming Me." And the mysteries of the growth process are explained in terms that the child can understand in the section "Watch Me Grow." Volume 14 will answer many of the child's "Why?" questions.

Free access to *Childcraft* will bolster the child's growing sense of competence and independence. In addition, he will find in *Childcraft* references to material he encounters each day in school.

Childcraft in the intermediate grades
(Grades 4 through 6)

It is in the intermediate school years that a child's attention focuses almost exclusively on other children. The codes, styles, and expectations of the peer group will determine most of the child's behavior. The familiar practice of sharing *Childcraft* with a parent may shift to sharing *Childcraft* with a friend or group of friends. The important thing is that *Childcraft* remains a reliable source of enjoyment and information.

Since most of the volumes relate to school subjects, *Childcraft* serves as a valuable home reference library for children in the intermediate grades. While homework may be a problem for many children, the habit of browsing through *Childcraft* is a pleasurable experience. Children will find in *Childcraft* material that refers directly to a needed social studies report, proposed science project, and many other school assignments.

Childcraft is also a valuable resource for the older child's important peer-group activities. Volume 11, *Make and Do,* contains group games, directions for puppet shows, tips on how to give a party, and other helpful hints that fit into the child's need for group interaction.

Childcraft aids in child development and guidance

Train up a child in the way he should go:
and when he is old, he will not depart from it.
—Proverbs 22:6

Child development is a gradual, stage-by-stage process. Every child passes through the same developmental stages, but not at the same time or at the same rate of speed. *Childcraft* provides numerous ways to handle individual differences, whether these differences be physical, emotional, intellectual, or social. The following pages suggest ways parents can use *Childcraft* to help guide the development of their children, and ways children can use the books to inform themselves about the development of their bodies, their emotions, their minds, their relationships with other people, and their moral, ethical, and spiritual values.

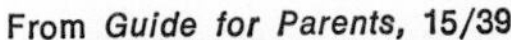
From *Guide for Parents,* 15/39

He was not an intellectual Croesus,
but his pockets were full of sixpences.
—Benjamin Disraeli

Intellectual development

For a child, wanting to know is as natural as breathing in and breathing out. He is a bundle of curiosity about practically everything. There is no question that early guidance and a life rich with conversation, books, music, art, and varied experiences will do much to stimulate the development of natural intelligence. *Childcraft* offers firsthand help by providing materials with high motivational content, yet presented at a level and in such a way that the child can use and understand them at an early age.

In Volume 4, *World and Space,* his question, "Where does rain come from?" leads naturally to a study of the water cycle. Among other facts, children learn that the real difference between hail and sleet is how they are formed, that snowflakes are always six-cornered crystals, and that fog is just a cloud near the ground. If they are intrigued by superstitions, they can delve into more than a dozen superstitions from different cultures in Volume 9, *Holidays and Customs.* The simple, practical, interesting, and stimulating presentations, especially of factual materials, afford the child every chance for successful learning experiences, thereby encouraging his further search for knowledge. He need not grow up with, as Oliver Wendell Holmes once put it, "a one-story intellect and a one-horse vocabulary."

Poetry is the spontaneous overflow of powerful feelings;
it takes its origin from emotion recollected in tranquility.
—William Wordsworth

Emotional development

Sound emotional development is related to every other aspect of a child's development. It is a continuing process, taking place at home, in the classroom, and at play.

Childcraft contributes to this process by showing children how people express their emotions—whether in a poem in Volume 1, *Poems and Rhymes;* as characters in a story in volumes 2 and 3, *Stories and Fables* and *Children Everywhere;* by acting without words in Volume 12, *Look and Learn.* Volume 11, *Make and Do,* also suggests ways for children to express their emotions at play and in creative activities. And Volume 14, *About Me,* is especially rich in material dealing with emotional development, and shows how such emotions as happiness, sadness, love, anger, and fear affect our actions.

The social, friendly, honest man,
Whate'er he be,
'Tis he fulfills great Nature's plan,
And none but he!

—Robert Burns

Social development

A child's social development starts right after birth, the moment he starts breathing. Then begins the lifelong adventure of being the individual he is, with not another soul in the world exactly like him, and being at the same time a social creature dependent upon others and with others dependent upon him. In the pages of *Childcraft,* children see man as an individual and as a part of society. They find, or can be shown, examples of ceremonies in many different societies, how people work together for a common goal, and especially how people work to help others. In Volume 14, *About Me,* they can ponder the question, "What does it mean to be *me*?" and discover ways to answer it. In Volume 8, *How We Get Things,* major sections discuss cooperative efforts to improve society. And in Volume 3, *Children Everywhere,* "Helmut in the City" is a moving story of a brother and sister who settle a quarrel without involving their parents.

Just as the twig is bent, the tree's inclined.

—Alexander Pope

Moral, ethical, and spiritual values

A child's world can be a confusing one. He constantly encounters new ideas, values, and philosophies. Often these conflict, and each day may bring on problems, hurt feelings, or even a bloody nose. To make some sense out of the confusion, a child needs to develop standards that help him to distinguish between right and wrong, truth and falsity, beauty and ugliness, reality and fantasy. He must learn, sometimes painfully, the difference between momentary pleasure and long-term happiness. His living models are adults, from whom he takes his examples.

His reading matter can enhance the values he learns. In terms of right and wrong conduct, what moral values can children find in the stories "How the Camel Got His Hump" and "Pandora" (Volume 2, *Stories and Fables*)? When a doctor treats an illness (Volume 8, *How We Get Things*), is he practicing a code of ethics? How are spiritual values reflected in the fact that medieval churches were the highest buildings in town (Volume 12, *Look and Learn*), or that people the world over celebrate days of thanksgiving (Volume 9, *Holidays and Customs*)? Through these stories and other materials, parents can use *Childcraft* to provide examples of moral, ethical, and spiritual values in action. By discussing these examples, parents will help children understand themselves and their fellow man, help them shape their character in terms of such virtues as loyalty and courage, help them become aware of their responsibilities as members of society, and awaken in them a reverence for life.

O, wad some Pow'r the giftie gie us
To see oursels as ithers see us!

—Robert Burns

Self-Knowledge underlies the development of all moral, ethical, and spiritual values. Unless a person understands himself he cannot expect to find standards to live by. Volume 14 includes a wealth of factual information that will help a child begin to understand himself. Here he can see himself not just in terms of physical growth and development, but as a *person.* He will recognize that he needs to be able to relate to other people, and that if he understands his own mental processes and emotional responses, he will be able to adjust to the outside pressures he is and will be experiencing.

In Volume 1, *Poems and Rhymes,* a poem as simple and as beautiful as *"Spring Morning"* raises the fundamental question, "Where am I going?"; "Bed in Summer" queries adult-imposed rules; and "Leisure" asks what life is worth if "We have no time to stand and stare." In volumes 2 and 3, *Stories and Fables* and *Children Everywhere,* there are stories that will enable the listener or reader to share situations in which the characters learn much about themselves and the reader learns by example. What child will not share with the Ugly Duckling the realization that "a good heart never becomes proud"?

Let the character be formed by poetry, established
by the laws of right behavior, and perfected by music.

—Confucius

Character means moral firmness, self-control, and such virtues as integrity, loyalty, and courage. Throughout *Childcraft* there are many examples of character in this sense. Sometimes character can be illustrated best with negative examples. Children will quickly realize that in the story "The Flight of Icarus" (Volume 2, *Stories and Fables*), Icarus fell to his death because he lacked moral firmness and self-control; he disobeyed his father and gave way to the impulse to glory in his new-found freedom.

At other times, positive examples are the best medium. In Volume 8, *How We Get Things*, children will see that the virtues of integrity and courage are implied in the way fire fighters and police officers help others. In Volume 5, *About Animals*, they will recognize the loyalty of a guide dog and the faith that a blind person must have in his "eyes." These examples of character will make a lasting impression on all children.

We shall not flag or fail; we shall go on to the end.

—Winston Churchill

Responsibility is a sense of obligation toward oneself, toward one's fellow man, and toward those creatures entrusted to one's care. Nowhere are the consequences of irresponsibility made more clear than in Aesop's famous fable about the boy who cried "Wolf!" (Volume 2, *Stories and Fables*). In learning about the causes and results of fires (Volume 6, *The Green Kingdom*), children will understand how carelessness can start a forest fire, and the lesson in personal responsibility will be much more meaningful than a stern injunction not to play with matches. And by finding out how to use the tools described in Volume 7, *How Things Work*, they will learn how to care for their own property and the property of others.

Let knowledge grow from more to more,
But more of reverence in us dwell.

—Alfred, Lord Tennyson

Reverence for life begins when a child first really opens his eyes, ears, heart, and mind to the wonders of the world. Then he will see and hear and feel, as never before, the swift flight of a bird, the mad rush of a scrambling squirrel, the glistening of dew on the grass, and the vastness of the sky above him.

A conscious awareness of nature in all its aspects is a product of knowledge. With knowledge comes understanding, and as a child begins to understand and appreciate the infinite variety of nature, so will he begin to understand the nature of God, to develop a set of moral and spiritual values. He will begin to feel, though he may not understand, what Albert Schweitzer meant when he wrote in *Out of My Life and Thought,* ". . . when, at sunset, we were making our way through a herd of hippopotamuses, there flashed upon my mind, unforeseen and unthought, the phrase, 'Reverence for Life.' Now I had found my way to the idea in which affirmation of the world and ethics are contained side by side. . . ."

The concept of reverence for life might be introduced with two poems by Rachel Field, "Barefoot Days" and "Something Told the Wild Geese" (Volume 1, *Poems and Rhymes*), both of which are full of feeling for the beauties of life and nature. This same volume also offers such prayers as "Father, We Thank Thee" and "The Prayer of a Little Bird," which are imbued with a sensitive appreciation for the wonders of nature.

The story "Ice" (Volume 2, *Stories and Fables*) will further the concept, for children will realize instinctively why Tim McGrath fed the wild stock—something he had not done before. In Volume 5, *About Animals,* and Volume 6, *The Green Kingdom,* there are related articles, such as the roles animals and plants play in ecological interrelationships, with which to pursue discussions of the concept.

A sound mind in a sound body.

—Juvenal

Physical development

Each person grows according to his own unique plan—a combination of his heredity and his environment. But there is a great deal more to growing than getting enough sleep, eating a nutritionally sound diet, and getting enough exercise. Children should be encouraged to learn more about their bodies, to understand the importance of physical development and exactly what it means. Many sections in *Childcraft*—but especially those in Volume 14, *About Me*—explain what takes place in the process of physical growth and development, thus helping children understand the changes they are undergoing. And in Volume 11, *Make and Do,* there are many indoor and outdoor games designed to contribute to a child's physical development.

'Tis Skill, not strength, that governs a Ship.

—Thomas Fuller

Skill development

The development of basic skills underlies all aspects of life and education. A child must master a wide variety of skills—from simple physical movements to complex intellectual processes. His ability to communicate, a skill basic to every part of life, will determine in large measure his success in school. His knowledge of problem-solving techniques can be applied to literature as well as to scientific problems, and his ability to develop concepts and to see relationships will be as useful in art as in social studies.

Using *Childcraft,* parents can develop and sharpen listening skills by means of the poems and stories in the first three volumes. The social skills involved in human relationships can be emphasized through an investigation of different cultures in Volume 9, *Holidays and Customs,* and by the study of the section "Me and My Family" in Volume 14, *About Me.* To show how computational skills are used in measuring with rulers and in measuring time, turn to Volume 7, *How Things Work,* and for measuring food for cooking and objects for construction, to Volume 11, *Make and Do.* Practice in a work-study skill such as map reading can be provided with Volume 4, *World and Space.* And in Volume 8, *How We Get Things,* there are sections that can be used to challenge children to exercise the judgmental skills involved in making civic and economic decisions.

Award-Winning Illustrators in Childcraft

Included in *Childcraft* are the specially commissioned works of many award-winning illustrators of children's books. These outstanding artists include recipients of the Randolph J. Caldecott Medal, as well as winners of the Hans Christian Andersen Medal and the Kate Greenaway Medal.

Randolph J. Caldecott Medal

The Randolph J. Caldecott Medal is awarded annually by the Children's Services Division of the American Library Association (ALA) "for the most distinguished American picture book for children." This medal, given each year since 1938, is named for Randolph J. Caldecott, an outstanding nineteenth-century English illustrator of children's books, and was established by the late Frederic G. Melcher, co-editor of *Publishers' Weekly* and founder of Children's Book Week. As a convenience for parents who want to bring beautifully illustrated books to the attention of their children, those Caldecott winners whose works appear in *Childcraft* are listed below, along with the titles of their award-winning books. Their illustrations in *Childcraft* are indicated by volume and page number.

Kate Greenaway Medal

The Kate Greenaway Medal, named in honor of another nineteenth-century Eng-

Caldecott Medal Winners and Their Books

Illustrator	Award-Winning Book	Art in Childcraft
Brown, Marcia	*Cinderella; or The Little Glass Slipper* *Once a Mouse*	2/252–257
Burton, Virginia Lee	*The Little House*	1/216
Cooney, Barbara	*Chanticleer and the Fox*	3/158–169
D'Aulaire, Ingri and Edgar Parin	*Abraham Lincoln*	2/166–171
Duvoisin, Roger	*White Snow, Bright Snow*	1/224, 276
Emberley, Ed	*Drummer Hoff*	2/76–77
Ets, Marie Hall	*Nine Days to Christmas*	1/17
Hader, Berta and Elmer	*The Big Snow*	1/90
Haley, Gail E.	*A Story, A Story*	1/264–265
Handforth, Thomas	*Mei Li*	1/66
Hogrogian, Nonny	*Always Room for One More* *One Fine Day*	1/242–243
Jones, Elizabeth Orton	*Prayer for a Child*	1/292
Keats, Ezra Jack	*The Snowy Day*	1/220–221
Lathrop, Dorothy	*Animals of the Bible*	1/199
Lawson, Robert	*They Were Strong and Good*	2/26–33; 8/17
Lent, Blair	*The Funny Little Woman*	1/282–283

lish artist, was instituted in 1955 and first awarded in 1956. It is presented by the Library Association (British) for distinguished work in the illustration of children's books. Medal winners in *Childcraft* are: William Stobbs (6/256); Brian Wildsmith (2/220–225); Victor Ambrus (2/258–261); Charles Keeping (3/50–59); and Pauline Baynes (6/262).

Hans Christian Andersen Medal

The Hans Christian Andersen Medal is awarded every two years by the International Board on Books for Young People. It was established in 1956 as an award for "a living author who, by an outstanding work (after 1960, by his complete work) has made an important international contribution to juvenile literature." Among the authors who have won the Hans Christian Andersen Medal are Eleanor Farjeon and Astrid Lindgren, and some of their works are in volumes 1 and 3 of *Childcraft*. Since 1966, there has been a second medal for an illustrator. One winner was Maurice Sendak, whose work appears in Volume 1.

Illustrator	Award-Winning Book	Art in Childcraft
McCloskey, Robert	*Make Way for Ducklings* *Time of Wonder*	1/67
Milhous, Katherine	*The Egg Tree*	1/94
Montresor, Benny	*May I Bring a Friend?*	1/294
Mordvinoff, Nicolas	*Finders Keepers*	1/78
Ness, Evaline	*Sam, Bangs & Moonshine*	1/26–27
Petersham, Maud and Miska	*The Rooster Crows*	1/146–147
Politi, Leo	*Song of the Swallows*	9/263
Rojankovsky, Feodor	*Frog Went a-Courtin'*	1/73
Sendak, Maurice	*Where the Wild Things Are*	1/151, 188–189, 192–193, 204, 214–215, 286–287
Shulevitz, Uri	*The Fool of the World and the Flying Ship*	1/45
Sidjakov, Nicolas	*Baboushka and the Three Kings*	2/142–143
Simont, Marc	*A Tree Is Nice*	1/20–21
Slobodkin, Louis	*Many Moons*	10/220
Steig, William	*Sylvester and the Magic Pebble*	1/74–75
Ward, Lynd	*The Biggest Bear*	2/132–139
Weisgard, Leonard	*The Little Island*	1/41, 48–49; 2/212–219
Zemach, Margot	*Duffy and the Devil*	1/260–261

How to use the general index

This General Index is a key to all of the material in volumes 1 through 15 of *Childcraft*—with the exception of the titles of the poems in Volume 1, which can be found in the Title Index in that volume.

The thousands of pages in *Childcraft* are filled with information on many subjects, in both text and pictures. Frequently, different aspects of a subject are covered in more than one volume. Although each of the other volumes has an index, this General Index is the only place to learn where in *Childcraft* you can find all the information on a subject.

The illustration on the opposite page shows the special features used in the General Index and in the individual volume indexes. To make the best use of any of the indexes, you should be aware of these various features.

The entries in dark type are of two kinds: specific and general. A specific entry is one that is the name of a person (**Adoma, Nana**), a place (**Acropolis**), or a thing (**acetone**). A general entry is one that covers a broad area or field of interest (**accidents, adult, Africa**). All general entries, and many specific entries, are subdivided to help you locate quickly the exact information you are looking for. One feature especially helpful for children is the use of an identifier in parentheses after many of the entries, as **acoustics** (study of sound).

The entries are arranged in alphabetical order, letter by letter, regardless of the number of words. The alphabetical arrangement applies only up to the comma in an inverted entry (one that has been turned around so that the key word is alphabetized, as Air Force, United States).

air
air conditioning
air conduction hearing aid
Air Force, United States
airline

The numbers following an entry or subentry (**15**/262) give the volume number in dark type and the page number or numbers in light type. If there is more than one page reference, the best information is listed first. When there are references to more than one volume, the volumes are listed in numerical order.

If there is information in both words and pictures, the words *with pictures* appear **after** the page number or numbers. If the reference is to a picture only, the word *picture* appears **before** the volume and page number or numbers.

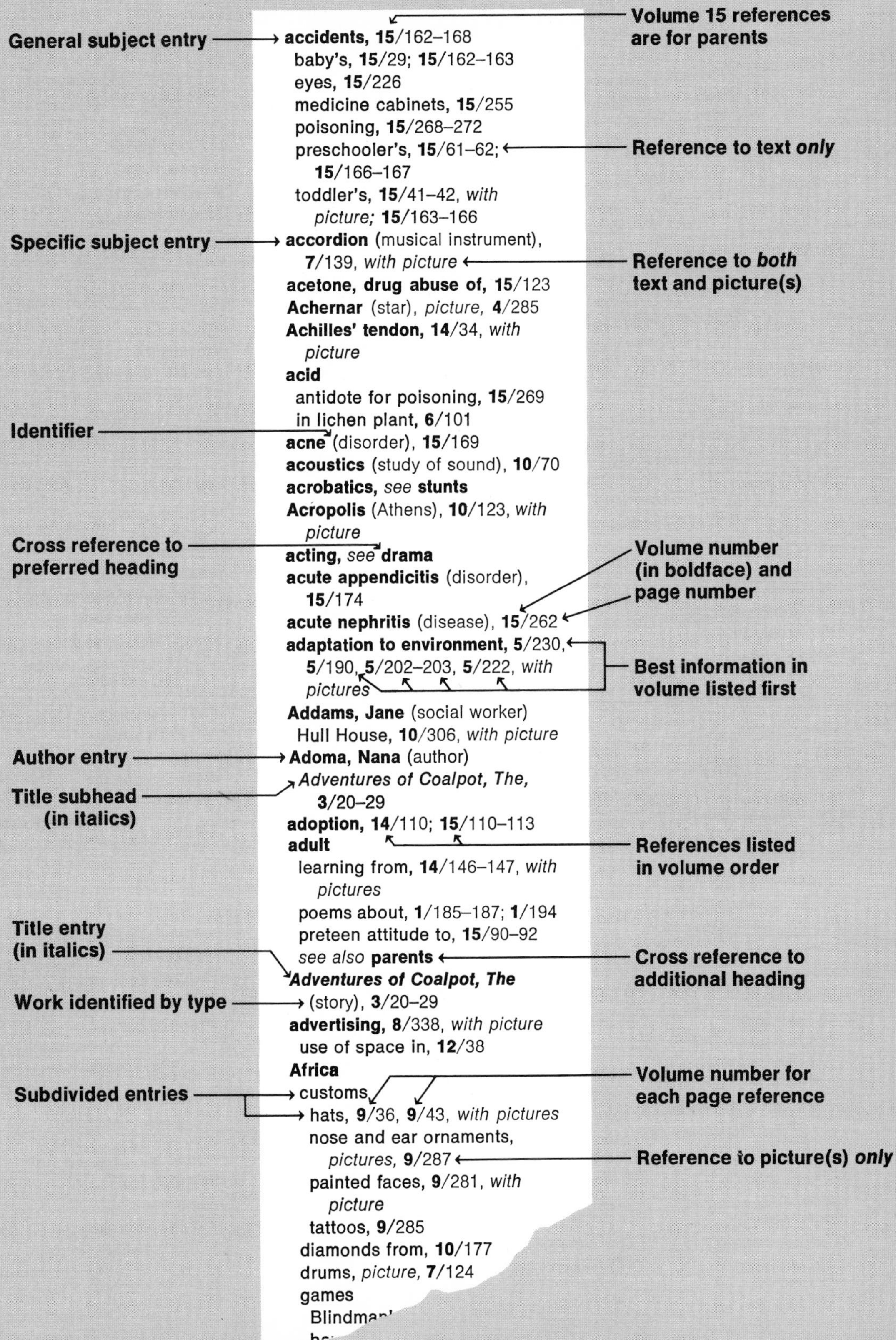
Volume 15 references are for parents
General subject entry
accidents, 15/162–168
baby's, 15/29; 15/162–163
eyes, 15/226
medicine cabinets, 15/255
poisoning, 15/268–272
preschooler's, 15/61–62; 15/166–167
Reference to text only
toddler's, 15/41–42, with picture; 15/163–166
Specific subject entry
accordion (musical instrument), 7/139, with picture
Reference to both text and picture(s)
acetone, drug abuse of, 15/123
Achernar (star), picture, 4/285
Achilles' tendon, 14/34, with picture
acid
antidote for poisoning, 15/269
in lichen plant, 6/101
Identifier
acne (disorder), 15/169
acoustics (study of sound), 10/70
acrobatics, see stunts
Acropolis (Athens), 10/123, with picture
Cross reference to preferred heading
acting, see drama
Volume number (in boldface) and page number
acute appendicitis (disorder), 15/174
acute nephritis (disease), 15/262
adaptation to environment, 5/230, 5/190, 5/202–203, 5/222, with pictures
Best information in volume listed first
Addams, Jane (social worker)
Hull House, 10/306, with picture
Author entry
Adoma, Nana (author)
Title subhead (in italics)
Adventures of Coalpot, The, 3/20–29
adoption, 14/110; 15/110–113
adult
References listed in volume order
learning from, 14/146–147, with pictures
poems about, 1/185–187; 1/194
preteen attitude to, 15/90–92
Title entry (in italics)
see also parents
Cross reference to additional heading
Adventures of Coalpot, The
Work identified by type
(story), 3/20–29
advertising, 8/338, with picture
use of space in, 12/38
Africa
Volume number for each page reference
Subdivided entries
customs
hats, 9/36, 9/43, with pictures
nose and ear ornaments, pictures, 9/287
Reference to picture(s) only
painted faces, 9/281, with picture
tattoos, 9/285
diamonds from, 10/177
drums, picture, 7/124
games

A

F

G

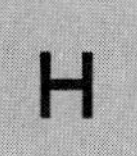

J

K

N

P

Q

R

S

V

Z